the Positive Side
of Interpersonal
Communication

Howard Giles
General Editor

Vol. 14

PETER LANG
New York • Washington, D.C./Baltimore • Bern
Frankfurt • Berlin • Brussels • Vienna • Oxford

the Positive Side *of* Interpersonal Communication

EDITED BY
Thomas J. Socha & Margaret J. Pitts

PETER LANG
New York • Washington, D.C./Baltimore • Bern
Frankfurt • Berlin • Brussels • Vienna • Oxford

Library of Congress Cataloging-in-Publication Data

The positive side of interpersonal communication /
edited by Thomas J. Socha, Margaret J. Pitts.
p. cm. — (Language as social action; v. 14)
Includes bibliographical references and index.
1. Interpersonal communication. 2. Interpersonal relations.
I. Socha, Thomas J. II. Pitts, Margaret Jane.
HM1166.P67   158.2—dc23   2011046178
ISBN 978-1-4331-1251-5 (hardcover)
ISBN 978-1-4331-1250-8 (paperback)
ISBN 978-1-4539-0536-4 (e-book)
ISSN 1529-2436

Bibliographic information published by **Die Deutsche Nationalbibliothek**.
Die Deutsche Nationalbibliothek lists this publication in the "Deutsche
Nationalbibliografie"; detailed bibliographic data is available
on the Internet at http://dnb.d-nb.de/.

The paper in this book meets the guidelines for permanence and durability
of the Committee on Production Guidelines for Book Longevity
of the Council of Library Resources.

© 2012 Peter Lang Publishing, Inc., New York
29 Broadway, 18th floor, New York, NY 10006
www.peterlang.com

All rights reserved.
Reprint or reproduction, even partially, in all forms such as microfilm,
xerography, microfiche, microcard, and offset strictly prohibited.

Printed in the United States of America

Contents

Acknowledgments ix
Foreword. So Let It Be with Caesar. . . ? xi
   Steve Duck
Chapter One. Toward a Conceptual Foundation for Positive
Interpersonal Communication 1
   Thomas J. Socha and Margaret J. Pitts

Section One
Key Concepts

Chapter Two. Aesthetic Relating 19
   Leslie A. Baxter, Kristen M. Norwood, and Sarah Nebel
Chapter Three. Being in Concert: An Explication of Synchrony in
Positive Intercultural Communication 39
   Young Yun Kim
Chapter Four. Communication Excellence: Embodying Virtues in
Interpersonal Communication 57
   Julien C. Mirivel
Chapter Five. Reflective Conversation as a Foundation for
Communication Virtue 73
   Nathan Miczo
Chapter Six. "Holding Each Other All Night Long:"
Communicating Intimacy in Older Adulthood 91
   Jon F. Nussbaum, Michelle Miller-Day, and Carla L. Fisher

Section Two
Fundamental Processes

Chapter Seven. Listening as Positive Communication 109
   Graham D. Bodie

Chapter Eight. Better Health, Better Lives: The Bright Side
of Affection 127
   Kory Floyd and Douglas M. Deiss
Chapter Nine. Fun with Friends, Pranks with Partners: How we
Play in Our Closest Relationships 143
   Krystyna S. Aune and Norman C. H. Wong
Chapter Ten. Humor as Personal Relationship Enhancer: Positivity
for the Long Term 161
   John C. Meyer
Chapter Eleven. The Bright Side of Conflict: Dialogic
Communication, Telesmatic Moments, and Deep Narrative Learning 179
   Peter M. Kellett
Chapter Twelve. Forgiveness as Restoration: The Search
for Well-Being, Reconciliation, and Relational Justice 193
   Douglas L. Kelley
Chapter Thirteen. Supportive Communication: A Positive
Response to Negative Life Events 211
   Erina MacGeorge, Bo Feng, Kristi Wilkum, and Eileen Doherty
Chapter Fourteen. Celebratory Support: Messages that Enhance
the Effects of Positive Experience 229
   Jennifer Dane McCullough and Brant R. Burleson

Section Three
Illustrative Applications

Chapter Fifteen. Engaging Health Communication 249
   Gary L. Kreps
Chapter Sixteen. Positive Religious/Spiritual Coping Among
African American Men Living with HIV in Jails and/or Prisons 259
   E. James Baesler, Valerian J. Derlega, and James Lolley
Chapter Seventeen. Nurturing Children as Assets: A Positive Approach
to Preventing Child Maltreatment and Promoting Healthy Youth
Development 277
   Steven R. Wilson and Patricia E. Gettings
Chapter Eighteen. Promoting Personal, Interpersonal, and Group
Growth through Positive Experiential Encounter
Communication Pedagogy 297
   Lawrence R. Frey and Angie B. White

Epilogue. The Power of the Dark Side 313
    Brian Spitzberg and William Cupach
Coda. Positive Interpersonal Communication as Child's Play 323
    Thomas J. Socha and Margaret J. Pitts

Contributors 325
Author Index 329
Subject Index 345

Acknowledgments

I have worked with many wonderfully positive and smart people in my professional life that includes my co-editor and friend, Maggie Pitts—a rising star in the communication field. For this volume, I want to pay special tribute to a couple individuals. First, one of my life's most positive friends: David A. Dawes. Dave and I were communication students together at the University of Illinois at Chicago, roommates at the University of Iowa, and like brothers. Although Dave passed away, far too young, over a decade ago, I can still hear his infectious laugh as I continue to try to emulate his positive way of being. So, along with remembering my long-time friend and fellow constructivist, Brant Burleson, and dedicating this volume to his memory, I also personally dedicate my contributions to this volume to Dave, and his family in Iowa, Karen and Hannah.

—TJS

I would first like to acknowledge Tom Socha for his mentoring and support in the five years that I have known him. I am thankful that our paths crossed early in my career and that together we can work toward a future that engages the full potential of positive communication. I also acknowledge my Penn State friends and colleagues Jon Nussbaum and Michelle Miller-Day. My work and thinking has been tremendously and positively influenced by these scholars who have encouraged me to consider interpersonal communication as the most powerful everyday act we engage in across our lifespan. And finally, I would like to acknowledge my new colleagues at the University of Arizona who see potential in my work and contributions to the field of communication.

—MJP

• F O R E W O R D •

So Let It Be with Caesar . . . ?

Steve Duck
University of Iowa

> The evil that men do lives after them; the good is oft interred with their bones.
> —Shakespeare

Apart from a lifelong interest in the study of personal relationships, one of my abiding passions is history, particularly Roman history and Medieval/English Tudor history. This is mostly for amusement and mental development, but also because of awareness of the risks of ignoring history and repeating its mistakes.

In the course of this dedicated leisure activity, I have learned that it was not until the late 1890s that any city—in this case, New York—was able to provide its inhabitants with such an efficient, reliable and voluminous on-tap water supply as was available in ancient Rome at the time of Julius Caesar. Likewise I have learned that the medieval invention of the mantled chimney, replacing the previous hole in the communal roof towards which smoke was optimistically directed, created the possibility of heating separate rooms.

Each of these changes in physical capacity had relational consequences that we all too often overlook in the search for the interestingly unique psychological or communicative activity while ignoring the commonplaces and ordinary activities of life (Duck, 2011). When people do not need to meet at wells in order to draw their daily rations of water, social community is affected; the private running water tap isolates members of the community who had previously gathered to draw water but also to share stories, news and relational updates. The heating of private room encourages separation of the wealthy from the rest of the group that had previously lived and performed all daily functions in one common hall. Social division is figuratively and literally represented in spatial separation (Duck, 2011).

On top of the relational consequences of technological growth, represented these days as if it were something new when that is by no means true

(Andrejevic, 2007), it is equally untrue to represent the study of relationships as a new science. It is often surprising to note that what the Romans took for granted disappeared with the fall of the Western Roman Empire and was not rediscovered or taken for granted again until relatively recent times. Many comforts of life and ingenious solutions to life's problems were nevertheless ready at hand, including, obviously, personal relationships about which Romans and Greeks both wrote quite a lot. Evidently an interest in relationships by thinkers and scholars has been long-lasting, though just as today there are some good and bad elements to relationships, so too for the Romans. Julius Caesar was, after all, murdered by some of his closest former friends and other people whom he had graciously forgiven for their past defaults. His dying words were not "Et tu Brute" but Greek, και συ τεκνον ["kai su teknon"], which translate as "you too, my son?" leading to long and unresolved debate about Brutus' paternity, given Caesar's lifelong notoriety as a seducer of his friends' wives.

Chapters in this volume represent such activities as forgiveness as positive influences on relationships, emphasize the clarity and the value of good listening and excellent communication, discuss the many sided nature of affectionate communication, indicate the importance of recognition and celebration of other people's performance, and stress the importance of nurturing, comfort, and support. Clearly, these are important and it is time that someone focused in a single volume on these positive aspects of relationships. One is nevertheless forced to recognize, even from the brief historical references above, that forgiveness can have negative consequences, nurturance can lead to betrayal, friendship can sometimes be a path way to adultery, and that support can end at the point of a dagger.

It is therefore necessary to praise the attempt of the editors to bring together such a variety of smart people to write chapters for this volume, but to contextualize their efforts which must be planted amidst the range of other circling activities in relationships. Only rarely do we experience friendship and nothing else, with no disturbances, no arguments, no disputes, no conflicts of opinion, no ongoing tedium of normality. Positive though friendship, forgiveness, intimacy, and other relational elements may be in themselves, they always have other accompaniments in the swirling, blooming, buzzing, boring confusion of everyday life. In order to elaborate on this point, made by Duck and Wood (1995), it is valuable to take another look at history of a more recent kind.

Resurgam

In an excavation in London in the late 1600s, workers preparing the site for the new St. Paul's Cathedral came upon a Roman burial ground and in particular a votive offering containing the word "Resurgam," I will rise again. It is something of a delight to learn repeatedly, as above, about the state of things so long ago, their disappearance, and their resurgence. It is also worth reflecting in the context of the current volume that similar patterns of existence, disappearance and resurgence besiege modern academic research. Although we like to think of research as driven by theory and strictly academic concerns, there is necessarily a pattern of fashion and it influences the topics that we consider worth studying. Against this pattern of fashion, it is commendable that the editors have chosen a relatively unpopular topic—or at least have managed to recognize a latent pattern in the work of many different scholars which can be brought together in this volume. Of course, work on positive aspects of relationships has been done before, but it has not been collected previously into a single important volume. Topics come and go, but their resurgence depends on the vision of those who recognize patterns.

Indeed, I must confess to an ironic repetition of a point that I first made in 1980 (Duck, 1980) that there is a cyclicity in research, as people become bored with some topics and wish to establish a reputation for inventing something new. In the 1980 chapter, I drew attention to the loss of the taken-for-granted as PhD advisors steer their students towards the *criticism* of current research and they, in their turn, did the same until we reached the point where those things that the original PhD advisor knew for certain were either crumbling under the assault of sharper minds or had been entirely discarded and forgotten. Thus, some certainties of research become lost, decline and decay, and all too often it is the case that someone will claim a new topic of research (e.g., "context" Karney et al., 2005), which is new only to those who have not sufficiently reviewed existing research that has already discussed the topic in detail (Duck, 1993).

It is also characteristic that scientists and scholars overlook research in disciplines other than their own, so that there is a continual rediscovery of piles and piles of discarded wheels. Likewise, it is the case that scholars are concerned with being up-to-date or connected to the famous, and therefore neglect other work as they follow the recognized leaders of a field treading a well-established path, preferably one with simple but exciting names, such as the Pygmalion effect, SPEAKING, or the Michelangelo effect (Innes, 1980).

One History of the Study of Relationships

The belief that relationships were an important positive and satisfying part of life was one of the earliest claims made on their behalf, and dates back to Aristotle and Cicero, both of whom, rather interestingly, wrote not only about rhetoric and persuasion, but also about friendship. It was however a 20th century trend for books to be written about the way in which relationships could be improved, with many trade books earning their authors satisfying retirements (Carnegie, 1936 for example). Early researchers on marital satisfaction such as Hamilton (1924) were more energetic but less well cushioned against the evening of life. Physical attractiveness, explored in detail by Perrin (1921), did not become fashionable again until the mid-1970s (Dion & Berscheid, 1974). After a brief, beautiful, flurry it declined and fell until a resurgence accompanied the development of third wave feminist theory and in particular an interest in transgendered identities (Norwood, 2010) and the role that physical attractiveness played in rejection of women by other women (Norwood, 2007). Attachment theory, developed in the 1940s by Bowlby (1951) was seen to have no obvious connection to the general theory of personal relationships until Hazan and Shaver (1987) reconceptualized romantic love as an attachment process, after which even a dying Gaul could not avoid encountering some research paper attaching attachment to all known forms of relational life.

One broad history of relationships therefore is a history of the discovery and resurgence of ideas that have previously declined and fallen. One is tempted to answer the question of whether it is a matter of human nature that this cycle of discovery is embedded in our psychological makeup, and that generation after generation is necessarily rediscovering the beliefs of our forebears. After all, one thing that is simply not transmissible from one person to another is "experience". To some degree, we must all stand on the shoulders of giants, and yet are required to relearn what they knew.

The ability to comprehend a broader picture that represents the contributions of previous researchers necessarily requires that we stop and think. The fact that this volume requires us to do just that, and to place our recent efforts in some larger framework, is all to the good. That is, it is all to the good as long as researchers actually take account of it and do not start their "historical contextualization" only with research dating from the 1990s.

Research as an Influence on Research

The nature of research itself encourages researchers to focus on specific issues, particularly in experimental paradigms, and to isolate them from the greater flow of life so that they may be studied more effectively. Despite the fact that physical and prevailing social characteristics are imported by everybody into their interactions with one another, the isolation of the influence of physical attraction from other factors is a necessary requirement of its study in the laboratory, for example. Almost every other topic which has been studied in the field provides a further example. Hence, many researchers happily plow their own furrows—or in Levinger's (1972) arresting analogy, play in their own sandboxes—while overlooking the broader picture that relationships present for analysis. This of course is one reason why isolated pockets of positive relationships have remained unconnected until the editors of this volume thought to pull it all together.

I'm not sure if this isolationism is a feature of research which is avoidable or simply one that is embedded in the academic structures in which we all earn our daily bread and circuses. Nevertheless, as the pace of research on relationships picked up in the 1980s and '90s, there was a tendency first to notice the importance of the positive influence of relationships on mental health before the pattern switched to concern with the negativity that relationships also brought—and then a resurgence of the important recognition that specific and isolated elements of positive relationships must be a major part of life. Individual researchers and teams of researchers pursue their own specific topical influences and interests. For example, Brant Burleson's energetic and consistent studies of comforting represent a programmatic approach to one specific element of positivity in relationships. A general overview of positivity, however, has had to wait for this particular volume.

Interestingly, one of the first places that an emphasis on positive relationships was developed was in the area of management theory, where many distinguished researchers were as unaware of the 25 years of research carried out by their colleagues in what is now the field of personal relationships as we were of their own efforts. Dutton and Ragins' (2006) volume on positive relationships at work was the first that I know of to have the words "positive relationships" in the title, but it is, somewhat predictably, not cited outside the field of business management. Nevertheless, the authors in that edited volume have done significant work about the way in which positive relationships influence productivity and satisfaction in the workplace as well as management styles and leadership techniques. Their definition of "positive relationships" may not be one that we recognize fully, and yet it is an important resource where opportunities for interaction between the two separate fields of business management and personal relationships are legion.

What Is Positive about Positivity?

The editors of this volume wisely focus on "prosocial/antisocial communication, communication ethics, religious/spiritual communication, positive psychology, and ... sketch a preliminary conceptual framework of 'positive interpersonal communication'" (Socha & Pitts, chapter 1, this volume). They cite several authors who have equated positive relationships with happiness and virtue. The topics of happiness and virtue are immediately reminiscent of those issues which taxed Aristotle and Cicero, to say nothing of Socrates, Seneca, and more ancient philosophers than you could shake an Ideal stick at. So do we come again to a resurgence of something that our forebears—every one of us must have at least some genetic connection to ancient Greece and Rome – were as equally thoughtful and concerned about, as we are?

Of course, it is conventional to suggest that the recent "science of relationships" is far too advanced from any ideas and suggestions proposed nearly 2500 years ago. On deeper inspection, however, it appears at best that the speculations of the millennia have merely been confirmed in detail by people in white coats using Hierarchical Linear Modeling methods. Similarity is preferred to dissimilarity, as Aristotle indicated. Individuals are drawn to those who have similar ways of viewing the world, as Cicero suggested. Physical attractiveness is an influence on patterns of social activity, as both of them indicated. Secrets and hurtful remarks influence relational outcomes as Herodotus, Thucydides, and other ancients described. Love takes many forms and styles, as Plato suggested.

So what is positive? As the Editors noted in chapter 1, several researchers have shown that positivity and negativity are not absolutes but are themselves either matters of opinion or re-negotiated by the participants. Despite the fact that researchers recognize this, at some level, the tendency persists for writers to act otherwise. For example, if Baxter et al. (chapter 2, this volume) place realistic emphasis on the balance between the two, their approach still suggests that the two elements are somehow defined in advance. In this sense, dichotomous thinking is the enemy of progress and an emphasis on the balance between extremes in a dichotomy is less progressive than the recognition that ... well, really relationship life is a bit of a muddle. Of course, in the life of a scientist, "muddle" does not exist; scientists are organized and methodical, and therefore the possibility that other people are not so structured is something that does not enter into a scientist's mind. Indeed the scientific method is one based on beliefs in hygiene and cleaning up of mess almost typical of the Roman baths.

But what if life is essentially, for the regular human being, an experience of confusion and compromise? What if everyone experiences relationships as an essentially positive activity, except for the negative parts? What if every human being is used to balancing the good and the bad, the ugly and the pretty, the predictable and the unpredictable, the negative and the positive? Perhaps our very subjects could instruct us on the fact that our focus on positivity or negativity is itself oversimplified. They are wrestling with contradictions and improbabilities in every moment of their relational life, and yet we persist in studying them as if they live in a dichotomous world of special behaviors when we have virtually no understanding of the day-to-day commonplaces that stitch that world together.

One of the advantages of the perspective taken in this volume, however, is that it allows us to represent the positive activities of relationships within the broader context of other activities whereon researchers have all too often made hard and fast distinctions that fit the experimental paradigm, but do not fit human experience. Humans will tell you that they love relationships and that they experience the greatest joys in relationships. However, they are not so naïve as to assume that all relationships are positive all the time every minute of the day. Nevertheless, it is important that researchers focus on the fact that people most often feel positive about their relationships and that relationships are a positive influence on their daily lives.

One of the main outcomes of the publication of this volume, therefore, is clearly going to be that researchers pay more attention to the balance of influences on relational life. It would be a huge mistake for the field of social and personal relationships to ignore the dilemmas that face individuals day by day. It would equally be a serious mistake for researchers to review experience in relationships in a way that ignores their positive influence on most people's lives.

One of the key values of this volume, then, is its recognition of the fact that the positive balance of relationships is overdue for recognition in social and personal relationship research. It is also important that many chapters in this volume recognize the innocence of separation between positive and negative and pay significant attention to the balancing act that real human beings perform each day in conducting their relationships. For too long the field of social and personal relationships has focused on small activities separated from their broader context and wholeness (Duck, 1993). The value of this volume, as compared to research in social and personal relationships more generally, lies in its emphasis on balance: the resurgence of emphasis on the positivity of relationships is a significant advance for the field.

Et tu Brute?

Am I then suggesting that the field of personal relationships has made no advances, worthy of the name? No. I do not come to bury the field of personal relationships but to praise it. Of course, the field of research has its limitations and researchers too often fail to recognize the significance of separating small pieces of the body from the whole routine background against which they are conducted. However, it is healthy to lend our ears to other points of view and the editors' emphasis on positivity should stimulate discussion about the proper ways to conceptualize beyond dichotomy. Thus, the debate about the negative and positive aspects of relationships is healthy to the extent that it encourages researchers to reflect more thoughtfully on the multiple interactions that take place between "variables" in any interpersonal interaction. That does not mean that we have failed in our task of clarifying the nature of relationships, but rather that we must more vigorously recognize the larger picture, the historical background, the multiple influences, the normal routine scenery, and our very own involvement in the activities that we study in order to make greater progress.

This latter might sound like a variation on the regular theme "more research needs to be done." This has only ever been true if it is *good* research. "Good research" recognizes and reconnects those parts which were separated for analytic purposes at the beginning of a given study. "Good research" does not simply limit itself, bare its neck and play the Roman fool by appearing to fall on the sword of a "limitations" section that is then effectively ignored. "Good research" really takes its limitations seriously, and recognizes the ways in which limitations really do affect the interpretation of results, including that fact that we lack a base of understanding of everyday routine behaviors against which the influence of the negative or the positive critical event can be placed. "Good research" is humble enough to recognize the very small part of the jigsaw that it is working on. As Baxter et al. note in Chapter 2 of this volume, the interplay between negativity and positivity is important to recognize. In addition, the interplay between large influences on relationships and small influences on relationships is also important to recognize, as is the daily routine of ordinary experience.

This volume makes a course correction for research in relationships and offers researchers many opportunities for greater advancement of the larger enterprise. While I sometimes wish that research would be suspended for four years to allow scholars to reflect more carefully on what it is they are doing, it is important that the role of positive relationships is fully recognized. We must not focus on the evil of relationships and inter the good. When these reflections occur, then we will have come, seen, and conquered.

References

Andrejevic, M. (2007). *iSpy: Surveillance and power in the interactive era*. Lawrence, KS: The University Press of Kansas.

Bowlby, J. (1951). *Maternal care and mental health*. Geneva: WHO.

Carnegie, D. (1936). *How to win friends and influence people*. New York: Simon and Schuster.

Dion, K. K., & Berscheid, E. (1974). Physical attractiveness and peer perception among children. *Sociometry, 37,* 1-12.

Duck, S. W. (1980). Taking the past to heart: One of the futures of social psychology. In R. Gilmour & S. W. Duck (Eds.), *The development of social psychology* (pp. 211-238). London: Academic Press.

Duck, S. W. (1993). Preface on social contexts. In S. W. Duck (Ed), *Understanding relationship processes 3: Social contexts of relationships*. Newbury Park: Sage.

Duck, S. W. (2011). *Rethinking relationships: A new approach to relationship research*. Thousand Oaks, CA: Sage.

Duck, S. W., & Wood, J. T. (1995). For better for worse, for richer for poorer: The rough and the smooth of relationships. In S. W. Duck & J. T. Wood (Eds.), *Understanding relationship processes 5: Confronting relationship challenges* (pp. 1-21). Thousand Oaks, CA: Sage.

Dutton, J., & Ragins, B. (Eds.) (2006). *Positive relationships at work*. Mahwah, NJ: Erlbaum.

Hamilton, G. V. (1924). *A research in marriage*. New York: Lear.

Hazan, C., & Shaver, P. (1987). Romantic love conceptualized as an attachment process. *Journal of Personality and Social Psychology, 52,* 511-524.

Innes, J. M. (1980). Fashions in social psychology. In R. Gilmour & S. W. Duck (Eds.), *The development of social psychology* (pp. 137-162). London: Academic Press.

Karney, B. R., Story, L. B., & Bradbury, T. Among newlyweds. In T. A. Revenson, K. Kayser, & G. Bodenmann (Eds.), *Emerging perspectives on couples' coping with stress* (pp. 13-32). Washington DC: American Psychological Association Press.

Levinger, G. (1972). Little sandbox and big quarry: Comment on Byrne's paradigmatic spade for research on interpersonal attraction. *Representative Research in Social Psychology, 3,* 3-19.

Norwood, K. M. (2007, October). *Gendered conflict? The "cattiness" of women on flavor of love*. Paper at the meeting of the Organization for the Study of Communication Language and Gender, Omaha, NE.

Norwood, K. M. (2010). *Here and gone: Competing discourses in the communication of families with a transgender member* (Unpublished doctoral dissertation). Department of Communication Studies, University of Iowa, Iowa City, IA.

Perrin, F. A. C. (1921). Physical attractiveness and repulsions. *Journal of Experimental Psychology, 4,* 203-217.

• CHAPTER ONE •

Toward a Conceptual Foundation for Positive Interpersonal Communication

Thomas J. Socha
Old Dominion University

Margaret J. Pitts
University of Arizona

Like government, human relationships can be regarded as "imperfect embodiments of . . . common will" (L. Pitts, 2010). Human relationships are messy, perpetually unfinished (Duck, 2011), and can elicit humans' most noble and most sinister sides (Duck, 1994). They are contexts for the realization of dreams and nightmares, for celebrations and diminutions of human potentialities and human spirit. Building on past research that includes prosocial-antisocial communication (e.g., Kinney & Pörhölä, 2009a), positive psychology (e.g., Csikszentmihalyi, 1990, 1993; Peterson, 2006; Seligman, 2002), and more, as well as complementing the dark side of interpersonal communication (e.g., Cupach & Spitzberg, 1994, 2004; Spitzberg & Cupach, 1998; 2007), this volume brings together veteran interpersonal communication scholars to begin to frame a conceptual foundation for studies on the "positive" side of interpersonal communication, or in general terms, relational communication facilitative of happiness, health, and wellness.

Our approach to building a conceptual foundation for positive interpersonal communication is inclusive of a wide array of theories and methods (social scientific, qualitative, and critical) and flexible so as to accommodate existing areas of inquiry as well as what we anticipate will be many new areas. Given this approach, some chapters in the volume feature essays where communication scholars expand on established areas of interpersonal communication theory and research that are considered to be positive such as affection (Floyd & Deiss, chapter 8, this volume) and humor (Meyer, chapter 10, this volume). Other chapters offer full reports of groundbreaking empirical research studies that yield new data about positive interpersonal communication phenomena. And, still other, shorter chapters suggest new horizons of inquiry and application such as positive interpersonal communication in healthcare (e.g., Kreps, chapter 15, this volume). Collectively, the volume offers a primer to a variety of concepts, processes, and applications that comprise interpersonal communication's positive side, as well as commentary that connects this work to interpersonal communication's dark side.

We organize the volume and our emerging conceptual foundation into three major sections that include: key concepts, fundamental positive interpersonal communication processes, and illustrative applications.

Section one, *Key Concepts*, contains five chapters that examine a number of important concepts which we argue should be among the significant building blocks in a conceptual foundation for positive interpersonal communication theory. These key concepts include: relational aesthetics (Baxter et al., chapter 2), relational synchrony (Kim, chapter 3), interpersonal communication excellence (Mirivel, chapter 4), virtues and interpersonal communication (Miczo, chapter 5), and a lifespan approach to intimacy, with a particular focus on later life (Nussbaum et al., chapter 6). Although certainly not exhaustive, together these chapters begin to delineate many primary concepts upon which future positive interpersonal communication theory-building and research can be built.

Section two, *Fundamental Processes*, contains eight chapters that examine fundamental interpersonal communication processes considered by most to be "positive." Some of the chapters in this section cover familiar positive interpersonal communication processes such as appreciative listening (Bodie, chapter 7) and affectionate communication (Floyd & Deiss, chapter 8). Other chapters examine important but understudied interpersonal communication processes such as: play (Aune & Wong, chapter 9), humor (Meyer, chapter 10), the positive sides of conflict (Kellett, chapter 11), and forgiveness (Kelley, chapter 12). Finally, although communicating support (MacGeorge et al., chapter 13) is certainly familiar, communicating celebratory support (McCullough & Burleson, chapter 14) represents an exciting new horizon. Together, the chapters in this section demonstrate that positive interpersonal communication consists of many multi-faceted and complex processes, and also that future research is needed that begins to examines how these positive processes and those yet to be considered, alone and together, comprise effective, appropriate, and positive interpersonal communication, as well as how communicators go about elevating these processes to even higher levels of refinement and sophistication.

Finally, section three, *Illustrative Applications*, features four chapters that illustrate the potential of applied positive interpersonal communication in the contexts of healthcare, spirituality, and human development. Gary Kreps (considered the father of health communication) sketches an outline of some of the features of positive communication in healthcare (chapter 15). This is followed by Baesler, Derlega, and Lolley (chapter 16) who examine prisoners' spiritual communication as they cope with HIV and prison life. These chapters spotlight the potential of positive interpersonal communication as a force in healthcare and also begin to connect spiritual communication processes and relational communication in new and important ways. These chapters also anticipate a positive interpersonal communication volume that is in the works which will focus on health and wellness (e.g., see Pitts & Socha, in preparation).

The final two chapters of this section and the volume focus on the critical importance of the development of positive interpersonal communication across the lifespan. Wilson and Gettings (chapter 17) remind us of the need to ensure that children's early communication experiences with caregivers are positive so as to create solid development footings for future growth. And, Frey and White (chapter 18) conclude the volume by demonstrating that positive interpersonal communication instruction and learning can, and should, continue into adulthood so as to serve as a force for the betterment of human relationships.

In short, together, the chapters in this volume present some of the many benefits of rethinking how we approach interpersonal communication theory and research by adopting a positive perspective that examines strengths and assets as well as deficits and weaknesses, and also seeks to spur new thinking about interpersonal communication by engaging our imaginations in service of the development of human communication potentialities. However, throughout the volume (and in an epilogue) readers will also notice that we remain cognizant and wary of the power of the dark side of interpersonal communication, as any of the concepts and processes covered in this volume can employed in destructive and debasing ways.

The volume also pays special tribute to the life's work of the nationally-regarded, interpersonal communication scholar, Brant Burleson (Purdue University), who passed away before the volume was completed. Brant's research on comforting and support spans over three decades and in many respects has been at the forefront of increasing our understanding of positive communication. We are particularly honored that this volume contains a chapter that Brant was coauthoring at the time of his death with a one of his many Purdue Communication PhD students, Jennifer McCullough, as well as chapters coauthored by Brant's wife, Erina MacGeorge and her Purdue students, and by Brant's former student, longtime friend, and Purdue colleague, Steve Wilson and one of his Purdue students, Patricia Gettings. As they, and all of us, grieve the loss of Brant, we cannot think of a better exemplar of positive interpersonal communication research than Brant's decades of studies on comforting, and are very proud to celebrate Brant's important work by dedicating this volume to his memory.

Chapter Overview

Over 17 years ago, at the dawning of the dark side of interpersonal communication studies (i.e., Cupach & Spitzberg, 1994), Duck (1994) pointed out a "positivity bias" in the literature on personal relationships, that is, the literature to that point was heavy on "nice" topics like "love . . . ideal courtships . . . deep personal intimacy . . . fairness . . . closeness [and more]" (p. 4), but light on topics like abuse, bullying, deception, humiliation, jealousy, revenge, stalking, and the like. Since that landmark volume, studies of the dark side of interpersonal communication have become commonplace in the landscape of relational communication scholarship and have contributed significantly to advancing a fuller understanding of interpersonal studies communication.

As research on the dark side of interpersonal communication developed, the historical landscape of interpersonal communication research continued to be dotted with many examples of the kinds of "positive" topics mentioned by Duck (1994). However, these kinds of studies continued to be scattered widely across the interpersonal communication literature, and lacking an organizing scheme, they existed amorphously in the interpersonal communication mainstream: everywhere and nowhere. To begin to give form to this work, this volume offers an organizing conceptual framework, the "positive side of interpersonal communication," as a means to: help connect the dots of past positive interpersonal communication studies, suggest new vistas for future interpersonal communication research on the positive side, as well as, facilitate connections between the positive interpersonal communication studies and an exciting new area in psychology—positive psychology.

For the past decade, while interpersonal communication research, both dark and bright sides, continued to grow, major developments on the positive front were also occurring under the banner of positive psychology (e.g., see Peterson, 2006; Seligman & Csikszentmihalyi, 2000). We believe this work holds substantial promise for communication studies in general, and relational and family communication in particular (e.g., see Socha, 2006, 2009) and are pleased to begin to explore prospective connections between positive psychology and interpersonal communication theorizing and research in this volume.

In this chapter, we draw on studies of prosocial/antisocial communication, communication ethics, religious/spiritual communication, positive psychology, and more to begin to sketch a preliminary conceptual framework of "positive interpersonal communication" that is intended to aid the field of interpersonal communication by advancing and deepening its understanding of interpersonal communication processes facilitative of happiness, health, and wellness. These concepts also appear in various ways throughout the chapters in the volume as will be noted below.

Core Elements of a Conceptual Foundation for Positive Interpersonal Communication

Happiness

A core concept in positive psychology is "happiness" (e.g., see Seligman, 2002) and discussions of meanings of "happiness" in positive psychology spotlight two important forms: hedonic and eudemonic. Hedonic happiness refers to "maximizing pleasure and minimizing pain," while eudemonia refers to "identifying one's virtues, cultivating them, and living in accordance with them" (Peterson, 2006, p. 78). In contrast to a contemporary culture driven by commercial advertising touting pleasurable, hedonic pursuits, research finds hedonic pursuits to actually be a weaker predictor of overall life satisfaction than eudemonic pursuits (Peterson, 2006, chapter 4; Seligman, 2002). According to Peterson (2006) the finding of eudemonia's relatively greater impact on life satisfaction "is robust, occurring across the adult years, for males and females, and for residents of the United States, Canada, and other nations" (p. 79). Further, research finds that humans adapt quickly to hedonic pleasures and must continue to seek more and higher levels of pleasure to achieve the same levels of satisfaction. Referred to as the "hedonic treadmill" (Peterson, 2006, p. 54), this condition is highlighted, for example, by studies of the happiness levels of lottery winners who, over the long haul, are found to be not much more happy than non-lottery winners, and who also experience less everyday-pleasure than non-lottery winners (Brickman, Coates, & Janoff-Bulman, 1978). Positive psychologists are, however, not suggesting that hedonic pursuits be abandoned, but rather that both forms of happiness are inherent in living full lives, but urge that eudemonia should receive greater attention in future work.

In an article cited in many positive psychology works, Lyubomirsky, Sheldon, and Schkade (2005) theorized that overall happiness (eudemonic and hedonic) can be conceptualized as the sum of three factors: individuals' happiness set point, their life circumstances, and their volitional activities. First, a person's genetically determined "set point for experiencing positive affect" contributes to his/her general levels of happiness (e.g., see Floyd & Deiss, chapter 8, this volume). Although research on this front is emerging, it seems reasonable to accept, to some extent, that personal happiness is not fully under conscious control, but rather is fundamentally shaped, to some degree, by genetic inheritance and human bio-chemistry that drives conditions from depression to optimism, sadness to happiness. However, for a fuller picture we must also include what is under our control, that is, our life-circumstances and volition (nurture).

The second factor of happiness, "life circumstances," includes: "number of friends, being married, religiousness, and conscientiousness," (Peterson, 2006, p. 92) (found to have a moderate effect on happiness) as well as "optimism, being employed, frequency of sexual intercourse, percent of time experiencing positive affect, [and] self-esteem" (Peterson, 2006, p. 92) (found to have a strong effect on happiness).

Life circumstance factors (positive and negative) are, of course, connected in essential and fundamental ways to interpersonal communication. That is, if we desire to augment our levels of happiness by increasing our number of friends, marrying (assumed happily), and maintaining a job, feeling good about ourselves, and so on, then we must consider the integral role that interpersonal communication processes play in relational pursuits (e.g., see Mirivel, chapter 4, this volume, for a discussion of interpersonal communication excellence).

Lyubomirsky et al.'s (2005) third and final factor in their happiness equation—volitional activity—refers to individual choices made concerning the engagement in thoughts and behaviors demonstrated to be facilitative of happiness (eudemonic and hedonic). Understanding the impact of positive volitional activities on happiness represents a major thrust of the theory, research, and pedagogy of positive psychology and, within positive psychology, has also fueled the development of an expanding array of experiential learning tools for use in classrooms, clinical, and self-therapeutic settings. These exercises have become commonplace in positive psychology courses and are intended to facilitate gaining insights, learning, and monitoring a host of positive aspects of self and relationships such as gratitude, mood, hope, flourishing, and more (e.g., see University of Pennsylvania Positive Psychology Center, 2011; Peterson, 2006; and in communication, see Frey & White, chapter 18, this volume; as well as Socha, 2008).

Extending the concept of "volitional activities facilitative of happiness" to interpersonal communication raises many questions that include how we chose to spend our interpersonal communication resources and time, especially in light of the current proliferation of interaction via social media. That is, in everyday life there is a finite amount of time and personal resources available for engagement in interpersonal communication. We therefore must choose how to optimally invest our time and resources in service of eudemonic and hedonic happiness through interaction with others (e. g., see Wilson & Gettings, chapter 17, this volume, concerning youth mentoring programs).

Csikszentmihalyi (1990), in his landmark book, *Flow*, found that only particular kinds of activities have the potential to provide high levels of engagement (e.g., artistic pursuits, athletics, meaningful debate and discussion, playing chess and similar games, building things, etc.) and also increase the chances of experiencing a positive psychological state called "flow" (Csikszentmihalyi, 1990). During experiences of genuine flow, we lose track of time and lose focus on ourselves as we become totally immersed in the activity. Activities where there are clear and challenging goals that require the use of skills and where feedback about our progress is received during engagement have the potential to produce flow. And, why are flow experiences important? They are strongly correlated with eudemonic happiness and, in the long run, contribute to life satisfaction (Csikszentmihalyi, 1990).

Relevant to positive interpersonal communication studies, and according to conditions in which the state of flow has been documented to occur (Csikszentmihalyi, 1990), it would seem that flow might likely to be elicited in interpersonal communication situations such as: old friends getting lost in hours of conversation at a reunion (e.g., see Nussbaum et al., chapter 6, this volume); newly romantically involved couples engaging in marathon sessions of self-disclosure; honeymooners spending days shut away from the outside world; families discussing and debating meaningful dinner topics far beyond dinnertime; friends, loved ones, and caring others engaging in episodes of therapeutic and caring listening about troubles, obstacles, illness, and problems (see Bodie, chapter 7, this volume; Kreps, chapter 15, this volume); spiritual/religious believers sharing meditation and prayer as conjoint communication (see Baesler et al., chapter 16, this volume), and more. Of course, let us not forget, that it also seems likely that flow might also be experienced during engagement in dark-side relational communication activities such as stalking (see Cupach & Spitzberg, 2004; and Spitzberg & Cupach, epilogue, this volume).

In sum, while humans may not have control of inherited genetic foundations of happiness, humans' choices do matter in shaping the qualities of interpersonal relationships, and experiences in interpersonal relationships figure largely in hedonic and eudemonic happiness (as well as in unhappiness and misery). And, as relationships are social constructions, it is clear that the quality of interpersonal communication is a contributing factor to positive (and negative) relational quality as well as personal and relational happiness and suffering (e.g., see Duck, 2011; Gottman, 1993). Thus, if we accept eudemonic and hedonic happiness as integral human pursuits, we must then ask about the qualities of interpersonal communication that can facilitate eudemonic and hedonic happiness—a general aim of what we are calling positive communication studies.

Although there is conceptual overlap between the concepts of eudemonic and hedonic happiness—helping others can produce feelings of eudemonia as well as experiences of pleasure—to begin to fashion a foundation for future studies, we first consider interpersonal communication foci that in some way have potential to contribute to boosting eudemonic happiness that include: prosocial communication, interpersonal communication ethics, religious/spiritual interpersonal communication, and interpersonal communication and positive character strengths. We then consider potential connections between interpersonal communication and augmenting hedonic happiness.

Eudemonic Happiness and Interpersonal Communication

Prosocial. In a groundbreaking volume on prosocial and anti-social communication, Kinney and Pörhölä (2009b) used the properties of "helpfulness" and "hurtfulness" to organize interpersonal research of communication's positive and negative sides:

> Antisocial communication is conceptualized generally as characteristic of relationships that function to harm or disadvantage individuals, often manifesting as detrimental or unsupportive messages. Similarly, prosocial communication is conceptualized as characteristic of relationships that function to help or assist individuals, often in the form of beneficial or supportive messages. (p. viii)

Thus, using Kinney and Pörhölä's (2009b) definition, prosocial messages promoting helping, assisting, and similar behaviors would seem, at least conceptually, and by definition, to have the potential to boost one's own (and perhaps one's partner's) eudemonic happiness. Thus, one important goal for future positive interpersonal communication studies is to empirically gauge the nature, direction, and strength of potential connections between a communicator's engagement in prosocial interpersonal communication behaviors and feelings of eudemonia (one's own and one's partners).

In the epilogue of the Kinney and Pörhölä's (2009a) volume, Giles and Speer (2009) also posed five useful questions intended to help frame future work on the prosocial/anti-social communication front (and by extension the positive/negative communication front). Their first two questions wonder about the kinds of concepts that might be included under a positive/negative communication banner and how these concepts are to be defined. Giles and Speer suggest that besides supportive and comforting messages (which appear in their volume as well as this one) such concepts as "accommodative messages, politeness, praise, caring, sympathy and empathy, compassion, and encouragement" (p. 192) might be considered (all of which would seem to support eudemonic happiness). However, Giles and Speer, echoing Duck (1994), also cautioned that the subjective nature of deciding, a priori, whether a concept or process is indeed to be viewed as "positive" is problematic. For example, effective humorous messages prompt mirth and laughter and laughter is viewed as having positive psychological and physical benefits. However, laughter can be prompted using antisocial means (dark side). Thus, if a communication vehicle is perceived to be "antisocial," but its message effect is "positive," does this count as an example of positive interpersonal communication? These kinds of complex philosophical and conceptual problems require further theoretical and conceptual work of which some is launched in the chapters by and Baxter et al. (chapter 2, on aesthetics, Mirivel (chapter 4, on excellence) and Miczo (chapter 5, on virtues).

Giles and Speer's third and fourth questions point out that instead of dichotomous thinking in prosocial/anti-social terms (positive/negative; bright/dark, etc.), that it is conceptually richer to regard the dark side and positive side as separate continua as well as unique forms of message processes that can vary in degrees (high to low). Their claims echo Spitzberg and Cupach's (1998, 2007) initial argument justifying the dark side of interpersonal communication as an important and unique topic area in its own right worthy of investigation. Of course, we also agree that positive communication is a different from, yet connected to, the dark side and that is a unique and important organizing metaphor to guide future interpersonal communication studies.

And, finally, in question five, Giles and Speer remind us that positive and negative processes reside at multiple levels that include individuals, relationships, groups and intergroup relationships, with prosocial/antisocial message activities occurring in numerous contexts across the human lifespan. Although most of the present volume on positive communication is devoted to adult communicators (Wilson & Gettings, chapter 17, this volume, is an exception), it is clear that future positive interpersonal communication research should consider a lifespan developmental approach (cradle to grave) as well as conduct research into how different groups view and manage what is regarded as standards of positive interpersonal communication (see also Socha, 2006, 2009; and Socha & Yingling, 2010).

Ethical. In a different but related vein, communication ethics scholars Arnett, Harden-Fritz, and Bell (2009) also invoke a positive/negative framing in their discussion of interpersonal communication ethics. They point out that, ethically speaking, on the dark side, interpersonal communication can function as a means of "interpersonal colonization" in the forms of "control, obsession, and manipulation" (p. 129), and, on the positive side, as *"hesed*, a Hebrew term, [referring to] something done . . . that protects and promotes the good of relationships [given freely, not demanded]" (Arnett et al., 2009, p. 128). As positive interpersonal communication is subjective, it is important to understand the interpretive frameworks that relational participants employ within and across similar kinds of relationships to determine what is, and what is not, considered to be ethical interpersonal communication behavior. And, although this is also left to future study, it would seem that engagement in ethical interpersonal communication may also boost eudemonic happiness (while unethical interpersonal communication would diminish eudemonia).

Religious/Spiritual. Another conceptually related, yet underexplored, area of interpersonal communication that employs a positive/negative framing is religious/spiritual communication. Although this area of inquiry has remained relatively separate from mainstream interpersonal communication inquiry, studies of prayer as communication by Baesler (1999) features the development of an interpersonal communication model of prayer (also see Baesler et al., chapter 16, this volume). Jacobi (2009) draws connections between spirituality, prosocial behavior and the use of positive social skills. Specifically, Jacobi pointed out at that "social skills [serve] as a mediator between spirituality and prosocial behavior . . . [and] it is [also] not a surprise that . . . spirituality leads to a desire to help others" (p. 123). Praying, meditating, engaging in helping and the like are clearly connected, at least by definition, to eudemonic happiness and should have a greater presence in future positive interpersonal communication studies.

Positive Character Strengths. Peterson and Seligman's (2004) book, *Character Strengths and Virtues: A Handbook and Classification* (and see Peterson, 2006, chapter 6), represents a landmark positive psychology work that identifies and offers extensive descriptions (including measures) of 24 positive virtues organized into six areas of strength. Extensive research into each area of strength is reported as well as extensive discussion of the criteria used to develop the classification scheme (e.g., virtues must be recognized across cultures, be measurable, have an obvious negative, be morally valued, and so on). Let's review each area and begin to consider points of connection for interpersonal communication inquiry.

Peterson and Seligman's (2004) strength area number one—*wisdom and knowledge*—contains five virtues: creativity, curiosity, love-of-learning, open-mindedness, and perspective (wise counsel). Interpersonal relationships where participants communicate, for example, in ways that are creative (see Baxter et al., chapter 2, this volume) would be a resource that could be used especially when facing a wide variety of problems.

Area two—*strengths of courage*—contains four virtues: authenticity, bravery, persistence, and zest (see Aune & Wong, chapter 9, on play, this volume). Authenticity would seem to represent interesting challenges in today's world of on-line social networking where the presentation of self could include the use of avatars (see Turkle, 2011), and persistence (although, on the dark side, equally applicable to stalkers) is also something that is a core part of work on relational maintenance.

Area three—*strengths of humanity*—contains three virtues that would seem to be essential defining qualities of positive interpersonal communication: kindness, love, and social intelligence. In this volume, chapters by Kim (chapter 3, synchrony), Mirivel (chapter 4, excellence), Floyd and Deiss (chapter 8, affectionate communication), and Wilson and Gettings (chapter 17, preventing child abuse) are examples of potential points of connection with the strengths of humanity.

Area four—*strengths of justice*—contains the three virtues of fairness, leadership, and teamwork. Although perhaps a bit more conceptually connected to past work on group communication, it is clear that fairness is a hallmark of interpersonal relationships from a social exchange perspective, and celebrating "we-ness" seems important, especially when sharing good news (see McCullough & Burleson, chapter 14, this volume). Also, the positive negotiation of conflict (see Kellett, chapter 11, this volume) would seem to fit into the strengths of justice area.

The fifth area—*strengths of temperance*—includes the virtues of forgiveness/mercy, modesty/humility, prudence, and self-regulation. The topic of forgiveness (Kelley, chapter 12, this volume) is clearly a significant part of positive interpersonal communication, but topics like prudence, and modesty would also seem to be important as a part preventing a variety of interpersonal conflicts.

And last, area six—*strengths of transcendence*—includes the virtues of appreciation of beauty/excellence (see Baxter et al., chapter 2, this volume; Miczo, chapter 5, this volume), gratitude, hope, humor (see Meyer, chapter 10, this volume), and religiousness/spirituality (see Baesler et al., chapter 16, this volume).

In general, Peterson and Seligman's work on character raises many interesting and potentially significant questions for interpersonal communication scholars, such as, how does positive virtue shape interpersonal communication? How does interpersonal communication facilitate the presentation of these positive virtues, such as, how do participants in relationships communicate so as to evoke hopefulness? The study of positive interpersonal communication virtues represents an important horizon for future positive interpersonal communication.

Summary. Positive interpersonal communication includes message processes that display prosocial, ethical, spiritual/religious, and positive character qualities somehow perceived to help and benefit a relationship and/or relational participants (as hesed, or blessing), or in general, promote eudemonic happiness. It is also commonly recognized that attitudes, feelings, and values can be framed positively (and negatively), and that communication (in all of its forms) plays a significant role in forming positive (and negative) attitudes, feelings, and values, such as those created and held by participants in personal and social relationships about each other as well as the relationship itself. To help us to further frame the role of interpersonal communication in bringing about positive psychological outcomes, as well as continue to expand the conceptual foundation for positive interpersonal communication we once again consult positive psychology.

Hedonic Happiness and Interpersonal Communication

Positive attitudes. Peterson's, *A Primer in Positive Psychology* (2006), offers an insightful chapter on positive thinking that includes the topics of optimism, the Pollyanna Principle (preferences to seek out positive stimuli, framings, memories, and more; see Matlin & Stang, 1978), explanatory style (how we choose to explain unhappy events) and hope. With respect to hope, Snyder's Hope Theory (1994, 2000) is included that considers hope as the product of two kinds of thinking—agentic thinking (determination to reach a goal and the worthiness of a person to reach a goal) and pathways thinking (belief in the ability to see multiple ways to overcome obstacles to reach a goal). From an interpersonal communication perspective, how do communicators use messages so as to increase agentic and pathways thinking? For example, when communicating support effectively it would seem that hope is also being increased (see MacGeorge et al., chapter 13, this volume). A positive outlook towards self, other, and the relationship itself would seem to clearly be a product of particular qualities of interpersonal communication that require future study,

Positive emotions. Positive psychologist Fredrickson (e.g., 2001, 2009) wondered about the role of positive emotions in human evolution. It seemed clear to Fredrickson that negative emotions like fear and anger served protective functions, keeping humans safe when confronting real or perceived dangers, but what about joy, contentment, and other similar positive feelings? Her lab-based research studies that support her broaden-and-build theory of positive emotions show that experiencing these kinds of positive feelings (and not just eliminating negativity) helps us to expand (broaden) our perspective and open ourselves to growth and positive changes (build). Further, Fredrickson (2009), similar to Gottman (1993, although his suggested ratio is 5-to-1), demonstrated that a minimum positivity ratio of 3-to-1 (positives to negatives) was necessary for flourishing, but that 11-to-1 seemed to represent an upper limit after which adding more positives would cease to have an effect (p. 135). Although this remains uncharted territory, research of extremely happy relationships (if such an ideal exists) would seem to be needed in interpersonal communication studies. However, studies of humor (Meyer, chapter 10, this volume), play (Aune & Wong, chapter 9, this volume), and affectionate communication (Floyd & Deiss, chapter 8, this volume), would seem to be three important areas concerning the cultivation of positive emotions in relationships that have potential to contribute to maintaining as well as increasing a positivity ratio.

Summary

Positive interpersonal communication is clearly much more than happy talk. We need to increase our understanding of the role of interpersonal communication in eudemonic as well as hedonic happiness, as well as on the three fronts that organize this volume: conceptual and philosophical foundations of positive interpersonal communication, positive interpersonal communication processes, and applications of positive interpersonal communication. The chapters that follow are intended to start the conversation about the many sides of positive interpersonal communication and we are happy to have you join us.

References

Arnett, R. C., Harden-Fritz, J. M., & Bell, L. M. (2009). *Communication ethics literacy: Dialogue and difference*. Thousand Oaks, CA: Sage.

Baesler, E. J. (1999). A model of interpersonal Christian prayer. *Journal of Communication & Religion, 22,* 40–64.

Brickman, P. Coates, D., & Jannoff–Bulman, R. (1978). Lottery winners and accident victims: Is happiness relative? *Journal of Personality and Social Psychology, 36,* 917–927.

Csikszentmihalyi, M. (1990). *Flow: The psychology of optimal experience*. New York: Harper Perennial.

Csikszentmihalyi, M. (1993). *The evolving self: A psychology for the third millennium*. New York: HarperPerennial.

Cupach, W. R., & Spitzberg, B. H. (Eds.). (1994). *The dark side of interpersonal communication*. Hillsdale, NJ: Lawrence Erlbaum.

Cupach, W. R., & Spitzberg, B. H. (2004). *The dark side of relational pursuit*. Mahwah, NJ: Lawrence Erlbaum Associates.

Duck, S. (1994). Stratagems, spoils, and a serpent's tooth: On the delights and dilemmas of personal relationships. In W. R. Cupach & B. H. Spitzberg (Eds.), *The dark side of interpersonal communication* (pp. 3–24). Hillsdale, NJ: Lawrence Erlbaum.

Duck, S. (2011). *Rethinking relationships*. Thousand Oaks, CA: Sage.

Fredrickson, B. L. (2001). The role of positive emotions in positive psychology: The broaden-and-build theory of positive emotions. *American Psychologist, 56,* 218–226.

Fredrickson, B. L. (2009). *Positivity*. New York: Crown Publishers.

Giles, H., & Speer, R. (2009). Exploring the efficacy of the anti- and pro-social divide: An epilogue. In T. A. Kinney, & M. Pörhölä (Eds.), *Anti and pro-social communication: Theories, methods, and applications* (pp. 183–196). New York: Peter Lang.

Gottman, J. M. (1993). *What predicts divorce? The relationship between marital processes and Martial outcomes*. Mahwah, NJ: Lawrence Erlbaum.

Jacobi, L. (2009). Spirituality, social skills, and pro-social behavior. In T. A. Kinney, & M, Pörhölä, M. (Eds.), *Anti and prosocial communication: Theories, methods, and applications*. (pp. 117–126). New York: Peter Lang.

Kinney, T. A. & Pörhölä, M. (Eds.) (2009a). *Anti and pro-social communication: Theories, methods, and applications*. New York: Peter Lang.

Kinney, T. A., & Pörhölä, M. (2009b). Introduction: An Integrative approach to anti-social and pro-social communication. In T. A. Kinney, & M. Pörhölä (Eds.), *Anti and pro-social communication: Theories, methods, and applications* (pp. vii–xii). New York: Peter Lang.

Lyubomirsky, S. Sheldon, K. M., & Schkade, D. (2005). Pursuing happiness: The architecture of sustainable change. *Review of General Psychology, 9*, 111–131.

Matlin, M., & Stang, D. (1978). *The Pollyanna principle*. Cambridge, MA: Schenkman.

Peterson, C. (2006). *A primer in positive psychology*. New York: Oxford University Press.

Peterson, C., & Seligman, M. E. P. (2004). *Character strengths and virtues: A handbook and classification*. New York: Oxford University Press; Washington, DC: American Psychological Association.

Pitts, L. (2010, May 29). Singing a new tune in oil spill's wake. *The Miami Herald*. Retrieved From http://www.miamiherald.com/2010/05/29/1654166/singing-new-tune-in-oil-spills.html.

Pitts, M. L., & Socha, T. J. (Eds.). (in preparation, 2012). *Positive interpersonal communication in health and wellness*. New York: Peter Lang.

Seligman, M. E. P. (2002). *Authentic happiness*. New York: Free Press.

Seligman, M. E. P, & Csikszentmihalyi, M. (2000). Positive psychology: An introduction. *American Psychologist, 55*, 5–14.

Snyder, C. R. (1994). *The psychology of hope*. New York: Free Press.

Snyder, C. R. (2000). *Handbook of hope: Theory, measures, and applications*. San Diego, CA: Academic Press.

Socha, T. J. (2006). Orchestrating and directing domestic potential though communication: Towards a positive reframing of "discipline." In L. Turner & R. West (Eds.), *The family communication sourcebook* (pp. 219–236). Thousand Oaks, CA: Sage.

Socha, T. J. (2008, November). *Building positive communication pedagogy: Positive experiential communication learning in human relating*. A paper presented at the annual the National Communication Association, San Diego.

Socha, T. J. (2009). Family as agency of potential: Towards a positive model of applied family communication theory and research. In L. Frey & K. Cissna (Eds.), *Routledge handbook of applied communication*. New York: Routledge.

Socha, T. J., & Yingling, J. A. (2010). *Families communicating with children: Building positive developmental foundations*. Cambridge, UK: Polity.

Spitzberg. B., & Cupach, W. (Eds.). (1998). *The dark side of close relationships*. Mahwah, NJ: Erlbaum.

Spitzberg, B., & Cupach, W. (Eds.). (2007). *The dark side of interpersonal communication*. Mahwah, NJ: Erlbaum.

Turkle, S. (2011). *Alone together: Why we expect more from technology and less from each other*. New York: Basic Books.

University of Pennsylvania Positive Psychology Center. (2007). *Positive psychology course syllabi*. Retrieved June 2, 2011 from http://www.ppc.sas.upenn.edu/teachingpp.htm.

Section One
Key Concepts

• CHAPTER TWO •

Aesthetic Relating

Leslie A. Baxter
University of Iowa

Kristen M. Norwood
Trinity University

Sarah Nebel
University of Iowa

> [W]ithout the ability to create moments that are beautiful, thrilling, and awe inspiring, life is empty.
>
> —Cronen (1998, p. 22)

For over a decade, communication scholars have illuminated the "dark side" of interpersonal communication, often differentiated from positive or "bright side" communication based on two conceptual criteria: (a) what is regarded as (im)moral/(in)appropriate, and (b) what is regarded as (dys)functional (Spitzberg & Cupach, 2007). In addition to the criteria of moral appropriateness and functionality, this chapter introduces a third way of understanding interpersonal relating as "dark" or "bright": the lens of aesthetics. A number of communication scholars echo Cronen's (1998) position, captured in the epigram, that more attention needs to be given to aesthetic communication (e.g., Baxter & DeGooyer, 2001; Crick, 2004; Stroud, 2008), in part as an alternative to a research tradition dominated by a means-end, rational focus. By way of preface, aesthetic communication is that which is experienced as beautiful in its enactment. The particular focus of this chapter is aesthetic interpersonal communication, or what we refer to as aesthetic relating. Our argument is that interpersonal relating can be beautiful or ugly (or sometimes both at once), and that interpersonal communication scholars could benefit from understanding communication as a verbal (and nonverbal) *art* (Bakhtin, 1990c). We organize our discussion of aesthetic relating into four main sections. The first section conceptualizes aesthetic relating, and the next three sections discuss three specific kinds of aesthetic relating—aesthetic love, semantic beauty, and beauty of style and form.

Conceptualizing Aesthetic Relating

As Williams (1983) has indicated, an aesthetic experience is a subjective feeling of deep pleasure, stimulation, and joy evoked in one's encounter with what is regarded as beautiful. Certainly, communication in our social, personal, and familial relationships often evokes intense positive (and negative) emotions. The emotions of romantic love, platonic liking, and relational satisfaction, for example, are of central concern in much interpersonal communication research, demonstrating the perceived importance of emotion to experiences of relating. Study of aesthetic relating has a place in this growing body of work that seeks to understand emotion in relating. However, aesthetic relating centers on a particular kind of emotion: the pleasurable experience of aesthetic beauty.

What exactly are the characteristics of interpersonal communication that evoke feelings of aesthetic pleasure? Although aesthetics theorists have long debated what characterizes phenomena experienced as aesthetically pleasing, we emphasize the conceptual work of two early twentieth century social theorists who address aesthetic communication in particular, Bakhtin[1] (1981, 1984, 1986, 1990a, 1990b, 1990c) and Dewey (1934), and highlight four interdependent features of aesthetic communicative enactments: uniquely creative action; participant absorption in the process rather than the product of the interaction event; noninstrumentality of focus; and the unity of disparate elements. Although our focus is on aesthetic relating, we note with interest that these four features show some similarity with the broader concept of "flow," or optimal experience, identified by the psychologist Csikszentmihalyi (e.g., Csikszentmihalyi, 1990; Csikszentmihalyi & Robinson, 1990).

Uniquely Creative Action

Aesthetic communication is first and foremost a departure from the mundane, routine, and mechanized communicative enactments that frequent our everyday lives. In fact, our everyday lives are so riddled with these kinds of communicative events that it is far too easy to think of creative activity as

---

[1] Bakhtin wrote the majority of his work in Russian from 1919–1975, some of which appeared under other authors' names (e.g., Voloshinov, 1986, originally published in 1929). However, for a variety of reasons, this work was slow to reach publication in English. For a discussion of the chronology of Bakhtin's work, see Baxter (2011).

something apart from the everyday. Bakhtin (1990a) captures this widespread belief of separation of art from life in this way: "Life has no hope of ever catching up with art. . . . 'That's too exalted for us'—says life. 'That's art, after all! All we've got is the humble prose of living.'" (p. 1). But we would be too pessimistic in giving up on everyday life so easily, for all communication holds potential to be artistic—to create a unique meaning in the moment and to transcend business-as-usual to construct "a new plane of existence" (Bakhtin, 1990b, p. 90). Dewey (1934) similarly notes that while much communication consists of statements that merely transmit already-formed meanings, it holds potential for artful expression in which new meanings are constituted, "the possibilities that are interwoven within the texture of the actual" (p. 346). So, the potential for aesthetic beauty exists in everyday communication even if it is rare in relation to the mundane.

When it does occur, aesthetic communication is a dynamic, ephemeral form of art. Aesthetic communication is not a thing—a product, a message; rather, it is action. As such, it happens in a given moment that cannot easily be recreated or captured for posterity. Stroud (2008) summarizes Dewey's view of art as motion: "Dewey shifts the focus of his definition [of art] from *objects* to certain processes; he indicates that 'art denotes a process of doing or making'" (p. 157). Bakhtin (1990c) similarly underscores that aesthetic communication is an activity of production and construction, one not understandable by focusing on material objects of art. Csikszentmihalyi and Robinson (1990) make the same point in observing that optimal experiences of living—those occasions of flow in which we feel exhilarated in the aesthetic experience—are activities not things.

The meanings created in the aesthetic moment are not final but instead fleeting. In this sense they are unique, never seen before and never to be experienced in exactly the same way again. Meanings constructed in one moment always are subject to the meaning making of the next interactional moment. According to Bakhtin (1990b), "complete chaos still holds sway in this regard in the aesthetics of verbal art" (p. 9). Dewey (1934) points to the same feature in underscoring that aesthetic communication has an individualizing quality, a sense of an experience that is one of a kind.

In sum, aesthetic, communicative enactments are experienced as unique acts of creation. However, other features are implicated, as well, in evoking aesthetic pleasure.

Participant Absorption in the Process over the Product of Communication

An element of aesthetic communication related to the fleeting uniqueness of a moment is the level of involvement in the process of relating. Participants in aesthetic communicative enactments do not focus on the products—the outcomes—of the interaction event. Instead, their attentions are absorbed in the process itself: the journey of the communicative process rather than its destination. This heightened sense of involvement that characterizes aesthetic relating departs from less meaningful or less pleasing interactions, with which participants may be less enthralled. As Dewey (1934) notes, "In much of our intercourse with our surroundings we withdraw; sometimes from fear, if only of expending unduly our store of energy; sometimes from preoccupation with other matters" (p. 53). Such partial and distanced engagement is antithetical to the aesthetic experience, which involves steeping ourselves in the moment, fully and completely immersed in its unfolding. Such "surrender" (Dewey, p. 53) to the moment is often a sensory experience of intense emotion. Bakhtin (1990b) similarly notes that the aesthetic experience is one of total and complete involvement, a "uniquely active form-giving energy" (p. 8). Participants do not act in a partial, disconnected manner, but fully engage the whole of the moment—the situation, the other, and the complexity of multiple systems of meaning. Csikszentmihalyi (1990) echoes this same feature in arguing that optimal experiences of all kinds—both communicative and noncommunicative—are characterized by an intense absorption or involvement in the process of enactment.

Noninstrumentality of Focus

To understand noninstrumentality as a feature of aesthetic relating, it is important to contrast it with its opposite of means-end instrumental communication. Csikszentmihalyi (1990) uses the terms "autotelic" and "exotelic," respectively, to mark this distinction, although his frame of reference includes all forms of "flow," not just communicative enactments. Related to this distinction, Dewey (1934) bemoans the plight of modern society which has been reduced, in his view, to a mechanical means-end orientation, devoid of deeply felt value and meaning. A number of scholars note a similar presumption of means-end rationality in interpersonal communication scholarship (e.g., Duck, 1998): communication as an intentional enterprise, organized around speaker goals (ends) and the strategic communication planned and deployed in order to accomplish those goals.

By contrast, aesthetic relating is not goal-driven, nor can it be strategically planned and deployed. Stroud (2008) interprets Dewey's work to suggest that communicators can be open to aesthetic communication by adopting an orientation that he labels "orientational meliorism" (p. 176), characterized by efforts to consciously avoid a focus on remote goals and attending instead to the present communication situation. Bakhtin's earlier work (i.e., that originally written before 1929) seems to advance a similar argument in his explication of answerability, a concept elaborated upon in the next section.

Bakhtin's later work (after 1929), also developed below, decenters the individual communicator and argues that the potential for aesthetic relating is located in the system of language itself and thus cannot be understood as strategic activity on the part of an individual speaker (Baxter, 2007a, 2011).

In short, aesthetic relating is an emergent process, an adventure to be appreciated for its unpredictable detours and discoveries along the way.

4. Unity of Disparate Elements

Arguably the most significant feature of aesthetic relating is its construction of unity or completion, however fleeting that might be. Dewey (1934) emphasizes that the form and rhythm of the aesthetic act is characterized by a "grace or dignity" and its "exquisite sense of the relations" of its elements, "its fitness" (p. 49). As he elaborates, "The existence of this unity is constituted by a single quality that pervades the entire experience" (p. 37), a quality in which "every successive part flows freely, without seam and without unfilled blanks, into what ensues" (p. 36). Bakhtin (1990b) similarly refers to the quality of "completeness," "wholeness," or "consummation" that characterized aesthetic communication. Csikszentmihalyi (1990) similarly underscores this feature in optimal experiences of all kinds, especially in his discussion of the sense of transcendent oneness or harmony that a person experiences while "flowing."

The quality of unity appears to be quite central in laypersons' sensemaking of aesthetic relating. In their study of aesthetic characteristics of interpersonal conversations, Baxter and DeGooyer (2001) found that participants, asked to provide accounts of beautiful and ugly incidents of interpersonal communication, identified many different kinds of unity. Participants most frequently identified unity as a completion of Self through Other, in which they felt as if they were somehow made whole through interaction. Participants also identified unity as a sense of oneness between themselves and another person. Cosmic oneness was experienced when participants felt complete connection between themselves and some non-human entity, for example, god or nature. Participants also reported experiencing temporal unity characterized by a seamlessness between the past and present or between the present and the anticipated future. Eisenberg's (1990) description of musical "jamming" nicely exemplifies the feature of unity, as well.

Although we have emphasized throughout this section the theoretical works of Bakhtin and Dewey in identifying features of aesthetic communication, we note that these show remarkable convergence not only with Csikszentmihalyi's (1990) work in optimal experiences but additionally with the more general work in aesthetics theory (e.g., Dickie, Sclafani, & Roblin, 1989). The challenge, of course, is how to translate these rather abstract characteristics into a more concrete treatment of aesthetic relating, a task we turn to in the next three sections in order to discuss several different kinds of aesthetic relating.

Aesthetic Love

Aesthetic love (Bakhtin, 1993) is the early Bakhtinian term to describe a kind of love one person enacts toward another. It is not to be mistaken with romantic love; aesthetic love is not an internal feeling of attraction or sentiment; instead, it is a way of co-enacting a kind of joint Being with another. Aesthetic love is a process of absorption in Other in which a communicator constructed the Other's consciousness through the unity of their different positions. Emerson (1991, p. 665) describes it as "a concentration of attention." In Bakhtin's (1993, p. 64) words, this attention, which he calls *answerability*, is an "intent power to encompass and retain the concrete manifoldness of Being [of Other] without impoverishing it," the act of "slow[ing] down and linger[ing] intently over [Other], to hold and sculpt every detail and particular in [him or her], however minute." Aesthetic love is "a confirmative acceptance" (Bakhtin, 1990b, p. 90) of the Other. Furthermore, it is not motivated by self-interest (Bakhtin, 1993, p. 64). The consequence of such totalizing attentiveness to Other is "aesthetically productive" (Bakhtin, 1993, p. 64). That is, in giving undivided attention to the Other, he or she is consummated—made more complete or whole.

But how are aesthetic love and the consummation of Other accomplished? According to Bakhtin (1990b), aesthetic love is a three-part process in which unity and difference are in play. The first element, empathy, builds on unity with Other: "I must experience—come to see and to know—what [Other] experiences; I must put myself in his [or her] place and coincide with [Other]" (p. 25). The second element is located in difference, a return to one's own position and unique perspective separate from Other: "My projection of myself into [Other] must be followed by a return into myself, a return to my own place outside . . . for only from this place can the material derived from my projecting myself into the Other be rendered meaningful" (p. 26). The final element of aesthetic love interanimates unity and difference in responding to, or answering, the Other, replying to him or her based on one's empathy in combination with one's own unique position. These three elements do not necessarily occur in a linear sequence; rather, they are temporally intertwined.

The consummation of Other—the completion of his or her consciousness or Self—is the result of enacting aesthetic love. According to Bakhtin (1990b), Self always holds potential for further growth through interacting with answering others. That is, Self is a process of ongoing construction, an unfinalized "yet-to-be" (p. 16). Thus, to Bakhtin, aesthetic love is a profoundly creative act in which Other is constituted. It is unmotivated by self-interest, and therefore can be described as noninstrumental in nature.

The early Bakhtinian concept of aesthetic love bears some resemblance to Martin Buber's (1970) notion of I-Thou relating. Buber contrasts I-Thou relating, or an orientation to Other as a unique subject, against I-It relating, an orientation to Other as an object in which communication is simply functional based on scripted roles and individual goals. When we go to the grocery store, we engage the checkout clerk as an It, not a Thou; we don't engage the totality of the clerk's consciousness and instead deal only with his or her role-based behaviors that serve our instrumental goal of making a purchase. Substantial scholarly attention has been given to Buber's paired constructs of I-It and I-Thou relating (for elaboration, see Anderson, Baxter, & Cissna, 2004). Researchers have amassed substantial empirical work in such conceptually related areas as: perspective-taking and person-centered communication (e.g., Burleson & Rack, 2008), empathy (e.g., Stiff, Dillard, Somera, Kim, & Sleight, 1988), confirming communication (e.g., Cissna & Sieburg, 1981); immediacy (e.g., Jones, 2004), and compassionate communication (e.g., Miller, 2007).

Although this humanistically inspired body of work has contributed much to our understanding of relating, it is deeply embedded in what Baxter (2007b) describes as the unity project characterizing much interpersonal and family communication. In privileging unity (similarity over difference, integration over separation, commonality over individuation), difference is understood as a problem to be contained, managed, and ultimately overcome in favor of similarity and becoming one with another. The first and third elements of aesthetic love—empathy and confirming responsiveness—have been well represented in extant research and fit well within the overall unity project. But aesthetic love is the interplay of unity *and* difference, and it is difference—the second element of aesthetic love and integral to the third element as well—that researchers have tended to overlook.

Difference has rarely been studied in its own right as a positive feature of communication; instead, it has been framed as a problem to be overcome (Baxter, 2007b). Interactants appear to position difference with substantial ambivalence, at once appreciating its potential to help parties grow as individuals at the same time that they seek to limit and contain it because of its dangers of conflict, discomfort, and alienation (Baxter, Foley, & Thatcher, 2008; Baxter & West, 2003). Even Buber's (1970, p. 75) conception of I-Thou tends to privilege unity, positioning difference as characteristic of I-It relating.

In an attempt to concretize our understanding of aesthetic love, we cite an example drawn from Baxter and DeGooyer's (2001) study of aesthetic conversation. A woman had been away on a trip, leaving her husband to assume all domestic responsibility for their household consisting of three children. She describes her homecoming as moments of lavished attention and love. The husband gained empathy for his wife's life in assuming domestic responsibility in her absence. However, his experience was different from his wife's, in his view. He found himself overwhelmed, in contrast to her skill in managing children and the household. His act of answerability displayed increased respect for and appreciation of his wife, which made her feel "like a queen." Clearly, he had moved beyond his everyday posture of taking her for granted to a different kind of engagement which made her feel better about herself.

Aesthetic love is not limited to romantic relationships. Baxter and Akkoor (2008) argue that Bakhtin's (1990b) concept of aesthetic love is fundamentally different in three ways from romantic love. First, romantic love is an internal feeling state (e.g., Hendrick & Hendrick, 1992). By contrast, answerability is focused on communicative action. Second, romantic love is usually understood through the logic of individualistic self-interest, in contrast to the noninstrumental basis of aesthetic love. Bellah and his colleagues (Bellah, et al. 1985) refer to the therapeutic ideal of love that dominates the cultural landscape of mainstream U.S. society, an ideal of "utilitarian individuals maximizing their own interests" (p. 104). This ideal of love stands in stark contrast to the noninstrumental, Other-orientation of aesthetic love. Third, romantic love presupposes finalized selves who precede the feeling of love. The Other is a pre-formed person whose rewarding qualities are a source of attraction to a prospective romantic partner. Love is not a creative act of consummating selves according to the logic of romantic love; instead, it is an antecedent variable that predicts partner satisfaction and relational longevity. By contrast, aesthetic love can only take place in the process of relating when parties are constituted through their answerability to one another.

The early Bakhtin (1919–1928) conceives of aesthetic relating as a person-qua-person process in which interacting parties consummate one another's whole being through the interplay of their similarities and differences. However, after his linguistic turn in 1929 (Voloshinov, 1986), Bakhtin shifts ground to envision aesthetic relating in a more expansive way, to which we turn next.

Semantic Beauty

A decade into his fifty-year dialogism project, Bakhtin re-envisions aesthetic relating as a discourse-qua-discourse process, located in the utterance. The shift from a narrower focus on one kind of meaning making—the constitution of consciousness—to a broader focus on the general meaning making process reflects Bakhtin's intellectual shift to center language and language use in his dialogism theory (Voloshinov, 1986; for an elaboration, see Baxter, 2007a, 2011). Meaning making is conceptualized as the centripetal-centrifugal struggle of different, often competing, systems of meaning (discourses) that circulate in utterances. The interanimation of these competing discourses usually takes place on an unequal playing field in that some discourses (the centripetal) occupy the discursive center, whereas other discourses occupy the centrifugal margins; centered discourses are the taken-for-granted claims that carry high legitimacy compared to less-accepted marginalized discourses. For example, individualism is often a discourse that organizes our interpersonal relating. In labeling individualism a discourse, we are envisioning it as a system of various interrelated beliefs and values (e.g., the importance of self-actualization, the importance of individual autonomy, the importance of individual need fulfillment) that parties orient to in shaping their friendships, romantic relationships, and familial relationships. The discourse of individualism, however, competes with a counter-discourse of community, captured by such beliefs as putting Other's needs above one's own and voluntarily giving up individual freedom to uphold obligations. Which discourse is dominant in a given moment of relating is a result of the joint negotiation between relating partners.

Baxter (2011) argues that relating in mainstream U.S. society is awash with myriad systems of meaning that adds discourses of rationality, romance, expression, and silence. These discourses can be viewed as a web of interdependent beliefs and values that "hang together" in their vision of what exists and what can be evaluated as good/bad. For example, the discourse of rationality views human action as oriented toward means-and-ends. Related, the discourse of rationality positions communication as a goal-driven activity in which speakers communicate in order to achieve their goals. Certainty is a valued commodity, according to the discourse of rationality, for a speaker cannot function rationally in the absence of the perceived ability to predict the likely outcomes associated with given actions. In interpersonal relating the discourse of rationality is often in discursive tension with an opposite discourse of romance in which emotions and spontaneity are valued and "having an agenda" is eschewed.

The struggle of discourses implicates the past, present, and anticipated future of meanings. Some discourses that animate a given utterance in the moment reflect meanings that already exist and are circulating in the larger culture. Other discourses animating a given utterance find their origin in the prior interactions of a relating pair, a meaning that the dyad has already constructed in the past. Not only does an utterance take prior utterances into account, but is also crafted in anticipation of a partner's response, and the systems of meaning implicated in that response. Finally, a given utterance is crafted in anticipation of how it might be judged by generalized others against cultural conventions and ideals. This utterance chain (Bakhtin, 1986), spanning past-present-future, positions a given utterance, and meaning making, as a site of intertextuality (Allen, 2000). The specific meanings that emerge from a given utterance depend on the discursive struggles at the moment—the particular discourses that are animating in a given utterance chain, the centripetal-centrifugal power of these discourses, and their particular interplay. Meaning making is thus a dynamic process, ultimately fleeting and unfinalized.

Although all communicative exchanges hold potential for idealized dialogue—aesthetic relating—most of our everyday meaning making is nonaesthetic in nature. Idealized dialogue is meaning making that is characterized by emergent creativity—a new, transformational meaning emerges from the interplay of equal discourses that are no longer framed as oppositional. It is easiest to understand aesthetic meaning making by contrasting it against nonaesthetic relating. One kind of nonaesthetic relating is single-voiced monologue (Bakhtin, 1984); where authoritative meaning silences alternative meanings. It is fused with overpowering authority and tradition becoming taken-for-granted truth. The risk of monologue, for Bakhtin, is semantic calcification in which meaning becomes rigidified and inflexible, due to the absence of alternative meanings. For example, a society that constructs the meaning of marriage as a bond-for-life, with no conception of divorce, is monologic in its orientation, and its conception of marriage can too easily become fixed and inflexible.

Many of our everyday exchanges are characterized by the interplay of competing discourses that are unequally powerful—some discourses are more centered whereas others are marginalized. Meaning making in these exchanges is polemic rather than aesthetic (Bakhtin, 1984). Meaning making in polemic exchanges features a power-laden jockeying of discourses to determine which discourse will be centered and which will end up marginalized. For example, a young married couple might be struggling with competing discursive demands for how to spend their time: a discourse of couple privacy supports the value of the couple spending their first Christmas together in their home, whereas a competing discourse of family embeddedness gives value to the couple spending the holidays at their parents' homes. This couple's discursive struggle might take an antagonistic turn, in which each party favors a different discourse and they end up engaged in conflict. Alternatively, both members of the couple might legitimate both discourses, in which case the discursive challenge is that of determining as a pair which to privilege in their decision-making. The pair might strike a compromise, deciding to spend Christmas Eve alone in their home, Christmas Day brunch with his parents, and Christmas Day dinner with her parents. Although there might be a certain creativity involved in striking a compromise, the underlying competing discourses—couple privacy and couple embeddedness in an extended family—are nonetheless still envisioned as competing with one another. Compromise is a form of discursive truce, if you will, between competing discourses.

By contrast, aesthetic relating—idealized dialogue—involves an interpenetration of discourses so profound that the competing discourses semantically dissolve in the emergence of a transformational meaning. Baxter and Braithwaite (2008) describe aesthetic relating by drawing a metaphorical comparison: "Think of aesthetic moments as akin to what chemists call 'reactions.' For example, two molecules of hydrogen combine with one molecule of oxygen to produce an entirely new entity—water" (p. 355). In aesthetic relating, a new meaning—a semantic reaction—emerges spontaneously from the interplay of different discourses. The integrity of the original discourses dissolves in a transformation of meaning. Aesthetic moments cannot be planned; they emerge spontaneously. They are often experienced emotionally as joyous and deeply pleasurable. They are semantic eruptions of beauty in which a transformational meaning is created in the moment. These fleeting revolutions of meaning are possible in instances in which each competing discourse "loses its composure and confidence" (Bakhtin, 1984, p. 198) and the discourses enter into a new "semantic bond" (Bakhtin, p. 189).

In the next section we shift from discussions of aesthetic love and semantic beauty to a discussion of the aesthetics of style and form.

Beauty of Style and Form

In discussing beauty of style and form, we shift our focus from a discourse-centered approach to a structural approach to aesthetic relating in attending to specific linguistic features and how interaction is organized. Focus on structural beauty is loosely inspired by Dewey's (1934) observation that rhythm and form are important to the aesthetic experience. Dewey argues that rhythm involves a symmetrical balancing across time, as some phenomenon moves back and forth in some pattern of alternation (p. 155). The beauty of rhythm resides in its sense of symmetry which constructs a sense of how parts relate to an organized whole. For example, one isolated swing of a pendulum becomes beautiful once we see an alternation with its counterbalanced swing in the opposite direction and we realize the larger organized back-and-forth patterning at play. Others have noted that rhythm appears, and is pleasing to us, in so many aspects of life that response to it may be innate, serving some evolutionary purpose. Cook (2000) points out that rhythms are essential to life in a physiological sense (e.g., important in respiration, circulation, and childbirth) as well as in a cultural sense (e.g., important in music, dance, prayer, poetry, and song). He argues that rhythm is a source of emotional expression, control, and comfort.

Rhythm is but one aspect of form, which Dewey (1934) defines as the coming together of elements in a fitting manner to create a sense of wholeness. The structural elements that constitute fit vary from one phenomenon to another:

> If the matter is of a jolly sort, the form that would be fitting to pathetic matter is impossible. If expressed in a poem, then meter, rate of movement, words chosen, the whole structure, will be different, and in a picture so will the whole scheme of color and volume relationships. (p. 137)

Although Dewey's discussion of rhythm and form is tantalizingly nonspecific (Crick, 2004; Stroud, 2008), he points us conceptually to how various structural features of a communicative enactment unfold in a given interaction to create a sense of symmetry, balance, and fit.

More recently, scholars have attended to specific ways that structural aspects of communication make for pleasing or beautiful experiences. Although literary works, such as novels or plays, are regarded as beautiful and poetic, everyday communication is not typically hailed for its potential as a work of art. As noted above, we tend to think of everyday communication as unrefined, simplistic, and functional, while literature stereotypically represents the creative and aesthetic potential of language (Tannen, 1998).

Scholars in folklore, sociolinguistics, and the ethnography of communication have argued for several decades now that communication, when viewed as performance, can be regarded as verbal art that contributes an aesthetic understanding of social and cultural life. Seminal to this approach is Bauman's (1977) essay on verbal art as performance, in which he views performance as an artistic enactment involving a performer, an art form (e.g., storytelling), an audience, and a setting of enactment. Central to the performance approach, argues Bauman, is a focus on the enactment and its form for its own sake, liberated from instrumental goals. The enactment captures attention and involvement in what is regarded as an uncommon moment of creative action. Performance involves reframing communicative messages through stylistic and structural features such that the audience understands the enactment not at a literal level but as an artistic accomplishment. A performance constitutes verbal art by shifting the audience's attention from the content of what is communicated to a focus on how the act is accomplished; a hearer is struck by the beauty of how the communicative act is done. An aesthetic performance is keyed, or framed, through any number of language practices which vary by culture, including such features as "special codes, figurative language, parallelism, special paralinguistic features, special formulae, appeal to tradition, and disclaimer of performance" (Bauman, p. 16).

Performances vary in their formality (Bauman, 1977). Sometimes, a performance is a formal communication event, as exemplified by the formal competitive talking matches among young men in the African-Caribbean speech community of St. Vincent to determine who earns a reputation for "talking sweet" (Abraham, 1972). However, many verbal performances are not formally organized events so much as speaker enactments of everyday communication, punctuated by artistic verbal utterances. For example, Basso (1979) provides a vivid ethnographic example of how Cibecue Apache men communicatively imitate "the Whiteman" in a parody celebrated for its aesthetic performative skill. What moves such everyday utterances to the aesthetic level is absorption by the process of expression; the enactment is accomplished in such a way that its symmetry, balance, and fit mark it as beautiful.

For Tannen (1998), poetic conversation means conversation that "creates involvement through audience participation in sense-making and rhythmic patterns" (p. 638). For example, Tannen (1989) cites the linguistic strategy of repetition as a device which creates a sense of poetry through the speaker's ability to establish a pattern, create a sense of seamless flow in talk, and make connections across content. Further, repetition, along with prosody, creates a sense of rhythm that invites the hearer to move along with the speaker, as a musical ensemble might cajole a listener to do (Tannen, 1998).

Although much of the scholarly focus on style and form is focused on the utterances of individual speakers, some scholars shift the unit of analysis from the individual to the relational system of interacting parties. Tannen (1984), for example, emphasizes the aesthetic quality that often characterizes matching styles between communicators. Her analysis of the talk of six people gathered together for a Thanksgiving dinner identifies some people who "clicked" (p. 54), or had similar, matching styles, and others who did not click and found conversation difficult and awkward. Those who did not click had styles that were nonsymmetrical.

Symmetry in conversational style seems quite related to the description of *conversational flow* offered by Baxter and DeGooyer (2001). In terms of structure, conversational flow or matched styles (Tannen, 1984) equates to similarity in both linguistic devices used and interpretation of meanings. Tannen's description of such symmetry of form between herself and another participant in the dinner conversation helps us to imagine what symmetry in linguistic devices might look like in conversation: "In some senses, Steve and I shared styles, for example, we tended to talk a lot; we used much overlap, latching, quick expressive responses, and fast, clipped questions" (p. 146). This type of interaction represents, for Tannen, aesthetic conversation by bringing a sense of coherence to the entirety of the exchange. She describes such symmetry of styles as beautiful in a transcendent way, and in doing so illustrates a potential link between structure of form and something like aesthetic love, discussed earlier.

But symmetry at the level of the interacting system is not limited to the matching of linguistic features that comprise speaker styles. Symmetry in other features of communicative enactments also can create aesthetic experience. To illustrate this point, we turn next to a description of the results of a study we recently conducted on the phenomenon of poetic justice (Baxter, Nebel, & Norwood, 2011) in which we identified two kinds of symmetry of form that construct revenge as aesthetically pleasing.

In a book about the "bright side" of communication, readers might wonder why we would draw an example from what is commonly regarded as a "dark side" phenomenon (Spitzberg & Cupach, 2007). We present the example of poetic justice to disrupt the tidy binary between dark and bright sides of communication, not only illustrating the concept of symmetry but additionally asserting that seemingly "dark sided" phenomena can have a "bright side." In the context of revengeful communication, there can be "ugly" as well as "beautiful" enactments of interpersonal revenge. Tripp, Bies, and Aquino (2002) highlight the frequency with which individuals engage in telling stories of revenge to one another as a means of entertainment, because revenge, when done right, "might not only serve the interests of justice, but also, in aesthetic terms, be poetic justice" (p. 967).

Our critical-incident survey study of university undergraduates solicited descriptions of poetic justice in family, friends, and romantic relationships (Baxter et al., 2011). Results of the study suggest that the two most common features characterizing poetic justice are symmetry of method and symmetry of consequence. Illustrative of symmetry of method is an event described by a female participant seeking revenge on her boyfriend. She explained that after a fight, her boyfriend Phillip would declare they were on a "break," during which "he would hook up (make out) with another girl" (Baxter et al., 2011, p. 18). So during the next break, the participant sought revenge by making out with one of Phillip's friends.

Participants also described revenge acts as poetic when there was a similarity in the quantity and/or quality of harm between what was experienced by the original victim (the revenge taker) and the harmdoer (the target of revenge) (Baxter et al., 2011). This symmetry of consequence indicated that the subsequent punishment was appropriate for the original crime and suggested a certain fittingness. Illustrative is an account provided by a male participant who described an act of poetic justice enacted by his brother, Joe, against his other brother, Matt. Joe and Matt shared a car, and it seems that Matt would always bring the car home with an empty gas tank, which presented obvious problems for Joe the next time he went to use the car. Rather than enacting revenge through a symmetry of method by returning the car empty for Matt's use, Joe retaliated by hiding some frozen chicken in the car just before he left for college. The smell was so terrible that Matt couldn't use the car. What made this act of revenge poetic to the participant was symmetrical consequences: an inability to use the car was matched by a reciprocal loss of use of the car, although the method by which the car became unusable was different.

Poetic justice underscores that an enactment can be aesthetic due to structural features that reach beyond the linguistic features of speaker style. Thus, aesthetic relating at the level of the interacting system can be constituted through more globalized, as well as more microscopic, practices. Poetic justice also underscores that the binary between dark side and bright side in interpersonal communication is far from tidy in that dark-sided communicative enactments such as revenge can be accomplished in aesthetically pleasing ways.

Conclusion

Grounded in the theoretical moorings of Bakhtin and Dewey, we have articulated four criteria that characterize aesthetic relating: the unique act of creativity, participant absorption in the process of enactment, noninstrumentality of goal, and the unity of disparate elements. Additionally, we identified three different kinds of aesthetic relating that collectively exemplify these features: aesthetic love, semantic beauty, and beauty of style and form.

Researchers of aesthetic relating could productively query whether the four criteria identified in this chapter are exhaustive and whether they are equally important in constituting an experience as aesthetic. On its face, we would anticipate that absorption and complete involvement in the process of enactment is requisite to aesthetic pleasure, but we suspect that this is not a sufficient feature to qualify a communicative moment as beautiful. We would expect, for example, that an enactment experienced as ugly would similarly draw its participants to the *how* of its unfolding, although with a completely different emotional reaction. It might be that symmetry of style and form, while aesthetic in its own right, is important in reframing participant attention to the process of enactment; such marking, as Bauman (1977) argues, reframes a communicative enactment as a verbal art and distinguishes it from ordinary, referentially based communication. Unity of disparate elements appears to be a transcendent criterion, evident across all three kinds of aesthetic relating identified in the chapter: aesthetic love involves a unity of similarity and difference between individuals; semantic beauty involves an emergent unity from disparate discourses; and the beauty of style and form involves a framing of the organized whole of an enactment in order for qualities of symmetry, balance, and fit to be discerned. Aesthetic relating is conceptualized as a fluid and fleeting experience, and future researchers could usefully pursue its temporal limits. Is it possible, for example, to regard a relationship as beautiful (or ugly)? Because relationships have a temporal continuity across interaction encounters, reference to a "beautiful relationship" implies that aesthetic relating is a sustained feature of the relationship that extends across time.

By introducing aesthetics to our evaluation of positive (and negative) interpersonal communication, a third dimension is added to the two traditional bases of judgment by which the bright side is distinguished from the dark side of relating: moral appropriateness and functionality (Spitzberg & Cupach, 2007). Communicative enactments can be gratifying if they are evaluated as appropriate to, and good for, the moral order of the social world. They also can be gratifying if they achieve participant goals. In this chapter we have examined a third basis for gratification—aesthetic pleasure. Relating can be appreciated simply for the beauty of how it is accomplished.

We would be remiss if we ended the chapter by allowing the reader to think that aesthetic relating, while pleasurable, is nonetheless a frivolous kind of communication. Although aesthetic relating is not enacted with a rational, instrumental goal in mind (in fact, to do so undermines its capacity to be appreciated as beautiful), aesthetic relating nonetheless can accomplish important interpersonal work. Aesthetic love constitutes selves, thereby growing identities as persons ongoingly change. Semantic beauty opens up space for novel meanings to emerge, reducing the likelihood that communicators will end up in calcified semantic ruts where old meanings grow stale. Beauty of style and form increases the coherence of talk and additionally creates opportunities for increased involvement between communicators, thereby encouraging increased closeness and intimacy between them. Aesthetically pleasurable enactments allow us to reframe potentially negative enactments, such as criticism of Whiteman dominance in the case of the Cibecue Apache or revenge in the case of poetic justice, along more positive lines and thereby increase their social acceptance. However, we must end where we began by reminding the reader that aesthetic relating, although it is often functional, should primarily be celebrated, and studied, because it adds pleasure to interpersonal life. As Cronen (1998) opined in the opening epigram, the emptiness of life is vast in the absence of beauty.

References

Abraham, R. (1972). The training of the man of words in talking sweet. *Language in Society, 1*, 15–29.
Allen, G. (2000). *Intertextuality*. New York: Routledge.

Anderson, R., Baxter, L. A., & Cissna, K. N. (2004). Texts and contexts of dialogue. In R. Anderson, L. A. Baxter, & K. N. Cissna (Eds.), *Dialogue: Theorizing difference in communication studies* (pp. 1–18). Thousand Oaks, CA: Sage.

Bakhtin, M. M. (1981). Discourse in the novel. In M. Holquist (Ed.), *The dialogic imagination: Four essays by M. M. Bakhtin* (C. Emerson & M. Holquist, Trans.; pp. 259–422). Austin, TX: University of Texas Press. (Original work published in 1975)

Bakhtin, M. M. (1984). *Problems of Dostoevsky's poetics* (C. Emerson, Ed. & Trans.). Minneapolis, MN: University of Minnesota Press. (Original work published in 1929)

Bakhtin, M. M. (1986). The problem of speech genres. In C. Emerson & M. Holquist (Eds.), *Speech genres & other late essays* (V. W. McGee, Trans.; pp. 60–102). Austin: University of Texas Press.

Bakhtin, M. M. (1990a). Art and answerability. In M. Holquist (Ed.), *Art and Answerability: Early essays by M. M. Bakhtin* (V. Liapunov, Trans.; pp. 1–3). Austin: University of Texas Press. (Original work published in 1919)

Bakhtin, M. M. (1990b). Author and hero in aesthetic activity. In M. Holquist (Ed.), *Art and Answerability: Early essays by M. M. Bakhtin* (V. Liapunov, Trans.; pp. 4–256). Austin: University of Texas Press. (Original work published in 1919)

Bakhtin, M. M. (1990c). The problem of content, material, and form in verbal art. In M. Holquist (Ed.), *Art and Answerability: Early essays by M. M. Bakhtin* (V. Liapunov, Trans.; pp. 257–326). Austin, TX: University of Texas Press. (Original work published in 1919)

Bakhtin, M. M. (1993). *Toward a philosophy of the act* (V. Liapunov, Ed., & M. Holquist, Trans.). Austin: University of Texas Press. (Original work published in 1986)

Basso, K. H. (1979). *Portraits of "the Whiteman": Linguistic play and cultural symbols among the Western Apache*. New York: Cambridge University Press.

Bauman, R. (1977). Verbal art as performance. In R. Bauman (Ed.), *Verbal art as performance* (pp. 1–58). Prospect Heights, IL: Waveland Press.

Baxter, L. A. (2007a). Mikhail Bakhtin: The philosophy of dialogism. In P. Arneson (Ed.), *Perspectives on philosophy of communication* (pp. 247–268). West Lafayette, IN: Purdue University Press.

Baxter, L. A. (2007b). Problematizing the problem in communication: A dialogic perspective. *Communication Monographs, 74*, 119–125.

Baxter, L. A. (2011). *Voicing relationships: A dialogic perspective*. Los Angeles, CA: Sage.

Baxter, L. A., & Akkoor, C. (2008). Aesthetic love and romantic love in close relationships. In K. G. Roberts & R. C. Arnett (Eds.), *Communication ethics: Between cosmopolitanism and provinciality* (pp. 23–46). New York: Peter Lang.

Baxter, L. A., & Braithwaite, D. O. (2008). Relational dialectics theory. In L. A. Baxter & D. O. Braithwaite (Eds.), *Engaging theories in interpersonal communication* (pp. 349–362). Thousand Oaks, CA: Sage.

Baxter, L. A., & DeGooyer, D., Jr. (2001). Perceived aesthetic characteristics of interpersonal conversations. *Southern Communication Journal, 67*, 1–18.

Baxter, L. A., Foley, M., & Thatcher, M. (2008). Marginalizing difference in personal relationships: A dialogic analysis of partner talk about their difference. *Journal of Communication Studies, 1*, 33–55.

Baxter, L. A., Nebel, S., & Norwood, K. (2011). *Poetic justice: Aesthetic moments of revenge in three relationship types*. Unpublished manuscript, University of Iowa, Iowa City, IA.

Baxter, L. A., & West, L. (2003). Couple perceptions of their similarities and differences: A dialectical perspective. *Journal of Social and Personal Relationships, 20*, 491–514.

Bellah, R. N., Madsen, R., Sullivan, W. M., Swidler, A., & Tipton, S. M. (1985). *Habits of the heart: Individualism and commitment in American life*. Berkeley, CA: University of California Press.

Buber, M. (1970). *I and thou*. (W. Kaufmann, Trans.). New York: Scribner.

Burleson, B. R., & Rack, J. J. (2008). Constructivism theory. In L. A. Baxter & D. O. Braithwaite (Eds.), *Engaging theories in interpersonal communication: Multiple perspectives* (pp. 51–64). Los Angeles, CA: Sage.

Cissna, K. N., & Sieburg, E. (1981). Patterns of interactional confirmation and disconfirmation. In C. Wilder & J. H. Weakland (Eds.), *Rigor & imagination: Essays from the legacy of Gregory Bateson* (pp. 253–282). New York: Praeger.

Cook, G. (2000). *Language play, language learning*. New York, NY: Oxford University Press.

Crick, N. (2004). John Dewey's aesthetics of communication. *Southern Communication Journal, 69*, 303–319.

Cronen, V. E. (1998). Communication theory for the twenty–first century: Cleaning up the wreckage of the psychology project. In J. S. Trent (Ed.), *Communication: Views from the helm for the 21st century* (pp. 18–38). Boston: Allyn and Bacon.

Csikszentmihalyi, M. (1990). *Flow: The psychology of optimal experience*. New York: Harper & Row.

Csikszentmihalyi, M., & Robinson, R. E. (1990). *The art of seeing: An interpretation of the aesthetic encounter*. Los Angeles: Getty Publications.

Dewey, J. (1934). *Art as experience*. New York: Perigee Books.

Dickie, G., Sclafani, R., & Roblin, R. (Eds.). (1989). *Aesthetics: A critical anthology* (2nd ed.). New York: St. Martin's Press.

Duck, S. (1998). Helms and bridges: Relational communication as conceptual and personal linkage. In J. S. Trent (Ed.), *Communication: Views from the helm for the 21st century* (pp. 47–52). Boston: Allyn and Bacon.

Eisenberg, E. M. (1990). Jamming: Transcendence through organizing. *Communication Research, 17*, 139–164.

Emerson, C. (1991). Solov'ev, the late Tolstoi, and the early Bakhtin on the problem of shame and love. *Slavic Review, 50*, 663–671.

Hendrick, S., & Hendrick, C. (1992). *Romantic love*. Newbury Park, CA: Sage.

Jones, S. M. (2004). Putting the person into person–centered and immediate emotional support: Emotional change and perceived helper competence as outcomes of comforting in helping situations. *Communication Research, 31*, 338–360.

Miller, K. I. (2007). Compassionate communication in the workplace: Exploring processes of noticing, connecting, and responding. *Journal of Applied Communication Research, 35*, 223–245.

Spitzberg, B. H., & Cupach, W. R. (2007). Disentangling the dark side of interpersonal communication. In B. H. Spitzberg & W. R. Cupach (Eds.), *The dark side of interpersonal communication* (2nd ed.; pp. 3–30). New York: Routledge.

Stiff, J. B., Dillard, J. P., Somera, L., Kim, H., & Sleight, C. (1988). Empathy, communication, and prosocial behavior. *Communication Monographs, 55*, 198–213.

Stroud, S. R. (2008). John Dewey and the question of artful communication. *Philosophy and Rhetoric, 41*, 153–183.

Tannen, D. (1984). *Conversational style: Analyzing talk among friends.* Norwood, NJ: Ablex Publishing Corporation.

Tannen, D. (1989). *Talking voices: Repetition, dialogue, and imagery in conversational discourse.* Cambridge, UK: Cambridge University Press.

Tannen, D. (1998). Oh talking voice that is so sweet: The poetic nature of conversation. *Social Research, 3,* 631–651.

Tripp, T. M., Bies, R. J., & Aquino, K. (2002). Poetic justice or petty jealousy? The aesthetics of revenge. *Organizational Behavior and Human Decision Processes, 89*, 966–984.

Voloshinov, V. N. (1986). *Marxism and the philosophy of language* (L. Matejka & I. R. Titunik, Trans.). Cambridge, MA: Harvard University Press. (Original work published in 1929)

Williams, R. (1983). *Keywords: A vocabulary of culture and society.* New York: Oxford University Press.

• CHAPTER THREE •

Being in Concert: An Explication of Synchrony in Positive Intercultural Communication

Young Yun Kim
University of Oklahoma

When two people first meet and engage each other interpersonally, a wide range of behaviors is potentially possible between them. From the possible verbal and nonverbal messages, they select certain ones and, thus, succeed or fail to agree on what is and what is not to take place subsequently. In so doing, they form a mutual definition of the communicative relationship between them. More often than not, the process of coming to a positive relational term is meta-communicated through implicit, nonverbal messages of interest, respect, and cooperation; whereas interactants' sense of withdrawal, control, and conflict in each other's nonverbal messages generally form a negative communicative relationship leading to a less than satisfactory outcome on both sides.

Synchrony occurs when interaction behaviors are coordinated in form and timing, reflecting mutuality of attention, interest, and cooperation. As the unspoken dimension of dyadic face-to-face interactions, synchrony contributes to perceived relational "entitativity" (Lakens, 2010). Just as the sound from a radio station becomes crystal clear at the correct frequency level, synchrony is a state in which the interactants comprehend and respond to each other's messages with fidelity. Each party brings forth a "baseline synchrony" or "self-synchrony," in which the physical and vocal configurations constitute an internally congruent personal communication system. When two such baseline systems are meshed in a dynamic equilibrium, "no particular person is overburdened with or completely relieved of work, and, thus, the exchange of messages become efficient, clear, economical, and well timed" (Ruesch, 1951/1968, p. 34).

Although seldom considered, synchrony is crucial to smooth and efficient interpersonal coordination (Bernieri, Reznick, & Rosenthal, 1988). As such, synchrony is a foundational dimension of positive interpersonal communication. It is a "focused encounter" (Kendon, 1982) that "coherence" and "rapport" (Miles, Nind, & Macrae, 2009; Sadler, et al., 2009; Trout & Rosenthal, 1980; Valdesolo, Quyang, & DeSteno, 2010). It engenders perceived "personality similarity" (Feldstein & Welkowitz, 1978), "positive interpersonal judgment" (Cappella, 1981), "interpersonal warmth" and "contact enjoyment" (Feldstein & Welkowitz, 1978). In addition, synchrony promotes the "cooperative ability" allowing individuals to functionally direct their joint interactional goals (Valdesolo et al., 2010). Synchrony, when achieved, is likely to make it possible for communicators to experience a state of "flow" (Csikszentmihalyi, 1990) and "authentic happiness" (Seligman, 2002), both arising from a deep sense of interpersonal cohesion and resonance.

This chapter presents synchrony in interpersonal communication, particularly through the lens of culturally dissimilar individuals. First, based on an examination of pertinent literature, synchrony is described in terms of symmetric and asymmetric forms, along with variations in synchrony systems across cultures. Second, two categories of associative intercultural communication behaviors, individuation and consonance, are identified as being likely to help create intercultural synchrony: individuation and convergence. Third, two communicator factors, identity inclusivity and identity security, are proposed as indirectly facilitating synchrony by fostering associative intercultural behavior.

Synchrony: An Elaboration

Synchrony has been investigated in anthropology, psychology, and communication. Within and across these disciplines, synchrony has been conceived, explained, and observed in different ways depending on the particular focal interests of investigators.

Synchronic Forms: Symmetry and Asymmetry

All indicators of synchrony involve some notion of behavior adjustment or entrainment to another, and can be classified into two broad categories of synchronous forms: symmetric and asymmetric. In Japanese bowing rituals, for instance, two people lowering their heads and upper bodies follow either symmetrically or asymmetrically, primarily depending on the equal or hierarchical nature of their relationship.

Symmetric synchrony occurs when interactants pick up signals from each other's kinesic and paralinguistic characteristics to create forms that either directly mirror (or match) or converge. Symmetric configurations entail one or more similar non-linguistic forms, intensities, frequencies, and tempos— all of which contribute to cohesive interaction. Arrays of studies have examined specific forms of symmetric synchrony. In videotaped films of infant-mother interactions, Bernieri et al. (1988) assessed the degree of symmetry based on a similar timing or tempo of movements. Others operationalized symmetric synchrony in terms of "behavioral matching" (Bernieri & Rosenthal, 1991), "congruent limb configurations" (Trout & Rosenthal, 1980), "posture sharing" (LaFrance, 1982), "movement mirroring" (Schmais & Schmais, 1983), "mimicry" (Chartrand & van Baaren, 2009) or "reflection symmetry" (Bavelas, Black, Lemery & Mullett, 1986), and "mutual eye gaze" (Condon & Ogston, 1967). Along with these and related kinesic-temporal manifestations, symmetric synchrony is observed in paralinguistic aspects of speech (Cappella, 1996). When babies and mothers, or close friends, confide in each other, for example, they often speak "in one voice," each echoing, and converging to, the other's tempo, loudness, pitch, tone, and pauses.

While symmetric synchrony is based on displays of similar and simultaneous nonverbal behaviors, *asymmetric synchrony* is reflected in the cohesion achieved through two types of interactional configuration: concurrent and reciprocal. *Concurrent asymmetric synchrony* occurs when interactants simultaneously display dissimilar, but congruent, nonverbal configurations. In this situation, dissimilar individual behaviors "fit" together in harmony, each complementing or supporting the other's nonverbal activities (Bernieri et al., 1988). *Reciprocal asymmetric synchrony*, on the other hand, emerges over time through alternation ("give-and-take") of similar patterns of behavior. Chapple (1982) observes reciprocal asymmetric synchrony when two people engage in an interaction, adjusting their interaction tempos, so as to achieve reasonably smooth turn-taking. Relatedly, Sadler et al. (2009) identify "shared cyclical patterns" during interactions as forms of interpersonal complementarity.

Synchrony as Biopsychological and Sociocultural Entrainment

Synchrony is rooted in biology and then shaped by culture through social communication processes. From the biological perspective, synchrony is ubiquitous, in all its symmetric and asymmetric manifestations, and occurs naturally and largely without the awareness of the person or of the persons being in sync. While synchrony is innate in human biology, the synchronous responses are also a product of communicative social. Effectual communication, in turn, is made possible by humans calibrating their messages to one another, under the rubric of a cultural or subcultural norm of reciprocity.

The phenomenon of synchrony as a complex interplay of human biology, psychology, culture, and communication is captured in the social interaction theory proposed by biological anthropologist Chapple (1970, 1982). In this theory, synchrony is explained as a function of the nervous system. Employing the key concept, *entrainment*, the theory illuminates the fluid-like process of "drawing in" and transporting interaction rhythms between communicators. According to Chapple (1970), "[the] nature of existence, for animals as well as humans, compels each individual to change his [or her] patterns of interaction since the particular people with whom this interaction takes place come and go" (p. 123). As such, synchrony is conceived as interactive and systemic in nature and is simultaneously biopsychological and sociocultural. The theory recognizes that consistent individual differences, both biological and psychological, exist in interaction tempo parameters, including the duration of an action and the duration of the silence or inaction, as well as in the temperament with which individuals respond to their partner's interruptions or nonresponses that interfere with their personal interaction tempo.

The theory further interfaces individual interaction parameters with various social parameters with which one comes into close contact. Throughout the developmental process, individuals learn and adapt to an ever larger entrainment system as they are exposed to enlarging social circles. Beginning with infancy when one's interactions are almost entirely limited to his/her mother and other primary caregivers, to childhood when one establishes relationships with peers, then to adulthood of entering into new or different organizations, communities, and the like, the various progressive stages challenge the individual with many different entrainment systems, each of which requires a new equilibrium. Calling such social interfaces of systems "mutual entrainment," Chapple (1970) theorizes that the greater the number of individuals mutually "coupled," as in the case of a cultural system, the more stable and less transient are its norms for synchrony, and that, at any given time in the developmental process, an individual's patterns of interactional rhythm are likely to reflect the overall outcome of the significant entrainment experiences of the past. Such an internalized interaction system, in turn, serves as an endogenous system of the individual's "baseline interaction tempos" (Chapple, 1970).

Synchrony, Culture, and Intercultural Communication

As suggested in Chapple's theory, synchrony occurs naturally as it is rooted in human biology and formed through social communication experiences. Given the biological root, however, synchrony is also shaped by culture through social communication processes. Like language, the rhythmic entrainment patterns governing the communication behaviors of individuals exist in every culture, each with unique patterns of synchrony.

Synchrony across Cultures and Subcultures

Since cultural synchrony patterns are learned and internalized throughout early development, their use becomes virtually automatic and "second nature." Once enculturated, individuals are equipped with a common interpretive framework and the ability to attune and enter into synchronous coordination with others with similar cultural conditioning. Within this shared framework, individuals are able to move from one mode of sociality to another (family member to coworker and beyond), making subtle behavioral adjustments to accommodate for the idiosyncratic communication styles of their interaction partners.

Culture, thus, serves as a macro-level entrainment system, a basic and all-encompassing "program" that provide a set of broad parameters for patterns of interpersonal synchrony at the micro-level social processing. Within any given cultural community, most individuals' baseline interaction rhythms and tempos are likely to be within a "normal" range of interactional synchrony established by the cultural tradition, hence the term, "cultural microrhythm," employed by Condon (1982). Similarly, Hall (1983) interfaces personal and collective systems of synchrony when describing "micro time" and "cultural time," and explains that, at any given moment, an individual's personal time system reflects "complex hierarchies of interlocking rhythms . . . comparable to fundamental themes in a symphonic score, a keystone in the interpersonal processes between mates, co-workers, and organizations of all types on the interpersonal level" (p. 153).

Efforts have been made to identify cultural variations in synchronous configurations. Birdwhistell (1970) demonstrated, through slow motion film, the different postural kinesic forms of communication across cultures. Extending Birdwhistell's work, Hall (1976, 1983) provides insights into cultural variations in synchrony. Defining synchrony as "moving together," Hall describes many of the "situational dialects" across cultures in terms of the ways conversational partners move in some kind of choreographed dance creating interactional harmony. Hall's notion of cultural "adumbration" (Hall, 1979) and "action chain" (Hall, 1976) illustrate the mutuality of interaction rhythms within different cultural communities, as though each "runs" on a different communication "beat" resonating at a different level of vibration.

Hall (1976) captures variations in cultural synchrony systems along the continuum of "high-context" and "low-context" communication. Hall explains that, compared to people in relatively low-context cultures (i.e., North-American and Western European cultures), people in relatively high-context cultures (i.e., Latin American, African, and Asian cultures) tend to be more conscious of, and more seriously attend to, the synchronous movements between interactants. Accordingly, Hall characterizes high-context communication as taking a longer time to complete an "action chain" such as the normative sequence in greeting and parting rituals, just as they tend to take a longer time to develop, and terminate, an intimate relationship.

Cultural variations in synchrony are also observed at the level of subcultures within a society. From experience, we are able to discern differences in subcultural systems based on ethnicity. Ethnographic studies offer insights into subcultural variations, including the "call-response" and other traditional rhythmic interaction patterns among African Americans (Daniel & Smitherman, 1990), and the employment of silence as a shared communication practice in the Western Apache culture (Basso, 1990).

Asynchrony in Intercultural Communication

Since particularities of any cultural synchronic system are acquired and internalized from childhood, they generally elude people's awareness or intentionality except when they encounter interactions that are at variance with their presumed "cultural script." Because intercultural communication, by definition, involves communicators of dissimilar cultural conditioning, it presents special challenges beyond those routinely expected in communication within a cultural group. As such, cultural strangers often find themselves "out of sync" with each other, and, thus, feel some degree of psychological strain.

As Hall (1979) warns, what is most often underrecognized or misunderstood in intercultural encounters is the incongruence stemming from dissimilarities in patterns of synchrony and the feeling of being forced into an unfamiliar and unaccustomed conversational configurations and rhythms. Either in anticipation of, or in response to, stress-inducing and unpleasant miscues people often try to avoid similar future encounters. Or they may end up engaging in "counter-accommodating" or "over-accommodating" devices such as speaking louder, interrupting, abruptly changing topics, or answering questions for the non-native speakers (Berger & diBattista, 1993). Even with the best intentions, excessive eagerness may force someone to impose, unwittingly, his or her interaction rhythm on the other party, leading to a silent, but real, clash of cultural operating systems.

In some cases, the asynchronous state can be serious enough to prevent the real communication from ever emerging. As Chapple's (1970, 1982) entrainment-based theory of social interaction points out, there are limits to the flexibility of each individual's interaction system and, when the baseline for preferred activity levels between two people are strikingly different, mutual entrainment is unlikely to occur. Also relevant to the challenges of asynchrony in intercultural communication is the arousal-based explanation by Cappella and Greene (1982). Their account of "affiliative" or non-affiliative behavior is based on the arousal triggered by others' behaviors that deviate from one's internalized procedural knowledge. Furthermore, according to expectancy violation theory (Burgoon & Hale, 1988) and interpersonal adaptation theory (Burgoon, 1995), non-affiliative "compensatory" behaviors are likely in intercultural encounters due to the reactions to the target individual who deviates from one's nonverbal expectancies.

Factors Facilitating Intercultural Synchrony

Despite the inherent challenges of asynchrony cultural strangers' face, some studies, while not directly focused on synchrony, offer some indications that synchrony can, and does, occur in intercultural encounters. Most of these studies examine how individuals make adjustments in verbal messages or speaking styles, so as to engender a greater congruence in their communicative relationships with cultural strangers. Native speakers try to assess the listener's common sense for an additional information base for conversation (Chen, 1997), and compensate for "communication deficits" when communicating with non-native speakers by choosing simpler conversation topics (Long. 1981). Analysis of naturally-occurring conversations between Japanese and American coworkers provides further indication of synchronic behavior by focusing on "verbal listening" patterns (Miller, 1991). Miller found that, whereas most American coworkers engage in the American cultural modes of expressing their listening by making minimal verbal responses, thereby failing to create cohesion in interacting with the Japanese, one American skillfully adapts his listening to the Japanese mode of more active and frequent vocalizations and nodding.

Other experimental studies, using speech accommodation theory, report indications of convergent paralinguistic responses to intergroup situations by making accommodating choices of speech dialects and accents (Giles & Smith, 1979). Gallois, Jones, Barker, and Callan (1992), in a study of interaction between Chinese and Anglo-Australian students and academic staff members in situations of potential conflict, reports a positive relationship between accommodative, convergent behavior and positive interpersonal evaluations.

Synchrony-Facilitating Behaviors: Individuation and Consonance

Research findings suggest that, although difficult, synchrony can, and does, occur in intercultural encounters when at least one interactant can make adjustments in his/her habitual nonverbal patterns and, consciously or not, some individuals are able to make such adaptive moves better than others. Building on these basic insights, I propose two interrelated categories of specific communication behaviors, both internal and external, that can help create intercultural synchrony: individuation and consonance. In a contextual theory of interethnic communication (Kim, 2005), I identify these two categories as the key constituent facets of the "associative" behaviors that increase the likelihood of understanding, cooperation, and the "coming-together" of the involved parties into a cooperative relationship, at least temporarily.

The first category, *individuation*, refers to communication behaviors that focus on a given cultural stranger as a unique individual (vs. a group member) and making adjustments in one's communication behavior according to that person's communication patterns. Through individuation, the communicator is able to process information and design messages that are more closely aligned with the other person's messages and the underlying thoughts and emotions. Individuation, thus, serves as an inclusive concept that incorporates within it a number of existing terms pertaining to interpersonal communication competence and cooperative intergroup communication. Among such concepts are: "cognitive differentiation" (Brewer & Miller, 1988), "particularization" and "decategorization" (Billig, 1987), and "multiple categorization" (Crisp, Hewstone, & Rubin, 2001), as well as "attentiveness" (Bell, 1987), "fully-focused gathering" (Goffman, 1979) of information, "nonverbal receiving ability" (Buck, 1983), and "mindfulness" (Langer, 1989).

The second category, *consonance*, represents the behaviors that reflect the communicator making adjustments in his or her habitual behaviors in such a way that is more congruent with the behaviors of the other. Like individuation, the term, consonance, incorporates concepts pertaining to interpersonal communication competence or cooperative intergroup communication. Such concepts include "person-centered messages" (Applegate & Sypher, 1988) that generally require speakers to recognize another person's perspectives and contain a quality of sensitivity, engagement, and concern for relational cohesion. Such behavioral characteristics are consistent with the meaning of related concepts including "convergent behavior" (Gallois, Ogay, & Giles, 2005), "empathic listening" (Rosenfeld & Hancks, 1990), and "responsiveness" (Cegala et al., 1982), to name a few.

Together, individuation and consonance constitute a cornerstone of intercultural communication competence, defined here as "the overall capacity of an individual to enact behaviors and activities that foster cooperative relationships with culturally (or ethnically) dissimilar others" (Kim, 2009, p. 54). To be interculturally competent means that one has the "capacity to improvise" (Sanders, 1987) by suspending group stereotypes and, instead, focusing on the particularities of a specific cultural stranger. It is individual people, after all, who are communicating, with each individual bringing something unique to the situation. Furthermore, a competent intercultural communicator is someone who is willing and able to modify at least some of his or her current cultural as well as personal communication habits, so as to creatively enter into the other person's communication style and engender mutuality with each interaction partner. In this regard, intercultural communication competence, built on individuation and consonance, is a self-altering capacity that invites alternations in the interaction partner, consistent with Ruesch's (1951/1968) idea that "successful communication with self and others implies correction by others as well as self-correction" (p. 18).

Synchrony-Facilitating Identity Orientations: Inclusivity and Security

An individual's capacity to engage in individuated and consonant intercultural behaviors is likely to be a function of his or her identity orientation. The term, identity, is conceived here holistically as the general self-other orientation of an individual, that is, the routinized way or "personal schema" (Horowitz, 1991), with which the individual receives and responds to communication messages from a social milieu. As such, identity is regarded as the more or less enduring core constitution of a personhood that influences the individual's communication behaviors including behaviors in intercultural settings.

Based on close examination of many theoretical ideas and research findings in intercultural and intergroup communication, I identify two interrelated, but conceptually distinct, identity orientations—inclusivity and security—as key communicator characteristics pertaining to an individual's ability to facilitate intercultural synchrony and, thereby, contributing to his/her overall "intercultural communication competence" (Kim, 2009).

Identity inclusivity refers to the extent that an individual's self-other orientation discourages rigid ingroup-outgroup differentiation of others based on social categories such as culture and ethnicity. This identity orientation serves as a cognitive and motivational basis of associative communication behavior in intercultural interaction (Kim, 2005). That is, individuals more inclusive in identity orientation tend to be more motivated to accommodate culturally dissimilar interaction partners and more mindful of the particularities of each intercultural encounter, including the unfolding of nonverbal activities. In contrast, individuals more exclusive in identity orientation are expected to be less interested in attending to such subtle details and less willing to make adjustments in their own habitual behaviors. The widely observed tendency of individuals to categorize themselves and others exclusively as "in-group" and "out-group" is likely to impede genuine person-to-person engagement, as suggested in social identity theory (Tajfel, 1974; Tajfel & Turner, 1986) and its twin theory of self-categorization (Turner, 1982).

A body of research findings provides some indirect empirical support for the present conception of identity inclusivity as a factor that contributes to intercultural synchrony. Kim, Lujan, and Dixon (1998), for instance, analyze the subjective identity experience of American Indians in Oklahoma, and report a preponderance of the inclusive "intercultural" identity orientation and its significant relationship to interpersonal engagement with non-Indians. Likewise, Thijs (2002), based on a study of Dutch and Turkish adolescents in the Netherlands, observe that, among the Turkish adolescents, their strong ingroup identification is positively related to ethnic maintenance, but not to adaptation in Dutch society. Agreement with cultural adaptation is lowest among those who strongly identified with Turkish ethnic background. A similar finding is reported by Polek, Oudenhoven, and Berge (2007), who find that, among immigrants in the Netherlands, those immigrants whose identity orientation is more "cosmopolitan" are better adapted in the host society than those with a strong attachment to their in-group identity.

The second identity orientation, *identity security,* is reflected in an individual's overall "ego strength" (Lazarus, 1966). As a broad concept, identity security integrates several more narrowly defined terms including "self-esteem" (Padilla, Wagatsuma, & Lindholm, 1985), "self-efficacy" (Harrison, Chadwick, & Scales, 1996), "personality strength" (Kim, 1988, 2001), and "hardiness" (Walton, 1990). Relatedly, "positivity" (Kim, 1988, 2001), or an affirmative and optimistic outlook, is also an important element of identity security, working as a source of "metamotivation" (Maslow, 1969), a kind of self-trust that allows individuals not to cripple oneself with irrational feelings of inferiority or defensiveness and instead to seek more practical and adaptive alternatives when interacting interculturally.

In this sense, along with identity inclusivity, the degree to which individuals are secure in their identity adds to the overall intercultural competence that enables them to engage in associative intercultural behaviors. As a personal inner resource, identity security accords the capacity to empathize with others and to be creative in responding to impending problems, in contrast with feelings of inferiority or defensiveness, when interacting with out-group members. Identity security, as such, allows for qualities of flexibility and relaxedness in one's behavior, that is, the ability to "bend" and empathize with others without losing the ability to maintain one's integrity, and to be creative and effective in responding to impending problems. As Worchel (1979) observes, "Cooperation could be induced by having each side set aside its weapons or reduce its potential to threaten or harm the other. The less the two parties fear each other the greater should be the likelihood that they will cooperate" (p. 266).

Social psychological studies provide additional indirect support for the link between identity security and associative intercultural behavior. Nesdale (2003), in a survey in Australia of immigrant adults from Hong Kong, Vietnam, Bosnia, Sri Lanka, and New Zealand, reports that "personal self-esteem," but not "ethnic self-esteem," is a significant predictor of the immigrants' relational involvement with Australians, as well as of their individual achievements. Also, Goff, Steele, and Davies (2008), in a four-part sequenced experimental study, find that White American participants distance themselves more from African American participants under conditions of threat, and this distance correlates with the activation of a "White racist" stereotype. Conversely, Thijs (2002), in the previously mentioned study of minority and majority adolescents in the Netherlands, report that Turkish adolescents who strongly identified themselves as Turks tend to perceive greater discrimination from the majority group.

Theoretical Synthesis

In this chapter, synchrony has been presented as an implicit dimension of interpersonal communication essential to generating focused engagement and relational cohesion, particularly between cultural strangers. The key ideas pertaining to these basic ideas about synchrony are summarized here in the form of four basic assumptions about the nature of synchrony.

Assumptions

1. Synchrony is a positive state of a simultaneous contagion and rapport in dyadic interpersonal communication, created by the interactants' rhythmic configurations of kinesic and paralinguistic nonverbal behaviors.

2. Synchrony takes two forms of configurations: symmetric and asymmetric. Symmetric synchrony is reflected in configurations of one or more similar nonverbal forms, intensities, frequencies, and tempos. Asymmetric synchrony occurs either in concurrently configurations of dissimilar, but complementary, nonverbal behaviors, or through reciprocation or alternation of similar behaviors.

3. Synchrony is a phenomenon of both biopsychological and sociocultural origins. It is, therefore, both universal and varied across cultures. Specific forms of synchrony are established through the process of entrainment. Culture serves as a macro-level entrainment system, within which individuals and subgroups coordinate their personal and interpersonal communication activities.

4. Because of cross-cultural variations in synchrony, intercultural interactants often experience asynchrony. Despite inherent challenges, however, it is possible for culturally dissimilar interactants to help create synchrony, so as to foster cohesion and mutuality in their communicative relationship.

Theorems

Based on the above framing, I propose the following four theorems as a way of explaining how an individual's associative communication behaviors and identity orientations are likely to foster synchrony in intercultural interaction. These theorems are presented as an initial set of ideas for future studies that are aimed at finding ways to facilitate the development of synchrony in intercultural communication.

1. The more individuated an individual's communication behavior, the more likely he/she is to initiate synchrony in intercultural interaction.

2. The more consonant an individual's communication behavior, the more likely he/she is to initiate synchrony in intercultural interaction.

3. The more inclusive an individual's identity orientation, the more likely he/she is to initiate synchrony in intercultural interaction.

4. The more secure an individual's identity orientation, the more likely he/she is to initiate synchrony in intercultural interaction.

Together, these theorems provide a behavioral and psychological profile of the intercultural communicator who is likely to play an active role in fostering mutuality in interactions with cultural strangers. Note that the two factors of associative behavior (individuation and consonance) as well as the two factors of identity orientation (inclusivity and security) are culture-general in nature, that is, they are universally applicable to all situations and events of intercultural communication regardless of specific cultural, social, and relational particularities involved.

Conclusion

Synchrony is an elusive, but real and potent, force behind our experience of positive interpersonal engagement. Equipped with a natural tendency of entrainment, we acquire our personal and cultural synchronic systems through communication. To the extent that cultures differ in defining parameters and normative expectations for synchrony, intercultural contexts present challenges in attaining synchrony between culturally dissimilar individuals. The four theorems, then, serve as a call for a greater recognition of the importance of synchrony in intercultural communication.

While achieving synchrony may not guarantee successful outcomes in any given intercultural encounter, it lays a necessary foundation on which we may pursue mutual interactional goals. As individuals, we may strive to achieve greater efficacy in our interactions by attending to the implicit, nonverbal undercurrents of communication. A clear understanding of the nature and potential power of synchrony in communication can help us foster cohesion and mutuality vis-à-vis culturally dissimilar individuals. Such an understanding can motivate us to make adjustments in our habitual ways of communicating, so as to communicate in a more individuated and consonant manner with respect to the person with whom we interact. It can also encourage us to move away from the common "us-and-them" psychological posture of an exclusive and insecure identity orientation that views a cultural stranger as "one of them." Rather, as the present theoretical account suggests, we need to make an effort to orient ourselves inclusively and attend to the other person as "one of us," and be willing and eager to form a partnership with that person.

Humans are creatures of habit, much of which is shaped by culture. For most of us, moving beyond the psychological habit of categorizing people does not come naturally. Synchrony, then, must be ultimately "the gift of the individual" (Steele, 1990). Achieving synchrony in interpersonal communication in general, and in intercultural communication in particular, calls for a certain degree of "character strength" (Peterson & Seligman, 2004), the inner resource that enables us to expand our communication repertoire and versatility. Indeed, each of us has some capacity to do so by opening ourselves to new experiences beyond our comfort zone, by endeavoring to cultivate a new habit of being attentive to the particularities of our culturally dissimilar interaction partners, and by being willing to make adjustments in our habitual ways. In Buber's (1965) words, "community is where community happens" (p. 31). With genuine motivation and through trial and error, we can increase our chances for being able to create a community—with one person at a time.

References

Applegate, J., & Sypher. H. (1988). A constructivist theory of communication and culture. In Y. Y. Kim & W. B. Gudykunst (Eds.), *Theories of intercultural communication* (pp. 41–65). Newbury Park, CA: Sage.

Basso, K. (1990). "To give up on words": Silence in Western Apache culture. In D. Carbaugh (Ed.), *Cultural communication and intercultural contact* (pp. 303–320). Hillsdale, NJ: Lawrence Erlbaum.

Bavelas, J., Black, A., Lemery, C., & Mullett, J. (1986). I *show* you how you feel: Motor mimicry as a communicative act. *Journal of Personality and Social Psychology, 50,* 322–329.

Bell, R. (1987). Social involvement. In J. McCroskey & J. Daly (Eds.), *Personality and interpersonal communication* (pp. 195–242). Newbury Park, CA: Sage.

Berger, C. R., & diBattista, P. (1993). Communication failure and plan adaptation: If at first you don't succeed, say it louder and slower. *Communication Monographs, 60*(3), 220–238.

Bernieri, F., Reznick, J., & Rosenthal, R. (1988). Synchrony, pseudo–synchrony, and dissynchrony: Measuring the entrainment process in mother–infant interactions. *Journal of Personality and Social Psychology, 54,* 243–253.

Bernieri, F. J., & Rosenthal, R. (1991). Interpersonal coordination: Behavioral matching and interactional synchrony. In R. S. Feldman & B. Rime (Eds.), *Fundamentals of nonverbal behavior (pp. 401–432).* Cambridge: Cambridge University Press.

Billig, M. (1987). *Arguing and thinking.* Cambridge, UK: Cambridge University Press.

Birdwhistell, R. (1970). *Kinesics and context.* Philadelphia: University of Pennsylvania Press.

Brewer, M., & Miller, N. (1988). Contact and cooperation: When do they work? In P. Katz & D. Taylor (Eds.), *Eliminating racism* (pp. 315–326). Newbury Park, CA: Sage.

Buber, M. (1965/1976). *Between man and man*. New York: Macmillan.

Buck, R. (1983). Nonverbal receiving ability. In J. Wiemann & R. Harrison (Eds.), *Nonverbal interaction* (pp. 20–242). Beverly Hills, CA: Sage.

Burgoon, J. (1995). *Interpersonal adaptation: Dyadic interaction patterns*. New York: Cambridge University Press.

Burgoon, J., & Hale, J. (1988). Nonverbal expectancy violations. *Communication Monographs, 55*, 58–79.

Cappella, J. (1981). Mutual influence in expressive behavior: Adult–adult and infant–adult dyadic interaction. *Psychological Bulletin, 89*, 101–132.

Cappella, J. (1996). Dynamic coordination of vocal and kinesic behavior in dyadic interaction: Methods, problems, and interpersonal outcomes. In J. Watt & C. van Lear (Eds.), *Dynamic patterns in communication processes* (pp. 353–386). Thousand Oaks, CA: Sage.

Cappella, J., & Greene, J. (1982). A discrepancy-arousal explanation of mutual influence in expressing behavior for adult-adult and infant-adult interaction. *Communication Monographs, 49*, 89–114.

Cegala, D., Savage, G., Brunner, C., & Conrad, A. (1982). An elaboration of the meaning of interaction involvement: Toward the development of a theoretical concept. *Communication Monographs, 49*, 229–248.

Chapple, E. (1970). *Culture and biological man*. New York: Holt, Rinehart &Winston.

Chapple, E. (1982). Movement and sound: The musical language of body rhythms in interaction. In M. Davis (Ed.), *Interaction rhythms: Periodicity in communicative behavior* (pp. 31–51). New York: Human Sciences.

Chartrand, T., & van Baaren, R. (2009). Human mimicry. *Advances in Experimental Social Psychology, 41*, 219–274.

Chen, L. (1997, December). Verbal adaptive strategies in U.S. American dyadic interactions with U.S. American or East–Asian partners. *Communication Monographs, 64*, 302–323.

Condon, W. (1982). Cultural micro–rhythms. In M. Davis (Ed.), *Interaction rhythms: Periodicity in communicative behavior* (pp. 53–77). New York: Human Sciences.

Condon, W., & Ogston, W. (1967). A segmentation of behavior. *Journal of Psychological Research, 5*, 221–235.

Crisp, R., Hewstone, M., & Rubin, M. (2001). Does multiple categorization reduce intergroup bias? *Personality and Social Psychology Bulletin, 27*, 76–89.

Csikszentmihalyi, M. (1990). *Flow: The psychology of optimal experience*. New York: Harper & Row.

Daniel, J., & Smitherman, G. (1990). How I got over: Communication dynamics in the Black community. In D. Carbaugh (Ed.), *Cultural communication and intercultural contact* (pp. 27–40). Hillsdale, NJ: Lawrence Erlbaum.

Feldstein, S., & Welkowitz, J. (1978). A chronography of conversation: In defense of an objective approach. In A. Siegman & S. Feldstein (Eds.), *Nonverbal behavior and communication* (pp. 329–378). Hillsdale, NJ: Lawrence Erlbaum.

Gallois, C., Jones, E., Barker, M., & Callan, V. (1992, May). *Communication accommodation between Chinese and Australian students and academic staff*. Paper presented at the International Communication Association, Miami, Florida.

Gallois, C., Ogay, T., & Giles, H. (2005). Communication accommodation theory. In W. B. Gudykunst (Ed.), *Theorizing about intercultural communication* (pp. 121–148). Thousand Oaks, CA: Sage.

Giles, H., & Smith, P. (1979). Accommodation theory: Optimal level of convergence. In H. Giles & R. St. Clair (Eds.), *Language and social psychology* (pp. 45–65). Oxford, UK: Blackwell.

Goff, P., Steele, C., & Davies, P. (2008). The space between us: Stereotype threat and distance in interracial contexts. *Journal of Personality and Social Psychology, 94*(1), 91–107.

Goffman, E. (1979). Facial engagement. In C. Mortensen (Ed.), *Basic readings in communication theory* (2nd ed., pp. 137–163). New York: Harper & Row.

Hall, E. T. (1976). *Beyond culture*. Garden City, NY: Anchor Books.

Hall, E. T. (1979). Adumbration as a feature of intercultural communication. In C. Mortensen (Ed.), *Basic readings in communication theory* (2nd ed., pp. 420–432). New York: Harper & Row.

Hall, E. T. (1983). *The dance of life*. Garden City, NY: Anchor Books.

Harrison, J., Chadwick, M., & Scales, M. (1996). The relationship between cross-cultural adjustment and the personality variables of self-efficacy and self-monitoring. *International Journal of Intercultural Relations, 20*, 167–188.

Horowitz, M. (1991). Person schemas. In M. Horowitz (Ed.), *Person schemas and maladaptive interpersonal patterns* (pp. 13–31). Chicago: The University of Chicago Press.

Kendon, A. (1982). Coordination of action and framing in face-to-face interaction. In M. Davis (Ed.), *Interaction rhythms: Periodicity in communicative behavior* (pp. 351–363). New York: Human Sciences.

Kim, Y. Y. (1988). *Communication and cross–cultural adaptation: An integrative theory*. Clevedon, UK: Multilingual Matters.

Kim, Y. Y. (2001). *Becoming intercultural: An integrative theory of communication and cross–cultural adaptation*. Thousand Oaks, CA: Sage.

Kim, Y. Y. (2005). Association and dissociation: A contextual theory of interethnic communication. In W. B. Gudykunst (Ed.), *Theorizing about intercultural communication* (pp. 323–349). Thousand Oaks, CA: Sage.

Kim, Y. Y. (2009). The identity factor in intercultural competence. In D. K. Deardoff (Ed.), *The Sage handbook of intercultural competence* (pp. 53–65). Thousand Oaks, CA: Sage.

Kim, Y. Y., Lujan, P., & Dixon, L. (1998). "I can walk both ways: Identity integration of American Indians in Oklahoma. *Human Communication Research, 25*(2), 252–274.

LaFrance, M. (1982). Posture mirroring and rapport. In M. Davis (Ed.), *Interaction rhythms: Periodicity in communicative behavior* (pp. 279–297). New York: Human Sciences.

Lakens, D. (2010). Movement synchrony and perceived entitativity. *Journal of Experimental Social Psychology, 46*(4), 701–708

Langer, E. (1989). *Mindfulness*. Reading, MA: Addison–Wesley.

Lazarus, R. (1966). *Psychological stress and the coping process*. New York: McGraw–Hill.

Long, H. (1981). Questions in foreign talk discourse. *Language and Learning, 31*, 135–157.

Maslow, A. (1969). A theory of metamotivation: The biological rooting of the value–life. In H. Chiang & Abraham H. Maslow (Eds.), *The healthy personality* (pp. 35–56). New York: Van Nostrand Reinhold.

Miles, L., Nind, L., & Macrae, C. N. (2009). The rhythm of rapport: Interpersonal synchrony and social perception. *Journal of Experimental Social Psychology, 45*(3), 585–589.

Miller, L. (1991). Verbal listening behavior in conversation between Japanese and Americans. In J. Blommaert & J. Verschueren (Eds.), *The pragmatics of international and intercultural communication* (pp. 111–130). Amsterdam: John Benjamins.

Nesdale, D. (2003). Ethnic identification, self-esteem and immigrant psychological health. *International Journal of Intercultural Relations, 27*(1), 23–40.

Padilla, A., Wagatsuma, Y., & Lindholm, K. (1985). Acculturation and personality as predictors of stress in Japanese and Japanese–Americans. *Journal of Social Psychology, 125*(3), 295–305.

Peterson, C., & Seligman, M. (2004). *Character strengths and virtues.* New York: Oxford University Press.

Polek, E., Oudenhoven, J. P., & Berge, J. (2007, July). *Cosmopolitan identity—the overlooked element in policies on immigrants' adaptation.* Paper presented at the International Academy for Intercultural Research, Groningen, The Netherlands.

Rosenfeld, H., & Hancks, M. (1990). The nonverbal context of verbal listener responses. In M. Key (Ed.), *The relationship of verbal and nonverbal communication* (Student Edition, pp. 193–206). The Hague: Mouton.

Ruesch, J. (1951/1968). Communication and human relations: An interdisciplinary approach. In J. Ruesch & G. Bateson, *Communication: The social matrix of psychiatry* (pp. 21–49). New York: Norton.

Sadler, P., Ethier, N., Gunn, G., Duong, D., & Woody, E. (2009). Are we on the same wavelength? Interpersonal complementarity as shared cyclical patterns during interactions. *Journal of Personality and Social Psychology, 97*(6), 1005–1020.

Sanders, R. (1987). *Cognitive foundations of calculated speech.* Albany, NY: SUNY Press.

Schmais, C., & Schmais, A. (1983). Reflecting emotions: The movement–mirroring test. *Journal of Nonverbal Behavior, 8,* 42–54.

Seligman, M. (2002). *Authentic happiness.* New York: Free Press.

Steele, S. (1990). *The content of our character: A new vision of race in America.* New York: Harper Perennial.

Tajfel, H. (1974). Social identity and intergroup behavior. *Social Science Information, 13,* 65–93.

Tajfel, H., & Turner, J. (1986). The social identity theory of intergroup behavior. In S. Worchel & W. Austin (Eds.), *Psychology of intergroup relations* (2nd ed., pp. 7–17). Chicago; Nelson–Hall.

Thijs, J. (2002). Multiculturalism among minority and majority adolescents in the Netherlands. *International Journal of Intercultural Relations, 26*(1), 91–108.

Trout, D., & Rosenthal, H. (1980). The effect of postural lean and body congruence on the judgment of psychotherapeutic rapport. *Journal of Nonverbal Behavior, 4,* 176–189.

Turner, J. (1982). Towards a cognitive redefinition of the social group. In H. Tajfel (Ed.), *Social identity and intergroup relations* (pp. 15–40). Cambridge, England: Cambridge University Press.

Valdesolo, P., Quyang, J., & DeSteno, D. (2010). The rhythm of joint action: Synchrony promotes cooperative ability. *Journal of Experimental Social Psychology, 46*(4), 693–695.

Walton, S. (1990). Stress management training for overseas effectiveness. *International Journal of Intercultural Relations, 14*(4), 507–527.

Worchel, S. (1979). Cooperation and the reduction of intergroup conflict: Some determining factors. In W. Austin & S. Worchel (Eds.), *The social psychology of intergroup relations* (pp. 262–273). Monterey, CA: Brooks/Cole.

• CHAPTER FOUR •

Communication Excellence: Embodying Virtues in Interpersonal Communication

Julien C. Mirivel
University of Arkansas at Little Rock

> What moves the Greek warrior to deeds of heroism, Kitto comments, is not a sense of duty as we understand it—a duty towards others: it is rather duty towards himself. He strives after that which translates as 'virtue,' but is in Greek aretê, 'excellence'.
> —Pirsig (1974, p. 340)

The most significant choice in interpersonal communication is to act with character. In personal and professional relationships, we can choose to show compassion, offer gratitude, express forgiveness, or communicate with courage. Unfortunately, few researchers document this kind of communicative conduct; most scholarship in interpersonal communication focuses on problems, issues, or the "dark side" (Spitzberg & Cupach, 2007). To date, few published studies have described interpersonal communication at its best. Sometimes, it has been done philosophically or theoretically, other times, empirically. There also is burgeoning research on mercy (Brann, Rittenour, & Myers, 2007; Ronel & Lebel, 2006; see also Kelley, chapter 12, this volume) and compassion (Miller, 2007). But, we still do not know what form excellent communication takes or what principles of communicative conduct should ground it.

In this chapter, I argue that communication excellence is a practical art that should be guided by virtues. Virtues like compassion, generosity, or prudence can stretch "our daily conduct toward a standard of principled and courageous living" (Jensen, n.d.). Viewed this way communication excellence includes speaking and acting ethically. Nicomachean ethics, an ethical system developed by Aristotle based on virtue (see MacIntyre, 1984), can guide reflection on the nature of excellence. As Kim (2004) explained,

"Aristotle's is an ethics not of principles and rules, but of character . . . proper and appropriate relations to others . . . it is an ethics of self-development, and duties to oneself" (p. xiii). Virtue, in fact, comes from the Greek word "arête," which translates as excellence. The word "arête" also "implies a respect for the wholeness or oneness of life" (Pirsig, 1974, p. 341). In this chapter, I propose that excellence in interpersonal communication is virtuous activity that implicates a person's character.

Virtues can guide a person to lead an ethical life. If communication excellence means striving toward virtue, the challenge for communication researchers is to articulate how virtues can be enacted through communication. There is a difference between compassion as a virtue and compassion as a communicative act. Researchers can thus ask: How is courage expressed as a speech act? How can a person enact compassion in human communication? How should communicators preserve justice in their talk? This chapter moves in that direction. To proceed, I draw on the French philosopher André Comte-Sponville (2001) to describe five virtues: gentleness, generosity, courage, justice, and compassion.[1] For each virtue, I use communication research and examples of human interaction to suggest how it can be embodied communicatively.[2]

Gentleness

In his *Last Lecture*, Pausch (2008) narrates a moment with a mentor:

> He put his arm around me and we went for a little walk and he said: Randy, it's such a shame that people perceive you as so arrogant because it's going to limit what you're going to be able to accomplish in life. What a hell of a good way to word: you're being a jerk.

The words we choose matter. This is why communication excellence should begin with gentleness. Gentleness is "a kind of peace, either real or desired: it is the opposite of war, cruelty, brutality, aggressiveness, and violence" (Comte-Sponville, 2001, p. 186). To be gentle includes the ability to monitor one's impulsive violence and anger. As Comte-Sponville explains:

> Aggressiveness is a weakness; anger is a weakness, even violence, when unmastered, is a weakness. [...] Gentleness is a strength, which is what makes it a virtue; it is strength in a state of peace, serene and gentle, full of patience and leniency. (p. 186)

If gentleness implies nonviolence, it can be embodied in communication by being face-attentive. Face attentiveness is a communicative approach that considers how an utterance will impact another person's sense of self. As Goffman (1967) explained, face is "the positive social value that a person effectively claims for himself" (p. 213). According to politeness theory (Brown & Levinson, 1978), every communicator in every culture has face needs that are managed during interaction with others. Communicators enter interaction needing love, inclusion, and respect (i.e., solidarity face needs). Communicators also need to be free from impositions from others and make their own decisions (i.e., autonomy face needs). And, communicators have a need for competency. These needs are constantly maintained or challenged in the course of human communication. Face attentiveness, then, occurs when a communicator speaks in a way that supports another person's face needs in spite of possible difficulties or challenges.

Face attentiveness functions positively in human interaction. Everyday communicators, however, tend to use face-threatening actions in conflict situations or under pressure (Tracy, 2008, Tracy & Tracy, 1998). During conflict especially, people can move quickly from face-threats to face-attacks. Face attentiveness is thus counter-intuitive; it moves against our natural tendency. To do it well, communicators need to design their talk in ways that are attentive to the other person's face needs. The practice involves communicating a sometimes difficult message by including particles of talk that will make it more receptive to another person. It also includes mitigating anticipated face-threats and using politeness jewelry such as "deferential address forms, expression of disagreement with mitigation markers or apologies" (Tracy, 2008, p. 187). The face-attentive communicator is thus someone who chooses her words wisely in light of their possible impact.

Gentleness, Comte-Sponville reminds us, "Refuses to produce or increase suffering" (p. 186). To be gentle is "to limit our violence." When gentleness becomes a leading virtue of communication excellence, it can be embodied in conversation when it matters most.

Generosity

Generosity is "the virtue of giving—giving money (whereby it touches on liberality) or giving of oneself (whereby it touches on magnanimity or even sacrifice)" (Comte-Sponville, 2001, p. 93). Comte-Sponville (2001) demonstrates that "generosity is both awareness of one's own freedom (or oneself as free and responsible) and the firm resolution to make good use of that freedom" (p. 94). Generosity is about realizing what one is capable of doing and deciding to act otherwise. As he put it, "To be charitable is to renounce the fullness of the ego, of power and potency" (p. 276). A bit later, he adds: "The generous man is not a prisoner of his emotions or of himself; on the contrary, he is master of himself" (p. 94). If generosity is choosing to control our capability, then this virtue translates well for communication excellence. Most communicators, if they so choose, can display anger, rage, or violence. They also can display love, kindness, or affection.

Generous communication can take place in three forms: by interpreting others' actions positively, offering their best move when they design an utterance, and monitoring their communicative actions for effect. To exemplify generous communication, I describe how behavioral instructors are taught to interact with children and adolescents with a traumatic past.

Behavioral instructors who work in addiction recovery and youth centers must learn to communicate with children to foster their growth. They also must be able to handle clients who turn violent or tantrum and discipline in a productive fashion. Ethnographic research I conducted at *Women Recovery Center* (for mothers and children) revealed that behavioral instructors were trained to communicate with clients by modeling positive behaviors (e.g., consistently greeting children), noticing and describing the positive behaviors that clients enacted rather than what they did wrong (e.g., praising rather than criticizing), and staying calm under pressure by being gentle rather than aggressive (Mirivel, 2011). During the training, the BIs were taught to "stay calm and in control at all times" and to "not threaten the children, punish them, or use any punitive means" because many clients suffer from a violent past. Enacting this communication approach, however, requires effort and tactfulness that exemplify what generous communication is about.

In a 40-hour workshop, I observed the BIs taught to praise children effectively and to consistently focus on what children were doing well. This perspective challenged the instructors to draw on a positive lens through which to view children's behaviors. The behavior structure taught was: (1) initiate praise and identify the behavior (e.g., "You did a good job greeting this morning"), (2) describe the appropriate behavior (e.g., "What you did was you initiated the greeting, you made good eye contact, you smiled, and you offered your hand so that we could shake hands. This is very good"), (3) state the positive consequences (e.g., "So you have earned 1000 positive points for greeting"), (4) seek acknowledgment (e.g., "do you understand?"), and (5) finish with general praise ("You did a good job"). Instructors awarded points so that the clients could keep track of what they earned, learn mathematics and budgeting, and later used the points to purchase various items in the facility. In the process of learning how to praise, the behavioral instructors fought the tendency to focus on the negative.

Praising clients models appropriate behavior, but it is not enough when conflict emerges. In the training, the BIs used corrective teaching to prevent conflict from deepening. Participants avoided rushing to conclusions quickly, labeling behaviors as "out of control" or to order children to "calm down." Instead, participants learned to describe what a child is doing and to "avoid judgmental terms by not evaluating their actions" (e.g., "you're becoming angry"). This advice echoed Rogers (1961) who wrote: "The major barrier to mutual interpersonal communication is our very natural tendency to judge, to evaluate, to approve or disapprove, the statement of the other person" (p. 330). Punishment is never used "because it produces the flight, fight, or freeze response." Instead, participants learned to: (a) praise and display empathy (e.g., "I understand that it's sometimes difficult to greet others..."), (b) describe inappropriate behavior (e.g., "But what you did was you looked down at the floor and you ignored me"), (c) state the consequences (e.g., "So you've earned 2000 correctives for "greetings."), (d) describe appropriate behavior (e.g., "What you should have done is make eye contact with me, introduce yourself, and..."), (e) state the rationale (e.g., "It's important to greet people because you will be able to make a good impression on them..."), (f) seek acknowledgement (e.g., "Do you understand?"), (g) offer to practice (e.g., "okay, let's practice"), and (h) give feedback and positive points (e.g., "Much better. What you did was you initiated the greeting, you made good eye contact . . . This is very good, so you've earned 1000 positive points for greeting"). When instructors engage in this sequence of actions, they are acting generously, in part because they are communicating in the interest of the child's well-being.

To summarize, generosity is the virtue of giving of oneself; "it elevates us toward others" (Comte-Sponville, 2001, p. 102). From a communication perspective, generosity can be enacted in interpersonal communication by producing our best move and interpreting others' utterances in a positive light. The generous communicator, thus, realizes the impossibility of perfect communication and the challenges of communicating well.

Courage

Courage, according to Ernest Hemingway, is "grace under pressure." As Nepo (2007) explained, "The word courage comes from the Latin cor, which literally means heart. The original use of the word courage means to stand by one's core" (p. 10). The virtue has a rich history among philosophers and thinkers. In his ontological study of courage, Tillich (1952), for example, describes how the Greek philosophers equated courage with strength of mind, "capable for conquering whatever threatens the attainment of the highest good" (p. 7). Later, he explained, the Stoics framed courage as a response: "the affirmation of one's essential being in spite of desires and anxieties" (p. 14). In his own work, he offers a refined definition: "Courage is self-affirmation 'in spite of,' that is in spite of that which tends to prevent the self from affirming itself" (p. 32). How does courage, thus, become embodied in the act of communication?

To be courageous, a person must often overcome challenges or risks. In his work, Comte-Sponville (2001) places courage against the notion of fear: "virtuous courage is not absence of fear, but the capacity to overcome it by a stronger and more generous will" (p. 49). He reinforces this notion later by writing that courage "is not the absence of fear; it is the ability to confront, master, and overcome fear" (p. 51). In his discussion, he aligns with Tillich's (1952) definition: "to be courageous is to persevere in our beings" (p. 53). Courage, then, involves the will to be who one is in the face of fear.

In interpersonal communication, courage can be embodied in the act of disclosure. Courage is to reveal information when there are risks or consequences. This argument is well-aligned with Michel Foucault's discussion of the Greek concept of parrhesia, which involves speaking the truth and taking a risk.

> The parrhesiastes is someone who takes a risk. Of course, this risk is not always a risk of life. When, for example, you see a friend doing something wrong and you risk incurring his anger by telling him he is wrong, you are acting as a parrhesiastes. In such a case, you do not risk your life, but you may hurt him by your remarks, and your friendship may consequently suffer for it. (Foucault, 2010, para. 14)

The parrhesiaste, then, is someone who speaks the truth when there are risks. In the workplace, great examples of parrhesia take place when employees "blow the whistle" on their organization (Seeger, 1997). Recall, for example, the story of Jeffrey Wigand, who single-handedly fought against the tobacco industry. Speaking the truth can also take place when subordinates confront their superiors (i.e., upward communication; Kassing, 2009). At home, it may mean telling friends that a joke that perpetuates racism is not funny, or telling one's father that a comment that dehumanizes others is inappropriate, or stopping a neighbor who uses derogatory language when telling a story. We can thus embody the virtue of courage in communication.

Disclosure is an essential part of relational communication (see Petronio, 2002). Researchers also know that the desire to be loved or accepted is so strong that it sometimes prohibits communicators to disclose what they wish they could say. Researchers have shown, for example, that tensions arise in disclosing information about one's sexual identity to family members or co-workers (Dindia, 1996). Scholars also have noted the ways in which family members manage information or avoid topics of conversations with certain members (Golish & Caughlin, 2002). In organizations, employees frequently struggle to confront those above them even though they are behaving or communicating unethically. The recent case of the horrors at Abu Graib (Zimbardo, 2007) is an unfortunate example. Other research suggests that employees keep information to themselves to keep or acquire power (Ipe, 2003). Although withholding information can be an act of courage too, research suggests that there are many circumstances in which the act of speaking is an act of courage.

One example of courageous disclosure is well-illustrated by research on coming out stories (e.g., Dindia, 1996). To disclose one's sexual identity is to act in spite of the contradictory demands that such disclosure implies. As Cain (1991) described, "Gay individuals, then confront a dilemma . . . By choosing to be open, they risk being seen as different and being harassed or ridiculed; they may also risk losing friends, family ties, or their jobs" (p. 72). On the other hand, "secrecy may create a sense of distance in relationships or may lead them to feel they are dishonest with trusted others" (p. 72). The fear of rejection and risk may sometimes prevent the self from acting in line with who one is. When they interviewed participants, Dindia and Tieu (1996) discovered that this tension is very real: "I want to tell—hard to lie—hate to lie. Something pulls the other way, I don't know what" (p. 17). Perhaps, it is courage that "pulls the other way." When an interpersonal message is an act of disclosure that is performed in spite of risks and fear, it is an act of courage.

Disclosure is a fundamental part of healthy interpersonal relationships. Speaking truthfully to friends, loved ones, or professional colleagues aligns with the virtue of courage. Confronting others about what we believe, experience, or feel demands our best. When it is done, others often perceive the action to be valuable. Of course, not every act of disclosure qualifies as the embodiment of the virtue. One key criterion is whether truth is being spoken. The second criterion is whether a risk is being taken in spite of fear. The most courageous act of communication is to reveal information that grows the self.

Justice

Justice, like courage, is a cardinal virtue. In his treatise, Comte-Sponville (2001) explains that "Justice hinges entirely on this twofold respect, a respect for legality in the *polis* and for equality among individuals" (emphasis in original, p. 63). The second form of justice, equality among individuals, best reflects how justice can be fostered in communication. Justice, after all, is "first and foremost the equality of men with respect to one another" (p. 13). With this in mind, I argue that justice can be embodied in interpersonal communication by (a) enabling others to make informed decisions and (b) refusing to engage in dehumanizing practices.

Justice and Significance Choice

Communicators have an ethical responsibility to foster well-reasoned decision making. As Nilsen (1974) argued, "When we communicate to influence the attitudes, beliefs and actions of others, the ethical touchstone is the degree of free, informed, and critical choice on matters of significance in their lives that is fostered by our speaking" (p. 46). When a communicator discloses pertinent information, acknowledges several sides to an issue, or provides alternatives, she is enabling the other party to make an informed decision that is free of coercion. According to Nilsen, this is one way to show "respect for the integrity of the [other] person" (p. 46). Justice, thus, can be fostered by messages that enable significant choice.

Making significant choice possible is crucial in political and organizational communication (Lyon, 2007; Ulmer & Sellnow, 1997). It also is desirable in interpersonal communication (see Lyon & Mirivel, 2011). Physician-patient encounters are a case in point. By professional codes of conduct, physicians have an ethical responsibility to help patients make good decisions about their health. But, physicians increasingly face institutional and economic pressures to sell their services. My research on cosmetic surgery revealed that plastic surgeons manage a thin line between selling services for profit and acting as gatekeepers of surgery (e.g., Mirivel, 2010). Ethically, plastic surgeons should educate clients without short-circuiting their ability to make rational decisions. For the most part, they walked the fine line. The data, however, also showed that they sometimes downplayed the risks of surgery. Consider, for example, how one surgeon describes pulmonary embolism, a serious post-surgery complication.

> Surgeon: the other problem that we get into with the pulmonary complications or pulmonary just means lung, is what they call pulmonary embolism. And what this is,

potentially where blood clots form in the veins typically in the legs and the blood clots can break off and migrate to the lungs. So ways to avoid this is number one shorten the operation that we were talking about. We are better off at times to do multiple smaller operations rather than one big large operation. Number two, we have special devices that we put on the legs that help pulsate and move the blood faster. When you go under anesthesia, the vessels dilate so the blood flow is more sluggish and we use pulse (stockings) after in recovery and we send you home with stockings, you know special stockings, and that helps a lot. It's good to stay hydrated, take plenty of fluids, and it's good to get up and move around. Uh, and even though it may be sore, but it is good to get up to go to the bathroom. If you need assistance and so forth that all helps.

The risk that is introduced here is very serious. The U.S. Food & Drug Administration's (FDA) Web site explains the risk in this way:

Embolism may occur when fat is loosened and enters the blood through blood vessels ruptured (broken) during liposuction. Pieces of fat get trapped in the blood vessels, gather in the lungs, or travel to the brain. The signs of pulmonary emboli (fat clots in the lungs) may be shortness of breath or difficulty breathing. If you have the signs or symptoms of fat emboli after liposuction, it is important for you to seek emergency medical care at once. Fat emboli may cause permanent disability or, in some cases, be fatal. (paragraph, 4)

Notice how the web site describes "pulmonary embolism" with a biomedical lens by stressing how "fat cells" may "gather in the lungs" or "travel to the brain." After explaining signs that may indicate this medical condition, the FDA's account ends by directing the reader to "seek emergency at once," as it may cause "permanent disability" and can be "fatal."

In comparing these two accounts, several differences appear. Rather than describing the signs and consequences of embolism (as seen in the FDA description), the surgeon instead emphasizes how to avoid the risk: performing multiple operations rather than one, the use of special devices, and special stockings, all of which serve the important purpose of maximizing safety in the face of risks. As a comparison, "permanent disability" and "fatality" are absent from his talk. Avoiding this topic may make sense if the main objective is to sell surgery, but surgeons have an ethical responsibility to enable clients to make an informed decision. Research shows in fact that women interested in cosmetic surgery want to be informed and that being informed does not alter their desire to proceed with surgery (Davis, 1995). In short, enabling clients to make a significant choice is a win-win situation for surgeons and clients.

Justice and Dehumanizing Communication

Justice "exists only to the extent that human beings want it [...] and bring it into being" (Comte-Sponville, 2001, p. 75). One way to do so is to enable others to make informed decisions free of coercion. A second approach is to avoid and confront dehumanization practices that naturally endanger equality between, and among, people.

To dehumanize someone, by definition, is to deprive them of their humanity, "their qualities, personality, or spirit" (dehumanize, 2011). Unfortunately, dehumanizing practices occur everywhere. Insults and name-calling are salient examples of dehumanization. In schools, it takes the form of bullying. Recent cases include a 15-year-old Phoebe Prince who hung herself (Eckholm & Zezima, 2010) and Tyler Clementi, an 18-year-old freshmen at Rutgers who jumped off a bridge (see Schwartz, 2010). Bullying, unfortunately, is pervasive in schools and at work (see Lutgen-Sandvik, 2006). A survey of 40,000 students revealed that 47% of teen students had been bullied and that 52% of the students hit someone in anger (Jayson, 2010). Bullying often leads to depression, anxiety, suicidal thoughts, and lowered self-esteem (Sunwolf & Leets, 2004). Insults also happen at home during parental conflict or in parent-child interaction (e.g., Pelzer, 1995). In a socio-cultural context, insults and name-calling also cultivate genocide. In the Rwandan genocide, for example, the Hutus, one ethnic group, referred to the Tutsis, another ethnic group, as "Inyenzi." The term stands for "cockroach" and thereby implied that the Tutsis were vermin. As another example, research by Bloch (2003) showed how the use of the term "Freier" in everyday conversation and political messages nudged Israelis to devalue "the good of society in favor of the pursuit of individual gain" (p. 132). In short, name-calling and insults are communication behaviors that create injustice. Refraining from the use of such terms is a way to embody just communication.

Hate talk is another example of injustice. According to contemporary research, sexism and racism are created and maintained by micro-discursive practices (Wetherell & Potter, 1992). In one study, Myers and Williamson (2001) revealed that people are often racist behind closed doors with friends and acquaintances. Consider an example from the data:

Chris:	Why is that Black guy standing by that tree?
Dave:	He's waiting to be hung in it.
Chris:	(laughs) Oh man . . . we can get some rope.
Dave:	(laughs) String him up!

In this excerpt, people who know each other actively participate in making racist remarks. However, there is no one present to challenge those statements. Hate against individuals, ethnic, or racial groups prevails by the interpersonal communication that takes places between people. Communication that cultivates justice, thus, involves the absence of those practices in the first place and the courage to challenge those who speak against the principle of equality. I witnessed a communicative event that embodies what I am calling forth.

A man entered a local gas station and asked for directions. His voice and demeanor was feminine. The cashier responded politely and the client subsequently left. Upon his exit, a friend of the cashier who waited on the side reacted to the encounter; he laughed and imitated his speech. The cashier immediately confronted her "friend." She said: "don't make fun of other people; be nice." The cashier's behavior embodied justice: she confronted injustice in the moment of interaction.

Interpersonal communication can produce as much injustice as it can produce justice. This section showed that justice can be fostered by excellent interpersonal communication. The behaviors include making significant choice possible by disclosing information honestly and appropriately, avoiding dehumanization practices, and, with a pinch of courage, confronting individuals who practice dehumanization.

Compassion

Compassion is a fifth virtue that can be embodied in the act of communication. By definition, "To have compassion means to suffer with" (Comte-Sponville, 2001, p. 103). Compassion is close to sympathy or empathy, but it actually is best seen as "participation in the suffering of others" (p. 105). If compassion means engaging with the suffering of others, then listening is one way to enact compassion.

Whether in philosophical work or empirical studies, listening is seen by many as an ideal, albeit necessary, form of communication (see Bodie, chapter 7, this volume). Frank (1995), for example, argued that "One of our most difficult duties as human beings is to listen to the voices of those who suffer" (p. 25). Listening, he suggested, is "a fundamental moral act" (p. 25). Similarly, Rogers (1961) encouraged practitioners to listen with unconditional positive regard. Listening can foster change in the other, he argued, but it demands courage from the individual: "The great majority of us could not listen; we would find ourselves compelled to evaluate, because listening would seem too dangerous" (p. 333). For scholars of dialogic communication, listening is essential. Martin Buber (1993), for instance, saw that "the mark of contemporary man is that he does not really listen . . . only when one really listens . . . does one attain to that sphere of the between" (p. xiv). In short, when listening functions as an interpersonal response to another's suffering, it is compassion.

Compassionate communication may take place at work or at home. Counselors, therapists, reverends, teachers or physicians, may communicate compassionately regularly. Miller's (2007) study, for example, revealed that employees in the human services professions often practice compassion. In particular, she found that touch, active listening and silence are communication behaviors that professionals use to enact compassion. In another study, Kanov et al. (2004) suggested that compassionate communication in organizations involves (a) noticing, (b) feeling, and (c) responding. Based on the research on supportive and comforting communication (see McCullough & Burleson, chapter 14, this volume), we also know that compassionate communication affects another person's well-being and that when people are listened to, they heal.

Listening as compassion is well-illustrated in the writings of Mitch Albom. In *Tuesdays with Morrie*, Albom (1997) narrates the final months of his relationship with his professor. For months, Mitch becomes a listener and a future messenger of Morrie's life lessons. During these dialogues, Morrie emphasizes the importance of listening. In one conversation, he tells Mitch: "But really listening to someone—without trying to sell them something, pick them up, and recruit them, or get some kind of status in return—how often do you get this anymore?" (p. 13). Later, Morrie strengthens his point:

> He paused, then looked at me. "I'm dying, right?" Yes. "Why do you think it's so important for me to hear other people's problems? Don't I have enough pain and suffering of my own? Of course I do. But giving to other people is what makes me feel alive."

Compassion can be experienced within, but it is enacted in interpersonal communication. As I showed, compassion is the ethical act of listening to someone who is suffering. Compassion "allows us to pass . . . from the emotional realm to the ethical realm, from what we feel to what we want, from what we are to what we must do" (Comte-Sponville, 2001, p. 116). Communication excellence, thus, includes responding to another's suffering.

Conclusion

Communication excellence is inspired by abstract virtues, but it is people who choose to enact them. In this chapter, I chose five virtues to describe how they could be embodied in interpersonal communication. To define the nature of each virtue, I drew on the philosopher Comte-Sponville. His ontological analyses enabled reflection about the nature of virtuous communication. First, I argued that gentleness can be embodied in the form of face-attentiveness. Second, I proposed that generous communication includes producing a best possible utterance and interpreting another person's discursive actions positively. In the third section, I suggested that when an act of disclosure involves taking a risk, it exemplifies courage. The fourth virtue, justice, can be cultivated by enabling others to make a significant choice and by refusing to engage in dehumanization. Finally, I proposed that to communicate compassionately is to listen to the suffering of others. Positive communication, thus, includes stretching the self in these directions.

From the perspective of this chapter, virtuous communication is not an impossible set of ideals that can never be attained. Instead, when virtues are defined as communication behaviors, they are possible to enact. This is precisely why Aristotle (2004) described virtue as "a habit of or trained faculty of choice" (p. 31); that is, it is an activity. This chapter shows that interpersonal communication is laden with fleeting moments of virtuous communication. When a mother responds calmly to an attack from her daughter, she is embodying gentleness. When a woman announces her sexual identity to her family, she is exhibiting courage. If a surgeon describes the risks of surgery appropriately, she is acting justly. If a son listens to his father's experiences with illness, he is acting compassionately. When thought about in these terms, virtues thus take a more central, possible, role in our lives.

The question for interpersonal communication researchers is not whether people can act virtuously, but to see when and how they choose to. In the future, scholars need to document specific instances of virtuous communication in naturally occurring interaction. Researchers, for example, can ask: What are examples of courageous communication? When and where do laypersons and professionals communicate generously or justly? What are model examples of listening that function as compassion? By documenting the best of communication, communication researchers can stretch the human kind and truly cultivate positive communication praxis.

Notes

1. In his work, Comte-Sponville (2001) suggests nineteen virtues, including fidelity, prudence, temperance, courage, mercy and gratitude. In their classification system, Peterson and Seligman (2004) suggest six central virtues that are valued in many cultures, including wisdom and knowledge, courage, humanity, justice, temperance, and transcendence. For this chapter, I chose five virtues that I believe are important for positive communication and that align with communication theory and research.
2. For each virtue, I propose how it can be embodied communicatively. Obviously, there are other ways that each virtue could be enacted. Future research should consider other practices that could exemplify a specific virtue.
3. Interruptions and overlapping talk are different discursive practices. Typically, an overlap is seen as an interruption when it takes over the other person's talk and conveys dominance or asymmetry (see West & Zimmerman, 1983). Research in language and social interaction, however, also shows that overlaps can function positively in relationships (Tannen, 1994).
4. The word "earned" is use to teach children that the consequences are the result of their actions. Said differently, children learn to become responsible for their own behaviors.

References

Albom, M. (1997). *Tuesdays with Morrie: An old man, a young man and life's greatest lesson.* New York: Doubleday.

Aristotle (2004). Nicomachean ethics (F. H. Peters, Trans). New York: Barnes & Nobles.

Bloch, L-R. (2003). Who's afraid of being a Freier: The analysis of communication through a key cultural frame. *Communication Theory, 13,* 125–159. doi: 10.1111/j.1468-2885.2003.tb00285.x

Brann, M., Rittenour, C. E., & Myers, S. A. (2007). Adult children's forgiveness of parents' betrayals. *Communication Research Reports, 24,* 353–360. doi: 10.1080/08824090701624254

Brown, P., & Levinson, S. C. (1978). Universals in language usage: Politeness phenomena. In E. N. Goody (Ed.), *Questions and politeness: Strategies in social interaction* (pp. 56–310). Cambridge, UK: Cambridge University Press.

Buber, M. (1993). *Between man and man.* New York: Routledge.

Cain, R. (1991). Disclosure and secrecy among gay men in the United States and Canada: A shift in views. *Journal of the History of Sexuality, 2,* 25–45.

Comte-Sponville, A. (2001). *A small treatise on the great virtues* (C. Temerson, Trans.). New York: Holt Paperbacks. (Original work published 1996)

Davis, K. (1995). *Reshaping the female body: The dilemma of cosmetic surgery.* New York: Routledge.

dehumanize. (2011). In *Merriam-Webster.com.* Retrieved June 22, 2011, from http://www.merriam–webster.com/dictionary/dehumanize

Dindia, K. (1996). "Going into and coming out of the closet": The dialectics of stigma disclosure. In B. M. Montgomery & L. A. Baxter (Eds.), *Dialectical approaches to studying personal relationships* (pp. 83–109). Mahwah, NJ: Erlbaum.

Dindia, K., & Tieu, T. (1996, November). *The process of self–disclosure of homosexual identity*. Paper presented at the Speech Communication Association Convention, San Diego, CA.

Eckholm, E., & Zezima, K. (2010, March 30). 6 teenagers are charged after classmate's suicide. *New York Times*, A14.

Frank, A. W. (1995). *The wounded storyteller: Body, illness, and ethics*. Chicago: The University of Chicago Press.

Foucault, M. (2010). *Discourse and truth: the practice of Parrhesia*. Retrieved from http://foucault.info/documents/parrhesia/foucault.DT4.praticeParrhesia.en.html

Goffman, E. (1967). *Interaction ritual: Essays on face-to-face behavior*. New York: Anchor.

Golish, T. D., & Caughlin, J. P. (2002). 'I'd rather not talk about it': Adolescents' and young adults' use of topic avoidance in stepfamilies. *Journal of Applied Communication Research, 30*, 78–106. doi: 10.1080/00909880216574

Ipe, M. (2003). Knowledge sharing in organizations: A conceptual framework. *Human Resource Development Review, 2*, 337–359. doi: 10.1177/1534484303257985

Jayson, S. (2010, October 26). Teens say bullying is widespread. *USA Today*, 1A.

Jensen, M. (n.d.). *A perspective for teaching communication ethics*. Unpublished manuscript.

Kanov, J. Maitlis, S., Worline, M. C., Dutton, J. E., Frost, P.J., & Lilius, J. (2004). Compassion in organizational life. *American Behavioral Scientist, 47*, 808–827. doi: 10.1177/0002764203260211

Kassing, J. W. (2009). "In case you didn't hear me the first time": An examination of repetitious upward dissent. *Management Communication Quarterly, 22*, 416–436. doi: 10.1177/0893318908327008

Kim, H-K. (2004). Introduction. In *Aristotle, Nicomachean ethics* (pp. xi–xix). New York: Barnes & Nobles.

Lutgen-Sandvik, P. (2006). Take this job and: Quitting and other forms of resistance to workplace bullying. *Communication Monographs, 73*, 406–433. doi: 10.1080/03637750601024156

Lyon, A. (2007). "Putting patients first": Systematically distorted communication and Merck's marketing of Vioxx. *Journal of Applied Communication Research, 35*, 376–398. doi: 10.1080/00909880701611052

Lyon, A., & Mirivel, J. (2011). Reconstructing Merck's practical theory of communication: The Ethics of pharmaceutical sales representative–physician encounters. *Communication Monographs, 78*, 53–72. doi: 10.1080/03637751.2010.542578

MacIntyre, A. (1984). *After virtue* (2nd ed.). Notre Dame: University of Notre Dame Press.

Miller, K. I. (2007). Compassionate communication in the workplace: Exploring processes of noticing, connecting, and responding. *Journal of Applied Communication Research, 35*, 223–245. doi:10.1080/00909880701434208

Mirivel, J. C. (2010). Communicative conduct in commercial medicine: A discourse analysis of initial consultations between plastic surgeons and prospective clients. *Qualitative Health Research, 20*, 788–804. doi: 10.1177/1049732310362986

Mirivel, J. C. (2011, November). *Communicating to enrich others*. Paper to be presented at the annual meeting of the National Communication Association, New Orleans.

Myers, K. A., & Williamson, P. (2001). Race talk: The perpetuation of racism in private discourse. *Race and Society, 4*, 3–26. doi:10.1016/S1090–9524(02)00032–3

Nilsen, T. R. (1974). *Ethics of speech communication* (2nd ed.). Indianapolis, IN: Bobbs–Merrill.

Nepo, M. (2007). *Facing the lion, being the lion: Finding inner courage where it lives.* San Francisco, CA: Conari Press.

Pausch, R. (2008). *The last lecture.* New York: Hyperion.

Pelzer, D. (1995). *A child called it: One's child story to survive.* Deerfield Beach, FL: Health Communications, Inc.

Peterson, C., & Seligman, M. E. P. (2004). *Character strengths and virtues: A handbook and classification.* Oxford: Oxford University Press.

Petronio, S. (2002). *Boundaries of privacy: Dialectics of disclosure.* New York: State University of New York Press.

Pirsig, R. (1974). *Zen and the art of motorcycle maintenance: An inquiry into values.* New York: Bantam Books.

Rogers, C. (1961). *On becoming a person.* Boston, MA: Houghton Mifflin Company.

Ronel, N., & Lebel, U. (2006). When parents lay their children to rest: Between anger and forgiveness. *Journal of Social and Personal Relationships, 23,* 507–522. doi: 10.1177/0265407506064212

Schwartz, J. (2010, October 3). Bullying, suicide, punishment. *New York Times,* WK1.

Seeger, M. W. (1997). *Organizational communication ethics: Decisions and dilemmas.* Cresskill, NJ: Hampton Press.

Spitzberg, B. H., & Cupach, W. R. (Eds.). (2007). *The dark side of interpersonal communication* (2nd ed). Mahwah, NJ: Erlbaum.

Sunwolf, & Leets, L. (2004). Being left out: Rejecting outsiders and communicating group boundaries in childhood and adolescent peer groups. *Journal of Applied Communication Research, 32,* 195–223.

Tannen, D. (1994). *Gender and Discourse.* New York: Oxford University Press.

Tillich, P. (1952). *The courage to be.* New Havens, CT: Yale University Press.

Tracy, K. (2008). "Reasonable hostility": Situation-appropriate face attack. *Journal of Politeness Research: Language, Behaviour, Culture, 4,* 169–191. doi: 10.1515/JPLR.2008.009

Tracy, K., & Tracy, S. J. (1998). Rudeness at 911: Reconceptualizing face and face-attack. *Human Communication Research, 25,* 225–251. doi: 10.1111/j.1468-2958.1998.tb00444.x

Ulmer, R. R., & Sellnow, T. L. (1997). Strategic ambiguity and the ethic of significant choice in the tobacco industry's crisis communication. *Communication Studies, 48,* 215–233.

West, C., & Zimmerman, D. H. (1983). Small insults: A study of interruptions in cross-sex conversations between unacquainted persons. In B. Thorne, C. Kramarae, & N. Henley (Eds.), *Language, gender and society.* Cambridge, MA: Newbury House.

Wetherell, M., & Potter, J. (1992). *Mapping the language of racism: Discourse and the legitimation of exploitation.* New York: Columbia University Press.

Zimbardo, P. G. (2007). *The Lucifer effect: Understanding how good people turn evil.* New York: Random House.

• CHAPTER FIVE •

Reflective Conversation as a Foundation for Communicative Virtue

Nathan Miczo
Western Illinois University

Scholars of interpersonal communication are often called upon to justify their focus: Why is interpersonal communication important? In attempting to answer that question, two arguments seem especially prominent. One argument is that improving interpersonal communication skills allow individuals to be more competent communicators in their achievement of personal goals (Canary, Cody, & Manusov, 2008). The other argument is that successful management of close relationships produces fruits in terms of increased physical and psychological health, and enhanced well-being (Floyd, 2009). Without disputing the validity of these answers, they may nevertheless be subject to further interrogation. What if individuals become more effective at achieving their goals, but those goals are base? Or, what if individuals are relationally satisfied or display superior immune functioning, but feel a deep sense of discontent about the ultimate aim of their lives? It is possible there is room for an additional answer to the question, Why is it important to understand interpersonal communication? The claim of this paper is that the ability to stop and reflect, to consider the potential consequences of one's actions, to critically evaluate them from multiple perspectives, is a bulwark against committing acts that harm relational partners (i.e., relational transgressions). This ability is fostered and developed through a form of virtuous communication referred to as reflective conversation.

A Model of Communicative Virtue

Following Aristotle, we begin with the assertion that virtue is excellence. Since there are many ways and areas of life that admit of excellence, we can bound the concept by stating that communicative virtue is excellence in "words and deeds" (Arendt, 1958/1998, p. 176). Insofar as communication involves conversation and interaction between partners, or social actors, the qualities of "words and deeds" that lend them their excellence are bound up with the notion of engagement. Such an interaction may be conceived of as a form of vital engagement (Nakamura & Csikszentmihalyi, 2003), where "the relationship to the world is characterized by completeness of involvement or participation and marked by intensity" (p. 86). In this case, that world revolves around the partners and the shared object of discourse that lies between them. This form of engagement is the hallmark of virtuous communication.

Communicative virtue, as excellence in "words and deeds," comprises the performance of behaviors indicative of engagement. The emphasis on performance is important because it suggests that engagement behaviors are observable aspects of interactions that can be evaluated or judged. Research on such concepts as partner attention (Jones, Hobbs, & Hockenbury, 1982) and other orientation (Spitzberg & Hecht, 1984) has revealed a host of behaviors indicative of conversational involvement. A partial list of those behaviors includes paying attention to the partner, continuing partner's topic, asking questions of partner, fluency, eye contact, smiling, turn-taking skills and proximity. When we observe the excellent performance of these engagement behaviors, we may claim that the communicators are acting with virtue. Yet, such an assertion seems less than satisfying insofar as a wicked or selfish communicator may exhibit the same behaviors in all apparent sincerity, as a means of pursuing a questionable, or selfish, plan. It is clear that when we speak of engagement, though it is observable in behavior, we are referencing the underlying sense of connection and intensity. We are wanting to speak of the underlying orientation to one's behavior, a virtuous disposition.

Focusing upon a virtuous disposition allows us to reframe the question as involving the qualities necessary for one to be a virtuous communicator. This is potentially a very long list so I will concentrate on a subset of four interlocking virtues that seem particularly suited to conversation. The first of these dispositions is politeness. Comte-Sponville (1996/2001) argues that politeness is not itself a virtue but that it "serves as a foundation for the moral development of the individual" (p. 9). When children are socialized in politeness, they are schooled in the outward form of attentiveness to partners. Outward form does not guarantee inner disposition, however. Politeness, in other words, is "a compliance with usage and its established rules, with the normative play of appearance—a compliance with the world and the way of the world" (p. 10). Nevertheless, that compliance with the way of the world is a necessary component of supporting the face, or public identity, of the other person.

Arendt (1958/1998) argued that individuals need a "space of appearance" that allows them to come together to potentially seek and give validation. Those spaces of appearance can be provided by the social order, and if so, then conventional usage will dictate what is expected behavior in that venue. Interactants can also establish a space for themselves by how they choose to orient themselves within a venue, regardless of its conventionalized usage. Much is often made of the importance of listening in the dialogic response to the other's otherness. That listening presumes that the other is speaking but the willingness to speak depends on the behaviors of the partner that signal engagement, involvement, immediacy, and support for the speaker's position as well as his/her freedom to express it. In a word, my politeness provides the "space of appearance" for you to express something worth listening to. Insofar as politeness is the conventionalized expectation, it only provides a starting point.

If my politeness encourages the other to speak, then, of course, continued speaking depends upon my ongoing response to the other. It may sound odd to label that response as compassion, but Comte-Sponville (1996/2001) speaks of compassion as "attentive openness, solicitude, patience, and listening" (p. 109). While these are all behaviors associated with engagement, what is the inner disposition indicated by that compassionate response? What is demanded in my response is that I enter into your perspective, empathically trying to understand your position in the world. Slote (2010) speaks of empathy as the thoughts and feelings that are appropriate to the person being empathized with, rather than the empathizer. More importantly, the empathizer will "have some desire to help those who need or could benefit from help" (p. 46). When I possess a virtuous disposition, my compassion motivates my desire to help you.

Help you do what? Essentially, to help you articulate your thoughts. Consider what Arendt (2005) said of Socrates:

> Every man [sic] has his own doxa, his own opening to the world, and Socrates therefore must always begin with questions; he cannot know beforehand what kind of *dokei moi*, or it-appears-to-me, the other possesses. He must make sure of the other's position in the common world. Yet, just as nobody can know beforehand the other's doxa, so nobody can know by himself and without further effort the inherent truth of his own opinion. Socrates wanted to bring out the truth which everyone potentially possesses. (p. 15, italics in original)

Thus, Socrates' compassion moved him to want to help his fellow citizens by getting them to articulate, to express, what they thought they knew.

My politeness facilitates your openness, and my compassion moves me to want to help you articulate your position. But what about my contribution to the conversation? In a genuine dialogue, we are both orienting to some aspect of the world we share in common, and we both must articulate the "inherent truth" of our own opinions. To do this, I must willingly be open about my position, and this giving of my opinions is generosity. Comte-Sponville (1996/2001) offers that generosity "elevates us toward others, as it were, and toward ourselves as beings freed from the pettiness that is the self" (p. 102). Similarly, Nietzsche (1883/1995) said of the gift-giving virtue: "Insatiably your soul strives for treasures and gems, because your virtue is insatiable in wanting to give. You force all things to and into yourself that they may flow back out of your well as the gifts of your love" (p. 75). Generosity is about freely giving to others what I possess, and in conversation what I possess is my "opinion" (i.e., my inner thoughts). To contribute to the dialogue I must be willing to share that opinion, even when I desire to hold onto it. It is this letting go of what I might prefer to keep to myself that elevates me toward the other, toward my conversational partner. To be open, to be forthcoming about my opinion is to freely choose moving toward you rather than drawing back (see Mirivel, chapter 4, this volume).

To move toward you by expressing my opinion is to commit myself to a point of view. The final communicative virtue that grows out of my openness is fidelity, which Comte-Sponville (1996/2001) called "the virtue of sameness, thanks to which sameness exists or persists" (p. 20). One of the dangers of action, of coming together to express ourselves in words and deeds, is its ephemeral nature. After helping each other to express our "inherent truths," we depart and go our separate ways and what is there to mark our coming together? Only our memory of it. And what is there to remember other than the positions that were expressed. Having expressed that opinion, I am linked to it as its author. As such, I am obligated to remain committed to the truth I have created. This is why the freedom from coercion in this kind of conversation is so important. I may be less likely to own my viewpoint, even as others rely on me to endorse it.

Given that the consequences of our actions are unknowable and the future is uncertain, to make a commitment is to "act into" the future, to reduce our uncertainty about it. When we gather information about our partner by self-disclosing, we are taking it on faith that our partner stands behind his/her words. And they expect the same from us. This is one interpretation of

Nietzsche's (1887/1967) discussion about breeding "an animal with the right to make promises" (p. 57). We only have the right to make such promises if we can stand behind them, despite the vagaries of fortune. This idea also underlies the role of self-control as a "moral muscle" (Baumeister & Exline, 1999). To exercise fidelity is to remember and to stand behind, to promise to remain committed to our expressed viewpoints.

Fidelity is a difficult virtue because our memories are imperfect, and our social identities are always at stake. If my expression of opinion is frivolous, or if I easily forget my opinions, then my commitment is shallow, and I am likely to express a different viewpoint on every different occasion. Such a pattern of behavior may give rise to a reputation for "waffling" which may deter my partner from an honest expression of her/his own. Additionally, there may be a tension between my desire for openness and my desire for maintaining my face. For example, in a study of public versus private reasons for turning down date requests, Weiner, Figueroa-Muñoz, and Kikihara (1991) found that the reasons for discrepancies between the two included such goals as not wanting to hurt the other's feelings, not wanting to make the other angry, and not wanting to make oneself look bad (as cited in Wilson, 2002). As Nietzsche (1886/1966) said, "It is no more than a moral prejudice that truth is worth more than mere appearance" (p. 46). In this case, that appearance is the public face of both self and other. Thus we often sacrifice truth to preserve our relationships, placing ourselves in the curious position of remaining committed to public statements we don't believe in.

A related danger of fidelity is that my partner will not allow me to change my opinion; that she/he will attempt to "fix" me in place. On the one hand, this is impolite insofar as it constrains me, aggravates negative face, and this lack of politeness may cause me to withdraw the hand which before I had freely extended. Consequently, I will become less open. On the other hand, reflective conversation is premised on the notion that we have created a safe space in which to appear to each other. Being willing to re-examine my own viewpoint and/or to enter into yours, means that I am open to changing my opinion or at least expanding it to accommodate yours. There must be certain conditions, therefore, that allow for changing one's mind. Fidelity "means refusing to change one's idea in the absence of strong, valid reasons, and—because one cannot always be examining—it means holding as true, until subsequent re-examination, ideas whose truth has been clearly and solidly established" (Comte-Sponville, 1996/2001, pp. 24–25). This too can oftentimes be difficult. Is your viewpoint a strong, valid reason in its own right or will I perceive that you are trying to go beyond expressing your opinion to deliberately trying to change mine? And is that acceptable in reflective conversation or antithetical? And how many opinions are rooted in truths that have been clearly and solidly established? Seeking truth through reflective conversation presumes that many of the opinions we hold as true are not clearly and solidly established but rather that's one of the benefits of questioning and being questioned on them. Nevertheless, despite these difficulties, as we encounter new others, or even as we re-encounter the familiar, we must have the latitude to revise our opinions; yet, our dependability as a relational partner hinges on weighing that revision with a certain amount of gravitas.

There is a great deal of interdependence and tension among these virtues. Politeness is a starting point, yet politeness exerts a strong pressure to modify our openness. So, we must transcend politeness, developing a sort of "thick skin" (Cupach & Metts, 1994, p. 99) to our relationship that allows it to tolerate our search for truth. Citing the irreversibility of words and deeds, Arendt (1958/1998) argued for the importance of forgiveness in human action. That is, the capacity to forgive and be forgiven fosters the freedom to express opinions without regard to consequences. On the other hand, the notion of reflective conversation as safe space for the expression of opinion is not intended to be another instantiation of the "ideology of openness" (Parks, 1982). The field has grown more sophisticated than this. The permeable boundary of the biological cell wall provides a better metaphor than the hard layers of the onion. People make decisions about what to disclose, to whom, and how to disclose it (Petronio, 2002). At times, however, it still comes down to having the courage to speak one's opinion regardless of the consequences. Thus, the delicacy of these interconnections means they are easily sundered, and nowhere is this more true than when one partner seeks to subvert the workings, the virtuousness, of the conversation. If your politeness is simply attention to a secondary goal as you seek to effectively gain my compliance, then there is no need for my openness. If I am merely seeking to change your opinion under the guise of a genuine dialogue, then I am unlikely to feel compassion or empathy for your position and unlikely to want to help you articulate your view. But when both partners possess a virtuous disposition, and demonstrate a willingness to engage each other, then the conversation I have sketched here becomes more probable.

From Virtue to Morality

Insofar as the conversation I have described is excellent, and therefore, one which communicators should strive for, it is ethical. But any ethics, even a virtue ethics, can be fitted to a variety of different moralities. In what way, then, is this virtuous conversation also morally good? We can begin by adopting Slote's (1992) position that a communicator has moral obligations to both self and other. This allows us to dispense with the notion that acts are only morally good if they benefit someone other than the self. Nevertheless, it remains to be shown that the type of virtuous conversation advanced generates, or creates, good for both self and other.

In the same sense in which Socrates likened himself to a midwife, we can begin by asking what I am doing when I attempt to deliver you of your "inherent truth?" The presupposition of that delivery is that your opinion is composed of two parts: a part which is given by your culture and a part that represents your unique standpoint in the world (see Kim, chapter 3, this volume, regarding individuation and consonance). Your "inherent truth," the truth that is yours as your unique standpoint in the world, is therefore obscured by the truths of your culture. Of course, this view is oversimplified, but retaining it has several advantages. If we want to talk about the relationship between culture and communication, then we must define those terms so as to minimize the overlap between them. If conversation involves "words and deeds," then culture concerns meaning, or "shared mental representations" (Baumeister, 1991, p. 15). Further, if a culture is to be viable, those meanings must be widely shared and they must be transmitted across generations (Spiro, 1987). Therefore, we can take it as a given that a cultural portion of our mental life exists. And, even though cultures are not monoliths, and may allow for multiple, competing discourses, there will still exist canonical narratives (Bochner, Ellis, & Tillmann-Healy, 2000) that unite those voices, providing the unrealized common assumptive ground from which the voices speak, or at least, from which the voices cannot escape.

If we assume that your viewpoint contains two parts, one part that has been received by your culture, class, socialization, etc., and one part that is uniquely yours, then to truly enter into your viewpoint and bring your truth into the light of day, I need to dissolve or shrink the cultural portion of your view. This assumes that a great deal of our everyday interactions are highly scripted and routinized, and even the contents of our conversations are a repetition of positions and arguments that have long ago been divorced from their founding contexts. From the cultural standpoint, this is as it should be. The culture would not survive if we did not parrot its precepts. From an individual standpoint, the familiarity of routines is comforting and reassuring, reducing our uncertainty about our social worlds. To the extent that we believe such security is good, then it remains to be shown why it might also be good to re-examine the bases of that security from time to time (see Baxter et al., chapter 2, this volume).

Thoughtfulness

Arendt (1958/1998) draws a distinction between two types of mental activities: thinking and cognition. Cognition, as a mental activity, "always pursues a definite aim" (p. 170). Cognition, therefore, can easily fit within a goals-plans-action (GPA) framework (Dillard, 1990a). In the GPA model, actors formulate a primary goal, or desired end state, consider a host of secondary goals, and then engage in a planning process, considering various means for accomplishing that goal, before settling on a plan and putting it into action. During conversation they must monitor the ongoing flow of turns, maintaining conversational coherence even as they make ongoing decisions about whether to continue goal pursuit. Often, initial ideas are never expressed as conversation takes on a life of its own (Hjelmquist, 1990). Despite that, the formulation of goals as culturally viable explanations of behaviors, telling us what the interaction was about (Dillard, 1990b), is consistent with the notion of cognition as a mental activity with a definite aim.

Thinking, on the other hand, is the silent dialogue between me and myself. To engage in thinking requires a withdrawal from the world of the senses and appearances, a retreat into a private world of solitude that is potentially boundless. In many ways, this withdrawal from the world of appearances is antithetical to the immersion into conversation that exemplifies engagement. To be completely involved with my partner is to be attentive and responsive to what my partner is doing and saying. To think too much about his/her words and deeds while we are speaking risks missing something important as well as being perceived as uninvolved (i.e., impolite). Of course it is preposterous to claim that reflective conversation entails no reflection while it is occurring. So we can flip the assertion around and ask what a reflective conversation would look like compared to one guided by cognition.

Thinking requires time to process, to think through what was said and consider its many implications. We should therefore expect more "silences" (Bruneau, 2008) in reflective conversation and a slower pace as individuals juggle multiple, sometimes competing perspectives. In conversations driven by cognition, silences are most apt to occur where individuals are juggling multiple conflicting goals, and the indicators of cognitive load (e.g., filled pauses, longer response latencies) are usually taken to mean that they are experiencing anxiety as they take time to formulate their utterances (Lindsey,

Greene, Parker, & Sassi, 1995). In reflective conversation, we take time to think precisely because we are trying to think through our cultural schemas to formulate our own unique response; by contrast, the quick pace of ordinary conversation requires that we often revert to cultural truisms or habitual responses merely to keep pace with the interaction. So, a reflective conversation will look and feel differently than a goal-driven conversation, but it is still talk between partners and as such requires adherence to conversational forms.

If engaged conversation demands my full involvement, my immersion, in what my partner is saying, then thinking as the silent dialogue between me and myself has to be given full play in between conversations. Recall that integral to fidelity is remembering what was said. I remember those perspectives by thinking about them. As Taylor (2004) argued, after our conversation has ended and we depart, I take the raw material of our talk and turn it into a text, or set of texts. If thinking is a dialogue between me and myself, then we need positions from which to converse. Those positions come from the texts that have been created from our engaged interactions. Therefore, when I am able to participate in excellent conversation, my mental life is richer afterwards. I can now withdraw into thinking and have something to think about. The outcome of thinking may be new insights, new questions, and these reflections may inform my future engaged conversations.

The question remains, however: why or how is the capacity for thoughtfulness morally good? One answer is provided by Arendt (2005) in her earlier writings. As people talk about something, it becomes more common to them. Eventually, what they have oriented toward "begins to constitute a little world of its own which is shared in friendship" (p. 16). Whereas natural abilities and social roles make people unequal, so long as they are free to express their opinions, talking about what they have in common serves an equalizing function. When they have become "equal partners in a common world" (p. 17), they constitute a community. Thus, the individual who strove to make friends of everyone would possess the virtue of the true statesperson, which "consists in understanding the greatest possible number and variety of realities . . . as these realities open themselves up to the various opinions of citizens; and, at the same time, in being able to communicate between the citizens and their opinions so that the commonness of this world becomes apparent" (p. 18). In other words, the interplay of thinking and conversing is good because it builds communities.

A second answer appears throughout Arendt's (1964/1992, 2003, 2005) writings but it becomes especially pronounced following her reflections on the trial of Adolf Eichmann. The idea centers around her interpretation of two statements of Socrates: "it is better to be in disagreement with the whole world than, being one, to be in disagreement with myself" and "it is better to be wronged than to do wrong." The earlier gloss on these statements is that the individual who contradicts him/herself is unreliable. The possibility of contradiction arises because even though I appear to others as one, in thinking I become two-in-one. Therefore, I need to be in agreement with myself in my own thoughts in order to appear as someone who is reliable. Since my own "inherent truth" can only emerge in dialogue, to contradict myself is to foreclose the possibility of arriving at that truth. In this earlier sense, the ability to talk to myself conditions me to talking with others. I have to be a friend with myself before I can take on another friend (another self) by helping him/her deliver his/her own truth.

In Eichmann, Arendt (1964/1992) encountered the epitome of thoughtlessness. The phrase she coined, the "banality of evil," was never intended to account for all evil. Clearly, there were Nazis who were evil in the sense of being moral monsters, criminals, and just plain brutes. Eichmann did not fit these categories and yet he was a willing participant in the orchestration of the monstrous crimes of the Final Solution. In reconciling these two realities, Arendt noted certain characteristics about the man: His overreliance on stock phrases and clichés, his excessive concern about his own career and advancement, and his apparent ability to adjust himself to every policy change handed down from his superiors. What these characteristics share at bottom is thoughtlessness. Eichmann was at loss for words only when his well-worn and over-rehearsed phrases failed him; he was not able to take the perspective of, or truly empathize with, his victims; and, he never stopped to think about, to really think through, the implications of those policy changes. Claiming that Eichmann was thoughtless does not imply that his mind was devoid of mental activity. Rather, it seems he deliberately avoided thoughtfulness by engaging a form of mental activity that was more cognition-driven. For example, over-attention to administrative and bureaucratic detail involves the same sort of low-level concrete thinking that Baumeister (1999) posited as a way of dealing with guilt. Or again, failing to take the perspective of the Jews allowed Eichmann to remain in pursuit of his career and identity goals as a "good Nazi." Since he wasn't on trial for thoughtlessness, what was disturbing about Eichmann was that, as a type, he could be lifted out of Nazi Germany and placed in any bureaucracy in the world and his mental life might have continued in the same thoughtless manner.

The obvious answer to the problem of Eichmann, then, is that thoughtlessness allowed him to participate in Nazi atrocities. Yet, is the converse also "obvious"? Can thoughtfulness provide a bulwark against the commission or perpetuation of evil and injustice? Here we return to Socrates. According to Arendt (2003), his claim "it is better to be wronged than to commit wrong" rests upon the notion that criminal acts are subject to punishment from state and/or society. Therefore, the criminal cannot bring those acts into the light of day; cannot, in other words, speak about them in the public world where people and their deeds appear and receive validation. Criminals' acts must remain hidden. Of course, the most effective way to do that is to not think about them, to not admit them even in the silent dialogue between me and myself. The more I think about them, the more likely I may be to express them aloud during conversation. What this may mean is that I need to stop thinking altogether. For Socrates, therefore, in order to continue talking openly with himself and to engage his fellow Athenians in dialogue, it was essential that he not commit any act that would require secrecy. To commit wrong would interfere with the ability to engage in dialogue.

Pitfalls of Virtuous Communication

The type of virtue-based conversation I have sketched here is an ideal type. As an interactional accomplishment, its realization will be rare. Should we strive to make it more common? There are at least two potential pitfalls in encouraging this kind of communication. The first is the perception that nothing is getting done. Deetz and Simpson (2004) describe an exhibit where people were encouraged to place sticky notes on displays with their anonymous thoughts. The authors express apparent disappointment that although people enjoyed the exhibit there was a sense afterward that it was "just talk" and now it was time to get down to serious business. It's possible that the very anonymity that was intended to provide a safe space for expression may have fostered this attitude insofar as opinions lacked authors. In other words, I can agree with an opinion scratched into the side of a wall, but can only dialogue with an author who is willing to be associated with the sentiment. Thus, seeing the post-its may have encouraged my own thoughtfulness, but without an author to engage and carry on dialogue with, my thoughts remain ephemeral. Yet, even our reflective conversations, full of engagement, may be ephemeral. Even if I am able to put aside the cares of the day and forego purposeful activity, enter into a co-authored dialogue where we help deliver each other of our own inherent truths, and I walk away with a richer mental life, I may still have difficulty translating that richness into practical activity. In other words, being morally good (empathic and thoughtful) may not necessarily result in being an effective communicator who can pursue goals efficiently and appropriately at every opportunity.

Second, the type of virtuous communicator described here will not necessarily be more obedient. Villa (2001) introduces the notion of "Socratic citizenship" and it is worth quoting him at some length:

> Socrates' relentless questioning and ferocious intellectual honesty remain essential for anyone who cares about justice, citizenship, and democratic political action. He helps us to recognize the inevitable moral distortions introduced by any creed or ideology, including that of a "post-ideological" pragmatism. He forces us to acknowledge that by far the greater part of both are activism and apathy is unexamined, no matter how well it has been "theorized" or rationalized. He is the enemy of all forms of self-righteousness, but especially those that congeal around groups. He exposes the manifold corruptions of solidarity. (pp. 4–5)

The interplay between an interpersonal conversation that truly seeks to increase one's unique viewpoint at the expense of unexamined cultural conceptions and an intrapersonal thoughtfulness that is boundless and prone to thinking through cultural conceptions is as likely to produce a "moderately alienated" citizen as one who is the first to sign up to build shelters as a resume-building activity.

The type of thoughtfulness advocated here cuts across boundaries of positionality. Wood (2004), for example, poses the following question: "Why should a CEO engage in dialogue with a line worker who wants better working conditions but cannot afford to risk her or his job?" (p. xix). If the line worker simply desires better working conditions, then she or he might be better served by adhering to a competence model that frames the desire in terms of a goals-plans-action (GPA) sequence. But if she or he truly desires to enter into dialogue with that CEO, that line worker better be prepared to be as open to the standpoint of the boss as she or he expects that boss to be open to her/his standpoint. And of course, the worker must be willing to risk the result that both parties walk away with a deeper understanding of each other and a richer mental life, even while conditions on the line remain unchanged. In other words, rather than offering alternatives to the GPA model, some forms of dialogism may be read as further extensions of it, even though the goal they posit is a noble one (e.g., social justice). The whole point of Socratic citizenship is to think through the simple dichotomy of powerful-powerless which always assumes the powerless would be willing to enter into dialogue if only the powerful would "take responsibility for identifying and reducing socially determined asymmetries that dictate who gets to speak, what forums and forms of speech are deemed legitimate, whose speech counts, and to whom it counts" (p. xx). How do the powerful themselves view things? What "webs of bio-power" and "techniques of self-discipline" do they perceive being exerted upon themselves, constraining them to reproduce privileged positions? Conversely, one could ask complementary questions of the powerless. Do they wish to be released from those webs and techniques altogether? Do they wish to trade places with the powerful?

Conclusions

One of the advantages of the virtue model is that it directs attention to a set of qualities that are observable. Several coding schemes exist that focus on various facets of immediacy and partner involvement. Further, there are self-report based measures of virtue (Proyer & Ruch, 2009; Strom, 2003). One might begin by predicting that virtuous individuals will display greater engagement. But what are the links between enacted virtuous behaviors and the underlying disposition indicative of genuine engagement? Most likely, then, that prediction will have to be tempered by identifying certain situational features that allow for preparation for virtuous communication. It may turn out to be the case that only the four communicative virtues of politeness, compassion, generosity, and fidelity will relate to observable behavior, or, it may be that the ability to engage with one's partner opens up to a host of additional moral and intellectual virtues. Nevertheless, the model is intended as a testable set of constructs.

The underlying moral claims of the model direct our attention to solitude as a core feature. Bruneau (2008) distinguishes between silence, referring to "contemplation and meditation, psychic fugues, nostalgic raptures, fantasies, day-dreaming, mind-wandering, sleep, and unconscious journeys" and silences involving "verbal thought, speaking, language and linguistics, and a linear sequencing of words and ideas" (p. 78). Insofar as solitude as conceived here is a silent dialogue between me and myself, it tends toward the latter definition. It may be, however, that the ability to live with oneself, to be a friend to oneself in the silent dialogue of thinking, unites both forms, and therefore provides a bulwark against cruelty and injustice, or it may be that the critical questioning of the dialogue between me and myself in solitude is what matters most. One might also ask if this capacity for solitude is changing with the widespread adoption of portable forms of communication technology. While the inability to go 15 minutes or to walk from point A to point B without texting or phoning someone may increase a sense of solidarity, does it reduce our ability to reflect upon the "manifold corruption" that Villa (2001) speaks of?

In addition to providing empirically testable statements about the role of virtue in communicators' lives, the model also stands in a definable relationship to current models of communication. The field has been well-served by a competence model that centers on concerns with effectiveness and appropriateness. In this model, individuals form goals, and a competent communicator pursues those goals by formulating plans that are appropriate to the situation. Since there is no assumption that goals are necessarily selfish, communicators can pursue goals that benefit others. How then does the virtue model differ from the competence model, at least in cases where my goal promotes the interests of, or helps, another (i.e., is the virtue model just a special case of the competence model)? Conceptually, the idea of the virtue model is that our truths emerge during the course of our reflective conversation. That helps you in terms of gaining a new perspective and self-understanding, or stretching your capacity for empathy. But the open-ended nature of the conversation means there's no criteria for determining if that is the help you wanted, or even needed, at that time. Under the competence model, to formulate a goal and to try and move the conversation toward that endpoint requires that I treat many parameters of the interaction as fixed. For example, I have to "know" your problem if I am to give you advice about it. And the criterion of effectiveness allows me to assess whether or not I have successfully met my goal. The kind of engaged, reflective conversation I have described here requires a suspension of goal pursuit, and not simply a switching of an instrumental goal to a relational goal.

Dialogism is an umbrella term for a number of approaches which frequently focus on conversation as the fundamental unit of analysis. This focus means that they tend, to varying degrees, to exhibit a critical stance toward the individualism of the GPA model. The preceding discussion of virtue in relation to competence might imply that the virtue model is another variant of dialogism. Certainly the focus on reflective conversation supports that implication. Nevertheless, the virtue model differs from many forms of dialogism in two respects. One, by starting with the dialogue, dialogic approaches have less to say about what individuals are enjoined to do in between dialogues. What sort of person is capable of recognizing and creating the conditions necessary for dialogue? My approach begins with a form of moral individualism that relates it to a tradition of Western thought that goes back at least to Socrates. The individual who is capable of dialogue is one who is thoughtful in between dialogues. Such an individual seeks out the friend in both self and others, and therefore is not another example of the "sovereign self." Two, and not unrelated to the first, many dialogic approaches adopt a Protean view of the self. That is, they adopt a view of the self as shifting and unstable, constantly changing and becoming in response to encounters with the otherness of others. If this Protean self idea merely states that people adjust their presentations to their roles and audiences, then it seems little different from the advice one would give someone whose goal was to manage his/her impression effectively. Or, if it means that people grow and change in response to their experiences, that's not inconsistent with a competence model either. It seems that something more is implied by dialogic approaches. If that something more is a view of the self as genuinely unstable and constantly changing, with no "person" able and willing to stand behind and guarantee his/her position, a social actor who lacks "the right to make promises," then that is a dangerous position, according to the present view. While reflective conversation requires us to be open to the perspective of the other and willing to re-examine our own views, the virtuous statesperson whom Arendt describes has an ever enlarged view of the self rather than one which is constantly changing.

This paper began with a question: "Why is it important to understand interpersonal communication?" Understanding interpersonal communication can make us more competent communicators. At times however, it is necessary to let go of our goals and engage our partners in the flow of the conversational moment. The virtue model suggests qualities that can assist us in this "letting go" process. Another answer is that communication, especially in our close relationships, can bring physical and psychological benefits, in particular a sense of meaningfulness. Without thoughtfulness, however, that meaning may simply reflect cultural frameworks. What happens when those cultural narratives fail us? For example, the loss of meaning and the need to re-narrativize is a common theme among the chronically ill (Miczo, 2003). The thoughtfulness that underlies communicative virtue fosters the ability to create our own unique meanings. In one sense, the proposed model cannot be revolutionary: if people never acted with virtue, we would truly see Hobbes's "war of all against all," a situation where everyone pursued his/her own self-interest, whether that involved seeking pleasure or benefitting others. To the extent that such is not the case, we may assume that individuals already act with some degree of virtue. A fuller understanding of how virtue complements competence and well-being may promote the development of citizens with the characteristics of Arendt's (2005) "true statesperson."

References

Arendt, H. (1992). *Eichmann in Jerusalem: A report on the banality of evil* (Rev. ed.). New York: Penguin Books. (Original work published 1964)

Arendt, H. (1998). *The human condition* (2nd ed.). Chicago: University of Chicago Press. (Original work published 1958)

Arendt, H. (2003). *Responsibility and judgment*. New York: Schocken Books.

Arendt, H. (2005). *The promise of politics*. New York: Schocken Books.

Baumeister, R. F. (1991). *Meanings of Life*. New York: Guilford Press.

Baumeister, R. F. (1999). *Evil: Inside human violence and cruelty*. New York: W. H. Freeman and Company.

Baumeister, R. F., & Exline, J. J. (1999). Virtue, personality, and social relations: Self-control as the moral muscle. *Journal of Personality, 67*, 1165–1194.

Bochner, A. P., Ellis, C., & Tillmann–Healy, L. M. (2000). Relationships as stories: Accounts, storied lives, evocative narratives. In K. Dindia, & S. Duck (Eds.), *Communication and personal relationships* (pp. 13–29). Chichester: John Wiley & Sons.

Bruneau, T. J. (2008). How Americans use silence and silences to communicate. *China Media Research, 4*, 77–85.

Canary, D. J., Cody, M. J., & Manusov, V. L. (2008). *Interpersonal communication: A goals-based approach* (4th ed.). Boston: Bedford/St. Martin's.

Comte-Sponville, A. (2001). *A small treatise on the great virtues* (C. Temer son, Trans.). New York: Holt Paperbacks. (Original work published 1996)

Cupach, W. R., & Metts, S. (1994). *Facework*. Thousand Oaks, CA: Sage.

Deetz, S., & Simpson, J. (2004). Critical organizational dialogue: Open formation and the demand of "otherness." In R. Anderson, L. A. Baxter, & K. N. Cissna (Eds.), *Dialogue: Theorizing difference in communication studies* (pp. 141–158). Thousand Oaks, CA: Sage.

Dillard, J. P. (1990a). A goal-driven model of interpersonal influence. In J. P. Dillard (Ed.), *Seeking compliance: The production of interpersonal influence messages* (pp. 41–56). Scottsdale, AZ: Gorsuch Scarisbrick.

Dillard, J. P. (1990b). The nature and substance of goals in tactical communication. In M. J. Cody & M. L. McLaughlin (Eds.), *The psychology of tactical communication* (pp. 70–90). Clevedon, England: Multilingual Matters LTD.

Floyd, K. (2009). *Interpersonal communication: The whole story*. Boston: McGraw–Hill.

Hjelmquist, E. (1990). Planning and execution of discourse in conversation. *Communication & Cognition, 23*, 277–294.

Jones, W. H., Hobbs, S. A., & Hockenbury, D. (1982). Loneliness and social skill deficits. *Journal of Personality and Social Psychology, 42*, 682–689.

Lindsey, A. E., Greene, J. O., Parker, R. G., & Sassi, M. (1995). Effects of advance message formulation on message encoding: Evidence of cognitively based hesitation in the production of multiple-goal messages. *Communication Quarterly, 43*, 320–331.

Miczo, N. (2003). Beyond the "fetishism of words": Considerations on the use of the interview to gather chronic illness narratives. *Qualitative Health Research, 13*, 469–490. doi: 10.1177/1049732302250756

Nakamura, J., & Csikszentmihalyi, M. (2003). The construction of meaning through vital engagement. In C. L. M. Keyes & J. Haidt (Eds.), *Flourishing: Positive psychology and the life well-lived* (pp. 83–104). Washington: American Psychological Association.

Nietzsche, F. (1966). *Beyond good and evil: Prelude to a philosophy of the future* (W. Kaufmann, Trans.). New York: Vintage Books. (Original work published 1886)

Nietzsche, F. (1967). *On the genealogy of morals and ecce homo* (W. Kaufmann, Trans.). New York: Vintage Books. (Original work published 1887)

Nietzsche, F. (1995). *Thus spoke Zarathustra* (W. Kaufmann, Trans.). New York: The Modern Library. (Original work published 1883)

Parks, M. R. (1982). Ideology in interpersonal communication: Off the couch and into the world. In M. Burgoon (Ed.), *Communication Yearbook 5* (pp. 79–107). New Brunswick, NJ: Transaction.

Petronio, S. (2002). *Boundaries of privacy: Dialectics of disclosure*. Albany: State University of New York Press.

Proyer, R. T., & Ruch, W. (2009). How virtuous are gelotophobes? Self- and peer-reported character strengths among those who fear being laughed at. *HUMOR, 22*, 145–163. doi: 10.1515/HUMR.2009.007

Slote, M. (1992). *From morality to virtue*. New York: Oxford University Press.

Slote, M. (2010). *Moral sentimentalism*. Oxford: Oxford University Press.

Spiro, M. E. (1987). *Culture and human nature: Theoretical papers of Melford E. Spiro* (B. Kilborne & L. L. Langness, Ed.). Chicago: The University of Chicago Press.

Spitzberg, B. H., & Hecht, M. L. (1984). A component model of relational competence. *Human Communication Research, 10*, 575–599.

Strom, B. (2003). Communicator virtue and its relation to marriage quality. *Journal of Family Communication, 3*, 21–40.

Taylor, J. R. (2004). Dialogue as the search for sustainable organizational co-orientation. In R. Anderson, L. A. Baxter, & K. N. Cissna (Eds.), *Dialogue: Theorizing difference in communication studies* (pp. 125–140). Thousand Oaks, CA: Sage.

Villa, D. (2001). *Socratic citizenship*. Princeton, NJ: Princeton University Press.

Weiner, B., Figueroa-Mūnoz, A., & Kikihara, C. (1991). The goals of excuses and communication strategies related to causal perceptions. *Personality and Social Psychology Bulletin, 17*, 4–13.

Wilson, S. R. (2002). *Seeking and resisting compliance: Why people say what they do when trying to influence others*. Thousand Oaks, CA: Sage.

Wood, J. T. (2004). Foreword: Entering into dialogue. In R. Anderson, L. A. Baxter, & K. N. Cissna (Eds.), *Dialogue: Theorizing difference in communication studies* (pp. xv–xxiii). Thousand, Oaks, CA: Sage.

• CHAPTER SIX •

"Holding Each Other all Night Long:" Communicating Intimacy in Older Adulthood

Jon F. Nussbaum
Pennsylvania State University

Michelle Miller-Day
Pennsylvania State University

Carla L. Fisher
George Mason University

"La vita e bella; la vita e amore.— Life is beautiful; life is love."
— Braschi & Ferri (1997)

The film *Life Is Beautiful*, quoted above, captures the essence of this chapter. To some, the film may seem an overly romantic vision of love and intimacy because it argues that one can transcend all forms of hardship and oppression as long as intimates have one another. However, in our book *Communicating Intimacy in Older Adulthood* (Nussbaum, Miller-Day, & Fisher, 2010) we discussed how this may indeed be the case. For older adults, looking back on years past and anticipating years to come, "life is love" and "intimacy is what matters" are themes that cut across the narratives of the 36 older adults we interviewed. In the book we pointed out that poets and storytellers from every culture have consistently glorified the importance of close, intimate relationships, and that the story of a meaningful, full human life has always been placed within the context of relating to others. Across most of the arts, depictions of rich, meaningful lives have centered on the closeness found among lovers, family members, and friends. In this chapter we summarize and extend our arguments that intimate relationships *are* central to a meaningful life across the human lifespan. Intimacy is positive. Intimacy enhances our well-being. The main purpose of this chapter is to tell a (not *the*) story of intimacy in later adulthood, at times offering a retrospective of lives, loves, and personal accounts of a sampling of older adults in the United States.

Intimacy

The feeling of intimacy is located within the individual. However, this feeling is dependent upon our social interactions with others (Nussbaum et al., 2010). Intimacy cannot be achieved and maintained without active social engagement. A focus upon the individual feeling of intimacy without a recognition of the importance of the other individual(s) and the communication process necessary to promote the development of intimate relationships simply will not capture the true domain of intimacy in our lives. Intimacy is a feeling located within, but co-constructed through, communicative interactions with others. Intimacy is not a given in any relationship. According to the older adults we interviewed intimacy is:

> warmth, satisfaction, closeness, connection, friendly, touching, caring, spiritual union, emotional union, feeling safe and secure, sharing daily lives, a sense of understanding and a patient attitude, being there for each other, being partners and a team ... all kinda intertwined. (Nussbaum et al., 2010, p. 15–16)

Intimate relationships are socially important across the world. In Spanish and Latin American cultures intimate relationships are greatly valued and highly prioritized. *Personalismo*, or intimacy in relationships and talk can be perceived by Latinos as more important than life accomplishments. Likewise, people of these cultures appreciate a high degree of intimacy in their interactions. *Personalismo* is a cultural value in Spanish and Latin American cultures and is actively displayed in social interactions (Santiago-Rivera, 2003). The term encompasses many meanings and explanations of behavior, all of which convey the value these cultures have for expressing and maintaining intimacy in relationships across the life span. Recently, Underwood (2008) was among a group of researchers from the World Health Organization developing the concept of "compassionate love." This particular kind of intimacy centers on a "self-giving, caring love that values the other highly and has the intention of giving full life to the other" (p. 18). This term compassionate love is intended to capture aspects of altruism, positive passion, and caring connection inherent in this kind of intimacy.

Definitional difficulties aside, intimacy is health promoting. Intimate relationships seem to buffer people from the stressors of life. People who have intimate relationships experience less stress, demonstrate fewer stress-related physical symptoms, and recover faster than people who do not (Prager, 1995). Having caring, supportive relationships can lead to improved immune function (Carrere & Gottman, 1999, and see MacGeorge et al., chapter 12, this volume). Additionally, intimacy with others may impact health indirectly by encouraging and reinforcing preventative behaviors. Intimates are likely to encourage one another to reduce or quit the use of tobacco and alcohol, eat diets low in cholesterol and high in fruits and vegetables, and schedule checkups (Miller-Day, 2010) as well as offer positive, celebratory support (see McCullough & Burleson, chapter 14, this volume).

As we age, the importance of intimacy becomes more central to a high quality of life. Intimacy becomes more vibrant, more diverse, more attainable and more fundamental to our overall well-being as we age into our 60's, 70's, 80's, 90's, and beyond (Nussbaum et al., 2010). It may very well be that, for many, a lifetime of practicing may result in the communication skills necessary to achieve optimal intimacy across a wide variety of relationships. Yet for those in older adulthood, optimal intimacy may be restricted to a core group of family and friend relationships (Nussbaum, Pecchioni, Robinson, & Thompson, 2000).

Intimacy in Older Adulthood

Intimacy is truly a lifespan feeling. Throughout the lifespan, including older adulthood, intimacy is felt and remains a critical component of anyone's ability to lead a rich, meaningful life. Older adulthood is a time of significant transition (Williams & Nussbaum, 2001). Modern industrialized countries have established a retirement norm. Older adults are leaving their work life. This could mean leaving those intimate work friendships that have lasted over several decades. The older worker is moving from spending the majority of his or her day at work to spending the days at home, and will spend significant time with his or her spouse attempting to re-negotiate the relationship. During this time, older adults are also adapting and coping with less financial security and often several chronic health conditions that may slow down an ability to accomplish tasks that were once taken for granted. The great majority of older adults do report high levels of satisfaction with their lives and report an acceptable level of good health. Those older adults who struggle with the challenges of old age, however, also report smaller social networks of family and friends. Janice, age 77, indicated that she is satisfied with a smaller network of intimates, saying:

> I am not a loner, I'm a person that needs people. But, I just can't envision being intimate with anyone else (other than my husband). Everything in my life is secure, status quo, and I am in control of it. I have my friends and my family. That is all I need to be happy. (Nussbaum et al., 2010, p. 18)

Perhaps, at no time in life, is intimacy within a broad range of relationships more important for good physical and mental health than are the older adult years (and within positive psychology, see Seligman, 2002).

For many older adults across the globe, the grandparent-grandchild relationship is one of the more satisfying relationships in later life. The grandparent role in most cultures is respected and admired. Within this role, older adults achieve intimacy with their grandchildren by providing positive emotional support and by educating the younger generation on family history and tradition. Research has shown that this notion of giving back to younger generations (generativity) not only creates a close intimate bond with grandchildren, but functions to create positive feelings of selfworth for the older adult (Hagestad & Burton, 1986). Grandparents who provide instrumental support can also help parents who may need a break from the constant demands of parenthood and, thus, provides an opportunity to reinforce intimacy between the parent and his or her mother/father.

In addition to grandparenting, the older-adult sibling relationship can reach a point of high intimacy during the later years of our lives. Research studies find that reported closeness levels of older-adult siblings often reflect the highest reported levels of closeness throughout the entire life span (see Cicirelli, 1995). Children, however, are typically not asked to complete surveys of their feelings of closeness with their siblings, so there is incomplete information for age comparisons on this subject. Nevertheless, when older adults are asked who they would rather ask for help with regard to emotional issues, travel problems, or with health care issues, siblings are frequently selected as often as are spouses and children. Intimacy in the older sibling relationship is most often compared to the intimacy felt in older life-long friendships. Siblings have a history of similar experiences which at times translates into similar values, attitudes, and beliefs.

Friendships in older adulthood have also been linked to high levels of overall well-being and life satisfaction (Williams & Nussbaum, 2001). Friends can discuss things that family members may not choose to discuss. Research has been very consistent supporting the importance of at least one close friendship relationship for maintaining a healthy lifestyle in our old age. The older adult who is able to maintain a combination of intimate family and friendship bonds has an excellent chance of maintaining a high quality of life throughout the aging process.

Numerous social theories have been proposed to help explain the social lives of older adults and any connection to quality of life (Williams & Nussbaum, 2001). Disengagement theorists suggest that for older adults to maintain a high level of satisfaction they should gradually withdraw from social relationships and "give in to" the fact that society is withdrawing from them. Activity theorists, on the other hand, suggest that for older adults to maximize feelings of well-being, the older adult needs to remain and even increase his or her social activity. Continuity theorists argue that whatever level of social activity made you happy as a young adult and as a middle-aged adult, should also be maintained into older adulthood. Research testing these theories is quite mixed.

Laura Carstensen, a Stanford University psychology professor, has advanced the socioemotional selectivity theory to address the often contradictory findings found in the gerontology literature that attempts to explain the link between older adult social activity and quality of life. As we age, Carstensen and her colleagues have found that older adults choose to intensify the feelings of intimacy in only a few selected relationships (Carstensen & Charles, 1998). Others that were within the older adult's social network and who may have, at one time, maintained an intimate relationship with the older adult, are slowly excluded from daily interactive activities. The factor that serves to fuel this process of downsizing and intensifying one's social relationships is time.

The older adult marriage, in particular, is the best candidate for one of the most intimate relationship across the life span. Internationally, a high percentage of marriages for this particular cohort of over-65-year-olds represent marriages maintained for well over thirty years. Catholicism remains the main religion in Spain, Latin American, and South America, even though it has declined in years. Likewise, divorce is less common in these cultures than in North America (Sharlin et al., 2000). Although separation and divorce are becoming more accepted in these cultures, in one South American country (i.e., Chile) divorce is still illegal. Thus, long-term marital bonds are common within Latin American and Spanish cultures. Individuals in these long-term marriages report the highest levels of marital satisfaction and well-being in life. Older married adults are the healthiest and most active older adults. Older adults who have maintained a long- term marriage have learned how to competently communicate within the relationship and have multiple strategies to provide emotional support for one another. The sexual activity that often communicated intimacy in this relationship continues to function in a similar fashion throughout the entirety of this relationship. Older spouses provide for many of the necessary physical, psychological, financial, and spiritual needs of their aging partners in ways not previously experienced at other points in the life span (Nussbaum & Coupland, 2004).

Interestingly, older adults in satisfying long-term marriages from around the world report similar characteristics of healthy long-term relationships. Nearly 900 long-term married couples (married 25–45 years) from five different continents (Africa, Europe, North America, South America, and Asia) recently participated in a global study (see Sharlin, Kaslow, & Hammerschmidt, 2000). Scholars examined what these older adult couples perceived made their long-term marriages satisfying. Their experiences and perceptions were similar, regardless of country of origin. These older adult long-term married couples consistently reported a number of common characteristics. One of these characteristics was intimacy—defined as a sense of belonging together. This sense of belonging extended beyond the couple into a sense of belonging together to a larger, extended family network and circle of friends. These couples also mentioned other traits that helped inform their intimate long-term connection. For instance, older-adult couples mentioned reciprocal consideration and sensitivity, love and affection, mutual empathy, concern for children and grandchildren, ongoing and enjoyable sexuality, understanding, and shared values as being key traits to a long-lasting satisfying marriage.

Intimacy and Sexuality in Older Adulthood

Although sexual intimacy is only one facet of intimacy in an older adult's life, we believe it deserves special discussion in this chapter. The "young is good and desirable" mentality that permeates all modern cultures has created an ageist world. The most notable and harmful stereotype that flows from our preoccupation with all things young is the notion that as we age our sexual encounters should diminish in frequency and quality. While it is true that several unique challenges do exist in the lives of older adults, old age is by no means a time of zero or even a significantly diminished level of sexual activity. Reasonably good health, availability of sexual partners, and medications that can aid in sexual performance have helped older adults in their quest to maintain an appropriate level of sexual activity in their intimate relationships.

A most destructive myth of the aging process uncovered by North American public opinion researchers is the notion that as we age beyond our 30's sexual activity will become increasingly uninteresting and ultimately nonexistent (Lindau et al., 2007). It is important to note that this negative stereotype linking sexual activity and the aging process is most strongly felt within North American cultures. Individuals living in Spain and Latin and South America do not report having such strong negative attitudes toward sexual activity as we age into adulthood as those individuals responding to surveys in North America (Sharlin et al., 2000). It is also interesting to note that several very recent and specific surveys (e.g., Global Study of Sexual Attitudes and Behaviors or GSSAB) have indicated that older adults themselves try to maintain an overall positive attitude toward sex and agree that sexual activity with a significant other is an important component of intimacy in their life adding to its overall quality (Laumann et al., 2005). Nevertheless, the negative attitudes toward sexual activity for older adults found within the media, the health care profession, young individuals, and by adult children when specifically asked about their older parents, has caused confusion for not only younger adults but also older adults who are attempting to maintain a healthy, intimate relationship that includes frequent, passionate, and fulfilling sexual activity.

All of the older adults interviewed for Nussbaum et al. (2010) and the majority of older adults worldwide maintain the ability and desire to engage in sexual activity for their entire lives. Pleasurable sexual encounters are the norm in older adulthood regardless of the negative stereotypes within given cultures or the misinformation of the medical profession. The sex actually gets better with age, according to Lee, aged 77. "Everything is just more natural and more comfortable" he says. "We may not make love as frequently as we used to, but we still have a hell of a lot of fun!" Tom and Lynette, in their mid-80's, are a case in point. Tom and Lynette reconnected after Tom's wife died and after a whirlwind romance they married. Now, 20 years later Tom says, "Our sex life is as fun as ever. We have some physical challenges to be sure, but we try and have sex as much as possible." Lynette shares that she "loves sex" and she tries to read up on ways she can keep their love life fresh. Her resources are magazines such as *Cosmopolitan* and *Glamour*. After a recent bout of rather energetic play, the couple laughs in recounting how they broke their bed when Tom attempted to throw Lynette on it "like one of those romance book guys" (p. 47–48).

We want to emphasize the fact that changes in our sexual abilities and desires do continue throughout the aging process. A Duke University study found that 20 percent of people over 65 report sex lives that are better than ever before. Sexual activity is maintained and continues to play an important role in our intimate relationships as we cope with our physical limitations directly related to the aging process (Butler & Lewis, 2002).

In a study published in *The New England Journal of Medicine,* Lindau et al. (2007) helps to shed light upon the sexual behaviors and sexual function of older adults. A sample of 3,005 adults living in the United States between the ages of 57 and 85 years of age were studied. Seventy-three percent (73%) of the respondents between the ages of 57 and 64, 53% of the respondents between the ages of 65 to 74, and 26% of the respondents between the ages of 75 to 85 years of age reported being sexually active. Participating in either vaginal intercourse or oral sex throughout the previous 12 month period served as the definition of sexual activity. Two-thirds of the older adults within this study participated in sexual activity at least twice a month into their 70's and more than 50% reported a continuation of this level of sex into their 80's. Fifty-eight percent (58%) of sexually active respondents in the age group 57–64 engaged in oral sex, while 31% of the oldest respondents reported engaging in oral sex. Twenty-three (23%) of the individuals aged between 75 and 85 reported engaging in sexual activity at least once a week.

Surprising to individuals who consider anyone over 40 to be "sexless," recent research suggests that older adults today have better sex lives than those in previous generations. Swedish scholars recently published research in the *British Medical Journal* based on the self-reports of 1,500 healthy 70-year-old Gothenburg residents over 30 years (Beckman, Waern, Gustafson, & Skoog, 2008). They collected surveys in 1971–1972, 1976–1977, 1992–1993, and 2000–2001. Results indicated that the frequency of sexual intercourse increased between the first survey and the last in all groups of individuals. 68 % of married men reported engaging in sex in the most recent survey in comparison to only 52% in 1971. Additionally, 56% of married women reported having intercourse, whereas only 38% had reported this activity during the first survey. Unmarried 70–year–old men also reportedly engage in sex more in today's generation. Only 30% reported this sexual activity in 1971 compared to 54% in 2001. Finally, 12% of unmarried women in the twenty-first century also reported engaging in sex in contrast to less than 1% in 1971.

While it may be true that the likelihood of being sexually active does decline with age, it is very important to note that the most striking decline in sexual activity occurs after the age of 75 (Lindau & Gavrilova, 2010; Lindau et al., 2007). The availability of a partner, health status, and gender have been found to be associated with the decline in sexual activity. Older adults who have a healthy, living spouse or who are currently involved in a committed relationship are more likely to engage in sexual activity than individuals whose spouse had passed away or who are not currently involved in a committed relationship. This proximity and commitment factor plays a rather significant role in whether older adults will maintain a lifestyle that includes sexual activity. We feel that an understanding of how older adults maintain their intimate relationships through competent communication will shed light upon the ability to remain sexually active well into old age.

The majority of the individuals participating in the Lindau et al. (2007) *New England Journal of Medicine* study between the ages of 57 and 75 reported that their health status was excellent to very good. Self-reported health status was lower for individuals over the age of 75. However, only 32% of men and 33% of women over the age of 75 reported their health to be fair or poor. The likelihood of maintaining a sexually active lifestyle was positively associated with self-reports of good health. An additional factor related to maintaining sexual activity is the reported health status of the intimate other. A total of 55% of men and 64% of women listed the health status of their intimate partner as a reason for diminished sexual activity.

Barriers to sexual activity in older adulthood are constructed by the culture, various religions, family members, and health institutions where relatively healthy older adults live (such as assisted care facilities and continuing care facilities). Strong feelings and beliefs are maintained that regard sexual activity for older adults as an inappropriate behavior. Rules may specifically state that sex outside the context of marriage or outside of the context to produce children is forbidden. Additionally, when an older mother or father moves into a child's home, the privacy needed to achieve and maintain an intimate sexual relationship can be effectively eliminated. Moreover, it is not uncommon to find a total lack of privacy within long-term care facilities. Research has also been quite clear that staff within long-term care facilities often have negative attitudes toward the older residents maintaining an active sexual relationship, especially when they are not married or living with their partner. One such U. S. case received a fair amount of media attention a few years ago. This "story", however, is repeated throughout the United States each and every day. She was 82, he was 95. They were living in a care facility, had dementia, and eventually fell in love. The problems began when they started having sex. Melinda Henneberger (2008) wrote in *Slate*:

> Bob's family was horrified at the idea that his relationship with Dorothy might have become sexual. At his age, they wouldn't have thought it possible. But when Bob's son walked in and saw his 95-year-old father in bed with his 82-year-old girlfriend last December, incredulity turned into full-blown panic. "I didn't know where this was going to end," said the manager of the assisted-living facility where Bob and Dorothy lived. "It was pretty volatile." Bob's son became determined to keep the two apart and asked the facility's staff to ensure that they were never left alone together. After that, Dorothy stopped eating. She lost 21 pounds, was treated for depression, and was hospitalized for dehydration. When Bob was finally moved out of the facility in January, she sat in the window for weeks waiting for him. This case created a flurry of responses, revealing the rather common practice of older adults in care facilities who "hook up." One care provider articulated that "I have witnessed at least five instances/cases of such love affairs among residents [in the past 4 years]. Sometimes both parties had some form of dementia and, at other times, only one, but the ending was always the same. Management forced them apart and one of the 'offending' parties was whisked away, never to be seen again. It was always done with terrible cruelty.

An issue of conscious consent exists despite the fact that sexual intimacy among individuals with Alzheimer's may vastly improve their spirits, outlook, and well-being. At times it may be impossible to know whether a person suffering from dementia might actually want to participate in sexual activity. There is the potential for "date rape" in these cases if an excited person takes sex to a higher level than the partner expected or was ready for. These make for a complicated array of legal, moral, and social issues. Nevertheless, these cases illustrate the ongoing need for basic sexual intimacy across one's lifetime, and (some may say) children's difficulty with acknowledging their parents as sexual beings.

A combination of maintaining good health well past the age of 75 and the various medications available to enhance sexual performance has resulted in enhancing the possibility of a number of sexual encounters and partners outside of a committed relationship for older adults. This increase in the number of sexual partners has also increased the risk of contracting STDs like HIV within the older population. Studies in the United States and England reveal that not only is sexual activity prevalent in middle and older adulthood, but so are the disease risks that accompany unprotected sex. In England's West Midlands Health Protection Agency's study of people aged 45 and older, STD rates more than doubled in the last 10 years (Bodley-Tickell et al., 2008). In addition, in a 2000 study of Washington State residents (a study that is reportedly one of the only investigations of STD infection in middle and older-adult populations), incidences of gonorrhea increased nearly 20% between 1997 and 1998 among people aged 45 and older (Xu et al., 2001). Some scholars and professionals believe that older adults are of a generation not familiar with practicing safe sex when pregnancy is no longer a concern. Jane Fowler, aged 74, admits this to be true of her experience. She is the co-founder of HIV Wisdom for Older Women, an organization she started after being diagnosed with HIV in later life. Tiffany Sharples writes in a Summer 2008 issue of *Time* about Fowler's sexual experience in older adulthood after her 24-year marriage ended in divorce.

> A self-dubbed "1950s good girl," Fowler had only ever had one partner - her husband. Newly single in her early 50s, she started dating a man she'd known her entire life, and pregnancy was no longer a concern. "If you know for a fact that you can't become pregnant and you don't know anything about sexually transmitted diseases," she says, "why would you use a condom?" Five years later, a routine blood test revealed that she had contracted HIV. Thousands of adults like Fowler find themselves renegotiating sex in singlehood, after years or even decades of marriage, and they are in need of the same kind of sex-ed their grandchildren get. (Sharples, 2008)

We do not want to leave this chapter without a brief discussion highlighting the ability of older adults to achieve the highest level of physical satisfaction in their sexual activities. Orgasms are not only possible in our 80's but are as desired at this age as they are at any age! Some scholars feel that sexual satisfaction among older adults may have increased in recent decades as Western society has become more comfortable talking about sexual issues more openly. The recently published 30-year Swedish study compared the sexual activity and attitudes of healthy 70 year olds sampled in the 1970s, 1990s, and the twenty-first century (the H70 studies of the geriatric population in Gothenburg). The 70-year-old women in the twenty-first century reported being not only highly satisfied with their sex life but having more orgasms during sex than the previous generations of same-aged women. The individuals we interviewed in Nussbaum et al. (2010) complement this finding. When asked to describe the pleasure they received from their continuing sexual activity, Paul (age 82) and Mary (age 80) who both had been married before, laughed, looked at each other and said that "their best orgasms were two days ago and will be better tonight" (p. 63).

For many of the couples discussed in Nussbaum et al. (2010), especially those who met later in life, sexual activity was not deemed as essential to developing intimacy as was the act of touching. For these couples, touch alone was one of the more powerful indicators of intimacy in a relationship. Lois, 83, (who met her husband at the age of 81) recounts how her husband nurtured their growing intimacy with touch.

> Right after we had first met, um, we weren't really that sexually intimate. But he was here, he was staying with me and he was sitting in the rocking chair this one day and I was working around here and he goes, "Come here." He said, "Sit on my lap," and I said, "I can't sit on you" and he said "You can." And so he pulled me over on to his lap, put his arms around me, put my head on his shoulder and rocked me until we both fell asleep. That's a lovely picture. It was, it was just something else, you know, just little things and he holds me at night; I mean, his arms are around me. We have to touch each other; we're never apart. We're holding each other all night long. (Nussbaum et al., 2010, p. 75)

Interestingly, our physical ability to feel touch diminishes as we age. In certain cultures, touching an older adult can be viewed quite negatively. Touching by health-care professionals and their patients, by teachers and their students, by clergy and their parishioners, is often controlled and various limits are placed on the appropriateness of this professional touch. While these physical, cultural, and ethical barriers do serve a positive societal function, these same barriers have resulted in our concern over the lack of touch within the lives of older adults.

Touching an older adult often requires a longer stroking motion or a firmer grasp. Older adults who have a sexual relationship may hold onto one another in public much longer than would be appropriate for a much younger couple. The importance of hugging, caressing, stroking and kissing does appear to increase in an intimate relationship in older adulthood. Much to the displeasure of children at times, older adults may want to hug their grandchildren a bit closer and a bit longer than the children are accustomed to. Older adults who are married or have a sexual relationship with another individual have been known to hold hands or caress in public more than couples within other age groups. In some ways the frequency and duration of various public displays of affection by older adults can be similar to such displays by adolescents! Positive touch is soothing, touch lets you know that the other person is near, touch reminds us that we are still alive and vital.

Conclusion

Throughout this chapter we have discussed intimacy in older adulthood. Older adults must manage their relationship networks within a much different social context than individuals of other age groups. Older adults, for instance, can outlive their spouses and friends. The intimate relationships we form throughout our lives and attempt to maintain as we age function in rather miraculous ways to support our daily needs. As mentioned several times within this chapter, these intimate relationships have been shown to increase our overall physical health, to keep us socially active, to hold back the ravages of dementia, to create a climate where giving back to society is a frequent and reinforcing occurrence, and to generally make life worth living—in short to live Aristotle's the good life (see Seligman, 2002).

Each intimate relationship within the family can serve a unique, as well as, overlapping function in the life of an older adult. Married older adults live longer, are healthier, and are more satisfied with life than are non-married older adults. It is interesting to note that older men are much more satisfied with their life in general and with their marriage than older women. Older men who lose their wife to death or divorce are much more likely to re-marry than older women. The constant companionship of a long marriage is not only comforting but serves as a physical and mental health check for both individuals within the marriage. All of our activities of daily life are made easier and more fun when we share those activities with our spouse. A marriage that has lasted for 30, 40, 50, 60 and even 70 years becomes a pleasant, safe environment within which to share the remaining years of life. In addition to the companionship offered by romantic relationships in later life, healthy and active sexual intimacy is a large part of many older couples' lives. For many, the richness of the intimacy found within older marriages is unsurpassed in its passion and simple overall "goodness."

Summing up the overall message in this chapter we offer you this quote from Walter Bortz, author of three books on healthy aging and senior sexuality, who says, "People that have sex live longer. Married people live longer. People need people. The more intimate the connection, the more powerful the effects" (Bortz, 1996).

References

Beckman, N., Waern, M., Gustafson, D., & Skoog, I. (2008). Secular trends in self reported sexual activity and satisfaction in Swedish 70 year olds: cross sectional survey of four populations, 1971–2001. *British Medical Journal, 337*, 151–154.

Bodley-Tickell, A. T., Olowokure, B., Bhaduri, S., White, D. J., Ward, D., Ross, J. D. C., Smith, G., Duggal, H. V., & Goold, P. (2008). Trends in sexually transmitted infections (other than HIV) in older persons: analysis of data from an enhanced surveillance system. *Sexually Transmitted Infections, 84*, 312–317.

Bortz, W. (1996). *Dare to be 100*. New York: Simon and Schuster.

Braschi, G., Ferri, E. (Producers), & Benigni, R. (Director). (1997) *Life is beautiful* [Motion picture]. Italy: Cecchi Gori Distribuzione, Caravan Pictures.

Butler, R. N., & Lewis, M. I. (2002). *The new love and sex after 60.* New York: Ballantine Books.

Carrere, S., & Gottman, J. (1999). Predicting the future of marriages. In E. M. Hetherington (Ed.), *Coping with divorce, single parenting, and remarriages* (pp. 3–23). Mahwah, NJ: Erlbaum.

Carstensen, L. L., & Charles, S. T. (1998). Emotion in the second half of life. *Current directions in psychological science, 7,* 144–149.

Cicirelli, V. G. (1995). *Sibling relationships across the life span.* New York: Kluwer Academic / Plenum Publishers.

Hagestad, G., & Burton, L. (1986). Grandparenthood, life context, and family development. *American Behavioral Scientist, 29,* 471–484.

Henneberger, M. (2008, June). An affair to remember. *Slate.* Retrieved from http://www.slate.com/id/2192178/.

Laumann, E. O., Nicolosi, A., Glasser, D. B., Paik, A., Gingell, C., Moreria, E., & Wang, T. (2005). Sexual problems among women and men Aged 40–80 y: prevalence and correlates identified in the Global Study of Sexual Attitudes and Behaviors. *International Journal of Impotence Research, 17,* 39–57.

Lindau, S. T., & Gavrilova, N. (2010). Sex, health, and years of sexually active life gained due to good health: Evidence from two US population based cross sectional surveys of ageing. *British Medical Journal, 340,* 810–813.

Lindau, S. T., Schumm, L. P., Laumann, E. O., Levinson, W., Muircheartaigh, C. A., & Waite, J. (2007). A study of sexuality and health among older adults in the United States. *New England Journal of Medicine, 357,* 766–774.

Miller–Day, M. (Ed.) (2010). *Family communication, connections, and health transitions: Going through this together.* New York: Peter Lang.

Nussbaum, J., Miller-Day, M. & Fisher, C. L. (2010). *Communication and intimacy in older adulthood.* Spain: Editorial Aresta

Nussbaum, J. F., & Coupland, J. (Eds.). (2004). *The handbook of communication and aging research (*2nd ed.). Mahwah, NJ: Erlbaum.

Nussbaum. J. F., Pecchioni, L. L., Robinson, J. D., & Thompson, T. L. (2000). *Communication and aging (*2nd ed.) Mahwah, NJ: Erlbaum.

Prager, K. J. (1995). *The psychology of intimacy.* New York: Guilford Press.

Santiago-Rivera, A. L. (2003). Latinos values and family traditions: Practical considerations for counseling. *Counseling and Human Development, 35*(6), 1–12.

Seligman, M. E. P. (2002). *Authentic happiness.* New York: Free Press.

Sharlin, S. A., Kaslow, F. W., & Hammerschmidt, H. (2000). *Together through thick and thin: A multinational picture of long-term marriages.* Binghampton, NY: Haworth Press.

Sharples, T. (July 2, 2008). More midlife (and older) STDs. *Time Magazine.* Accessed http://www.time.com/time/health/article/0,8599,1819633,00.html

Underwood, L .G. (2008) Compassionate love: A framework for research. The science of compassionate love: Theory, research, and applications. In Fehr, B. & Sprecher, S., & Underwood, L. G. (Eds.), *The science of compassionate love: Theory, research, and applications* (pp. 3–25). Wiley-Blackwell.

Williams, A., & Nussbaum, J. F. (2001). *Intergenerational communication across the lifespan.* Mahwah, NJ: Erlbaum.

Xu, F., Schillinger, J. A., Aubin, M. St. Louis. M. E., & Markowitcz, L. E. (2001). Sexually transmited diseases of older persons in Washington State. *Sexually Trasmitted Diseases*, *28*, 287–291.

Section Two
Fundamental Processes

• CHAPTER SEVEN •

Listening as Positive Communication

Graham D. Bodie
Louisiana State University

At age 17, Byron Pitts was a first-year college student a midterm away from flunking out. One particularly memorable day began as his English professor handed back an essay marked with a D+. Shortly after hearing "You are wasting my time and the government's money," Mr. Pitts began filling out papers to withdraw from school. Fortunately for Mr. Pitts, a stranger took the time to listen to his story. As Mr. Pitts describes it, "She stopped. She helped me . . . she was encouraging . . . and she planted seeds of kindness in me and optimism."[1]

Although much could be said about this story, the relationship between Mr. Pitts and his unofficial mentor began with her willingness to listen. Indeed, listening is deeply rooted in the context of its ability to help create, maintain, and enhance positive interpersonal relationships. One might go as far as to say that listening is *the* quintessential positive interpersonal communication behavior as it connotes an appreciation of and an interest in the other. Such a statement is not without its empirical warrant. Research shows that feeling "listened to" (Notarius & Herrick, 1988) or "being heard" (Myers, 2000) is vitally important for many types of conversations and is an expected part of many relationships from early childhood to the end of life. Good listening is an important aspect of parenting (Duncan, Coatsworth, & Greenberg, 2009), marital relationships (Pasupathi et al., 1999), salesperson performance (Castleberry & Shepherd, 1993), customer satisfaction (de Ruyter & Wetzels, 2000), and healthcare provision (Watanuki, Tracy, & Lindquist, 2006); and the list could go on. Good listeners can enhance others' ability to cope with (Jones, 2011) and remember events (Pasupathi, Stallworth, & Murdoch, 1998); they are more liked, rated as more attractive (Argyle & Cook, 1976), and garner more trust (Mechanic & Meyer, 2000) than those less proficient; and they have higher academic motivation and achievement (Schrodt, Wheeless, & Ptacek, 2000) and a higher likelihood of upward mobility in the workplace (Sypher, Bostrom, & Seibert, 1989). Adding to the importance of listening, research finds that natural decrements in the ability to process speech can negatively impact individual and relational health and well-being (Villaume, Brown, & Darling, 1994).

Despite the recognition of listening as a positive element of communication, evidence suggest that educators have "spent a disproportionate amount of time on teaching speaking as opposed to teaching listening" (Janusik, 2010, p. 193); and scholarly attention allotted to listening has paled in comparison to that paid message production (Bodie, 2011a). Thus, listening seems "a kind of human behavior that almost everyone thinks important" (Weaver, 1972, p. 24), though this importance is not always matched by fervent academic inquiry (Bodie, 2010b).

One potential reason for this paradox is that although listening has been studied in a range of specific contexts like social support and physician-patient interaction, it is less often incorporated into theoretical frameworks that allow for more comprehensive empirical study. Indeed, most of the communication research employing the term listening has either focused so narrowly on its role in the classroom thus limiting listening to a type of information processing stripped from its inherent connection with human communication and relational processes (Bostrom, 2011), or cast such a broad net defining listening as a single behavior thus suggesting its component parts are unworthy of systematic study (Bodie & Jones, in press).
This chapter attempts to provide a broader conceptualization of listening and to serve as a ready resource of the myriad perspectives through which one can come to understand the positive potential of listening. In service of this aim, this review is organized in two primary sections. Section one sketches a brief history of the study of listening within the communication discipline. Drawing from the work of Kaplan (1964), the second section argues past work has treated listening primarily as a construct rather than a theoretical term. As a consequence, the term listening is used infrequently and a host of other terms have been developed that obscure the evidence for the positive potential of listening. Throughout, I highlight directions for future research and theory building efforts to advance listening as an essential component of human interaction.

Defining and Measuring Listening: A Brief History

Although earlier writings exist, many attribute Nichols's (1948) study of listening comprehension as the catalyst for the systematic study of listening in communication research. Undergraduates in this study were asked to listen to six, 10-minute lectures and answer a multiple choice test after each. Student participants averaged 68% on the composite listening test with higher scores related to both individual (e.g., intelligence) and situational factors (e.g., listener fatigue). Subsequent interviews with instructors of students scoring in the top and bottom tertiles of the test revealed that good, compared to poor, listeners were "more attentive during classroom activities and more conscientious in their…work habits" (p. 160). From these data, Nichols concluded that factors likely to discriminate among good and poor listeners should be afforded empirical attention and that instructional efforts should be aimed at improving student ability to comprehend aural input. This study was most important, however, because it suggested a conceptualization of listening that set the research agenda throughout the 1980s (see also Bodie et al., 2008).

Listening as Lecture Comprehension

Early listening research almost exclusively focused on designing standardized tests of lecture comprehension. In general, these tests included at least one measure of memory for facts presented in a lecture, and most utilized multiple choice questions scored as right or wrong (for review see Watson & Barker, 1984). The fact that these standard elements of listening tests were also found in tests of reading comprehension and tests of mental ability led Kelly (1965) to argue that these "tests consist essentially of . . . comprehension questions . . . whose accuracy perhaps depends primarily upon mental factors that are far from specific to audition" (p. 139). Kelly showed that the correlation between two commercially available and widely used listening comprehension tests—the Brown-Carlsen Listening Test (BCLT; Brown & Carlsen, 1955) and the Sequential Tests of Educational Progress (STEP; ETS, 1957)—was similar in magnitude to the correlation between each listening test and a test of general mental ability.[2] From these data he concluded that (a) "our traditional procedures for testing listening are sterile," (b) "currently published listening tests are not valid measures of a unique skill," and (c) "listening should be considered a complex of activities, not a unitary skill" (Kelly, 1967, p. 456).

Listening as a Complex of Skills

Viewing listening as a complex of skills meant conceptualizing listening as a set of abilities, some of which are related to other language abilities like reading, some of which are related to mental acuity and intelligence, and some of which are unique to aural processing (see Weaver, 1972, pp. 9–10). Research conducted prior to Kelly's critique suggested that processing speech was a distinct language ability (for review see Caffrey, 1955), and several large-scale factor analytic studies around the time of Kelly's work proposed "a constellation of interrelated listening abilities" (Lundsteen, 1966, p. 311).

This line of thinking, along with research questioning the validity of existing tests, spearheaded efforts in the 1970s and 1980s to develop multidimensional tests of listening comprehension. Each multidimensional test developed during this time held the assumption that there exists some identifiable set of skills that can be taught in order for a person to become a good listener, though agreement about which skills to include was far from universal (Ridge, 1993). The two leading tests were the Watson-Barker Listening Test (WBLT; Watson, Barker, Roberts, & Roberts, 2001) and the Kentucky Comprehensive Listening Test (KCLT; Bostrom & Waldhart, 1983), and each was quite influential for a variety of reasons. First, their development spawned a litany of research aimed to demonstrate their validity, constituting nearly the whole of listening research during the 1980s and 1990s (Rhodes, Watson, & Barker, 1990). Unfortunately, research has yet to generate a stable factor structure for either the WBLT or KCLT or to offer much published validity evidence (Bodie, Worthington, & Fitch-Hauser, 2011). Second, the "methodological fixation" driving research during this time (Bostrom, 2011) appears to have promoted concerns about how to "correctly define" listening (see ILA, 1995). A focus on defining listening was also extended to at leat two alternative views.

Listening as Responding

The first alternative view to listening as comprehension attempted to shift the focus from something internal to the listener to her overt behavior. Scholars began discussing listening competence (as opposed to comprehension), which was defined as a judgment made by an interlocutor based on a range of verbal (e.g., asking questions, paraphrasing) and nonverbal (e.g., eye contact, backchannel responses) behaviors that can be executed more or less skillfully (for a review see Bodie et al., in press). Primary among the concerns of these scholars were developing measures that could capture "good listening" in particular contexts and attempting to compare self-reports of competent listening to those obtained by close others and trained observers (e.g., Cooper & Husband, 1993). To date, "active listening" is used most often to describe how listeners should act in a range of contexts, though there is little agreement as to the specific skill set that constitutes active listening. Moreover, evidence suggesting the effecitveness of "active listening" is scant, and some research suggests that engaging in typical active listening behaviors (e.g., paraphrasing, non-directive reflecting) is counterproductive (Armstrong, 1998; Pasupathi et al., 1999).

Listening as Relating

Especially when used to refer to an action that occurs in close relationships, listening generally suggests an active presence of another individual who is typically acting with empathic tendencies (Bodie, 2011b; Gearhart & Bodie, in press). In general, listening as relating offers views of the active-empathic nature of listening, one from the perspective of the individual; the other from the perspective of the relationship. From the perspective of an individual, listening is an orientation toward being completely aware and open (i.e., "empty") to what is happening in and around us (Lipari, 2010). This "style" of listening is juxtaposed with ways of listening that are more oriented toward acquiring and critiquing information. From the perspective of the relationship, listening is a relationally constituted process (Rhodes, 1993), something that occurs within a dyadic system and helps to define that system (Halone & Pecchioni, 2001). Using this conceptualization, listening is defined in a manner similar to some definitions of intimacy (Reis, 1990) and social support (Burleson et al., 1994).

Though grounded in theory, little research has explored the ramifications of these speculations. For instance, measures for attitudes and predispositions toward listening have only recently been developed (Bodie, 2011b; Mishima, Kubota, & Nagata, 2000) or have questionable validity (Bodie & Worthington, 2010), and no research has sought to verify that these attitudes actually lead to more effective listening. Though some research suggests that "active engagement" may enhance relational satisfaction, the precise communicative actions that lead to such outcomes are largely unspecified (Bodie, Worthington, & Jones, in press).

Perspectives on Listening: A Synthesis and Selective Review

Though each perspective on listening reviewed above has its individual limitations, it is perhaps more informative to focus on a set of shared limitations and to offer a potential solution that fosters a conceptual space for the study of listening as an integrated part of positive interpersonal communication. The first general limitation of past work on listening is how the term has been treated. Grounded in pragmatism, Kaplan (1964) recognized that the utility of a concept depends on its use and suggested that terms can be conceptualized as either constructs or theoretical terms. While a construct is defined individually and in relation with observables, a theoretical term derives its meaning "from the part it plays in the whole theory in which it is embedded, and from the role of theory itself" (p. 56). Although some models of listening have been based on theoretical perspectives like human information processing (Goss, 1982) or theories of memory (Janusik, 2005), the goal of most extant research has been to create a consensual definition of listening and, subsequently, measures that assess all of its constituent parts. Even when scholars do discuss the need to theorize about listening, the sentiment is that "in order to develop a theory we must first agree upon a definition of the [construct]" (Barker, Barker, & Fitch-Hauser, 1987, p. 15).

Listening should, instead, be viewed as a theoretical term and allowed various meanings depending on the practical purpose pursued by an individual or team of scholars (see also Bodie, 2010b). Treating listening as a theoretical term moves us away from concerns over definitional harmony and towards attempting to understand listening in all its complexity. To borrow an analogy from Zebrowitz (2001): Communication scholars who lack a theoretical framework to explain listening are "like the blind men [in the John Saxe poem *The Blind Men and the Elephant*], who lacked an overarching theory of elephantness and could not find it through local observations" (p. 334).

The second general limitation of past work on listening seems to follow from the first—when scholars become primarily motivated to assemble *the* definition of a term, thus treating it as a construct, its theoretical association with other phenomena is largely ignored. Consequently, the extant literature becomes littered with a host of terms that seem to describe ostensibly analogous processes. Several have highlighted this problem in the literature on communication competence with terms such as social competence, interpersonal competence, social skills, and communicative competence being used interchangeably (Wilson & Sabee, 2003). Likewise, terms such as conversational involvement, conversational sensitivity, interpersonal sensitivity, and interaction involvement all seem to tap a component of what most would typically label listening.

In general, listening has been recognized as a multidimensional construct that consists of complex (a) cognitive processes, such as attending to, understanding, receiving and interpreting content and relational messages (Imhof, 2010); (b) affective processes, such as being motivated to attend to those messages (Weaver, 1972); and (c) behavioral processes, such as responding with verbal and nonverbal feedback (Bodie et al., in press). As a cognitive phenomenon, listening is linked to cognitive complexity (Burleson, 2011), interaction involvement (Cegala, 1981), conversational sensitivity (Daly, Vangelisti, & Daughton, 1988), perspective taking (Ebesu Hubbard, 2009), and various information processing dispositions (e.g., styles of thinking; Bodie, 2010a, Study 3). "Good" listeners are also described as more likely to hold certain attitudes like empathic concern (Bodie, 2011b) and a willingness to listen (Roberts & Vinson, 1998) or to formulate certain listening goals that increase attentiveness to others in conversation (Burleson, 2011). Similarly, listening seems to share conceptual space with other terms used to describe behavioral involvement including dimensions such as immediacy, expressiveness, interaction management, and altercentrism (Coker & Burgoon, 1987) and adaptation and coordination (Ebesu Hubbard, 2009).

Taken together, when we talk about "good listening" we are likely talking about a variety of skills and abilities, some of which have been afforded extensive empirical attention, though their nomological connection to listening has yet to be clearly specified. In many areas of interpersonal communication, especially those like social support and the communication of rapport that are inherently related to the "positive side," scholars largely ignore listening as a central and important component in their research (Bodie, 2011a). This is quite surprising given that a good deal of positive interpersonal communication research at least implicitly recognizes listening as an important concept, and the term is used quite often when scholars are asked about the practical implications of their research. It is likely, therefore, that myriad theories can be used to locate listening as a theoretical term.

A sample of those theories is provided in Table 7.1 with corresponding definitions of listening. While some of these definitions have been explicitly stated (e.g., Burleson, 2011; Powers & Witt, 2008), others were derived based on the use of similar terms within theories (e.g., Coker & Burgoon,

1987) and/or applications by other scholars (e.g., Schrodt, 2008). Though an in-depth analysis of each theory and the entire range of implications for listening is beyond the scope of this chapter, the sections that follow attempt to highlight relevant literature from within a sample of these frameworks to illustrate the positive potential of listening in its many definitional forms.

Table 7.1
Definitions of Listening within Various Theories of Human Communication

Theory	Definition of Listening
Affection Exchange Theory	A type of affectionate communication that fosters intimate interactions by enhancing feelings of being understood (Floyd, 2006)
Communication Fidelity Theory	The ability to accurately receive and interpret another's sensory output (Powers & Witt, 2008)
Constructivism	"The process of interpreting the communicative behavior of others in the effort to understand the meaning and implications of that behavior" (Burleson, 2011, p. 29)
Dialogic Theory of Public Relations	One among many skills needed to foster dialogue which "involves creating a climate in which others are not only encouraged to participate but their participation is facilitated" (Kent & Taylor, 2002, p. 27)
Family Communication Patterns	One of the fundamental theoretical mechanisms facilitating the coorientation process that family members undergo (Schrodt, 2008)
Implicit Personality Theory	One among many cognitive categories used to evaluate others during and after interaction (Bodie, St. Cyr, et al., in press)
Interpersonal Adaptation Theory	A complex behavior that helps signal involvement or "the degree to which participants are enmeshed in the topic, interpersonal relationship, and situation" Coker & Burgoon, 1987, p. 463)
Leder-Member Exchange Theory	Sensitivity and openness to the particular issues raised by each member of one's work team which leads to positive relationships, mutual trust, and increased job satisfaction (Graen & Uhl-Bien, 1995)
Planning Theory of Communication	Understanding of others' actions and discourse (Berger, 2008)

Table 7.1 Continued

Relational Framing Theory	The process of making sense of relational messages within social interaction (Dillard, Solomon, & Palmer, 1999)
Theory of Communicative Action	One half of coordinated action that involves the conscious selection of, attending to, and reflecting on interaction to reach a common understanding without the necessity for a cleansing of political (or other) interests (Habermas, 1984)

The Positive Potential of Listening within Affection Exchange Theory

According to affection exchange theory (AET), both the expression and reception of affection—"an emotional state of fondness and intense positive regard" (p. 4)—serves fundamental human needs (Floyd, 2006; see also Floyd & Deiss, chapter 8, this volume). From this perspective, listening is one type of affectionate communication (see Pendell, 2002) that fosters intimate interaction by enhancing feelings of being understood, a vital component of interpersonal need fulfillment (Prager & Buhrmester, 1998). When we feel "listened to," we are more satisfied with our relationships and life in general; this increased well-being can also have a profound effect on physical health. Not only does listening positively influence the recipient, but the listener can also garner positive outcomes (Notarius & Herrick, 1988). As reviewed by Floyd (2006), the communication of affection is vital to many close relationships, making a fruitful area for future research the documentation of specific roles listening plays in this process.

The Positive Potential of Listening within Constructivism

Constructivism attempts to explain how people accomplish social goals by appealing to the role of social perception (Burleson & Bodie, 2008). In general, this framework proposes that our cognitive structures help determine how we will produce and process messages and manage social interactions. Constructivist-based theories of communication propose that high quality messages, whether those messages are aimed at persuading, informing, or comforting, exhibit heightened awareness of and adaptation to multiple aspects of the communicative context (i.e., are more "person centered"; Burleson & Rack, 2008). From this perspective, skilled listening is defined as efficiently and effectively "interpreting the communicative behavior of others in the effort to understand the meaning and implications of that behavior" and to ultimately respond appropriately (i.e., in a person-centered manner; Burleson, 2011, p. 29). Using this definition, listening is located as an information processing task that can be done more or less competently, a view shared by several other theories listed above (e.g., planning theory, relational framing theory).

In place of the term listening, constructivist scholars have investigated interpersonal cognitive complexity (ICC) or the sophistication of others' understanding of people, relationships, and actions in the social world. People who are more cognitively complex are better able to (a) make competent social judgements; (b) take the perspective of another; and (c) craft highly person-centered messages (Burleson & Caplan, 1998). Accordingly, individuals high in ICC have been shown to process messages more deeply than their low ICC counterparts (Bodie et al., 2011). These more proficient listeners also tend to employ more sophisticated persuasive, comforting, regulative, and informative messages and model these competencies for their offspring (Burleson, Delia, & Applegate, 1995).

The Positive Potential of Listening within Family Communication Patterns

Like constructivism, research on family communication patterns (FCPs) suggests that communication within families and the values families place on communication help to explain the intergenerational transmission of communication attitudes, predispositions, and styles. That is, a primary reason that adult children manifest particular ways of relating and communicating with close relational partners (friends, romantic partners) is because of how they were taught to think about and value communication from their parents. Perhaps the most influential theory of FCPs has been aided by the two-dimensional typology of Fitzpatrick and her colleagues (for review see Koerner & Fitzpatrick, 2002). This typology asserts that FCPs are determined by two underlying orientations toward communication, orientations that reflect both how families talk and how families think about communication. The conversation orientation reflects "a climate in which all family members are encouraged to participate in unrestrained interactions about a wide array of topics," whereas the conformity orientation reflects a climate that places a premium on harmony, particularly concerning values and beliefs (Koerner & Fitzpatrick, 2002, p. 39). As listening is concerned, families exhibiting a higher conversational orientation are more likely than families with a high conformity orientation to entertain a variety of opinions, enjoy talking (and listening) to one another, and value the importance of understanding each other irrespective of agreement or dissention; indeed, several items on the primary instrument used to assess these orientations highlight the role played by listening (e.g., "My parents like to hear my opinions, even when they don't agree with me").

As stated by Schrodt (2008), however, "while listening is an implicit part of both the theoretical and methodological underpinnings of the FCP research tradition, researchers have generally neglected how listening facilitates the development and communication of family conversation and conformity orientations during the socialization of family members" (p. 2). The one study to date that has directly addressed relationships among listening attitudes and communication patterns within families found that adult children from families high in conversation and low in conformity orientation were less likely to report anxiety toward listening. The authors suggest that "when families create an environment where family members are encouraged to openly discuss a variety of topics, children may be more likely to learn how to process complex and ambiguous information without anxiety" (Ledbetter & Schrodt, 2008, p. 397). Schrodt (2008) further outlines three key developmental stages (early childhood, adolescence, emerging adulthood) representing the family life cycle "where listening may be particularly important for family socialization" (p. 3); future research thus seems bright for uncovering how listening can "carry conversation and conformity orientations from one generation to the next" (p. 4).

The Positive Potential of Listening within Leader-Member Exchange (LMX) Theory

The focus of leader-member exchange (LMX) theory is on enhancing organizational success and promoting "more effective leadership through the development and maintenance of mature leadership relationships" (Graen & Uhl-Bien, 1995, p. 220). In particular, LMX theory suggests "that effective leadership processes occur when leaders and followers are able to develop mature leadership relationships (partnerships) and thus gain access to the many benefits these relationships bring" (p. 225). As the quality of the exchange between leaders and followers increases, positive outcomes such as increased performance, commitment, satisfaction, and loyalty are more likely, and negative outcomes such as stress and burnout are less likely.

Although LMX theory does not detail specific behaviors likely to foster partnerships among leaders and followers, it stands to reason that "listening leaders" are more likely to foster partnerships than are leaders not perceived to understand subordinate needs (Steil & Bommelje, 2004). Some empirical work is available to back this speculation. For example, programs that train supervisors in listening and "feedback skills" as well as social support can increase the quality of partnerships, and research consistently mentions listening to problems and being attentive as important behaviors that assist the creation of partnerships (see Anderson & Williams, 1996). Likewise, items on a popular scale assessing organizational climate seem to suggest the importance of listening (e.g., "X values my contribution to its well-being"; "X would ignore any complaint from me") (Eisenberger, Huntington, Hutchison, & Sowa, 1986). In general, listening is proposed to be an important element of partnership building, which is linked to job satisfaction, commitment, and productivity. Since most past research on this topic only leads to informed speculations about the role of listening within organizations, however, research is needed to detail those specific elements of listening most important for fostering positive organizational relationships and a supportive organizational climate.

Conclusion

Scholars from a variety of fields have investigated listening from multiple perspectives, providing a rather large literature scattered across specializations (Bodie et al., 2008). Within communication scholarship, listening is often portrayed as a key component to effective communication and is cast as a fundamental competency in close, personal and professional relationships as well as for students of all ages. Research on social support demonstrates listening as one of the most helpful behaviors in times of distress, and scholars readily assert that listening is an important component of managing conflict, promoting intimacy, succeeding as a leader, and creating a client-centered business model (for reviews see Bodie, 2011a; Bodie & Fitch-Hauser, 2010). Indeed, when we provide "a sympathetic ear" we are doing more than receiving and processing information (Floyd, 2006, p. 34), we are displaying to others that they matter; we are, in essence, stopping, encouraging, and planting seeds of kindness and optimism.

From the extant literature across communication and allied fields, it is clear that listening is an important and positive communication behavior. Even so, the positive potential of listening has yet to be fully realized perhaps because the term has yet to be fully incorporated into a variety of theoretical frameworks that pose distinct roles and functions for the cognitive and behavioral components of this complex social skill. To date, the full realization of listening's positive potential has been limited by research treating it as a construct and by the proliferation of other terms that are merely synonyms for what we attempt to understand, listening. By treating listening, instead, as a theoretical term, scholars are warranted in defining listening in multiple ways and encouraged to incorporate the term into theoretical frameworks capable of explaining how listening works and functions to the betterment of people's lives. If our ultimate goal is to train or teach someone how to be a better listener (which it often is), a theoretical structure can aid in choosing relevant skills upon which to focus. This approach not only reduces the number of skills to a more manageable subset, thus allying concerns relevant to test construction, it also stands to aid in theory building (and presumably better training outcomes) (Ridge, 1993).

Overall, this chapter has attempted to provide an historical sketch of the research on listening and how the term has been treated in past communication scholarship. In addition, I have suggested a re-conceptualization of listening as a theoretical term, the purpose of which was to carve a more sophisticated conceptual space for its study. By unpacking the implicit recognition of listening and making the term a more central focus of our research we can begin to fully appreciate listening as the positive force it is suggested to be.

Notes

1. This is a summary of a story that aired on NPR in Baton Rouge, LA on November 16, 2009. The quotes were drawn from the transcript available here: http://www.npr.org/templates/story/story.php?storyId=120463986
2. Although not frequently cited, Kelly also reported the partial correlation between the listening tests after removing variance shared with the test of mental ability (Otis). That correlation, $r = .33$, suggests that BCLT and STEP, as measures of listening ability, were tapping something not assessed by the Otis. Whether that something was "aural-processing ability" was never addressed primarily because scholars seemed to focus on the strong correlation between each test and the Otis test.

References

Anderson, S. E., & Williams, L. J. (1996). Interpersonal, job, and individual factors related to helping processes at work. *Journal of Applied Psychology, 81*, 282–296.

Argyle, M., & Cook, M. (1976). *Gaze and mutual gaze.* London: Cambridge.

Armstrong, M. N. (1998). *Active listening and the speaker: How does that make you feel?* Unpublished Honors thesis, Department of Psychology, University of Victoria.

Barker, D. R., Barker, L. L., & Fitch-Hauser, M. (1987). *Listening as a hypothetical construct.* Paper presented at the annual meeting of the International Listening Association.

Berger, C. R. (2008). Planning theory of communication: Goal attainment through communicative action. In L. A. Baxter & D. O. Braithwaite (Eds.), *Engaging theories in interpersonal communication: Multiple perspectives* (pp. 89–101). Los Angeles: Sage.

Bodie, G. D. (2010a). The Revised Listening Concepts Inventory (LCI-R): Assessing individual and situational differences in the conceptualization of listening. *Imagination, Cognition, and Personality, 30*, 301–339.

Bodie, G. D. (2010b). Treating listening ethically. *International Journal of Listening, 24*, 185–188.

Bodie, G. D. (2011a). The understudied nature of listening in interpersonal communication: Introduction to a special issue. *International Journal of Listening, 25*, 1–9.

Bodie, G. D. (2011b). The Active-Empathic Listening Scale (AELS): Conceptualization and validity evidence. *Communication Quarterly, 59*, 277–295.

Bodie, G. D., Burleson, B. R., Holmstrom, A. J., McCullough, J. D., Rack, J. J., Hanasono, L. K., & Rosier, J. G. (2011). Effects of cognitive complexity and emotional upset on processing supportive messages: Two tests of a dual-process theory of supportive message outcomes. *Human Communication Research, 37*, 350–376.

Bodie, G. D., & Fitch-Hauser, M. (2010). Quantitative research in listening: Explication and overview. In A. D. Wolvin (Ed.), *Listening and human communication in the 21st century* (pp. 46–93). Oxford: Blackwell.

Bodie, G. D., & Jones, S. M. (in press). The nature of supportive listening II: The role of verbal person centeredness and nonverbal immediacy. *Western Journal of Communication*.

Bodie, G. D., St. Cyr, K., Pence, M., Rold, M., & Honeycutt, J. M. (in press). Listening competence in initial interactions I: Distinguishing between what listening is and what listeners do. *International Journal of Listening*.

Bodie, G. D., & Worthington, D. L. (2010). Revisiting the Listening Styles Profile (LSP-16): A confirmatory factor analytic approach to scale validation and reliability estimation. *International Journal of Listening, 24*, 69–88.

Bodie, G. D., Worthington, D. L., & Fitch-Hauser, M. (2011). A comparison of four measurement models for the Watson-Barker Listening Test (WBLT)-Form C. *Communication Research Reports, 28*, 32–42.

Bodie, G. D., Worthington, D. L., Imhof, M., & Cooper, L. (2008). What would a unified field of listening look like? A proposal linking past perspectives and future endeavors. *International Journal of Listening, 22*, 103–122.

Bostrom, R. N. (2011). Rethinking conceptual approaches to the study of "listening". *International Journal of Listening, 25*, 10–26.

Bostrom, R. N., & Waldhart, E. S. (1983). *The Kentucky Comprehension Listening Test*. Lexington, KY: The Kentucky Listening Research Center.

Brown, J. I., & Carlsen, G. R. (1955). *Brown-Carlsen Listening Comprehension Test* New York: Harcourt, Brace and World.

Burleson, B. R. (2011). A constructivist approach to listening. *International Journal of Listening, 25*, 27–46.

Burleson, B. R., Albrecht, T. L., Goldsmith, D., & Sarason, I. G. (1994). Introduction: The communication of social support. In B. R. Burleson, T. L. Albrecht & I. G. Sarason (Eds.), *Communication of social support: Messages, interactions, relationships, and community* (pp. xi–xxx). Thousand Oaks, CA: Sage.

Burleson, B. R., & Bodie, G. D. (2008). Constructivism and interpersonal processes. In W. Donsbach (Ed.), *The international encyclopedia of communication* (Vol. 3, pp. 950–954). Oxford, United Kingdom: Blackwell.

Burleson, B. R., & Caplan, S. E. (1998). Cognitive complexity. In J. C. McCroskey, J. A. Daly, M. Martin & M. J. Beatty (Eds.), *Communication and personality: Trait perspectives*. Cresskill, NJ: Hampton Press.

Burleson, B. R., Delia, J. G., & Applegate, J. L. (1995). The socialization of person-centered communication: Parental contributions to the social-cognitive and communication skills of their children. In M. A. Fitzpatrick & A. L. Vangelisti (Eds.), *Explaining family interactions* (pp. 34–76). Thousand Oaks, CA: Sage.

Burleson, B. R., & Rack, J. J. (2008). Constructivism: Explaining individual differences in communication skill. In L. A. Baxter & D. O. Braithwaite (Eds.), *Engaging theories in interpersonal communication* (pp. 51–63). Thousand Oaks, CA: Sage.

Caffrey, J. G. (1955). Auding. *Review of Educational Research, 25*, 121–138.

Castleberry, S. B., & Shepherd, C. D. (1993). Effective interpersonal listening and personal selling. *Journal of Personal Selling and Sales Management, 13*, 35–49.

Cegala, D. J. (1981). Interaction involvement: A cognitive dimension of communicative competence. *Communication Education, 30*, 109–121.

Coker, D. A., & Burgoon, J. K. (1987). The nature of conversational involvement and nonverbal encoding patterns. *Human Communication Research, 13*, 463–494.

Cooper, L., & Husband, R. L. (1993). Developing a model of organizational listening competency. *Journal of the International Listening Association, 7*, 6–34.

Daly, J. A., Vangelisti, A. L., & Daughton, S. M. (1988). The nature and correlates of conversational sensitivity. *Human Communication Research, 14*, 167–202.

de Ruyter, K., & Wetzels, M. G. M. (2000). The impact of perceived listening behavior in voice-to-voice service encounteres. *Journal of Service Research, 2*, 276–284.

Dillard, J. P., Solomon, D. H., & Palmer, M. T. (1999). Structuring the concept of relational communication. *Communication Monographs, 66*, 49–65.

Duncan, L. G., Coatsworth, J. D., & Greenberg, M. T. (2009). A model of mindful parenting: Implications for parent-child relationships and prevention research. *Clinical Child & Family Psychology Review, 12*, 255–270.

Ebesu Hubbard, A. S. (2009). Perspective taking, adaptation, and coordination. In W. F. Eadie (Ed.), *21st century communication* (pp. 119–127). Thousand Oaks, CA: Sage.

Educational Testing Service (ETS). (1957). Sequential tests of educational progress. Princeton, NJ: Educational Testing Service.

Eisenberger, R., Huntington, R., Hutchison, S., & Sowa, D. (1986). Perceived organizational support. *Journal of Applied Psychology, 71*, 500–507.

Floyd, K. (2006). *Communicating affection: Interpersonal behavior and social context*. Oxford: Cambridge University Press.

Gearhart, C. G., & Bodie, G. D. (in press). Active-empathic listening as a general social skill: Evidence from bivariate and canonical correlations. *Communication Reports*.

Goss, B. (1982). Listening as information processing. *Communication Quarterly, 30*, 304–307.

Graen, G. B., & Uhl-Bien, M. (1995). Relationship-based approach to leadership: Development of leader-member exchange (LMX) theory of leadership over 25 years: Applying a multi-level multi-domain perspective. *Leadership Quarterly, 6*, 206–212.

Habermas, J. (1984). *The theory of communicative action* (T. A. McCarthy, Trans. Vol. 1). Boston: Beacon Press.

Halone, K. K., & Pecchioni, L. L. (2001). Relational listening: A grounded theoretical model. *Communication Reports, 14*, 59–71.

Imhof, M. (2010). The cognitive psychology of listening. In A. D. Wolvin (Ed.), *Listening and human communication in the 21st century* (pp. 97–126). Boston: Blackwell.

International Listening Association (ILA) (1995). An ILA definition of listening. *Listening Post, 53*(April), 1, 4–5.

Janusik, L. (2005). Conversational Listening Span: A proposed measure of conversational listening. *International Journal of Listening, 19*, 12–28.

Janusik, L. (2010). Listening pedagogy: Where do we go from here? In A. D. Wolvin (Ed.), *Listening and human communication in the 21st century* (pp. 193–223). Oxford: Wiley-Blackwell.

Jones, S. M. (2011). Supportive listening. *International Journal of Listening, 25*, 85–103.

Kaplan, A. (1964). *The conduct of inquiry: Methodology for behavioral science.* San Francisco, CA: Chandler Publications.

Kelly, C. M. (1965). An investigation of the construct validity of two commercially published listening tests *Speech Monographs, 32*, 139–143.

Kelly, C. M. (1967). Listening: Complex of activities—and a unitary skill? *Speech Monographs, 34*, 455–465.

Kent, M. L., & Taylor, M. (2002). Toward a dialogic theory of public relations. *Public Relations Review, 28*, 21–37.

Koerner, A. F., & Fitzpatrick, M. A. (2002). Understanding family communication patterns and family functioning: The role of conversation orientation and conformity orientation. *Communication Yearbook, 26*, 37–68.

Ledbetter, A. M., & Schrodt, P. (2008). Family communication patterns and cognitive processing: Conversation and conformity orientations as predictors of informational reception apprehension. *Communication Studies, 59*, 388–401.

Lipari, L. (2010). Listening, thinking, being. *Communication Theory, 20*, 348–362.

Lundsteen, S. W. (1966). Teaching and testing critical listening: An experiment. *Elementary School Journal, 66*, 311–315.

Mechanic, D., & Meyer, S. (2000). Concepts of trust among patients with serious illness. *Social Science & Medicine, 54*, 657–668.

Mishima, N., Kubota, S., & Nagata, S. (2000). The development of a questionnaire to assess the attitude of active listening. *Journal of Occupational Health, 42*, 111–118.

Myers, S. (2000). Empathic listening: Reports on the experience of being heard. *Journal of Humanistic Psychology, 40*, 148–173.

Nichols, R. (1948). Factors in listening comprehension. *Speech Monographs, 15*, 154–163.

Notarius, C. I., & Herrick, L. R. (1988). Listener response strategies to a distressed other. *Journal of Social and Personal Relationships, 5*, 97–108.

Pasupathi, M., Carstensen, L. L., Levenson, R. W., & Gottman, J. M. (1999). Responsive listening in long-married couples: A psycholinguistic perspective. *Journal of Nonverbal Behavior, 23*, 173–193.

Pasupathi, M., Stallworth, L. M., & Murdoch, K. (1998). How what we tell becomes what we know: Listener effects on speakers' long-term memory for events. *Discourse Processes, 26*, 1–25.

Pendell, S. D. (2002). Affection in interpersonal relationships: Not just "a fond or tender feeling". *Communication Yearbook, 26*, 70–115.

Powers, W. G., & Witt, P. L. (2008). Expanding the theoretical framework of communication fidelity. *Communication Quarterly, 56*, 247–267.

Prager, K. J., & Buhrmester, D. (1998). Intimacy and need fulfillment in couple relationships. *Journal of Social and Personal Relationships, 15*, 435–469.

Reis, H. T. (1990). The role of intimacy in interpersonal relations. *Journal of Social & Clinical Psychology, 9*, 15–30.

Rhodes, S. C. (1993). Listening: A relational process. In A. D. Wolvin & C. G. Coakley (Eds.), *Perspectives on listening* (pp. 217–240). Norwood, NJ: Ablex.

Rhodes, S. C., Watson, K. W., & Barker, L. L. (1990). Listening assessment: Trends and influencing factors in the 1980s. *Journal of the International Listening Association, 4*, 62–82.

Ridge, A. (1993). A perspective on listening skills. In A. D. Wolvin & C. G. Coakley (Eds.), *Perspectives on listening* (pp. 1–14). Norwood, NJ: Ablex.

Roberts, C. V., & Vinson, L. (1998). Relationship among Willingness To Listen, Receiver Apprehension, Communication Apprehension, Communication Competence, and Dogmatism. *International Journal of Listening, 12*, 40–56.

Schrodt, P. (2008). The missing link: Listening processes as explanatory mechanisms for the intergenerational transmission of family communication patterns. Paper presented at the annual meeting of the National Communication Association.

Schrodt, P., Wheeless, L. R., & Ptacek, K. M. (2000). Informational reception apprehension, educational motivation, and achievement. *Communication Quarterly, 48*, 60–73.

Steil, L. K., & Bommelje, R. K. (2004). *Listening leaders: The then golden rules to listen, lead, and succeed.* Edina, MN: Beaver's Pond Press.

Sypher, B. D., Bostrom, R. N., & Seibert, J. H. (1989). Listening, communication abilities, and success at work. *Journal of Business Communication, 26*, 293–303.

Villaume, W. A., Brown, M. H., & Darling, R. (1994). Presbycusis, communication, and older adults. In M. L. Hummert, J. M. Wiemann & J. F. Nussbaum (Eds.), *Interpersonal communication in older adulthood: Interdisciplinary theory and research* (pp. 83–106). Thousand Oaks, CA: Sage.

Watanuki, S., Tracy, M. F., & Lindquist, R. (2006). Therapeutic listening. In M. Snyder & R. Lindquist (Eds.), *Complentary/Alternative therapies in nursing* (4th ed., pp. 45–56). New York: Springer.

Watson, K. W., & Barker, L. L. (1984). Listening behavior: Definition and measurement. *Communication Yearbook, 8*, 178–197.

Watson, K. W., Barker, L. L., Roberts, C. V., & Roberts, J. D. (2001). *Watson Barker Listening Test: Video version/Facilitator's guide.* Sautee, GA: SPECTRA.

Weaver, C. (1972). *Human listening: Process and behavior.* Indianapolis: Bobbs-Merrill.

Wilson, S. R., & Sabee, C. M. (2003). Explicating communicative competence as a theoretical term. In J. O. Greene & B. R. Burleson (Eds.), *Handbook of communication and social interaction skills* (pp. 3–50). Mahwah, NJ: Erlbaum.

Zebrowitz, L. A. (2001). Groping for the elephant of interpersonal sensitivity. In J. A. Hall & F. J. Bernieri (Eds.), *Interpersonal sensitivity: Theory and measurement* (pp. 333–350). Mahwah, NJ: Erlbaum.

• CHAPTER EIGHT •

Better Health, Better Lives: The Bright Side of Affection

Kory Floyd
Arizona State University

Douglas M. Deiss
Arizona State University

> Affection is responsible for nine-tenths of whatever solid and durable happiness there is in our lives.
> —C. S. Lewis (1960)

The time and energy humans expend demonstrating love and affection illustrate the extent to which we believe those concepts are the sine qua non of interpersonal relationships. We buy greetings cards and gifts in hopes of capturing just the right sentiment. Couples see romantic movies in which fictional characters express fictional love for one another in a fictional world. Individuals pine over the right time and manner to convey feelings of endearment to a significant other. We plan weekend getaways, romantic dates, and warm moments in an effort to create the intimate opportunities for affection. Indeed, communicating love and affection in personal relationships is a robust and ubiquitous characteristic of human behavior.

If pressed to explain *why*, however, most people are bound to be found wanting. Asking why we love may seem as sensible as asking why we breathe; yet, its very ubiquity raises the possibility that affection—like oxygen—is necessary for human survival and well being. C. S. Lewis's quote acknowledges that we *like to be loved*, but contemporary research provides reason to believe that we, in fact, *need to be loved*. This chapter will articulate many of the benefits that make both expressing and receiving affectionate communication so important to quality human relationships.

The mission of the positive psychology movement is often described as a focus on "the good life" or human flourishing (Sandage & Hill, 2001). Similarly, this chapter focuses on the ways that humans can flourish in many of their relationships across the lifespan. Unlike the research under the "dark side" metaphor, which might concentrate on the misuse of affection in relationships, this chapter illustrates the numerous benefits conferred to those individuals engaging in affectionate behavior. We begin our discussion by identifying the nature of affection and affectionate communication. Next, we describe a model of affectionate communication by explaining the three types of affectionate behavior followed by several theories offering explanations for the presence of affection. Then, we show the relational, mental, and physical benefits of affectionate behavior. We conclude with ideas for future research.

On the Nature of Affection and Affectionate Communication

Across the lifespan, affection is so pervasive within interpersonal communication that one might think volumes would have been written by now explaining why. On the contrary, relatively little scholarly attention has been paid to affectionate behavior until fairly recently, despite the fact that it characterizes the interactions of humans and multiple other species from birth to death. Theoretic and empirical work in the last decade and a half has cast light on the questions of how people communicate affection, why they do so, and why they benefit from doing so. We will summarize that work in this section.

Affection in Human Communication

To call affectionate communication an important part of human interaction is an understatement. Longitudinal research confirms that people who receive more affection as infants experience significantly less emotional distress in adulthood (Maselko et al., 2010). Even among the elderly, affectionate behavior benefits both those who receive it and those who express it (Weisberg & Haberman, 1989). Affection is so important, in fact, that a recent issue of *Scientific American Mind* dubbed it the single most important skill for effective parenting (Epstein, 2010). How is it that people accomplish this critical communication task?

Affection and affectionate communication. Before proceeding, it is instructive to define the term "affection" and to distinguish it from "affectionate communication." As used in contemporary scholarship (see

Floyd, 2006a), "affection" denotes an emotional state of fondness and intense positive regard that one entity experiences for a specific other. We *feel* affection, in other words, and we feel it for a particular person or other entity (such as a pet). Affectionate feelings need not be reciprocated.

By extension, "affectionate communication" encompasses the encoding of messages that connote affectionate feelings and the expression of those messages from the entity purportedly experiencing the affection to the entity to which the affection is directed. Whereas affection is something we *feel*, therefore, affectionate communication is something we *do*. Two clarifications on the definition of affectionate communication are important to note. First, the expression of affectionate feelings must be directed at the target of those feelings. If Megan feels affection for Luke, she is not engaging in affectionate communication if she discloses her feelings to Abby. Second, as we briefly note later in this chapter, the expression of affection need not be reciprocated.

Differentiating affection and affectionate communication is critical for at least two reasons, the first of which is that, although they overlap substantially, they do not necessarily covary. One can easily have affectionate feelings that, for a variety of reasons, one chooses not to convey to the target of those feelings. And, just as it is possible to have feelings one does not express, it is possible to express feelings one does not have. "Affectionate communication" includes the expression of insincere or false affection, as when one partner says, "I love you" only to induce sexual interaction on the part of the other. Although felt affection is often communicated, and expressed affection is often genuine, neither can be assumed.

The second reason why differentiating affection and affectionate communication is important is that the research reported in this chapter is about the benefits of affectionate communication, not affection per se. Although much of the research on the benefits of affectionate communication has focused on the positive aspects of *receiving* affectionate expressions, several recent studies have confirmed that *sending* affectionate messages is also beneficial, above and beyond the benefits associated with affection that is received in return. In either case, however, it is the communication of affection—rather than the emotional experience of it—that is associated with those benefits.

A tripartite model of affectionate communication. Specifying that "affectionate communication" comprises those behaviors through which feelings of affection are conveyed begs the question of what those behaviors are, exactly. Floyd and Morman (1998) recognized that affection can be—and is—expressed in myriad ways in personal relationships, and that some relationships may favor particular modes of expressing affection over others. Their tripartite model of affectionate behavior adds conceptual and operational clarity to the issue by distinguishing between three forms of affection display.

The *verbal* communication of affection consists of spoken or written affectionate expressions, such as "I love you," "I care about you," and "You mean so much to me." The *direct nonverbal* communication of affection includes non-linguistic or paralinguistic behaviors that denote affection within the relationship or speech community in which they are enacted. In North America, those behaviors routinely include hugging, kissing, and holding hands. In fact, the research conducted on adult "play" by Aune and Wong (see chapter 8, in this volume) may provide additional examples of both verbal and direct nonverbal forms of affectionate behavior. Finally, *indirect nonverbal* communication is composed of behaviors that connote—rather than denote—affection via the provision of social or material support. Those may include actions such as helping with a task or lending the use of a car. Unlike with verbal and direct nonverbal expressions, the affectionate message in indirect nonverbal expressions is ancillary to the behavior itself, and is consequently less overt.

Why People are Affectionate

Why is affectionate communication a part of the human behavioral repertoire in the first place? The available evidence immediately eschews a socio-cultural, anthropocentric explanation. Although cultural variation exists in *how* people express affection, there is no such variation in *whether* they do; affectionate behavior characterizes interpersonal interaction in every known human culture (Floyd, 2006a). Affectionate communication is likewise not limited to *Homo sapiens*, but characterizes a wide range of both mammalian and non-mammalian species (Floyd, 2006a). Those observations—especially when considered in tandem—warrant re-framing the question to ask *for what purposes would the tendency toward affectionate communication have evolved?*

Three theories, in particular, shed light on that question. Among those theories, the most commonly tested in affection research is Floyd's (2006a) *affection exchange theory* (AET). AET is a neo-Darwinian theory, meaning that it incorporates as axiomatic assumptions the foundational principles of Darwin's (1859) theory of evolution by means of natural selection. Specifically, Floyd, Pauley, and Hesse (2010) argue that engaging in affectionate expression is adaptive insofar as it enhances the ability of individuals to survive and procreate. AET reasons that if affectionate behavior is adaptive in those ways, then physiological systems exist to make it physically and emotionally rewarding. Indeed, as we describe below, experimental research has documented that reduction in stress hormones and increases in pleasure-providing hormones occur in the wake of affectionate behavior and are largely responsible for the physical and emotional rewards that accompany it. AET therefore provides that affectionate behavior produces positive outcomes because of the physiological activity it induces, but that it induces specific physiological activity *because of the adaptive benefits affectionate behavior conveys*. We will say more about the specific adaptive benefits of affectionate communication later in this section.

Two other theories offer similar but slightly divergent explanations for the benefits of affectionate behavior. First, Baumeister and Leary's (1995) *need to belong theory* (NBT) argues that close, intimate relationships are so fundamental a human need that failing to form and maintain them is physically and psychologically aversive. Importantly, NBT provides that, to satisfy their need to belong, people require not just the emotion of affection but also the manifestation of it. From that theoretic perspective, relationships are unsatisfactory if they provide affectionate feelings in the absence of affectionate interaction (as in a long-distance marriage) or if they provide affectionate interaction in the absence of affectionate feelings (as in an anonymous sexual encounter). According to NBT, affectionate behavior is positive because it meets a fundamental drive for attachment and affiliation. Second, Taylor et al.'s (2000) *tend-and-befriend theory* (TBT) proposes that expressing feelings of care to loved ones—and receiving such expressions in return—benefits people in times of acute stress by accelerating their physiological recovery from elevated stress. TBT further proposes that the stress-alleviating benefit of affectionate behavior is more pronounced for women than for men because it is driven principally by the peptide hormone oxytocin, which is more bioactive in females than in males.

Importantly, although each theory takes a slightly different focus, all three theories provide explanations for affectionate behavior that are not limited to particular species, specific cultures, or precise historical, political, or economic circumstances. Rather, the gist of all three theories' explanation for why humans (or other species) are affectionate is that *affectionate communication is adaptive,* meaning that it contributes in some way to the survival and/or replication of one's genes. For instance, the tendency to eat regularly is adaptive because it ensures a steady supply of nutrients, which are essential for survival. Likewise, the tendency to have sex is adaptive because humans are a sexually reproducing species, so sexual activity ensures species proliferation.

The tendency to give and receive affectionate communication may be similarly adaptive. Although a hug and kiss do not directly provide nutrients or facilitate insemination, they contribute benefits that are important for both survival and reproduction. Several specific examples follow in the next three sections. First, we examine the advantages of affectionate communication for mental health and well-being. Second, we investigate the role of affectionate communication in managing the body's stress response. Finally, we explore the contribution of affectionate communication for general physical health and competence.

Affectionate Communication has Mental Health Benefits

Expressing affection appears to be associated with enhanced mental health, as indexed by multiple operational outcomes. Floyd (2002) and Floyd et al. (2005) found that, in comparison to non-affectionate peers, highly affectionate people reported greater levels of happiness, self-esteem and comprehensive mental health. Further, non-affectionate individuals had higher levels of stress and depression. Those findings applied both to the sending and the receiving of affectionate messages. Importantly, however, Floyd et al. (2005) illustrated that although receiving and expressing affection share some variance, the expression of affection accounts for a significant portion of unique variance in mental and physical health measures even after the effects of received affection are controlled. For example, bivariate correlations between expressed affection and mental health were as follows: happiness ($r = .53$), self-esteem ($r = .40$), and comprehensive mental health ($r = .42$). In comparison, correlations between expressed affection and mental health controlling for received affection, were: happiness ($r = .37$), self-esteem ($r = .25$), and comprehensive mental health ($r = .20$). Although the strength of the relationships was reduced, the partial correlations remained significant: Those findings indicate that giving affection was associated with mental health benefits that were above and beyond those produced by any affection received in return.

In addition, studies on affection have illustrated relationships with several other mental health variables. The deprivation of love and affection is associated with psychosomatic illness in adults (Komisaruk & Whipple, 1998) and children (Janov, 2000). Experimentally, Shuntich and Shapiro (1991) found a negative association between affection and physical and verbal aggression in family relationships. Other mental health issues related to the exchange of affectionate communication include psychological well-being (Green & Wildermuth, 1993; Prager & Buhmester, 1998; Quinn, 1983), self-esteem (Barber & Thomas, 1986; Roberts & Bengtson, 1996), loneliness (Downs & Javidi, 1990), and depression (Mackinnon, Henderson, & Andrews, 1993; Oliver et al., 1993).

Affectionate Communication Aids Stress Alleviation

Although there is substantial research on the mental health benefits of affectionate communication, there is an equal focus of research on the effect of affectionate behavior on the human experience of stress. That is, affectionate communication has been shown to enhance recovery from stress, both cognitively and physiologically.

The Threat of Stress

Despite variation, most scholarly definitions identify *stress* as the body's response to any perceived threat to its well being (Cohen, Kessler, & Gordon, 1995; Selye, 1976). Such threats come in the form of *stressors*, which can be either acute (e.g., the threat of an upcoming performance review) or chronic (e.g., the threat of ongoing homelessness). Research on stress has tended to focus on the body's ability either to regulate it (*stress buffering*) or to recover from it (*stress recovery*).

Stress Buffering and Regulation

Affectionate communication has the ability to temper the threat of stressors on physical reactivity. Individuals who feel that they are receiving emotional help or support from their partner have been shown to experience a buffer against the experience of stress (Berkman, 1988; Kessler & Essex, 1982). A buffer is anything that offsets the adverse physiological effects of stress. Individuals who experience a stress buffer have comparatively lower-magnitude physiological responses to stressors. That is important to human health because exaggerated physiological reactivity to stressors has multiple comorbidities, including heart disease (Shively, Musselman, & Willard, 2009) and disruptions of immune system functioning (Cohen & Wills, 1985).

Some research has focused on the ability of affectionate communication to act as a buffer against the effects of acute (short-term) stressors. This research has often used the steroid hormone cortisol as a marker for stress. When exposed to physical, emotional, or mental stressors, cortisol is released into the body, thus giving it the nickname, "the stress hormone." For an individual who experiences an injury, cortisol has the role of suppressing one's immune system in an attempt to keep one's body from overreacting and damaging sensitive tissue (see Nicholson, 2008). Cortisol also suppresses the body's nonessential physiological systems once the body is exposed to a stressor. That has the advantage of allowing the body's energy to be devoted to the stressor itself instead of nonessential processes, including digestion and reproduction. Research analyzing the effects of various behaviors on one's stress levels examines the 24-hour variation of cortisol. Consequently, an indicator of chronic stress is a low level of 24-hour variation.

Floyd (2006b) hypothesized that giving and receiving high levels of affection, as a trait, would be adaptive with respect to stress management. This research analyzed the effects of both expressed and received affection on 24-hour variation in the healthy adults' level of the hormone cortisol. He found a correlation between trait levels of affectionate communication and the ability to handle stress. Additionally, affection was found to be strongly and positively related to the extent of morning-to-evening decrease in cortisol levels. This finding indicates an increased adaptive ability to handle stressful situations for highly affectionate expressers or receivers. That is, trait affection buffers the effects of stress on the individual's body. In another correlational study examining the diurnal variation in cortisol, Floyd and Riforgiate (2008) discovered that partner assessments of verbal, nonverbal, and supportive affection given predicted the degree of morning to evening cortisol change in their spouse. This research supports the notion that affectionate communication from one's significant other is positively associated with hormonal stress regulation and may provide stress-ameliorating physiological effects.

Further, experimental research has strengthened evidence of the buffering effect of affectionate communication. Floyd et al. (2007a) collected participants' assessments of the degree of affection present in their closest relationships to establish if affection reduces the physiological effects of acute stress on an individual. Those who indicated high levels of verbal and supportive affectionate communication had lower resting heart rate and a minimized increase of the stress hormone cortisol during an acute stressful interaction compared to those with low levels of affectionate communication. This supports the notion that affection from either a close romantic partner or more generally a member of our close social network can offset the physiological experience of stress (see also Floyd, Pauley, & Hesse, 2010).

Stress Recovery

In addition to stress buffering or regulation, affectionate communication has also been shown to provide a stress recovery effect. That is, individuals who experience affectionate communication find that their bodies return to physiological baseline after a stressful encounter quicker than those individuals who lack the experience of affection. The research of the effects of affectionate communication on stress recovery utilizes one of several stress-induction strategies. This section will examine the various ways in which affectionate communication speeds up one's return to baseline levels after such experimental stress inductions. Specifically, the work on affectionate writing offers support for the role that the expression of affection plays in recovery from the physiological effects of acute stress.

Just as affectionate writing buffers the stress experience by reducing one's total cholesterol levels, this form of affectionate communication can also quicken a person's recovery from a stressor. Floyd et al. (2007b) exposed participants to a series of standard laboratory stress inductions. These inductions involve several specific procedures that are commonly used in experimental stress research, including cold pressor, mental arithmetic, and Stroop Color-Word Test.

Floyd et al. (2007b) elevated participants' stress by utilizing the induction techniques above and then assigned participants to either the experimental or control groups. The experimental group wrote a letter to a loved one whereby they expressed their feelings of affection for that person, while those in control group 1 thought about their loved one without any writing, and those in control group 2 just sat quietly for the same period of time. Researchers then measured each individual's salivary free cortisol, the steroid hormone found in a person's saliva. In comparison to the control groups, those individuals in the experimental group experienced faster cortisol recovery—the return of cortisol to baseline values—following the various stress inductions.

Affection Aids General Physical Competence

In addition to stress buffering and regulation, affectionate behavior also increases an individual's general physical competence. Specifically, being able to direct one's affection toward a significant other can have health benefits for the affectionate communicator. Based on the work of Pennebaker's written disclosure paradigm (Pennebaker, 1993; Pennebaker, Hughes, & O'Heeron, 1987; Pennebaker, Kiecolt-Glaser, & Glaser, 1988), affectionate writing research has investigated the effects of having participants write for short periods of time to a loved one (Floyd et al., 2007). These writing periods have been structured to induce participants to express affectionate communication to a loved one in the physical absence of the other person.

The research of Floyd et al. (2007) focused on the ability of written affectionate expressions to modulate serum cholesterol levels. Cholesterol is a lipid that is elevated in response to stress (McCann et al., 1995). Chronically elevated cholesterol, or hypercholesterolemia, is a known contributor to coronary heart disease; thus, there are important health implications of the ability of affectionate behavior to affect lipid levels. In this research, healthy college students were randomly assigned either to control or experimental groups. Although control groups wrote about generic topics, those in the experimental groups wrote about their positive, affectionate feelings for romantic partners, relatives, and/or close friends for 20 minutes at three separate intervals. Participants' total cholesterol was measured at the beginning and end of the experimental trials. Those individuals writing affectionate letters exhibited statistically significant decreases in total cholesterol, compared to those in the control groups.

According to affection exchange theory, the communication of affection bolsters the body's capacity to deal effectively and efficiently with stressors. Based upon this premise, Floyd et al. (2010) argued that communicating affection should increase physical health thereby enhancing the body's capacity to manage stress. In order to measure this, individuals were invited to a clinical research center where they reported expressed and received trait affectionate communication and their resting pulse rate was assessed and blood samples were drawn through venipuncture. Their blood was assayed in order to assess natural killer cell cytotoxicity and immunoglobulins A and M.

These physiological indicators have direct implications for a person's health. Resting pulse rate indicates the number of cardiac contractions taking place during a specific time frame when a person is awake and resting. Chronic stress elevates resting pulse rate (Buckley & Kaloupek, 2001). Numerous investigations have indicated the link between resting pulse rate and cardiovascular mortality and coronary heart disease (Dyer et al., 1980; Gillum, Makuc, & Feldman, 1991; Kannel, et al., 1987; Schroll & Hangerup, 1977). Natural killer cells, a part of the innate immune system, protect the body against cells infected by viruses as well as tumors (Whiteside & Herberman, 1995). The cells' success in defending the body is known as their cytotoxicity, which can be reduced through exposure to chronic stress (Zorrilla et al., 2001). Finally, immunoglobulins A and M are a component of the body's immune response that help to recognize and deactivate pathogens that may cause harm to a person. These specific immunoglobulins have been shown to negatively relate to overall and psychological stress (Herbert & Cohen, 1993).

Floyd et al. (2010) found that after controlling for affection received, expressed affection significantly predicted resting pulse rate = -.40. Further, after controlling for participant sex and received affection, expressed affection significantly predicted natural killer cell cytotoxicity = .43. Finally, after controlling for participant sex and received affection, expressed affection did significantly predict immunoglobulin M = .36, but not immunoglobulin A. Therefore, the more affectionate individuals are, the lower their resting heart rate is and the better their immune system can react to external stressors.

Several studies have investigated the health benefits of affectionate touch, specifically. Physical affection in the form of touch has been associated with cardiovascular arousal modulation (Diamond, 1999), pain relief (Fishman, Turkheimer, & DeGood, 1995), and decreased blood pressure. Increasing the amount of warm touch—such as affectionate cuddling behavior—within couples has a significant and advantageous effect on stress systems including blood pressure and salivary cortisol (Holt-Lunstad, Birmingham, & Light, 2008).

Hugging is another specific form of physical affection that has health advantages. Light, Grewen, and Amico (2005) found that for women, the number of reported hugs they received from their male romantic partners was negatively related to their resting systolic and diastolic blood pressures. With elevated blood pressure being indicative of increased levels of stress, any affectionate behavior (e.g., hugs) that can reduce this physiological indicator suggests a reduction in the stress experience.

Future Looks at Affectionate Communication

The communication of affection is so fundamental to interpersonal experience that its study offers much promise for understanding and improving the human condition. Although current research has illuminated much of the "bright side" of affectionate communication, future work can extend that goal in at least three fruitful ways.

As we detailed in this chapter, one of the most important applications of current work—and directions for future research—relates to the improvement of mental and physical health. As experiments identify how affectionate communication is associated with stress management, immunocompetence, mental and emotional regulation, and other aspects of well-being, those findings may aid in the development of behavioral interventions that could serve as ancillary treatments for physical and mental disorders. Although that research is in its infancy, its promise is substantial.

AET's explanation of the relationship between affectionate behavior and reproduction also has potential for the understanding and prevention of sexual assault. To the extent that rape and other forms of sexual assault occur within familiar relationships, they may be preceded by insincere affectionate expressions that are intended to persuade the victim that sexual interaction is warranted. Indeed, in a survey of over a thousand American college students, Floyd et al. (2006; cited in Floyd, 2006a) found that "initiating sexual activity" was one of the most common reasons why individuals reported having expressed non-genuine verbal affection to others. With respect to understanding and preventing sexual assault, the important question is not why one person would use an affectionate expression to coax another into sexual interaction, but why such a strategy would be successful. The explanation offered by AET is that it is evolutionarily adaptive for humans to attend to affectionate expressions as signals of another's potential fitness as a mate and parent. Therefore, receiving an affectionate expression that is believed (by the recipient) to be sincere may be sufficiently persuasive, in many instances, to allow ill-advised or otherwise unwanted sexual interaction.

Finally, to the extent that expressed affection predicts relational stability and satisfaction, it may prove to be a successful ancillary to marital and relational therapy. Research by Floyd et al. (2009) has already shown that increasing nonverbal forms of affectionate behavior in romantic relationships elevates relationship satisfaction. It is possible that a type of subconscious feedback loop exists wherein the mind begins to perceive greater satisfaction with relationships in which the body is enacting more positive behaviors, such as affectionate expressions. Future experimental work could verify the pathways and limitations of such an approach.

Although there are real risks associated with the expression of affection, the benefits conferred to those individuals are so advantageous, it is easy to see why affection makes us feel as good as it does. One of the more positive themes derived from the affectionate communication research is that various relational types reap the benefits, thus expanding the inclusion criteria to behaviors experienced in families, romantic couples, and other relationships. At any one time, even those individuals devoid of a romantic partner can express affection to family members; and even those without family members can still write expressively in an attempt to offset the impact of life's stressors. For a behavior so ubiquitous, most individuals experience affection without any thought for its true advantages; yet, they acquire the advantages nonetheless. What this research suggests is that affection can be increased in an effort to bolster a person's relationships, mental or physical health, and finally the individual's stress response. Whether planned or unplanned, being affectionate increases our quality of life. Hopefully, after reading this chapter, not only can a person distinguish between affection and affectionate behavior, but also they can understand a little more about just how much of our happiness is shaped by the affectionate communication we share with those closest to us.

References

Barber, B. K., & Thomas, D. L. (1986). Dimensions of fathers' and mothers' supportive behavior: The case for physical affection. *Journal of Marriage and the Family, 48,* 783–794.

Baumeister, R. F., & Leary, M. R. (1995). The need to belong: Desire for interpersonal attachments as a fundamental human motivation. *Psychological Bulletin, 117,* 497–529.

Beckman, N., Waern, M., Gustafson, D. & Skoog, I. (2008). Secular trends in self-reported sexual activity and satisfation in Swedish 70-year-olds: Cross-sectional survey of four populations, 1971–2001. *British Medical Journal, 337,* 337-344. doi: 10.1136/bmj.a279

Berkman, L. F. (1988). The changing and heterogeneous nature of aging and longevity: A social and biomedical perspective. *Annual Reviews in Gerontology and Geriatrics, 8,* 37–68.

Buckley, T. C., & Kaloupek, D. G. (2001). A meta-analytic examination of basal cardiovascular activity in posttraumatic stress disorder. *Psychosomatic Medicine, 63,* 585–594.

Cohen, S., Kessler, R. C., & Gordon, U. L. (1995). Strategies for measuring stress in studies of psychiatric and physical disorder. In S. Cohen, R. C. Kessler, & U. L. Gordon (Eds.), *Measuring stress: A guide for health and social scientists* (pp. 3–26). New York: Oxford University Press.

Cohen, S., & Wills, T. A. (1985). Stress, social support, and the buffering hypothesis. *Psychological Bulletin, 98,* 310–357.

Darwin, C. (1859). *On the origin of species*. London: J. Murray.

Diamond, L. M. (March, 1999). Are friends as good as lovers? Attachment, physical affection, and effects on cardiovascular arousal in young women's closest relationships, *Dissertation Abstracts International, Section B: The Sciences and Engineering, 60*(8-B), 4272.

Downs, V. C., & Javidi, M. (1990). Linking communication motives to loneliness in the lives of older adults: An empirical test of interpersonal needs and gratifications. *Journal of Applied Communication Research, 18,* 32–48.

Dyer, A. R., Persky, V., Stamler, J., Paul, O., Shekelle, R. B., Berkson, D. M., ... Lindberg, H. A. (1980). Heart rate as a prognostic factor for coronary heart disease and mortality: Findings in three Chicago epidemiologic studies. *American Journal of Epidemiology, 112,* 736–749.

Epstein, R. (2010, November/December). What makes a good parent? *Scientific American Mind,* pp. 46–51.

Fishman, E., Turkheimer, E., & DeGood, D. (1995). Touch relieves stress and pain. *Journal of Behavioral Medicine, 18,* 69–79.

Floyd, K. (2002). Human affection exchange: V. Attributes of the highly affectionate. *Communication Quarterly, 50*, 135–152.

Floyd, K. (2006a). *Communicating affection: Interpersonal behavior and social context.* Cambridge: Cambridge University Press.

Floyd, K. (2006b). Human affection exchange: XII. Affectionate communication is associated with diurnal variation in salivary free cortisol. *Western Journal of Communication, 70*, 47–63.

Floyd, K., Boren, J. P., Hannawa, A. F., Hesse, C., McEwan, B., & Veksler, A. E. (2009). Kissing in marital and cohabiting relationships: Effects on blood lipids, stress, and relationship satisfaction. *Western Journal of Communication, 73*, 113–133.

Floyd, K., Hess, J., Miczo, L., Halone, K., Mikkelson, A., & Tusing, K. (2005). Human affection exchange: VIII. Further evidence of the benefits of expressed affection. *Communication Quarterly, 53*, 285–303.

Floyd, K., Mikkelson, A., Hesse, C., & Pauley, P. (2007). Affectionate writing reduces total cholesterol: Two randomized, controlled trials. *Human Communication Research, 33*, 119–142.

Floyd, K., Mikkelson, A. C., Tafoya, M. A., Farinelli, L., La Valley, A. G., Judd, J., ... Wilson, J. (2007a). Human affection exchange: XIII. Affectionate communication accelerates neuroendocrine stress recovery. *Health Communication, 22*, 123–132.

Floyd, K., Mikkelson, A., Tafoya, M., Farinelli, L., La Valley, A., Judd, J.,...Wilson, J. (2007b). Human affection exchange: XIV. Relational affection predicts resting heart rate and free cortisol secretion during acute stress. *Behavioral Medicine, 32*, 151–156.

Floyd, K., & Morman, M. T. (1998). The measurement of affectionate communication. *Communication Quarterly, 46*, 144–162.

Floyd, K., Pauley, P. M., & Hesse, C. (2010). State and trait affectionate communication buffer adults' stress reactions. *Communication Monographs, 77*, 622–640.

Floyd, K., Pauley, P. M., Hesse, C., Veksler, A. E., Eden, J., & Mikkelson, A. C. (2010). *Affectionate communication predicts immunologic and cardiologic health markers.* Manuscript submitted for publication.

Floyd, K., & Riforgiate, S. (2008). Affectionate communication received from spouses predicts stress hormone levels in healthy adults. *Communication Monographs, 75*, 351–368.

Gillum, R. F., Makuc, D. M., & Feldman, J. J. (1991). Pulse rate, coronary heart disease, and death: The NHANES I epidemiologic follow-up study. *American Heart Journal, 121*, 172–177.

Green, V. A., & Wildermuth, N. L. (1993). Self-focus, other-focus, and interpersonal needs as correlates of loneliness. *Psychological Reports, 73*, 843–850.

Herbert, T. B., & Cohen, S. (1993). Stress and immunity in humans: A meta-analytic review. *Psychosomatic Medicine, 55*, 364–379.

Holt-Lunstad, J., Birmingham, W. A., & Light, K. C., (2008). Influence of a "warm touch" support enhancement intervention among married couples on ambulatory blood pressure, oxytocin, alpha amylase, and cortisol. *Psychosomatic Medicine, 70*, 976–985.

Janov, A. (2000). *The biology of love.* Amherst, NY: Prometheus.

Kannel, W. B., Kannel, C., Paffenbarger, R. S., & Cupples, L. A. (1987). Heart rate and cardiovascular mortality: The Framingham study. *American Heart Journal, 113*, 1489–1494.

Kessler, R. C., & Essex, M. (1982). Marital status and depression: The importance of coping resources. *Social Forces, 61,* 484–507.

Komisaruk, B. R., & Whipple, B. (1998). Love as sensory stimulation: Physiological consequences of its deprivation and expression. *Psychoneuroendocrinology, 23,* 927–944.

Lewis, C. S. (1960). *The four loves.* New York: Harcourt, Brace & World.

Light, K. C., Grewen, K. M., & Amico, J. A. (2005). More frequent partner hugs and higher oxytocin levels are linked to lower blood pressure and heart rate in premenopausal women. *Biological Psychology, 69,* 5–21.

Mackinnon, A., Henderson, A. S., & Andrews, G. (1993). Parental "affectionless control" as an antecedent to adult depression: A risk factor refined. *Psychological Medicine, 23,* 135–141.

Maselko, J., Kubzansky, L., Lipsitt, L., & Buka, S. L. (2010). Mother's affection at 8 months predicts emotional distress in adulthood. *Journal of Epidemiology and Community Health.* doi:10.1136/jech.2009.097873

McCann, B. S., Magee, M. S., Broyles, F. C., Vaughan, M., Albers, J. J., & Knopp, R. H. (1995). Acute psychological stress and epinephrine infusion in normolipidemic and hyperlipidemic men: Effects of plasma lipid and apoprotein concentrations. *Psychosomatic Medicine, 57,* 165–176.

Nicholson, N. A. (2008). Measurement of cortisol. In L. J. Luecken & L. C. Gallo (Eds.), *Handbook of physiological research methods in health psychology* (pp. 37–74). Thousand Oaks, CA: Sage.

Oliver, J. M., Raftery, M., Reeb, A., & Delaney, P. (1993). Perceptions of parent-offspring relationships as functions of depression in offspring: "Affectionless control," "negative bias," and "depressive realism." *Journal of Social Behavior and Personality, 8,* 405–424.

Pennebaker, J. W. (1993). Putting stress into words: Health, linguistic, and therapeutic implications. *Behaviour Research and Therapy, 31,* 539–548.

Pennebaker, J. W., Hughes, C. F., & O'Heeron, R. C. (1987). The psychophysiology of confession: Linking inhibitory and psychosomatic processes. *Journal of Personality and Social Psychology, 52,* 781–793.

Pennebaker, J. W., Kiecolt-Glaser, J. K., & Glaser, R. (1988). Disclosure of traumas and immune function: Health implications for psychotherapy. *Journal of Consulting and Clinical Psychology, 56,* 239–245.

Prager, K. J., & Buhrmester, D. (1998). Intimacy and need fulfillment in couple relationships. *Journal of Social and Personal Relationships, 15,* 435469.

Quinn, W. H. (1983). Personal and family adjustment in later life. *Journal of Marriage and the Family, 45,* 57–73.

Roberts, R. E. L., & Bengtson, V. L. (1996). Affective ties to parents in early adulthood and self-esteem across 20 years. *Social Psychology Quarterly, 59,* 96–106.

Sandage, S. J., & Hill, P. C. (2001). The virtues of positive psychology: The rapprochement and challenges of an affirmative postmodern perspective. *Journal for the Theory of Social Behaviour, 31,* 241–260.

Schroll, M., & Hangerup, L. M. (1977). Risk factors of myocardial infarction and death in men aged 50 at entry: A ten-year prospective study from the Glostrup Population Studies. *Danish Medical Bulletin, 24,* 252–255.

Selye, H. (1976). Forty years of stress research: Principal remaining problems and misconceptions. *Canadian Medical Association Journal, 115,* 53–56.

Shively, C. A., Musselman, D. L., & Willard, S. L. (2009). Stress, depression, and coronary artery disease: Modeling comorbidity in female primates. *Neuroscience and Biobehavioral Reviews, 33,* 133–144.

Shuntich, R. J., & Shapiro, R. M. (1991). Explorations of verbal affection and aggression. *Journal of Social Behavior & Personality, 6,* 283–300.

Taylor, S. E., Klein, L. C., Lewis, B. P., Gruenewald, T. L., Gurung, R. A. R., & Updegraff, J. A. (2000). Biobehavioral responses to stress in females: Tend-and-befriend, not fight-or-flight. *Psychological Review, 107,* 411–429.

Weisberg, J., & Haberman, M. R. (1989). A therapeutic hugging week in a geriatric facility. *Journal of Gerontological Social Work, 13,* 181–186.

Whiteside, T., & Herberman, R. (1995). The role of natural killer cells in immune surveillance of cancer. *Current Opinion in Immunology, 7,* 704–710.

Zorrilla, E. P., Luborsky, L., McKay, J. R., Rosenthal, R., Houldin, A., Tax, A., ... Schmidt, K. (2001). The relationship of depression and stressors to immunological assay: A meta-analytic review. *Brain, Behavior, and Immunity, 15,* 199–226.

• CHAPTER NINE •

Fun with Friends, Pranks with Partners: How We Play in Our Closest Relationships

Krystyna S. Aune
University of Hawaii at Manoa

Norman C. H. Wong
University of Oklahoma

Play is a pervasive activity associated with children and their psychosocial development. What is fascinating and yet perplexing is how there is no specific feature of a message or behavior that defines it as play. Play can include warm and pleasant behaviors such as hugging, but can also include antisocial activities such as kicking. What distinguishes play from other activities is the attitude and emotional state of the interactants. Play involves behaviors that are perceived as lighthearted, enjoyable, humorous, or entertaining (Carpenter & Aune, 1997).

Play has been shown to help foster cognitive and social development. Numerous studies have found that play helps to promote children's creativity and problem-solving skills, as well as contribute to their overall psychological well-being (Handler, 1999). The bulk of research on play focuses on children's play (e.g., Broadhead, 2009; Piaget, 1945/1951) or play between animals (e.g., Palagi, Cordoni, & Tarli, 2004). Comparatively less research attention has focused on play in adulthood. Some exceptions include Abramis' (1990) study of play at work, Lin's (2010) research on play between children and adults, Doster et al.'s (2006) study on the therapeutic benefits of play for adults, and Betcher's (1981) research on therapeutic play in couples.

Extending Betcher's (1981) clinical work, Baxter (1992) outlined a taxonomy of the forms and functions of adult play within personal relationships. Based on her research, play among adults was enacted in a variety of forms (e.g., idioms, role-playing, teasing, physical play, games, gossiping, and public performance) and hypothesized to serve a wide range of positive relational functions, including: providing an index of intimacy, a moderator of conflict, a strategy for testing potentially embarrassing actions, a creative outlet for individual expression, a way to communicate, and a promoter of intimacy. Play was significantly related to closeness in same-sex friendships and romantic relationships.

Since Baxter's study was published, a few communication studies have examined adult play: Bruess and Pearson's (1993) study of idiom use in marriage; Aune et al.'s (1993) study of relational messages associated with persona sharing (a public performance form of play); and Bombar and Littig's (1996) study on babytalk in romantic relationships and friendships. Aune and Wong (2002) found that humor orientation and self-esteem were significant predictors of playfulness in relationships, and playfulness was associated with the experience of positive emotions, which in turn was associated with relationship satisfaction.

Thus, play has been studied as positive relational behavior that serves multiple functions related to the development and maintenance of a personal relationship. This is likely because a variety of relational messages can be expressed through play, including similarity, informality, level of emotional arousal and activation, and intimacy (Burgoon & Hale, 1984). While it is apparent that play is a significant feature of childhood and adulthood, much more remains to be investigated. This chapter examines the nature and positive relational functions of play in two salient relationship types: romantic relationships and friendship. At the outset, we explore the literature on friendship and romantic relationships.

Friendship and Romantic Relationships

Friendship is a social context that reflects a wide range of relationships providing relational satisfaction and rewards. Informal rules are applied in friendships in order to maximize rewards and minimize the conflicts. Exchange rules in friendships involve such things as emotional support, sharing news, repaying debts, etc. Intimacy rules reflect the notions of trust and confidence. In contrast with romantic partners, third-party rules among friends include not being jealous of other relationships, not criticizing, and respecting privacy (Argyle & Henderson, 1984). Despite the lack of consistent conceptualizations, what is evident is that friendship allows people to be genuine, open, and less constrained than within other relationship types.

In contrast to friendships, people typically are more emotionally dependent on their romantic relationships. Romantic relationships are often more important to one's self-definition and more rewarding than other relationships (Aune & Comstock, 1991). Romantic relationships encompass emotional, cognitive, and motivational characteristics which Sternberg (1986) labeled intimacy, passion, and commitment. Intimacy involves psychological closeness, passion entails romantic desire, and commitment is the cognitive decision to remain with the partner. Friendship may involve the dimensions of closeness and commitment, however it does not traditionally entail passion.

Rules for romantic relationships generally prescribe interdependence and exclusivity, whereas friendship rules prescribe greater autonomy and equitable instrumental exchange (Argyle & Henderson, 1984, 1985; Baxter, 2001). A key aspect of friendship is simply having fun and relaxing together. Relative to acquaintances, friends use more idiomatic communication, joking and teasing. Baxter (1992) noted that the culture of friendship entails an activity orientation, behavioral rituals, and routines. In contrast, romantic pairs are marked by the centrality of feeling states. Canary et al. (1993) found that positivity, openness, and assurances were used more than expected in romantic relationships, but less than expected in friendship. Relative to friends, romantic partners use more maintenance strategies. This affective orientation in romantic relationships may be due to the importance of pair bonding.

The significance of specific play behaviors may be subordinate to the overall satisfaction experienced from playfulness in a romantic relationship, relative to a friendship. In fact, while Baxter (1992) found that overall playfulness was associated with closeness in both romantic relationships and friendships, quantitative indicators of play were not associated with closeness in romantic relationships. For friends, the number of play instances and the breadth of different play forms were positively correlated with perceived closeness.

Many questions remain regarding the nature, forms, and effects of play across these two salient relationship contexts. Play clearly serves important functions in both friendships and romantic relationships, and our goal here is to further examine the relationships between play and positive relationship outcomes across these contexts. As such, two studies were designed to revisit Baxter's seminal work on play. The first utilizes a diary method to examine the prevalence of use of the original types of play to determine the utility of Baxter's play typology. Further, this study compares friends and romantic partners on the types and prevalence of play forms. Study one utilizes a diary method to examine the following research questions:

> RQ1: How frequently do friends and romantic partners engage in play?
>
> RQ2: Is frequency of play associated with perceived relationship solidarity and satisfaction among friends and romantic partners?
>
> RQ3: Do the perceived appropriateness, effectiveness, and uniqueness of play differ between friends and romantic partners?
>
> RQ4: Do the perceived functions of play differ between friends and romantic partners?

Study One Method

Participants

The sample included 56 females and 36 males in a same-sex or cross-sex friendship, and 33 females and 31 males involved in a romantic relationship. Participants were recruited from various speech communication classes at a large Western university and via snowball sampling. Participation was voluntary and confidential.

The overall sample was culturally diverse, with the following breakdown: Japanese/Okinawan (20.5%), Caucasian (19.2%), Filipino (10.9%), Chinese (10.3%), Mixed (9.0%), Hawaiian/Part-Hawaiian (5.8%), Pacific Islander (3.8%), African-American (3.2%), and Hispanic (3.2%). Twenty-two participants (14.1%) marked "Other" as their response to the cultural background question. In terms of relationship status, participants included those currently in a same-sex friendship (26.9%) or cross-sex friendship (30.8%), serious/exclusive daters (23.7%), cohabitators (10.3%), engaged couples (4.5%), and married couples (3.8%). The mean relationship length among friends was 27.35 months, $SD = 33.01$ months, minimum = 1 month, maximum = 122 months. The mean relationship length among romantic partners was 31.81 months, $SD = 31.09$ months, minimum was 1 month, maximum was 140 months.

Procedures

Participants from several communication classes were given two survey packets, one for them to complete, the other to ask their friend or romantic partner to complete. The packet contained survey instructions, a copy of the play diary survey, and a return envelope. For each play instance, participants were asked to provide the following: (a) date of the play episode, (b) approximate time of the play episode, (c) the context in which the play occurred (e.g., school, home, work, etc.), (d) what prompted the playful act, (e) what was said/done, (e) what was the response, (f) who initiated the playful act, (g) who was the target of the playful act, (h) whether the play was reciprocated or not, and (i) whether the target's response was positive or negative. The researcher briefly defined play as "a lighthearted and spontaneous dyadic exchange that can be verbal or nonverbal in nature." Participants were told that play comes in many forms and the important thing to remember was to log down instances they considered to be "playful" in nature. The researcher instructed the participants to complete the survey independently and return it in the envelope provided after one week.

Measures

Interpersonal solidarity. A modified version of Wheeless' (1978) Interpersonal Solidarity Scale was used to assess perceptions of interpersonal solidarity. Samples items include, "my partner and I are very close to each other," and "I interact/communicate with my partner much more than with most people I know." Several of the items were reverse-coded. One of the items, "I distrust this person" was deleted from the scale due to its poor item-total reliability. Responses were rated on a 7-point scale, with (1) meaning "low relationship solidarity" and (7) meaning "high relationship solidarity." The alpha reliability was .90.

Relationship satisfaction. A modified version of Norton's (1983) Quality Marriage Index assessed perceptions of relationship satisfaction. Samples of the items include, "my partner and I have a good relationship" and "my relationship with my partner makes me happy." Responses were rated on a 7-point scale with anchors of (1) "not at all satisfied" and (7) "highly satisfied." Alpha reliability was .94.

Appropriateness, effectiveness, and uniqueness of play. Participants' perceptions regarding the appropriateness, effectiveness, and uniqueness of play, and whether it was self-initiated, partner-initiated, or mutually initiated was measured by averaging across the reported instances for each individual. Single Likert items on a 7-point scale (1 = not at all, 7 = very much) assessed appropriateness, effectiveness, uniqueness of, and how recurrent/routine each play instance was. On average, the sample perceived most play instances as being highly appropriate ($M = 5.43$, $SD = .99$), effective ($M = 5.54$, $SD =$

1.16), somewhat unique (M = 4.82, SD = 1.44), and spontaneous in nature (M = 4.99, SD = 1.37).

Frequency of play. To assess the frequency of play, two items were created, "my partner and I are frequently playful in our interactions with each other" and "my partner and I frequently engage in playful acts together in our interactions with each other." Anchors on the 7-point scale were (1) "low frequency of play" to (7) "high frequency of play." Alpha reliability was .93. As an additional measure of play frequency, the total number of play instances was also recorded. An average of 5.78 instances of play for the week were reported.

Relational functions of play. To assess the six relational functions of play posited by Baxter (1992), a 15-item scale was constructed. Nine items reflect the degree to which the six relational functions of play are served by the participants' own use of play in the relationship. A sample item included: "overall my use of play in the relationship has enhanced my feelings of intimacy towards my partner." Responses were rated on a 7-point scale from (1) strongly disagree to (7) strongly agree. Alpha reliability was .85. The other six items were designed to reflect the degree to which the functions of play are served by the participants' partner's use of play in the relationship. A sample item was: "overall my partner's use of play in the relationship has helped us to discuss more sensitive issues openly." Responses were rated on a 7-point scale from (1) strongly disagree to (7) strongly agree. Alpha reliability was .80.

Study One Results

Because dyadic diary data were obtained, analyses were conducted on both members of the friendship and romantic relationships separately. Given that same-sex data are included among the friendship dyads, partners are distinguished only as "partner A" and "partner B." They are referred to as "individuals" and "partners" respectively.

Coding of Play Instances

Two coders independently categorized the open-ended data. After discussion of Baxter's (1992) original typology and training using fictitious data, each coder independently categorized each respondent's original descriptions of play instances. An "other" category was added to capture types of play which may not have been present in Baxter's original typology. Three additional types of play were identified: joking (not teasing), physically intimate behaviors, and private nonverbal behaviors.

Frequency of Play

The first research question asked how frequently friends and romantic partners engage in play. Romantic partners reported 6.56 weekly play instances (SD = 3.89) and mean play frequency of 5.47 (SD = 2.25), with partners reporting 5.71 play instances (SD = 3.47) and mean play frequency of 6.23 (SD = 1.38). Friends reported 5.52 weekly play instances (SD = 1.13) and mean play frequency of 5.09 (SD = 2.07), with partners reporting 5.74 play instances (SD = 4.32) and mean play frequency of 4.81 (SD = 2.38).

T-tests were computed to test whether friends and romantic partners differed in the number of instances recorded on the play diary and perceived frequency of play. Only frequency of play reported by partners differed across the two groups, $t(76) = 3.32$, $p < .01$, with romantic partners reporting higher play frequency than friends.

Play, Solidarity, and Satisfaction

The second research question asked whether frequency of play is associated with perceived relationship solidarity and satisfaction among friends and romantic partners. Correlation analyses for both individuals and their partners revealed no significant associations between the number of instances of play recorded and perceived solidarity and relationship satisfaction among friends or romantic partners. No significant correlations were found between frequency of play and relationship solidarity and satisfaction among friends and romantic partners.

Appropriateness, Effectiveness, and Uniqueness of Play

Regarding the third research question, the perceived appropriateness of play was not found to be significantly different between friends and romantics. Individuals' perceptions of the effectiveness of play did differ with romantic partners reporting greater effectiveness of play episodes, (M = 5.86, SD = .97) compared to friends (M = 5.32, SD = 1.24), $t(76) = 2.15$, $p < .05$. Partners' ratings of effectiveness did not significantly differ between friends and romantic relationships.

Perceptions of the uniqueness of play did differ between friends and romantics with romantic partners reporting greater uniqueness of play episodes, (M = 5.50, SD = 1.11) compared friends (M = 4.44, SD = 1.50), $t(76) = 3.60$, $p < .05$. Partners' ratings of uniqueness did not significantly differ between friends and romantics.

Functions of Play

The fourth research question examined perceived functions of play. T-tests were computed for partners separately, with results showing significant differences between friends and romantics. Romantic partners reported that play enhanced their feelings of intimacy toward their partner (M = 5.69, SD = 2.28) to a greater extent than did individuals in friendships (M = 4.18, SD = 2.14), t(75) = 2.91, $p < .01$. Feelings of enhanced commitment were higher among romantic partners (M = 5.38, SD = 2.32) compared to friends (M = 3.87, SD = 1.96), t (75) = 3.10, $p < .01$. Romantic partners also disagreed that play decreased the quality of communication between them (M = 1.28, SD = 1.14) to a greater extent than did friends (M = 2.0, SD = 1.46), t(75) = -2.35, $p < .05$. Play helped romantic partners (M = 5.03, SD = 2.27) manage conflict to a greater extent than friends (M = 3.73, SD = 2.07), t (75) = 2.61, $p < .05$, and their identity as a couple (M = 5.28, SD = 2.26) more than friends (M = 3.18, SD = 1.06), t(75) = 4.17, $p < .01$.

A similar pattern of results was found for partners' perceptions of the functions of play. Romantic partners reported that play enhanced their feelings of intimacy toward their partner (M = 6.25, SD = 1.34) to a greater extent than did those in friendships (M = 4.28, SD = 2.35), t(76) = 4.67, $p < .01$. Play also helped romantic partners enhance feelings of commitment (M = 6.16, SD = 1.30) more than friends (M = 4.13, SD = 2.32), t (75) = 4.87, $p < .01$, manage conflict more (M = 5.69, SD = 1.42) than friends (M = 4.00, SD = 2.18), t (76) = 4.13, $p < .01$, enhance their couple identity (M = 5.81, SD = 1.49) more than friends (M = 4.00, SD = 2.19), t(75) = 5.74, $p < .01$, and enhanced overall relationship satisfaction (M = 6.13, SD = 1.41) more than did friends (M = 4.72, SD = 2.32), t(76) = 3.33, $p < .01$.

Study One Discussion

The first two research questions examined the frequency of play among friends and romantic partners. Romantic partners reported a higher mean perceived frequency of play than friends. But interestingly, no correlations between play and satisfaction were found. This finding does not replicate Aune and Wong's (2002) findings that showed a positive association between playfulness and relationship satisfaction. These findings did not confirm Baxter's (1992) results showing a positive correlation between play and closeness. Perhaps this is because the focus of this analysis was on perceived frequency and a count of number of instances recorded. What may be more important across friends and romantic relationships is the quality of play, and not the quantity of play engaged in. Emmers-Sommer (2004) found that indicators of communication quality were significant predictors of intimacy and relationship satisfaction, whereas communication quantity indicators only contributed an additional 10% of the variance in intimacy.

Regarding the third research question, while the perceived appropriateness of play did not differ across the two groups, romantic partners reported greater uniqueness and effectiveness of play than did friends. This may be due to several reasons. First, compared with friendship pairs, romantic couples may be more motivated to develop highly specialized forms of play between them, so that they can stand out as a "couple" from the rest of their social network. On the other hand, within friendships it may be more important for people to follow along with the rest of the crowd and mimic their playful behaviors rather than be unique in order to fit in better with the social network. Second, given the greater amount of time romantic couples are likely to spend together compared to friendship pairs, they may become bored with certain playful routines quicker than friends, and are likely to seek out new ways to play with one another to inject spontaneity into the relationship.

Lastly, regarding the effectiveness of play, romantic couples might report higher levels than friends because for them, play may be more of a goal-oriented behavior. Whereas friends are just having fun for its own sake, couples may view play as a more strategic attempt on their or their partners' part to accomplish some relational goal. Results seem to offer some support for this argument in that the enactment of play was perceived to be more "functional" among romantics than friends.

The fourth research question examined perceived functions of play. Both partners in romantic relationships reported that play enhanced their feelings of intimacy, commitment, and identity as a couple, more than did friends. Also, romantic partners disagreed that play decreased the quality of communication between them to a greater extent than did friends. As discussed, given that the enactment of play among romantics is likely designed to create a closer connection for the couple, while separating them from their social network, it is not surprising to find that play is perceived to bring them romantically closer together compared to friends. Among friends, while play may serve to enhance feelings of solidarity and closeness between the pair, and perhaps "group" identity, it is unlikely that play will help friends become closer together to the same extent that it does among romantic partners.

As for the finding that romantics perceived play as less likely to decrease communication quality between them compared to friends, it may simply be play tends to be biased more toward the positive than the negative for romantic partners. Romantic partners may choose to avoid negative forms of play (i.e., teasing your romantic partner may be too relationally risky to do).

The results of study one reveals that even though friends and romantic couples share some similarities in how they view play (e.g., appropriateness of enactment), there were important differences also. Of particular interest is that romantic couples reported that the enactment of play served more important functions in their relationships compared to friends. This finding is consistent with Betcher's (1981) earlier work on play among married couples. Closer examination of the different relational functions suggest that play may be a more effective relational management tool for romantic partners compared to friends. However, the lack of support for the relationship between interpersonal solidarity, relationship satisfaction, and frequency of play warrants some further exploration asthe positive association between these three variables has been a robust finding in the play literature. Moreover, given that romantic couples and friendship pairs for the most part differ in their views of how play "functionally" works in their relationships, it makes sense then to also compare and contrast the ways in which they "enact" play within these relationships. Whereas the first study focused on the functions of adult play that Baxter (1992) explored in her work, the second study focused on the forms of adult play and provides another test of the relationship between interpersonal closeness, relational satisfaction, and frequency of play.

Study Two

Study two was designed to confirm and extend the findings of the diary data from study one. In particular, the frequency of the different types of play identified by Baxter (1992) and the additional types found in study one were examined. A self-report instrument assessed the perceived frequency as well as numerical estimates of play. To further examine relationship context differences, play and satisfaction across friends and romantic partners was assessed. The following research questions guided this study.

> RQ1: What types of play are engaged in by friends and romantic partners?
> RQ2: Do friends and romantics differ in the types of play they engage in?
> RQ3: Do friends and romantics report different degrees of perceived playfulness overall?
> RQ4: Do friends and romantics report different frequencies of play instances overall?

RQ5: To what extent is playfulness associated with relationship satisfaction for friends and romantics?

Study Two Method

Participants

A total of 193 individuals (61 males and 130 females, with 2 people not identifying their sex) participated in the study. Partners included 111 females, 80 males, and two not identified. The sample was comprised of students as well as non-students. Specifically, the snowball sampling technique (Monge & Contractor, 1988) was used to solicit research participants from the community. The mean age of participants was 22.4 years, SD = 4.34 years, minimum = 18, maximum = 56.

As with Study 1, this sample was ethnically diverse. Sixty-one participants were of Japanese descent (31.6%), thirty-four were Caucasian (17.6%), eighteen reported mixed ethnicity (9.3%), seventeen were Filipino (8.8%), seventeen checked the "other" category (8.8%), sixteen were Chinese (8.3%), twelve were Hawaiian or part-Hawaiian (6.2%), seven were Korean (3.6%), four Hispanic (2.1%), four African American (2.1%), and one Native American (.5%).

Friends described the category of their relationship as follows: acquaintance (N=2, 2.5%), casual friend (N=9, 11.1%), good friend (N=33, 40.7%), best friend (N=26, 32.1%), and "other" (N=11, 13.6%). Romantic relationship categories were as follows: acquaintance (N=1, .9%), casual dater (N=8, 7.2%), serious dater (N=59, 53.2%), cohabiting (N=26, 23.4%), engaged (N=6, 5.4%), married (N=9, 8.1%), and other (N=1, .9%).

Questionnaire

Reference to relationship type was the only difference in the two versions of the questionnaire. For romantic relationships, respondents were asked to think about a romantic relationship and "indicate how frequently (if at all) you engage in these behaviors in this particular relationship." Participants were then asked to record the initials of the person they had in mind. The friendship version of the instrument asked participants to think about a platonic friendship they are currently in. Respondents to the friendship questionnaire were instructed that the relationship should not be a romantic relationship, but could be a same-sex or opposite-sex friend.

Based on Baxter's typology, items were created that assessed: a) the gestalt perceptions of the frequency with which each of the forms of play occur; and b) the number of times per week that they engage in each type of play. For the perceptual frequency measure, participants were asked "How frequently do you and your ____ (friend or partner) engage in the particular type of play." The Likert-type scale was anchored by 1 "never" and 5 "very frequently." In addition to Baxter's forms of play, three additional forms of play were included, based on the results from the first study. These included: joking (not teasing), physically intimate behaviors, and private nonverbal behaviors.

Hendrick's (1988) 7-item relational satisfaction scale was used with the addition of three items from Metts (1989). Individual scores were computed as means. Alpha reliability was .90.

Study Two Results

The first research question asked what types of play are engaged in by friends and romantic partners. A breakdown of the types of play by friends or romantic couples is provided in Table 9.1. The most frequent forms of play included: (a) teasing ($M = 3.83$, $SD = 1.27$), (b) private language (or idioms) ($M = 3.66$, $SD = 1.36$), (c) joking ($M = 3.55$, $SD = 1.24$), (d) nonverbal play ($M = 3.29$, $SD = 1.46$), and (e) gossiping ($M = 3.27$, $SD = 1.36$). The following forms of play were less frequently reported: (a) prosocial physical play ($M = 2.84$, $SD = 1.37$), (b) intimate play ($M = 2.81$, $SD = 1.67$), (c) anti-social physical play ($M = 2.48$, $SD = 1.48$), (d) role playing ($M = 2.21$, $SD = 1.27$), (e) games ($M = 2.05$, $SD = 1.24$), and (f) public performance ($M = 1.47$, $SD = .96$).

Frequency counts per week followed a similar pattern, with the following play forms scoring high counts: (a) private language use ($M = 10.26$, $SD = 14.29$), (b) teasing ($M = 9.72$, $SD = 13.87$), joking ($M = 8.39$, $SD = 13,19$), (c) nonverbal play ($M = 8.05$, $SD = 13.19$), and (d) gossip ($M = 5.91$, $SD = 9.31$). Lower counts of play were reported for: (a) Anti-social play ($M = 4.74$, $SD = 8.08$), (b) prosocial physical play ($M = 4.73$, $SD = 6.07$), (c) intimate play ($M = 4.52$, $SD = 8.86$), (d) role playing ($M = 3.17$, $SD = 4.06$), (e) games ($M = 2.30$, $SD = 3.45$), and (f) public performance ($M = 1.27$, $SD = 3.04$).

The second research question asked whether friends and romantic partners differ in the types of play they engage in. Length of relationship was found to be significantly associated with several play types. As such, a MANCOVA was conducted on frequency and number of times per week for each play type, controlling for relationship length. The overall multivariate test was significant, $F(22, 87) = 6.39$, $p < .001$, Wilks' lambda = .38.

Univariate tests revealed that romantic partners reported significantly higher perceived frequencies and counts on: (a) private language use, (b) prosocial physical play, (c) game play, (e) intimate play, and (f) nonverbal play compared to friends.

Table 9.1

Means and Standard Deviations for Types of Play Across Relationship Types

Play Type	Friends		Romantics	
	Mean	SD	Mean	SD
Private Language F*	3.38	1.40	4.08	1.17
Private Language C*	5.42	7.25	14.11	15.83
Teasing	3.58	1.54	3.92	1.28
Prosocial Physical Play F	2.00	1.28	3.29	1.23
Prosocial Physical Play C	2.29	4.75	6.58	6.73
Antisocial PhysicalPlay F	2.00	1.51	2.85	1.45
Antisocial Physical Play C	2.18	3.32	6.36	9.70
Games F	1.84	1.19	2.14	1.24
Games C	1.49	2.02	3.12	4.68
Jokes C	7.51	15.19	10.86	14.99
Intimate Play F	1.36	1.00	3.73	3.73
Intimate Play C	.93	3.29	7.47	12.20
Nonverbal Play F	2.56	1.49	3.92	1.17
Nonverbal Play C	3.53	4.66	10.26	11.73

*F = Frequency, C = Count

Additionally, univariate tests show that romantic partners reported significantly higher joke counts and teasing frequency than friends.

The third research question asked whether friends and romantics report different degrees of perceived playfulness overall. Using a composite of playfulness frequency scores across types of play, a t-test revealed that romantic partners (M = 3.11, SD = .66) reported significantly more play than did friends (M = 2.50, SD = .76), t (189) = -5.90, p < .001.

Research question four asked whether friends and romantics report different frequencies of play instances overall. A t-test was computed on the composite of play count scores across types of play. Romantic partners (M = 7.30, SD = 7.34) reported significantly higher frequencies of play than did friends (M = 3.66, SD = 3.28), t (181) = - 4.03, p < .001.

Research question five asked to what extent playfulness is associated with relationship satisfaction for friends and romantics. Pearson correlations were computed between relationship satisfaction and the composite playfulness score separately for friends and romantics. Relationship satisfaction and playfulness were significantly positively associated for friends, r(80) = .25, p < .03, but not for romantic partners, r(111) = .05, p > .05. The correlation between relationship satisfaction and playfulness was also computed, controlling for relationship length. The strength of the association for friends increased, r(68) = .31, p < .01. For romantic partners, the correlation was still not significant, r(104) = .11, p > .05.

Study Two Discussion

Study two set out to re-examine the forms of play in romantic relationships and friendships. Three additional types of play were studied in this project: joking, intimate play, and nonverbal play. These three types of play were reported by the respondents in study one. Not surprisingly, intimate play was found almost exclusively among romantic partners. Joking and nonverbal play were prevalent across relationship types.

Overall, romantic partners were found to report greater frequencies and more instances of each form of play relative to friends. It is likely that romantic partners make more opportunities to interact with one another, live within close proximity of each other, and communicate with one another more frequently than many friendships. Therefore, the frequency of play behaviors may be higher. Conversely, it may be that the greater variability in what counted as a "friend" may have resulted in fewer instances being reported among friends. Given that play is typically enacted when one feels most free and comfortable, perhaps those in less developed relationships are not yet able to engage in many of the types of play examined in this study. Arguably, those in romantic relationships have a greater likelihood of having the psychological intimacy necessary to engage in playful behaviors.

The association between playfulness and relationship satisfaction was significant for friends, but not for romantics, even after controlling for relationship length. This is consistent with Baxter's original findings that play frequencies were associated with relationship closeness for friends, but not romantic partners. Friendship may be characterized by the types of activities engaged in, whereas romantic partners may be more characterized by the gestalt affect associated with the relationship.

This study also provides data regarding how frequently these forms of play are typically engaged in on a weekly basis. An intriguing and not-so-trivial question is how often does this happen? Overall, it appears that idiomatic communication occurs frequently, about ten times per week, similar to teasing and joking. The distinction between teasing and joking is that teasing is humor specifically designed to make fun of an individual, whereas joking is a broader form of humor, not specifically designed to ridicule. These types of humor reported occur around eight or nine times per week, across the two relationship types. The least frequently reported form of play was public performances at just over once per week. This is nonetheless a relatively prevalent activity across both friends and romantics. So it appears that all the forms of play occur between once per week up to multiple times per day, in the case of private language. Any human behavior that occurs as frequently should merit empirical investigation.

General Discussion

While this research also used a convenience sample of undergraduate college students, it provides comparability to Baxter's original study. One exception is that the current study had predominantly participants of Asian descent whereas it is typical in many communication studies to have predominantly Caucasian participants. Future research should examine play among a non-college student sample, across a greater range of ages and members of different socio-economic groups.

Additionally, though we found that appropriateness of play is perceived the same between friends and romantics, what remains unclear is the process by which romantic partners or friends negotiate to establish what are and are not appropriate forms of play. Is this an explicit or implicit process? This study focused on various positive relational functions that play serves. An interesting follow-up study could explore the negative relational functions served by play. The evolution of play in a relationship would also be worthy of future longitudinal research. This could provide insights into how play helps individuals to initiate and maintain positive interpersonal relationships. Longitudinal studies could explore how play is initially negotiated, how partners develop different rules for play, and how these may change over time. How do rules of play affect the way playful behaviors are interpreted within a relationship as either positive or negative communication behaviors (e.g., expectancy violation)? Also of interest are the maintenance functions that play serves. Literature identifies several common strategies for maintaining positive relationships such as providing assurances, sharing tasks, being open, and engaging in positivity. Play is likely to help elicit positivity and may also express assurance that both partners are still interested in maintaining the relationship given that play is often dyadic and reciprocal in nature.

In addition to tracking the evolution of play as it unfolds within relationships, it would also be interesting to examine potential differences in the way play is enacted within specific types of romantic relationships and friendships. Different rules may apply as to what constitutes appropriate or inappropriate playful behavior. For example, in a same-sex relationship, antisocial physical play may be considered appropriate among males, but the same behavior is likely perceived as highly inappropriate in an opposite-sex relationship. This in turn may affect the degree to which play effectively functions to help foster relational closeness and satisfaction. Continued investigation of adult play will help us to understand a significant, pervasive, and intriguing relational phenomenon.

References

Abramis, D. J. (1990). Play in work: Childish hedonism or adult enthusiasm? *American Behavioral Scientist, 33*, 353–373.

Argyle, M., & Henderson, M. (1984). The rules of friendship. *Journal of Social and Personal Relationships, 1*, 211–237.

Argyle, M., & Henderson, M. (1985). The rules of relationships. In S. Duck, & D. Perlman (Eds.), *Understanding personal relationships* (pp. 63–85). London: Sage.

Aune, R. K., Aune, K. S., Dawson, E. J., & Pena, E. F. (1993). Relational messages associated with persona-sharing. *Communication Research Reports, 10*, 129–139.

Aune, K. S., & Comstock, J. (1991). The experience and expression of jealousy: A comparison between friends and romantics. *Psychological Reports, 69*, 315–319.

Aune, K. S., & Wong, N. C. H. (2002). Antecedents and consequences of adult play in romantic relationships. *Personal Relationships, 9*, 279–286.

Baxter, L. A. (1992). Forms and functions of intimate play in personal relationships. *Human Communication Research, 18*, 336–363.

Baxter, L., Dun, T., & Sahlstein, E. (2001). Rules for relating communicated among social network members. *Journal of Social and Personal Relationships, 18*, 173–200.

Betcher, R. W. (1981). Intimate play and marital adaptation. *Psychiatry, 44*, 13–33.

Bombar, M. L., & Littig, L. W. (1996). Babytalk as a communication of intimate attachment: An initial study in adult romances and friendships. *Personal Relationships, 3*, 137–158.

Broadhead, P. (2009). Conflict resolution and children's behavior: Observing and understanding social and cooperative play in early years educational settings. *Early Years, 29*, 105–118.

Bruess, C. J. S., & Pearson, J. C. (1993). 'Sweet pea' and 'pussy cat': An examination of idiom use and marital satisfaction over the life cycle. *Journal of Social and Personal Relationships, 10,* 609–615.

Burgoon, J. K., & Hale, J. L. (1984). The fundamental topoi of relational communication. *Communication Monographs, 54,* 19–41.

Canary, D., Stafford, L, Hause, K. S., & Wallace, L. A. (1993). An inductive analysis of relational maintenance strategies: Comparisons among lovers, relatives, friends, and others. *Communication Research Reports, 10,* 5–14.

Carpenter, B. M., & Aune, K. S. (1997. May). *Partners at play: The impact of playful behaviors on the experience of positive emotion in romantic relationship.* Paper presented at the International Communication Association, Montreal.

Doster, J. A., Mielke, R. K., Riley, C. A., Toledo, J. R., Goven, A. J., & Moorefield, R. (2006). Play and health among a group of adult business executives. *Social Behavior and Personality, 34,* 1071–1080.

Emmers-Sommer, R. M. (2004). The effect of communication quality and quantity indicators on intimacy and relational satisfaction. *Journal of Social and Personal Relationships, 21,* 399–411.

Handler, L. (1999). Assessment of playfulness: Hermann Rorschach meets D. W. Winnicott. *Journal of Personality Assessment, 72,* 208–217.

Hendrick, S.S. (1988). A generic measure of relationship satisfaction. *Journal of Marriage and the Family, 50,* 93–98.

Lin, Y. C. (2010). Improving parent-child relationships through block play. *Education, 130,* 461–469.

Metts, S. (1989). An exploratory investigation of deception in close relationships. *Journal of Social and Personal Relationships, 6,* 159–179.

Monge, P., & Contractor, N. (1988). Communication networks: Measurement techniques. In C. Tardy (Ed.), *A handbook for the study of human communication: Methods and instruments for observing, measuring, and assessing communication processes* (pp. 107–138). Norwood, NJ: Ablex.

Norton, R. (1983). Measuring marital quality: A critical look at the dependent variable. *Journal of Marriage and the Family, 45,* 141–151.

Palagi, E., Cordini, G., & Tarli, S. (2004). Immediate and delayed benefits of play behavior: New evidence from chimpanzees. *Ethology, 110,* 949-962.

Piaget, J. (1951). *Play, dreams, and imagination in childhood* (C. Gattegno & F. M. Hodgson, Trans.). New York: Norton. (Original work published 1945)

Sternberg, R. J. (1986). A triangular theory of love. *Psychological Review, 93,* 119–135.

Wheeless, L. R. (1978). A follow-up study of the relationships among trust, disclosure, and interpersonal solidarity. *Human Communication Research, 4,* 143–157.

• CHAPTER TEN •

Humor as Personal Relationship Enhancer: Positivity for the Long Term

John C. Meyer
University of Southern Mississippi

Humor, as a uniter and divider, can be a powerful communication tool in relationships. Many cite "a sense of humor" as a key personality characteristic looked for in friends and romantic partners. When two or more share humor, a common path for understanding a topic and a common value placed on it can build unity. But, some key questions include: How does humor positively enhance relationships? What topics elicit or serve as a focus for humor in relationships? This chapter reports a study that sought to discover the topics and effects of humor in the words of those experiencing it in relationships where a main goal was to characterize humor use as a positive force in close personal relationships.

This chapter explores sources of humor through a review of key theories as well as, humor's effects such as enhanced sharedness, unity, and a sense of togetherness. A study of humor content is then reported. The chapter concludes with a discussion of various elements that can help to build understanding of the unifying effect of humor on close personal relationships.

Sources of Humor

Humor is thought to have emerged as a part of survivability for humans: sharing the relief of a victory over a threatening group or hunted creature (Gruner, 1997), or as a signal for nonaggression and mutual cooperation (Morreall, 1983). Three major theoretical explanations of humor include: a form of physiological relief, psychological superiority, and as cognitive incongruity (Meyer, 2000; Morreall, 1983).

Relief theory holds that humor results primarily from a release of tension by an individual. The more tension is built up and released, the more humor is experienced (Shurcliff, 1968). Reasons for the tension relief may vary, but the humor experience is a change in physiological state, and can therefore be detected medically or biologically. Perceived humor may result from the relief of a danger reduced or removed, a riddle solved, or a story concluded that resolves contradictions. One key characteristic of the relief theory of humor is its focus on the physiological phenomenon—humor as experienced can actually be measured, through slower heart rate, lower blood pressure, and deep breaths. An alteration of a potentially threatening pattern is thus indicated by humor as relief.

Superiority theory holds that humor results primarily from a sense of accomplishment or elevation over other people (Gruner, 1997). Humor, according to this theory, is a symptom of winning. Superiority humor results when one gets a psychological "one-up" on others, whether it stems from accomplishing something, avoiding a danger or drawback that affects others, or winning over another through a verbal riposte, story, or memorable line. Perhaps the most common examples of superiority humor are jokes that ridicule certain groups. One person has noted that "one useless man is a shame, two together are a law firm, and three or more is a Congress." Many teases are readily explained by superiority humor as one points out a flaw to another through humor. A perceived ugly, old-fashioned shirt may draw the comment: "1980's called and wants its shirt back." Those who agree, laugh, and even the ugly-shirt wearers may laugh if they realize they have a personal weakness or quirk which has led them to a "lesser" status of violating a group norm. Thus, humor through superiority can serve to "discipline by laughter" (Duncan, 1962).

Incongruity theory holds that humor is a cognitive perception of a non-threatening violation of an expected pattern (Levasseur & Dean, 1996). Humor is perceived by someone who has learned a pattern that is suddenly violated. Social norms are often the key patterns violated, and thus humor can have a social unifying effect among those who recognize the pattern and understand its violation. One statement making its way around holds that "good health is merely the slowest possible rate at which one can die." That statement certainly violates expected social norms, albeit negatively framed, most notably the idea that people seek good health to avoid death. People in our culture understand the common pattern of conversations about good health seeking to avoid death, or even mentioning it. Thus, when a statement so dramatically equates good health with dying (just more slowly) humor may results from the reaction to the incongruity in the suddenly broken pattern.

These kinds of theories have been forwarded in efforts to explain the origin of humor in general. Morreall (1983) sought to define humor broadly by including all three theories and noting each of them were simply variations of the "pleasant psychological shift" (p. 39) that is the defining characteristic of humor. Morreall defined the humor experience broadly, holding that a pleasant change in cognition may be based on elements of superiority, incongruity, or relief, or certainly elements of all three. His was an integrative model of humor. Yet clearly a change, or violation of a pattern, was essential to Morreall's explanation of humor.

Veatch (1998) also claimed that humor resulted from violations of a pattern referred to as an expected moral order. For Veatch, humor is a cognitive function experienced only if an expected norm or expected moral order is perceived, a violation of that norm is also perceived, and both are perceived simultaneously. If only a pattern violation is perceived, humor may not be experienced. Similarly, if the norm is perceived along with no serious violation of it, humor may not be perceived. Yet, if a sense of normal and violation of that normal coexist in mind, humor is experienced. With Veatch, a change in perceptions or violation of an expected pattern is essential to humor, to exist simultaneously in mind with a perception of an expected pattern or moral order. So, perceiving humor together with another involves a shared script; both can recognize the pattern, as well as mutual understanding that the violation is manageable, nonthreatening, and therefore deserving of laughter. This can provide a shared connection.

Humor Enhances Sharedness

Long term relationships depend on a comfortable degree of sharing between the parties. Uncertainties within a relationship may be maintained to avoid having to manage undesirable outcomes (Brashers, 2007), although a large degree of uncertainty reduction is expected to occur as parties interact (Berger & Calabrese, 1975). Still, to maintain fun it is desirable that humor (and surprise) also play be a part. However, humor as a form of expressed superiority may not be used to create sharedness but rather as a form of control. Potential uncertainties may be turned into certainties albeit by a humorously resolved incongruity. Knowing one can trust one's partner allows laughter at potentially threatening situations. Given key needs for those in interpersonal relationships, discovery of how humor could meet those needs, and become so valued in relationships, is worthwhile.

Meyer (1997) unearthed three key aspects affecting how humor functions in a relationship: Humor is subjective—it depends on one's experiences and the patterns developed that influence what one finds funny; Humor is intentional—one must choose to find some symbol or action funny or not; and Humor is social—we often find funnier what others also find funny; laughter is contagious. These qualities were illustrated by studying humor in a workplace. Interviews of organization members discovered narratives that encapsulated values they shared in their work lives (Meyer, 1997). The only stories that were duplicated across multiple interviewees contained humor. Such stories, shared with one another and with the researcher, clearly demonstrated shared work values. For instance, two workers shared the story of a dumpster outside the workplace catching fire, both finding humor in the reactions of each person.

Research shows that people who display a higher degree of humor appreciation or sense of humor are more successful in their relationships. Studies pairing communicators demonstrating a highly developed sense of humor with those demonstrating a less developed sense of humor showed the power of a sense of humor within interpersonal encounters—those invoking humor were much more desired as potential future partners (Graham, 1995). Sharing humor reduces social distance between interactants and can enhance the relational growth. Couples who shared and accepted one another's humor showed more satisfaction in their marriage (Honeycutt & Brown, 1998). Workers with a relatively higher humor orientation (compared to those with low humor orientation) could cope with work stress better and express emotions more readily to one another (Wanzer, Booth-Butterfield, & Booth-Butterfield, 2005).

Humor provides one key avenue for reassuring ourselves in communication that we can relate to one another because we get a sense of valuing something similar. Conflicting social roles can be managed through humor as expectations become ambiguous. Women, for instance, use humor to let their managerial identities emerge through communication at work in ways that men do not need to worry about (Martin, Rich, & Gayle, 2004). Men, culturally expected to lead, may tease or joke with impunity as persons in power, yet women as managers must cope with fulfilling both female and managerial roles. Women thus may use humor less overall while seeking more affiliation and unity when invoking it. In the classroom, prosocial behaviors involving humor increase compliance-gaining (Punyanunt, 2000). Even across cultural boundaries, sharing humor can build a relationship (Kalbfleisch, 2009). People with higher humor orientation have less apprehension communicating with someone from another culture (Miczo & Welter, 2006).

Humor for Social Cohesion

Identification with others may be achieved by relieving uncertainty and tension through jokes, resulting in deeper relational bonds among individuals

(Graham, 1995). Humor in relationships reduces the social distance between people as one makes the other feel good through laughter (Ziv, 1984). Humor decidedly has ingratiation characteristics. People know how humor brings out good feelings when shared in communication. The relief theory of humor pinpoints this effect, as when one shares a laugh during communication, the sense of the situation becomes more open and relaxed. In turn, people then learn more about one another and develop stronger relationships with one another.

Crucial elements in relationships involving control, affection, and inclusion have been found to be enhanced through invoking humor. Humor use in messages can reassure people that they are in control of an issue and really can handle it, as laughing at something reduces fear of it (Morreall, 1989). People who have cancer, for instance, often deal with it by being refreshingly honest about its effects upon their bodies and telling jokes about them. Caregivers, too, can use humor to defuse tensions in uncomfortable situations, as humor serves to effectively comfort with affection through messages in relationships (Bippus, 2000b). Humor also can help smooth out conflictual communication, as the amount of humor use correlates with all conflict management styles except forcing (Smith, Harrington, & Neck, 2000). Children learn young that humor can be a powerful uniter in relationships (Socha & Kelly, 1994). For children, invoking and appreciating humor were a clear sign of an ability to understand multiple perspectives and developed reasoning patterns (Meyer, 2003). Children would treat humor use as an indicator of closer relationships, as shared laughter would lead to more eager initiation of messages with the same party. Additionally, humor's service for inclusion shows as people of similar races and classes employ humor with one another more (Smith et al., 2000).

In interpersonal relationships, humor has been shown to enhance intimacy (Hampes, 1992, 1994), empathy (Hampes, 2001), assertiveness (Bell, McGhee, & Duffey, 1986) and trust (Hampes, 1999).

Ambivalent Humor Functions in Relationships

Humor creation is facilitated by a sense of security, safety, and control (Miczo, 2004). Laughter can signal a play frame that promotes a humorous message—the initiation of one by the sender and acceptance of one by the receiver of the message. Taking humor as playful or not, unifying or not, creates four potential relational functions of humor. According to Miczo, crossing key humor functions of unification and division with playful and nonplayful aspects of humor produces a typology of objects of humor: playful unifying humor involves expressing feelings and creating affiliation; nonplayful unification humor involves using humor to cope or gain a new perspective or understanding; playful division humor involves mocking and disparagement that demeans or belittles others; finally nonplayful division humor is concerned with social control and enforcement of norms. Playful humor is produced for its own sake, while nonplayful humor is more rhetorical as it intends to send a message for another purpose.

Teasing often crosses such humor function lines, as it can be negative or positive; crucial to forming and enhancing relationships yet serving as a channel of aggression (Alberts, Kellar-Gunther, & Corman, 1996). Teasing involves aggression in the sense that one's identity is questioned in some way, yet it also involves a play frame that inserts ambiguity in the remark, so that it is "funny" or just in fun (Mills & Carwile, 2009). Teasing can thus enhance the level and amount of comfortable topics that can be addressed. Teasing invokes "off-record" communication that does not require taking literally (Keltner, 2008). Messages can therefore be sent with ambiguity, rather than complete earnest sincerity. This flexibility can enhance relationships by smoothing the rough edges of negative comments, and introducing an aura of play around the interaction as an alternative to complete seriousness. Teases also emerge as crucial for assessing potential romantic relationships as well as negotiating rank in social hierarchies (Keltner).

The acceptance of teases and humorous comments allows for a "safe space" in communication between parties. Messages of criticism hurt less in a relationship when delivered with humor (Young & Bippus, 2001). During conflicts, couples who attribute internal motives for a partner using humor responded negatively, while external motives led to a positive reception of the humor (Bippus, 2003). Humor showing a couple is "in this together" likely helps, while humor that makes light of the other for purposes of self-gain makes conflict worse.

Benign humor among couples in conflict includes jokes about the self, the relationship, or the partner in a gentle manner, according to Alberts et al. (1996). Hostile humor among couples in conflict includes sarcasm and jokes about the partner in a negative way. Teases about a person's identity and appearance are mentioned most often by those studied, but the topic of a tease does not primarily determine the response. Background knowledge of the relationship is the major factor in how one chooses to take a tease, along with the context of the tease, nonverbal messages, and one's own mood (Alberts et al., 1996).

Clearly, humor can be used both positively and negatively in relationships, and the propensity to use each, measured by the humor styles questionnaire, relates to effective social relationships, with positive humor the more effective route (Cann, Zapata, & Davis, 2009).

Humor as Key Relationship Enhancer

Humor use is a key factor in maintaining romantic relationships (Bippus, 2000a). For example, people come to expect and rely on humor as a form of comforting. Humor's capacity to distance one from an unhappy topic, through reduced ego-involvement necessary for appreciating the humor, can promote a reappraisal of the situation that helps one's comfort. Moreover, Alberts (1990) found that satisfied couples in conflict accept humor attempts by the partner, lightening the discussion and mood, while dissatisfied couples treated the humor attempt as further attack during the conflict (Alberts, 1990).

Measures of individual tendencies to use humor show that individuals high in humor orientation are less lonely, suggesting they use humor more effectively in relationships (Wanzer, Booth-Butterfield, & Booth-Butterfield, 1996). Those high in humor orientation find humor in more situations and by enacting it seem to demonstrate more flexibility in their communication (Wanzer, Booth-Butterfield, & Booth-Butterfield, 1995). The "entertainment" quality that people seek in close relationships is supplied by higher humor-oriented people. Those with high humor orientation, thus, are perceived as funnier and more entertaining by others. Their enhanced social attractiveness helps them adapt to and maintain more relationships (Wanzer et al., 1996).

The Study

The study asked two research questions: What topics or events sparked communication with humor during a selected two-week period of the relationship? Following that, did each instance of humor help, hurt, or have no effect on the relationship? Accounts in the words of participants were gathered to explore details of how humor fit uniquely in these relationships. Humor is thought to lead to a common path for understanding a topic and building unity in a relationship. Yet, humor use could also divide through superiority or harsh putdowns. Thus, specific accounts of humor by relationship members were collected to understand specifics of how humor works in relationships.

Method

Despite development of sound measures of humor tendencies and humor use researchers still lack specific descriptive evidence of how humor is used in everyday communication between relational partners. Therefore, this study took a qualitative turn, to discover what was said and laughed at to enact humor in relationships to get to such positive results. Accounts were sought from both parties in a relationship, over the course of two weeks, of any instances of humor that related to the couple on each given day. Thus, two-week journals were generated by both parties of each couple participating. Each day's reminder asked participants to "write down as complete a description as possible of anything that caused you to laugh or struck you as funny in or about your relationship." Then, participants were asked, "Did each instance of humor help your relationship, hurt it, or have no effect?"

Twenty participants constituting 10 couples participated in the research, keeping journals for most or all of two weeks. Seven couples completed all 14 days desired; three completed partial journals that still yielded rich and usable data. Individuals ranged in age from 24 to 80. The average age was 42, and couples had been together in a strong romantic relationship for at least one year. Couples listed their "number of years together" as ranging from 3 years to 65 years, for an average of 18.5 years. All couples but one were married; the one other was living together (the three-year-duration couple). Appeals for participants were sent through email as part of campus and alumni newsletters, along with a presentation made by the author at a seminar on humor given for a senior citizens education group. A cash payment was made to each couple participating.

Data were collected in the form of daily journal entries, most describing one event per day, but some included three or more shorter events involving humor on certain days. At times, both members of a couple would describe the same humorous incident on a given day, facilitating observation of shared humor with differing perspectives on an event. More often, each partner focused on different instances or aspects of their relationship each day. Each daily account of humor was given a code number, and names were changed for anonymity (although some participants wrote initials or "wife" or "husband" in their journal entries to facilitate this without being prompted to do so by the researcher, all initials were altered as well). Together, the entries supplied 36 typed, single-spaced pages of humor incidents, each separated by two lines of white space to facilitate categorization. Humor incidents analyzed from the journals totaled 156.

During data gathering, it became clear that the answer to whether or not each instance of humor helped, hurt, or had no effect on the relationship was too lopsided to facilitate further analysis. In short, in two incidents participants reported they were not sure whether they helped or hurt, and three incidents were said to hurt the relationship. Only two of the 20 participants supplied these five incidents, as well. Several expressed the view of a statement by one participant: "Might as well categorize them all as 'helped the relationship.'" Overall, so few instances were noted that hurt or had no effect on the relationship that they were dropped from further analysis. Not surprisingly, most of these involved teasing that the other party took too seriously—showing the paradox between aggressive and humorous attempts at teasing (Mills & Babrow, 2003). As noted below, further exploration of potential negative effects of humor on relationships would be warranted, but they were not tapped by this study.

The 156 humor incidents were categorized by a thematic analysis using constant comparison (Strauss & Corbin, 1998). The incidents were first read as they were turned in as part of each person's journal. Secondly, all included incidents were placed together in one document in random order. Each incident of humor was then labeled with a theme which illustrated its topic. Each humor incident was constantly and recurrently compared with the others, until a full list of theme categories was generated. The themes emerged from the descriptions and wordings of the participants rather than from any attempt to characterize humor according to earlier theory. If an incident did not fit well in initially created categories, a new one was formed. After a certain point, no further new categories emerged, as all instances clearly fit into those created earlier. Continued repeating of themes reified the category system and suggested conceptual saturation. The categories thus generated could provide a clear picture of the topics of humor used in close personal relationships.

Results

Ten categories of humor use in relationships emerged in answer to the question of what topics or events sparked communication with humor in close, personal relationships. Use of humor tended to cluster around the topics (in order of relative frequency): (a) animals, (b) the partner, (c) outsiders, (d) the self, (e) paradox, (f) surprise at the unusual, (g) imitation, (h) the sexual, (i) wordplay, and (j) physical behaviors. In addition, six instances where no humor was observed were recorded by participants. These humor categories are listed in order of amount of incidents generated for each (see Table 10.1), and following are more detailed descriptions with examples.

Table 10.1
Humor Topics in Close Personal Relationships

Humor Category	Explanation	Number of Instances	Number of Participants Citing a Category
Animal Behavior		28	10
Partner Characteristic	Quality of the dyad partner	25	9
Outsider Characteristic	Quality of a person not part of the dyad	24	9
Own Characteristic	Quality of the self in the dyad	20	10
Paradoxical Situation	A contrary or opposite event from that expected	17	10
Surprising/Unusual Situation	An unexpected or unplanned event	12	8
Imitation	Acting or sounding like someone else	10	7
Sexual Humor	Alluding to sexual activity	7	4
Wordplay	Using puns or altering word meaning	4	2
Physical Humor	Falling, hitting, or body motions	3	3
No Humor	Humor not noted that day	6	6
Total		156	20

Animal humor was surprisingly prevalent among all couples. People in relationships laugh a lot about their pets—and even couples who may not own a pet described animals encountered during daily life as worthy of laughter. One noteworthy entry recounted:

> Today as we got ready for the day our dog M was acting silly. He was laying on his back with all four paws in the air and his head arched to the side. H[usband] called me over from the bathroom to see how cute M was acting. Not only was our dog acting funny I also thought it was nice that once I heard H[usband] laughing I had to drop everything and see what was going on.

Partner humor involved classic teasing: bringing up partner behavior to laugh at. Among participating couples, this was almost universally responded to positively. One participant noted that her husband was notoriously frugal:

> The Dad turned the water off on his child in the shower, stopped the car a long distance from the children's school and turned off the lights leaving his family to eat in the dark. After each he said, "We are cutting back." I laughed and told Robbie how much this reminded me of him. He is quite frugal. We both laughed.

In this relationship, the husband separately noted in his journal the same incident, noting that being laughed at by his wife was normal and strengthened their relationship.

Humor based on the self involved self-deprecating humor, poking fun at oneself, and inviting the partner to laugh. One participant pointed out that "I don't mind when John gets great pleasure out of something I do wrong. I dropped an egg and made a big mess and it delighted him. I love to see him laugh." Others would use humor about the self to reinforce acceptance by the other in spite of errors or difficult personal characteristics:

> Kyla is always late to everything, she was born late literally. We were talking about tombstones and funerals of all things, guess that happens at our age or because my dear aunt is in hospice and my visits to her are so painful. This conversation was getting pretty serious about death and morose topics until Kyla said that her epitaph was a no brainer, the LATE KYLA ROWENA LARSEN. And she said it was the most accurate epitaph ever, no argument.

Humor about a paradox or contradiction was the strongest fit to an overall humor theory—the incongruity theory. Members laughed at a comeuppance or opposite sense of what they thought should be happening. One wife noted that her husband "Perry came back from the department office carrying a plate full of pizza and a container of ravioli. This food was to be shared between the two of us. He laughed about having to carry the whole lunch, saying 'you made me look like a fat kid carrying all this food!'" Another, older participant noted that one day "during our early morning walk it began to rain and it tickled our funny bone for some reason—the idea of two old people trying to hurry in out of the rain." The same wife later noted that "Every night I hand him his two pills and almost every night he asks, 'Are these my sleeping pills?' and I answer, 'No, they're your memory pills.' He answers, 'Well, they're not working are they?'" All couples noted these instances of humor helped their relationship.

Humor at the surprising or unusual similarly invoked the incongruity theory—but these instances were simply so unusual or out of the norm that no paradox or contradiction was noted, only that the daily routine was shockingly and unexpectedly disrupted. One wife said that

> I was watching an episode of "The Middle" where the characters discuss celebrating their 16th and 17th anniversaries together because they had postponed the 16th for so long, they had reached the 17th without celebrating. I turned to Perry and explained the set up. "That definitely sounds like something we would do," he said. "So our life is a sitcom?" I questioned. "I don't know if that is funny or depressing." "Our life is full of sad humor," he replied.

Imitation humor normally referred to movies or programs the couple had both seen. Although imitating media characters dominated this category, a few would imitate family or workplace personalities (e.g., Arnold Swatzenegger). Participants would imitate media or literary figures for effect, and the sharedness in the relationship became evident as the other party knew immediately to whom the partner was referring.

Sexual humor might be expected to occur among couples married or living together. Several participants alluded to such humor more than they were comfortable writing down! Thus, the final set of data obtained for this study likely underrepresents sexual humor as part of long-term relationships. For example:

> So much of the humor in our relationship revolves around that typical mid-life situation where the husband still has a strong desire to have sex quite often and the wife desires it less often. It's a lot like the conversations between Ray and Debra Barone on the sitcom "Everybody Loves Raymond." In fact, there is a scene in one of the episodes where Debra goes to bed in flannel pajamas sending the message to Ray that he will not be "getting lucky" that night. We cracked up when we saw that episode because it imitated our life so closely. When my husband sees me in flannel pajamas, his response is "Oh no! You've got your armor on tonight!"

Wordplay humor involved fun with puns. Notably, only two couples had humor that fit this category, with one couple recording most of these, to wit:

"a TV sports show mentioned a team that didn't 'cut the mustard.' I wondered just how one does cut it?"

Physical humor dealt with the pratfalls of daily life—spilling coffee everywhere or running into a tree while running. A touchstone instance was that "last night Carolyn, Katie, and I had a tickle fight. When Katie climbs into our bed, she has to pay a tickle penalty. She loves this game a lot and we played for half an hour tickling one another." Simple touching, hitting, or physical play was found to be humorous.

Discussion and Conclusions

Humor could be called glue that holds relationships together. Through mutually shared superiority via humor couples maintained their relationships. Two of the most frequent humor themes involved laughing together at animals (often pets) and persons outside the relationship (often children). The themes of laughing at characteristics of self and one's relational partner also point to a way to kindly or mutually process potential superiorities of one partner over the other. Violations of expected norms or knowledge or skills could result in shared humor, showing that the resulting sense of superiority was benign and simply became a reinforcing part of the relationship. "Triumphs" of knowledge or accomplishment were processed through humor to further unify the relationship, rather than bitter conflicts alienating the partner or third parties associated with the relationship.

Similarly, the incongruity theory of humor emerged in couple's humor use in the way it helped couples deal with the unexpected events of life, notably paradoxical or surprising situations. Rather than adopting an inflexible, regimented, serious response to such aspects of life, the couples participating in this study showed an optimistic, flexible, understanding tone of response to life's events. A third theme was imitation, showing a desire and ability to mock people in life that may raise questions or reinforce undesired norms. Without such humor, or without such flexibility and positive optimistic outlook, relationships could more easily be threatened or strained by life's events. The humorous interactions reported by couples showed ways that couples dealt with unexpected or potential problems and drew closer relationally to one another. Humor has been found to enhance interpersonal attraction and decrease social distance between couples (Graham et al., 1992). Laughing together at a topic reinforces shared scripts, knowledge, and values toward that topic, and enhances the relationship thereby. Participants drew forth the richness of humor in their lives that helped bind them together as couples. Humor used as relief was prominent in the themes of sexual and physical humor, as potentially threatening or uncomfortable situations were viewed as humorous. Notably, humor also served to relax tensions in responding to paradoxical or surprising situations as discussed above. Multiple theories of humor, thus, may be applied to identical instances of humor (Morreall, 1983).

Simply stated, humor indicated pleasure both in the other and in the potential responses to life situations. Humor could be used to avoid painful confrontations with the other, but more often humor served to approach or broach a topic that, taken in all seriousness, could be threatening to one or the other party's identity or to the relationship as a whole.

The ability to take a play frame in a relationship, or remain less concerned with practical goals or consequences in every unique situation, corresponds with enactment of a sense of humor (see also Aune & Wong, chapter 9, this volume). Miczo (2004), for instance, found that humor appreciation relates to a sense of security in interactions. Individuals differ in their willingness to play or invoke their senses of humor. Anxiety about attachment to significant others, beginning in infancy, relates to lower humor use. Positive uses of humor associate with one's willingness to communicate. Improving responses to stress and relationships with others results from affiliative, unifying humor use. The latter, in turn, relates to reduced anxiety, increased playfulness, and more effectiveness in interactions (Miczo, Averbeck, & Mariani, 2009). Participants in this study showed consistent levels of playfulness and humorous communication during their weeks. Humor served as a key positive tool in the communication repertoire of relationship participants.

Some drawbacks to this research approach, and thus its results, certainly must be noted. Given the requirement to write about humor daily for a time, since writing daily is not the normal habit of a wide swath of couples, other types of humor than those obtained here are likely. Still, one may consider the rich, detailed accounts obtained of humor in relationships to at last partially relate to most couples. Second, since the study required consent and participation by *both* members of a relationship, they had to communicate with each other and agree to participate. Since accounts were received of one party wanting to participate but the other not wanting to, results may bias toward strong, richly communicative relationships. More research on humor specifics in more troubled relationships would be welcome. Perhaps couples not participating in this study would show more use of aggressive humor, which relates to avoidance of attachments (Miczo et al., 2009). One can use divisive humor to set oneself apart socially and maintain distance from others. This kind of humor was extremely rare in journal entries, and was often overcome by the other partner returning to the same form of humor in a play frame after initially taking it seriously. Couples would describe how they responded to humor with humor, rather than with outrage or anger.

This kind of research allowed for sharing of the ins and outs of couples' daily lives, along with major events in life (for instance, attendance at weddings was mentioned by two couples). Key characteristics of each partner were expressed through humor. Journal entries showed exciting, entertaining lives, even if the humor stemmed from mundane events. Humor use was a key communication strategy that laid a solid foundation for couples to reinforce one another, support one another, and build stronger relationships. Humor clearly helped participants bind together in close personal relationships.

References

Alberts, J. K. (1990). The use of humor in managing couples' conflict interactions. In D. Cahn (Ed.), *Intimates in conflict* (pp. 105–120). Hillside, NJ: Lawrence Erlbaum.

Alberts, J. K., Kellar-Gunther, Y., & Corman, S. R. (1996). That's not funny: Understanding recipients' responses to teasing. *Western Journal of Communication, 60*, 337–357.

Bell, N. J., McGhee, P. E., & Duffey, N. S. (1986). Interpersonal competence, social assertiveness, and the development of humor. *British Journal of Developmental Psychology 4*, 51–55.

Berger, C. R., & Calabrese, R. J. (1975). Some explorations in initial interaction and beyond: Toward a developmental theory of interpersonal communication. *Human Communication Research, 1*, 99–112.

Bippus, A. M. (2000a). Making sense of humor in young romantic relationships: Understanding partners' perceptions. *Humor: An International Journal of Humor Research, 13*, 395–417.

Bippus, A. M. (2000b). Humor usage in comforting episodes: Factors predicting outcomes. *Western Journal of Communication, 64*, 359–384.

Bippus, A. M. (2003). Humor motives, qualities, and reactions in recalled conflict episodes. *Western Journal of Communication, 67*, 413–426.

Brashers, D. E. (2007). A theory of communication and uncertainty management. In B. B. Whaley & W. Samter (Eds.), *Explaining communication: Contemporary theories and exemplars* (pp. 201–218). Mahwah, NJ: Lawrence Erlbaum.

Cann, A., Zapata, C. L., & Davis, H. B. (2009). Positive and negative styles of humor in communication: Evidence for the importance of considering both styles. *Communication Quarterly, 57*, 452–468.

Duncan, H. D. (1962). *Communication and social order*. New York: Bedminster Press.

Graham, E. E. (1995). The involvement of sense of humor in the development of social relationships. *Communication Reports, 8*, 158–170.

Graham, E. E., M. J., & Brooks, G. P. (1992). Functions of humor in conversation: Conceptualization and measurement. *Western Journal of Communication, 56*, 161–183.

Gruner, C. R. (1997). *The game of humor: A comprehensive theory of why we laugh*. New Brunswick, NJ: Transaction Publishers.

Hampes, W. P. (1992). Relation between intimacy and humor. *Psychological Reports, 71(1)*, 127–130.

Hampes, W. P. (1994). Relation between intimacy and the Multidimensional Sense of Humor Scale. *Psychological Reports, 74(3*, Pt 2), 1360–1362.

Hampes, W. P. (1999). The relationship between humor and trust. *Humor: International Journal of Humor Research, 12*, 253–259.

Hampes, W. P. (2001). Relation between humor and empathic concern. *Psychological Reports, 88(1)*, 241–244.

Honeycutt, J. M., & Brown, R. (1998). Did you hear the one about?: Typological and spousal differences in the planning of jokes and sense of humor in marriage. *Communication Quarterly, 46*, 342–352.

Kalbfleisch, P. J. (2009). Effective health communication in native populations in North America. *Journal of Language and Social Psychology, 28*, 158–173.

Keltner, D. (2008). In defense of teasing. *The New York Times*, December 7.

Levasseur, D. G., & Dean, K. W. (1996). The Dole humor myth and the risks of recontextualizing rhetoric. *Southern Communication Journal, 62*, 56–72.

Martin, D. M., Rich, C. O., & Gayle, B. M. (2004). Humor works: Communication style and humor functions in manager/subordinate relationships. *Southern Communication Journal, 69*, 206–222.

Meyer , J. (1997). Humor in member narratives: Uniting and dividing at work. *Western Journal of Communication, 61*, 188–208.

Meyer, J. C. (2000). Humor as a double-edged sword: Four functions of humor in communication. *Communication Theory, 10*, 310–331.

Meyer, J. (2003). *Kids talking: Learning relationships and culture with children.* Lanham, MD: Rowman & Littlefield.

Miczo, N. (2004). Humor ability, unwillingness to communicate, loneliness, and perceived stress: Testing a security theory. *Communication Studies, 55*, 209–226.

Miczo, N., Averbeck, J. M., & Mariani, T. (2009). Affiliative and aggressive humor, attachment dimensions, and interaction goals. *Communication Studies, 60*, 443–459.

Miczo, N., & Welter, R. E. (2006). Aggressive and affiliative humor: Relationships to aspects of intercultural communication. *Journal of Intercultural Communication Research, 35*, 61–77.

Mills, C. B., & Babrow, A. S. (2003). Teasing as a means of social influence. *Southern Communication Journal, 68*, 273–286.

Mills, C. B., & Carwile, A. M. (2009). The good, the bad, and the borderline: Separating teasing from bullying. *Communication Education, 58*, 276–301.

Morreall, J. (1983). *Taking laughter seriously.* Albany: State University of New York Press.

Morreall, J. (1989). Enjoying incongruity. *Humor: International Journal of Humor Research, 2*, 1–18.

Punyanunt, N. M. (2000). The effects of humor on perceptions of compliance-gaining in the college classroom. *Communication Research Reports, 17*, 30–38.

Shurcliff, A. (1968). Judged humor, arousal, and the relief theory. *Journal of Personality and Social Psychology, 8*, 360–363.

Smith, W. J., Harrington, K. V., Neck, C. P. (2000). Resolving conflict with humor in a diversity context. *Journal of Managerial Psychology, 15*, 606–625.

Socha, T. J., & Kelly, B. (1994). Children making 'fun': Humorous communication, impression management, and moral development. *Child Study Journal, 24*, 237–253.

Strauss, A., & Corbin, J. (1998). *Basics of qualitative research* (2nd ed.). Thousand Oaks, CA: Sage.

Veatch, T. C. (1998). A theory of humor. *Humor: International Journal of Humor Research, 11*, 161–216.

Wanzer, M. B., Booth-Butterfield, M., & Booth-Butterfield, S. (1995). The funny people: A source-orientation to the communication of humor. *Communication Quarterly, 43*, 142–154.

Wanzer, M. B., Booth-Butterfield, M., & Booth-Butterfield, S. (1996). Are funny people popular? An examination of humor orientation, loneliness, and social attraction. *Communication Quarterly, 44*, 42–52.

Wanzer, M. B., Booth-Butterfield, M., & Booth-Butterfield, S. (2005). "If we didn't use humor, we'd cry": Humorous coping communication in health care settings. *Journal of Health Communication, 10*, 105–125.

Young, S. L., & Bippus, A. M. (2001). Does it make a difference if they hurt you in a funny way? Humorously and non-humorously phrased hurtful messages in personal relationships. *Communication Quarterly, 49*, 35–52.

Ziv, A. (1984). *Personality and sense of humor*. New York: Springer.

• CHAPTER ELEVEN •

The Bright Side of Conflict: Dialogic Communication, Telesmatic Moments, and Deep Narrative Learning

Peter M. Kellett
University of North Carolina at Greensboro

> The stories we tell about our lives and ourselves can play an important role in the ways in which we can learn from our lives. Such learning, in turn, can be important for the ways in which we live our lives.
>
> —Goodson, Biesta, Tedder, & Adair (2010, p. 2)

> Do what you can in your conflicts to bring peace to your relationships...take what you can from your conflicts to build the life-narrative that brings peace to you.
>
> —Kellett & Dalton (2001, p. 183)

It would be bordering on flippant to argue that conflicts are inherently positive or always have some sort of bright silver lining—they are not, and they do not. Throughout history much human suffering, loss, and missed opportunities can be assigned at least in part to the fact that people engage in conflict in destructive ways and for destructive purposes. Fighting with and destroying enemies of various sorts and competing for territories and boundaries are among the deep organizing archetypes for humans rhetorically, narratively, and behaviorally. At the same time there is a considerable allure and common sense to the idea that conflicts can be positive processes and that they can have positive consequences and "bright" results for people. It makes a good deal of sense, for example, to think through the now classic perspective that points to the energizing and creative forces that conflict can release for people (Walton, 1969). Conflicts do sometimes precede and lead to peaceful and brighter times. As I discuss in detail, conflicts can also lead to desired change, positive transformation, and more productive relationships between people (Kellett, 2001, 2007, 2009, 2011). They can even be associated with the achievement of peak experiences if they enable people to find and create changes in their lives that bring them greater happiness (Goodall & Kellett, 2004).

Mostly these positives, I want to argue in the spirit of Goodson et al. and Kellett and Dalton (quoted above), result from how people engage in conflicts, and from how they make a conscious effort to learn from conflicts in ways that change their communication practices and themselves. Confronting the archetypes that guide us toward negative or destructive conflict and imagining alternative possible storylines for everyday life can be a transforming and freeing activity when such confronting and imagining are possible choices for people and when people make those choices in a spirit of critical inquiry and learning (Kellett & Dalton, 2009). In this chapter I describe connections between narrative learning, communication, and the positive or bright side of conflict by exploring how people learn positive lessons from conflicts, and how these lessons translate into approaching conflict communication more *telesmatically* (Goodall & Kellett, 2004, p. 166; Kellett, 2007, p. 21–22). This concept is defined and illustrated below.

On Being and Becoming Telesmatic Communicators

A dialogic communication approach to conflict is not necessary for having telesmatic moments or transformational learning about one's conflict. I think we all know from everyday life experiences that transformative lessons can be learned from mismanaged conflict, and bad experiences and positive outcomes can occur when people do very little if nothing that our textbooks would say is optimal, communicatively. Sometimes good fortune—perhaps even destiny or fate—rather than good communication brings positive results. Sometimes conflicts, particularly complex ones and conundrums have a way of self-reorganizing, or they and the people in them simply burn out of energy for the fight and become transformed themselves as they invite the participants to collaborate. Peace can come through, and as a welcome alternative to, the wearying effects of long term conflicts. So, in short approaching conflicts with an ethos of dialogue and negotiation and a desire to learn and change is of course no guarantee of positive results. Similarly, approaching conflict with a less collaborative ethos is no guarantee of negative results.

However, these realistic caveats aside, I have found that there is frequently enough of a connection between the communicative intelligence that people bring to conflicts, and develop as they learn from conflicts, and the quality of how they manage conflicts, and the likelihood that conflicts will be positive experiences. This interpretive intelligence to understand how one's speech acts, thoughts, and behavior have a systemic impact on the layers and meanings of a conflict and its direction and outcomes has to do with being telesmatic (Goodall & Kellett, 2004, Kellett, 2007). A derivative of the Greek word *apotelesma apo* (after) and *telesma* (the words leave us), this intelligence implies the development of a keen interpretive understanding of the impact of our words on others as well as ourselves, and our conflicts with them, once our words leave us and their words leave them. Being telesmatic is similar in some ways to the concept of rhetorical sensitivity in that it implies sensitivity to the impact of speech (Hart, Carlson, & Eadie, 1980; Ward, Blumen, & Dauria, 1982). The idea of being telesmatic differs from rhetorical sensitivity as it suggests an interpretive intelligence rather than a behavioral or strategic/rhetorical competence, although being telesmatic implies a competent communicator as a dialogic negotiator. Differing also in the fact that telesmatic communication emphasizes not just an understanding of what I should and should not say for a particular audience, but rather a systemic understanding of the patterns that our own and others' communication could and does set in motion, impact, and possibly change when we engage in conflict. Put in a narrative frame this intelligence can be summed up in advice I give students. Thus, a key to being narratively telesmatic is to interpretively understand which archetypal conflict story you are in with the other, how you got into this story, why your stories are different and oppositional, where you want the story to go next, and how to get there through effective dialogic negotiation (e.g., Booker, 2004, Brooks, 1984). Approaching conflict this way has, I believe, a substantial impact on the positive outcomes of conflict experiences.

Assuming there is a connection between being/becoming more telesmatic where necessary and the quality of communication in our conflicts—ideally as dialogic negotiation, or being open in exchanging what's needed to make progress on and learn from a conflict—let's discuss how the learning moments of some of my recent students illustrate how being telesmatic leads to positive conflict experiences for them. I also draw upon a few recent discussions of conflicts by students in my conflict communication class to illustrate the three main ways that conflicts can be positive by leading to the development of telesmatic intelligence through narrative learning.

Types of Narrative Lessons and Their Positivity

Creating positive life learning and lessons is at least in part related to one's ability to narrate one's life skillfully and effectively (Bage, 2010; Clark, 2010; Glaser, Garsoffky & Schwan, 2009; Hammack, 2010; Jeong, 2008). Even on an intuitive level we know how important stories are in helping us learn about life from others and from our own experiences. I have, more specifically, discussed how using narrative methodology and the process of narration itself—telling and retelling conflict stories—is a key communicative process in learning from conflict experience and enabling those experiences to have positive results (e.g., Kellett & Dalton, 2001, pp. 94–99). More specifically, I argue that learning can be cyclical in that if one begins with a story that represents the lived reality of a conflict, and then learn to question it, understand it, and get smarter about how and why changes to communication might result in the living of different/improved/more positive conflict experiences—this will result in a person telling better stories (for example more productive, happier, more peaceful) about how they navigate differences with others. This process is ideally cyclical in that the person begins with a story (representing the actual lived reality of a conflict) and ends with ideas for how their stories (as representations of the possibility of how their conflicts could be lived) might be different next time. The difference between the beginning story and their hypothetical ending story is in some way a marker of their development as a telesmatic communicator.

Others, most notably Goodson et al. (2010) have made similar points in slightly different terms about the connection between narrative, learning, and positivity of experiences (e.g., Clandinin & Connelly, 1991; Czarniawaska, 2004). It is clear that much of the time more constructive conflict processes can be aimed for through improved communication which leads to more positive experiences (Rossiter 1999; Tedder & Biesta, 2009). I next explore several forms of narrative intelligence, based on the notion about telesmatic communication and the positive sides of conflict.

Proposition/lesson 1: Positives can come from learning to see conflict stories and their antecedents.

Positives come from understanding what story a person is in and how they got there. This aspect of telesmatic intelligence that has to do with being able to identify, represent (narratively), and understand the *actuality* or reality of the lived experience of a conflict. This is the intelligence to be able to ask "what" questions and build these questions into a descriptive account of our conflicts. What happened that made a given take on reality a conflict? What was said and done in the conflict and how is this connected to reactions or responses that created the conflicted moments that make up a conflict? What are the participants divided/oppositional on and why? What seems to be the meaning(s) behind the conflict, and how does (do) this/these meaning(s) set in motion a communicative collision? Who are the participants and what are they bringing to this conflict biographically, psychologically, and culturally that helps explain why this conflict happened? What is the plot structure and characterizations of self and other through which this conflict progresses? Given that there are only so many conflicts that people engage in, what archetypal conflict are these people co-creating? How are participants making important representational choices of self and other and their plot character (villain, hero, victim, etc.) motives and intents when I describe the conflict? These are some of the questions that enable people to understand the lived reality and meaning of a conflict episode in a way that lays it out for interpretive critique.

This narrative form of intelligence is based on communicators' ability to describe and interpret lived reality in a way that is as accurate and fair to the events of a conflict and the people in a conflict as possible, given that this is interpretive in nature. It leads to positives because it ought to enable—even compel us to see who we are and where we are in our conflicts and how we got there. This is a positive form of learning because it enables auto-critique and personal insight that leads to the recognition of how and why we have co-created an oppositional reality with another person. But why would this self-awareness be positive—after all aren't we then much of the time seeing our own and others' communication dark side? Simply, it is positive because the ability to describe what happened grounded in evidence is the basis of understanding why it happened as it did, and understanding why is the basis of learning more about who we are as communicators and who the other is as a communicator, and what confluence of dynamics between self and other lead to the conflict, and accounting for its qualities and characteristics as a conflict. Taking these insights to heart enables us to become more telesmatic communicators in that we gain insight into why we said and did what we said and did (and didn't say and do) and how our actions and reactions impacted the other(s) and the conflict we share responsibility for. Simply, the first proposition of engaging in positive conflicts is that we can become more critically aware and understanding of how and why we experience the conflicts that we do.

Perhaps the most positive learning within this type of intelligence is the realization that our conflicts are co-constructed—negotiated—and as such we can understand how and why they are negotiated as they are and perhaps learn to negotiate or renegotiate reality in different ways. Simply, there are ways that we can change in positive ways because if reality is at least in part negotiated—then it is logical to assume that it can be renegotiated.

For example, a student (Stuart—a pseudonym) recently began a story he shared in class with the claim that he always thought of himself as a "conflict free" person. He had a tendency to see conflicts as a sort of negativity that he is normally able to avoid. Yet, he began to tell a story that was indeed a conflict he found himself in with his then best friend (JG). He told us of his senior year in high school in which despite his upbringing that rebelling against norms "felt cool." It was around this time he began hanging out with JG who became his best friend. His parents did not like JG or JG's family's background. He was a "bad boy" who parents often dreaded having an influence over their own children. After Stuart received a large sum of money for graduation and JG did not, JG began using Stuart for loans and the relationship became one sided. JG was making drug deals with Stuart's money, and using him for rides and other favors. As soon as Stuart refused one favor, JG cut him off telling him that he was no longer his friend and in fact that he was "dead" to him. Stuart processed the events with friends and realized that he was much better off without JG as his friend.

Stuart created a story in which he naïvely became friends with someone who did not have his best interest at heart. The conflict with this so-called best friend was positive in the sense that he learned to avoid hanging out with the wrong kind of friend, was no longer likely to be used, and avoided dangers from someone who did not have his welfare in mind. As such, Stuart has created a sort of coming of age story—wisdom and good choices that occurred through a period of bad choices. For Stuart, the narrative choices represented himself as the fool who learned a valuable lesson at the hands of a "best friend" who turned out to be villainous (as his parents suspected). This is a "fool who learned a valuable lesson" story archetype and as such repositions the experience into a positive frame. Stuart avoids assuming the role of fool when it comes to judging people as potential friends. Stuart developed telesmatic intelligence through these experiences. He recognized that he will need to learn from conflicts instead of assuming they will never happen to him. He also learned valuable lessons about how he contributed to getting into this conflict and what it says about him at the time (naïve fool/victim) and subsequently (wise choices of friends that fit him and his family culture). The plot, characterization, and motives of the characters in his story center on the representation of the conflict as a positive experience—a bad event that made him smarter and affirmed the things he holds dear. This is a good example of how the construction of the story and the lessons he learns from it are positive—we might say even healthy. He has a clear sense of why he was in the conflict and what role it served in his life. He can also become more critically aware of why he is choosing to represent the events in this way and not in the other (negative) ways that it might have been possible to tell this story.

Proposition/lesson 2: Positives can come from learning to question conflict stories for possibilities.

This aspect of telesmatic intelligence is related to understanding how to look beyond lived realities for *possibility*—to be able to ask "why" questions, and to be able to answer those why question in a way that accounts for the lived reality of a conflict for the participants—that connects the dots to reveal the bigger picture or deeper dynamics of the conflict. Positives come when we are able to move beyond "why" questions to "what if" questions. The second proposition highlights that we can develop the ability to critically think through and map the interrelationships of speech acts (as well as thoughts and behaviors) that make up the systemic structure of a conflict, and from there begin to imagine alternate possibilities where desired. In short, this intelligence has to do with being able to see how and why a conflict occurred as it did, why it takes on the shape, form, intensity, patterns, and outcomes that it does, based on the communication of the participants and the meaning of the conflict for them. From critical mapping comes the systemic understanding of what happened, perhaps even what was effective and not effective if you will, and from this understanding alternative possibilities that build on the effective and that change the ineffective where possible should emerge.

This form of telesmatic intelligence also requires interpretive sensitivity to know that we cannot always know the motives and intents of others in conflicts. Nor can the participants in a conflict necessarily always be conscious of what they are doing and why, and we should not judge them as such. It requires the interpretive sensitivity to analyze the story from a nonjudgmental standpoint and with the spirit of peacemaking in mind. That is, we should explore our conflicts for lessons not about what we did wrong per se, but for the possibility for engaging alternative communication approaches where possible and where desired. Simply it is about asking what is possible for these people in conflict given the reality of what actually happened in the conflict.

Explicating possibilities carries the hope of being a positive experience in that it builds on a thorough interpretive account or narrative mapping of a conflict in ways that it suggests learning based growth. These moments lead to positives because they appeal to the desire people often have to make concrete steps to improve their conflict communication, and thus relationships.

Another example is useful to illustrate proposition two. Recently a student (Rachel—a pseudonym) shared a roommate conflict story with my conflict communication class in which a roommate relationship took a very conflicted turn and lead to may problems in the apartment. Rachel recognized that she just didn't "click" with one out of three of her new roommates (Kasey), and that she became close with the other two. This is a common roommate conflict in which a split around personality or likes devolves into a sort of us-versus-her dynamic. The roommate she didn't like began to want to hang out more with her and her roommates after she broke up with her boyfriend, but this caused tension because Rachel didn't like her. Rachel began to hang out less and less and her other three roommates grew closer. The conflict situation came to a head when they all went to an event, and while Rachel was in the restroom, Kasey took her seat which put Rachel on the outside of the group. Subsequently Kasey managed to turn the other roommates against Rachel and Rachel ended up being essentially shunned by the other three. She moved out without saying a word at the end of the semester and does not talk to the other former roommates.

All in all this appeared to most of us in the class to be a negative conflict experience. We then further discussed how the story contains the seeds for what might have been a more positive process and outcome. Rachel recognized that she seems to have a decision to make between engaging in a competitive power struggle with a roommate that she appears to have lost, or learning how to live with someone whom she appears at first meeting not to like for some reason. Perhaps she could also examine why she reacted so strongly to Kasey. Perhaps she could reflect on how it felt to be pushed to the margins of the apartment by Kasey when that is essentially what she did to Kasey from the start. Was this an equal and opposite reaction she set in motion? Perhaps she could also examine what dynamics and missteps her judgment and shunning of Kasey had on the roommate culture. Did she create the tension she talks about? Would her roommates assign her the bulk of the blame for this breakdown if we were able to talk to them? I also feel that she might reflect on what's missing from her story. I was not the only one listening to the story who wondered exactly what it was that made her react so strongly to Kasey before she even knew her. Might there be something valuable for her self-awareness and for her future roommate relationships in examining these and other questions?

What Rachel was later doing in class was asking questions of how telesmatically she approached her roommate relationships. She was able to see that much of her own communication, behavior, and thoughts helped create this competitive conflict that she essentially lost. She reflected that she saw Kasey as an "opponent" and that she set about—largely unconsciously—building an "imaginary fence" between them. She also admitted to "messing up" things in her room when she wasn't there. She was able also to see how she might do things differently next time—and not end up on the outside of the "fence" herself. Our discussion started to enable Rachel to examine her story for possibilities that she didn't take and from here to apply the communicative intelligence to approach roommate differences differently next time—with a view to creating positive conflict results.

Proposition/lesson 3: Positives can come from learning how to move a conflict story/reality in desired directions.

This form of communicative intelligence relies on our ability to create changes based on the skillful articulation, operationalization, and implementation of our *desire*—preferably our shared desire with the person with whom we are conflicting. Simply this intelligence is about knowing where you want the conflict story and/or the relationship to go next. Having developed a sense of where the story is currently, and a deep sense of possibilities, it should flow naturally to where we would like things to go from here based on the possibilities we have explicated.

This third proposition is basically that we often have substantially more choices for communication that move the conflict in desired directions than is evident to us when we are locked into a conflict with someone. In conflict the tendency is for us to narrow the possibilities—we see less as we focus on the specific issues of a conflict and become locked into our narrative characterization of self and other—and this has a limiting effect on the range of communication that seems available. This often in turn limits choices made, and that could be made. Recognizing this limiting effect of conflict and the fact that there are more possibilities than we might notice is the basis for the positives that come from expanding one's range of choices to match desire.

This expression of desire and its connection to strategy is based partly on our ability to view relational reality in narrative form—as a story that can be changed in strategic ways by changing particular communication tactics and strategies within the conflict story. It is also based on our ability to both know what we desire for a conflicted relationship, and on our ability to then see ways that this desire can be translated into the narrative and communication skills that mean we are able to change the conflict stories we live with others. Of course the other relationship implied here is that we are able to see the interconnections between a conflict and the relationship. Simply, the intelligence to know how changing a conflict with someone is likely to impact the relationship more broadly in desired ways can lead to very positive dynamics through conflict such as relational enrichment and reconciliation. Of course the lesson may be that a relationship is well and truly over and that more communication is inappropriate. This can also be a positive telesmatic learning moment. If every invitation to negotiate dialogically is rebuffed, then sometimes the most important thing to learn is how to end a relationship and move on.

It seems obvious how this lesson is connected to the positive possibilities for conflicts. Simply, the more telesmatically intelligent we become about being able to connect our desires to the way we engage conflicts then the more likely we are to have desired results from our communication. Also, the more skillfully we are able to externalize and see and treat conflicts as stories that are being co-authored as we communicate then the more likely we are to imagine and see real change possibilities. Knowing where you want the story to go from a certain point forward and developing the communicative intelligence to know how to move that story in a desired direction means that it is much more likely that communication itself gets tied to positive conflict processes and positive outcomes.

A third example is useful to further illustrate proposition three. Recently a student (Matt—a pseudonym) shared a story with my conflict communication class about his relationship with his half-sister. They grew up in different households and so were not close until they both ended up at the same college and even in a couple of the same classes. A closer relationship developed between them. His half-sister reached out to him and wanted to know why he did not share her commitment to Christianity. Matt on the other hand could not understand his sister's inability to think critically about the world in the same way that he does. A difference emerged in that initial conversation and she left the conversation assuming her half-brother was "lost" and he left the conversation with the belief that she had no interest in him but only to proselytize him. The difference started to become conflicted at this point. She began posting religious messages on Facebook and he would make joking and smart comments on the posts. His comments made her angry and she would "correct" him sometimes publicly on Facebook and sometimes simply delete his messages. She eventually sent him a Facebook message in which she accused him of being immature and disrespectful to her. He in return accused her of "passing judgment" and misunderstanding him. The rift grew as in the silence that ensued he began to post critical questions about religion that point to his perceived contradictions in religious discourse. Her response was to disengage this topic (and therefore him) and to continue posting religious messages on her Facebook wall. Their relationship had devolved through this often public (Facebook) conflict.

Through an analysis of the story Matt was able to recognize several things about their communication that contributed to the rapid rift and breakdown and he was also able to base some recommendations for change. He wants a close relationship with his sister, and realizes that their communication (as well as their related thoughts and behavior) is important to moving the story in that direction. This aspect of telesmatic intelligence is a key to the aforementioned conflict episode being a positive experience. Matt reflected that the first step in reconciliation would be for them to open up a dialogue about the conflict they had both gotten into. Specifically they should decide together what they want and recognize that it may be work to get their relationship back in a positive direction. The key, Matt sees is that their communication should reflect a respect for each other's boundaries, differences and beliefs. Both should become more keenly aware of the dangers of online communication and going public with messages about each other. Matt recognized his sister's attempt to engage rather than confront when she posted a mail privately, but that her tone and lack of engaging questions in that posting set in motion defensive reactions for him. If he were to listen carefully to her desires for his communication around their differences they are on their way towards an agreement about how they talk to and about each other in future. Finally he is able to conclude that they need to be able to either discuss different beliefs and look for commonalities or stay off the topic of religion altogether and focus on other topics that promote commonality. He concludes that approaching differences in this way might create a family atmosphere in which dialogue becomes the norm rather than the exception.

In this example, it is clear that the insights Matt comes to are quite simple but at the same time quite difficult to achieve when a rift has become entrenched between them. Much depends on his sister's desire—does she want to know him better or not? If so, the positive relationship he desires, and the positive outcome that might come from the conflict, depends on their common willingness to be more telesmatic about how they talk about and navigate their differences. Estrangement (negative) or greater intimacy as siblings (positive) lies in the balance.

Conclusion: The Centrality of Communication and Positive Conflict

Conflicts are inherently neither positive nor negative. They become defined as such depending on their meanings for people within relationships. If a conflict opens up a much needed space to redefine or renegotiate an issue of importance to the participants then it is usually defined—retrospectively at least—as positive. On the dark side of communication, if a conflict simply holds people in a never ending repeating pattern of difficulty, double-bind, or abuse then it is usually seen as a negative thing—at least by its "victims." Conflict are, as such, stories that are embedded in and impactful of broader (relational and life) stories in a variety of ways some of which might be characterized as negative or positive. The three main propositions explored in this chapter are keys to helping facilitate the positive or bright function of conflicts. Opening up relationships to desired change, enabling expression, dialogic negotiation, and so on are all constructive and sometimes reconstructive functions of conflict. At the same time we have seen that to learn these lessons and apply them to practice requires a good deal of communicative intelligence and competent practice—what we have defined as being telesmatic. The great challenge in all of this, I believe, rests on our ability to see and experience conflicts narratively—that is as stories that we help to co-create, and as stories that we therefore can learn to tell and retell in different ways, even if sometimes the reality behind the story has to catch up with our desire later.

References

Bage, G. *Narrative matters: Teaching and learning history through story.* London: Palmer.
Booker, C. (2004). *The seven basic plots: Why we tell stories.* London: Continuum.
Brooks, P. (1984). *Reading for the plot: Design and intention in narrative.* Oxford, Clarendon.
Clandinin, D., & Connelly, F. (1991). Narrative and story in research and practice. In D. Schon (Ed.). *The reflective turn: Case studies in and on educational practice.* New York: Teachers College Press.
Clark, M. C. (2010). Narrative learning: Its contours and possibilities. *New directions for adult and continuing education, 126,* 3–11.
Czarniawaska, B. (2004). *Narrative in social science research.* London: Sage.
Glaser, M., Garsoffky, B., & Schwan, B. (2009). Narrative-based learning: Possible benefits and problems. *The European journal of communications research, 34, 4:* 429–447.
Goodall, H. L., Jr., & Kellett, P. M. (2004). Dialectical tensions and dialogic moments as pathways to peak experiences. In R. Anderson, L. A. Baxter, & K. Cissna (Ed's.).

Dialogue: Theorizing difference in communication studies (2004) (pp. 159–174). Thousand Oaks, CA: Sage.

Goodson, I. F., Biesta, G. J. J., Tedder, M. & Adair, N. *Narrative learning*. London: Routledge.

Hammack, P.L. (2010). Identity as burden or benefit? Youth, historical narrative, and the legacy of political conflict. *Human Development, 53 (4),* 173–201.

Hart, R. P., Carlson, R. E., & Eadie, W. F. (1980). Attitudes toward communication and the assessment of rhetorical sensitivity. *Communication Monographs, 47,* 1–22.

Jeong, H. K. (2008). A romance with narrative inquiry: Toward an act of narrative theorizing. *Curriculum and teaching dialogue, 10*: 251–267.

Kellett, P. M. (2007). *Conflict dialogue: Understanding layers of meaning for more productive relationships*. Thousand Oaks, CA: Sage.

Kellett, P. M. (in press). Narrative and the teaching of peace and conflict studies. In T. Matyok & S. Byrne (Ed's.), *Critical issues in peace and conflict studies: Implications for theory, practice, and pedagogy*. New York: Lexington Books.

Kellett, P. M. & Dalton, D. G. (2001). *Managing conflict in a negotiated world: A narrative approach to achieving dialogue and change*. Thousand Oaks, CA: Sage.

Kellett, P.M. & Dalton, D.G. (2009). Games people play. In K. J. Gergen, S.M. Schrader, & M. Gergen (Ed's.). *Constructing worlds together: Interpersonal communication as relational process* (pp. 179–183). Boston, MA: Pearson, Allyn, & Bacon.

Rossiter, M. (1999). A narrative approach to development: Implications for adult education. *Adult Education Quarterly, 50 (1),* 56–71.

Tedder, M. & Biesta, G.J.J. (2009). What does it take to learn from one's life?: Exploring opportunities for biographical learning in the lifecourse. In B. Merrill (Ed.) *Learning to change? The role of identity and learning careers in adult education*. New York: Peter Lang.

Walton, R.E. (1969). *Interpersonal peacemaking: Confrontations and third party consultations*. Reading, MA: Addison-Wesley.

Ward, S. A., Blumen, D. L., Dauria, A. F. (1982). Rhetorical sensitivity recast: Theoretical assumptions of an informal interpersonal rhetoric. *Communication Quarterly, 30,* 189–195.

• CHAPTER TWELVE •

Forgiveness as Restoration: The Search for Well-Being, Reconciliation, and Relational Justice

Douglas L. Kelley
Arizona State University

"[You begin by] saying 'I forgive you in my heart.' And then you start building on that and actually the person doing the forgiving is the one that gets the gift. You give your soul a gift. Then you can both heal.... I got rid of the bondage, which was anger, sadness, negativism. Because it's a real bondage when you can't forgive."
—Margie

"Are we willing to throw away 32 years...just for a fling? I take it seriously, and it crushed me. And its probably changed me a lot, but I still don't know that I want to be alone and give up what we have, even though we were on real shaky ground there for a while."
—Susan

"She forgave me, but only because I apologized and admitted I was wrong."
—Sam

These opening quotes highlight three reasons to forgive. Margie refers to her own and her husband's well-being as she emphasizes, "Then you can both heal." Susan hopes that forgiveness will help her work through her husband's affair so she doesn't have to throw away their relationship, "just for a fling." And, Sam seeks forgiveness in order to fix a moral transgression, a perceived "wrong" in the relationship.

Family relationships create a unique context within which to study forgiveness (Kelley, 1998). The primarily nonvoluntary nature of sibling and parent-child relationships, the public nature of adult partner relationships, and the typically long-term nature of all family relationships generates distinctive pressures and responses to relationship hurt and transgressions (Kelley, 2012; Vangelisti & Crumley, 1998). As such, family members may experience unique demands to resolve conflict or "move on" in order to facilitate continued family functioning.

In each of the beginning scenarios forgiveness functions to restore one of three elements disrupted by a transgression: well being, the relationship, or the moral order. These three elements can be considered part of a positive psychological approach (Seligman & Csikszentmihalyi, 2000) to understanding relationships. Also, they represent three distinct motivations to be achieved through positive communication.

In the following pages I explore the restorative function of forgiveness. I begin by examining forgiveness as a form of positive communication. I follow with discussion of forgiveness motive as a desire to restore well-being, relationship, and/or the moral order. I finish with specific applications within the family context.

Forgiveness as Positive Communication

Positive communication is the means by which individuals pursue that which makes "life worth living" (Seligman & Csikszentmihalyi, 2000, p. 5). Theoretical work in positive psychology sets a sound framework from which to understand forgiveness as positive communication (Holter, Magnuson, & Enright, 2008; Kelley & Waldron, 2006; Peterson & Seligman, 2004). Seligman and Csikszentmihalyi (2000) identify the following as often neglected positive elements of psychology: hope, wisdom, creativity, future mindedness, courage, spirituality, responsibility, and perseverance. It is small stretch of the imagination to view these elements as related to positive communication and, specifically, forgiveness. Hope and future mindedness reflect individuals' desire to restore themselves, their relationships, or the moral order. Wisdom, creativity, and courage embody the skills needed to engage one's transgressor, or one who has been hurt, and renegotiate the relationship. Spirituality, responsibility, and perseverance move individuals to respond with mercy over time.

Conceptualizing forgiveness as a form of positive communication requires close examination of specific definitional components of forgiveness. A communication-based definition, developed by Vince Waldron and myself (Waldron & Kelley, 2008), highlights four essential elements critical to understanding forgiveness as positive communication:

> Forgiveness is a relational process whereby harmful conduct is acknowledged by one or both partners; the harmed partner extends undeserved mercy to the perceived transgressor; one or both partners experience a transformation from negative to positive psychological states, and the meaning of the relationship is renegotiated, with the possibility of reconciliation. (p. 19)

The first critical element of this definition is that it is relationally based. Positive communication by its very nature is relationally embedded. Second, it emphasizes the moral nature of the transgression when hurtful conduct, "a wrong," is identified. This aspect distinguishes forgiveness from nonforgiveness concepts (e.g., excuse, condoning; Enright & Fitzgibbons, 2000). Third, transforming negative responses to positive responses is a relatively common definitional feature of forgiveness (McCullough, Pargament, & Thorensen, 2000). Fourth, renegotiation of the relationship involves understanding relational meaning associated with the experience of the transgression and post-transgression partner response, as well as reorientation of the relational partners to reexamine essential relationship characteristics (e.g., trust and intimacy). In summary, forgiveness as positive communication focuses on relationship embeddedness; recognition of moral aspects of behavior; a shift from negative to positive emotion, thinking, and behavior; and renegotiation of the relationship.

In addition, Waldron and I (Waldron & Kelley, 2008) identified empathy and altruism as psychological responses to transgressions that can be conceptualized as positive communication responses. Empathy is identified by many researchers as essential to the forgiveness process (McCullough, Worthington, & Rachal, 1997; Tsuang et al., 2005). Malcolm, Warwar, and Greenberg (2005) suggest empathy be understood as cognitive and affective. Cognitive empathy represents the ability to understand the offender as human—acting in a manner similar to what others (or even oneself) might have done given similar background and circumstances. Affective empathy opens the injured party to compassion as he or she feels what the offender may have been feeling when the offense occurred. This affective connection to the offender then moves the injured party toward the possibility of forgiveness (Worthington, 2001).

Empathy may also trigger altruistic (helping) responses (Batson & Oleson, 1991; Tsuang et al., 2005). Smith et al. (2006) conceptualize altruism as "a voluntary act of helping or sharing that is intended to benefit others beyond simple sociability or duties associated with a role" (p. 711). As such, forgiveness when given voluntarily to benefit the offender can be seen as an act of altruism. In fact, Worthington (2001) identifies forgiveness as an "altruistic gift" which results from empathizing with the transgressor (Worthington, 1998; 2001).

Positive psychologists have also identified forgiveness as one of 24 character strengths recognized by various people groups around the world (Seligman et al., 2005). Each character strength is a component of one of six virtues. Forgiveness, a component of temperance (along with modesty and prudence) protects against excess (Seligman et al., 2005). For example, forgiveness inhibits unhealthy rumination and cultivating negative emotion as it moves the victim toward more positive responses.

Holter et al. (2008) identify four developments in positive psychology with particular relevance to forgiveness. The first development examines the role of positive emotions as related to creativity, problem solving, and ameliorating the effects of negative emotions (see Fredrickson, 2006). Managing the effects of negative emotions following a relational hurt, is crucial to moving forward in the process of forgiveness. In particular, positive emotions generated by the forgiveness process may neutralize negative emotions (Worthington, 2005).

The second development is research focusing on emotional intelligence. Because many forgiveness models posit a shift from negative to positive emotion (McCullough et al., 2000; Waldron & Kelley, 2008), emotional awareness and the ability to express emotions appropriately and discuss them with one's relational partner is crucial to the forgiveness process (see Grewal & Salovey, 2006). In previous work Waldron and I (2008) highlight managing emotion as one of seven central tasks of the forgiveness process.

The third development identified by Holter et al. (2008) is the relationship between intervention and prevention. They argue that while the transgression cannot be undone, the effects of the transgression can be reversed. In addition, possible future negative effects may be avoided.

The final development of positive psychology with implications for forgiveness is Seligman's concept of happiness, or the meaningful life. Seligman (Duckworth, Steen, & Seligman, 2005; Seligman et al., 2005) identifies three components of happiness: the pleasant life, the engaged life, the meaningful life. The pleasant life includes positive emotion related to the past, present, and future. Clearly one of the functions of forgiveness is to heal past hurt and bring hope to the future (Waldron & Kelley, 2008). The engaged life focuses on using specific individual traits, most specifically character strengths, as one engages the world. Strengths of character are those qualities considered virtuous across historical eras and culture, such as kindness, integrity, wisdom, valor, and leadership (Duckworth et al., 2005).

As previously discussed, forgiveness may function as a form of the virtue, temperance. The meaningful life pushes individuals outside themselves as they engage in positive institutions (e.g., strong families). Meaning is gained as one commits to something larger than oneself. As Duckworth et al. (2005) state, "positive traits and positive emotions flourish best in the context of positive institutions. Because meaning derives from belonging to and serving something larger than oneself, a life led in the service of positive institutions is the meaningful life" (p. 636). Holter et al. (2008) argue that the meaningful life is most germane to the study of forgiveness. For example, Freedman and Enright's (1996) forgiveness interventions with incest survivors discovered that many were able to find meaning in their suffering and new purpose in their lives. Likewise, Waldron and I (2008) identify sense-making as an essential task of the forgiveness process, as do Gordon, Baucom, and Snyder (2004, 2005) as they focus on forgiveness for couples in therapy.

Outcomes-based research supports a positive psychology approach to change (Duckworth et al., 2005). For example, in psychotherapeutic contexts with depressed clients, focus on positive emotion, engagement, and meaning have resulted in significant long-term effects (Seligman, Rashid, & Parks, 2006). However, as positive psychology research is still in its infancy, researchers have yet to tie forgiveness, and most specifically the communication of forgiveness, to living the happy life (Seligman et al., 2005). As such, I turn out attention to forgiveness motives as attempts to restore.

Forgiveness Motives

As with all human behavior, forgiveness is prompted by a variety of motivations. Although forgivers and transgressors have similar, though not identical, reasons to forgive (Kelley, 1998), motivations for both parties can largely be understood as a desire to restore personal well-being, the relationship, or the moral order (Kelley, 1998; Waldron & Kelley, 2008). In this sense, individuals pursue pleasant, engaged, and meaningful lives (Seligman et al., 2005).

Restoring well-being. Individuals forgive in order to restore their own personal (self) well-being or the well-being of their partner. In terms of personal well-being, respondents in my research (Kelley, 1998), focused on changing negative emotions that became damaging to self, such as harboring long-term anger: "I began to realize this anger was not only torturing him, but myself as well. It was eating me up inside and making me more of an angry person." Offender personal well-being focuses on negative feelings that resulted from the transgression, for example the elimination of guilt for wrong behavior. This may involve attempts to assuage or "heal" the victim's response to the transgression (e.g., eliminating the other's disappointment).

I also found other well-being to mirror self well-being (Kelley, 1998). Essentially, other well-being represents altruistic behavior toward one's partner (Waldron & Kelley, 2008). For example, forgivers reported their choice to forgive in order to help the offender feel better psychologically (e.g., remove guilt) or to help them "move on" with their lives. Interestingly, offenders desired other well-being in order to facilitate the wounded party's ability to forgive and get over feelings of hurt or disappointment.

Restoring the relationship/reconciliation. My research (Kelley, 1998) also revealed forgiveness motivations to restore the relationship. Forgivers reported that they were motivated to forgive in order to restore the relationship and because of obligation ("I had to forgive her because she is my sister"). Forgivers were also willing to restore the relationship when the infraction seemed minor compared to the worth of the relationship. Offenders were similarly motivated by, and specifically identified a desire to, restore trust.

Worthington (2001) identifies restoration of trust as the central element of reconciliation. While considered a part of forgiveness by many laypersons, most researchers make clear distinctions between forgiveness and reconciliation (Kanz, 2000; Kearns & Fincham, 2004; Waldron & Kelley, 2008). Forgiveness is often considered an internal process within an interpersonal context, and reconciliation a social process (de Waal & Pokorny, 2005; Enright & Fitzgibbons, 2000; McCullough et al., 2000). Although, it should be recognized that certain theorizing, particularly within applied contexts (e.g., marital therapy; Hargrave, 1994), views reconciliation as a part of the forgiveness process.

As a central motivation of both forgivers and offenders, reconciliation is an important consideration in the decision to forgive. Rusbult, Hannon, Stocker, and Finkel (2005) describe reconciliation as a process of partners enacting prosocial behaviors over an extended period of time. These include, for the forgiver, setting aside blame and indicating a willingness to begin with a clean slate. In addition, couple well-being is facilitated by the forgiver demonstrating empathy, letting go of hurt feelings, and forgiving. On the other hand, the offender needs to take responsibility for hurtful actions and make amends if possible. As such, couple well-being is facilitated by apology, amends, and promises not to repeat the offense. Reconciliation may also require renegotiation of relationship rules and norms (Rusbult et al.,

2005; Waldron & Kelley, 2008). Clearly forgiveness provides a means for the partners to engage in the positive communication necessary to successfully reconcile and renegotiate their relationships.

It is important to recognize that forgiveness and reconciliatory communication are often confounded. This is potentially problematic when couples presume that because some form of reconciliation has taken place, forgiveness has take place. For example, in my own research (Kelley & Waldron 2005; Waldron & Kelley, 2005) couples identify discussion, explanation, and setting conditions (conditional forgiveness) as strategies for granting or seeking forgiveness. Yet, interviews with couples indicate that discussion/explanation often results in reconciliation, with implicit forgiveness. That is, the granting or receiving of forgiveness is assumed, but never made explicit. The potential risk in these situations is that the work of forgiveness (see the essential communication tasks described in the following section, "Couple Applications") may be left undone, resulting in potential problems in restoring trust or managing subsequent transgressions.

Restoring the moral order. Forgiveness motivations identified in my research (Kelley, 1998; Waldron & Kelley, 2008) included moral obligation and religious obligation. Some individuals forgave because they believed it the "right" thing to do. This moral obligation often came from religious foundations. For example, several of the couples in my long-term marriage study (Waldron & Kelley, 2008) forgave their spouses' affairs because their religious beliefs valued forgiveness.

What is most significant is that forgiveness is used when a relational transgression is interpreted to be a break in the moral code (Freedman, Enright, & Knutson, 2005; Waldron & Kelley, 2008). When individuals interpret a relational behavior as "right" or "wrong," "good" or "bad," they are viewing the behavior within a moral context. Forgiveness, then, typically includes the goal of restoring the moral structure of the relationship. Negotiated morality theory (Waldron & Kelley, 2008) states that a desire to preserve moral codes motivates forgiveness and unforgiveness (e.g., revenge). Additionally, it purports that forgiveness interactions are dialogic spaces wherein individuals' moral codes are expressed and negotiated. As such, forgiveness communication may serve any of the following moral functions: defining moral standards, establishing accountability, engaging moral tensions, restoring relational justice through atonement, reimagining a moral future (hope), honoring the self, redirecting hostility, increasing safety and certainty, finding closure, and possible reconciliation.

From restoration to redemption. Before making specific application to the family context, it is necessary to reemphasize that while forgiveness is a process of restoration, relationships and individuals can never exactly achieve a previous state of being. Memory prevents achieving a past state exactly as it was. As such, while restoration may involve a return to certain previous conditions, it also involves transformation, hopefully toward new, positive conditions. Redemption, while often thought of as a religious term, involves the transformation of an object into that for which it was originally intended (e.g., think of soda bottles that can be redeemed at the grocery for five cents, in order that they may be used again for what they were originally intended). As such, the process of restoration involves the opportunity for relationships to be redeemed into that for which relational partners hoped they could be and for individuals to be redeemed by establishing personal well-being, in or out of the relationship. To this end, forgiveness as a positive-communication strategy moves individuals toward the development of strengths of character and personal happiness, particularly as it relates to living a meaningful life committed to strong, positive family systems.

Family Applications

My early research (Kelley, 1998) identified differences between forgiveness in family relationships as compared to nonfamily relationships. For example, narratives from participants revealed family members were less likely than those in voluntary relationships (e.g., dating and friendship) to forgive for love, because of the offender's apology, or to restore the relationship. As such, parent-child and marital forgiveness interactions may require special attention from forgiveness researchers and practitioners. The relative stability of family relationships (e.g., blood relations between siblings and parents and children, and the public nature of marital commitment) may lead individuals to devalue the need for forgiveness, or at least for more explicit expressions or processing of forgiveness. As a result, the following section explores application of forgiveness concepts to committed adult couple (married and long-term cohabitating) and family (parent-child and sibling) relationships.

Couple Applications

For application to long-term couples, I integrate the work of Gordon and Baucom (1999, 2003) and Gordon, Baucom, and Snyder (2004, 2005) with my own work (Waldron & Kelley, 2008). I begin by briefly reviewing Communication Tasks of Forgiveness (CTF; Waldron & Kelley, 2008) then integrate this framework with Gordon et al.'s (1999, 2003, 2004, 2005) three-stage process of managing relational trauma. CTF consists of seven communication-based tasks that contribute to enacting forgiveness. These tasks do not necessarily occur in the order presented and may be repeated. Task one is confronting the transgression. Recognition of the "relational wrong" is critical to eventual restoration of well-being, the relationship, and the moral order. In addition, it is a central element that distinguishes forgiveness from other similar concepts (e.g., acceptance). Task two involves managing one's emotional response. Managing emotion may entail expressing, labeling, or acknowledging strong negative emotions, such as anger, bitterness, and fear. Task three, sense-making, attempts to understand one's self, the relationship, and the offending partner in light of the offense. It may necessarily involve information sharing regarding motives or other situational details that can be used to reduce uncertainty. Task four, seeking forgiveness, occurs when the offending partner apologizes, explains, shows remorse, or directly requests forgiveness. Task five, granting forgiveness, can occur through somewhat direct means, such as the offended partner saying "I forgive you," setting conditions on the relationship, and discussing the transgression; less direct means, such as couple behavior returning to "normal," minimizing the event (e.g., "It was no big deal"), or simply responding to the offender nonverbally (e.g., hugging); or a combination of both direct and indirect approaches. Task six involves renegotiating the rules and values that will guide the relationship post-forgiveness/transgression. At this point, partners have moral-based discussions as to what constitutes a just or fair relationship given what has happened. Task seven, transition, recognizes that couples will need to continue to monitor the new relationship agreement and build trust. Often, individual partners continue to make sense of transgressions and responses to transgression over extended periods of time. For severe transgressions, this process may continue to evolve as individuals and relationships develop and grow across the lifespan.

It should be recognized that while the three primary forgiveness motivations occur across all of the preceding tasks, certain tasks may be most associated with certain motivations at any given time (see Table 12.1). For example, initially confronting the transgression and managing emotion are often related to pursuit of forgiver well-being. Sense-making is clearly associated with restoring one's moral sense of the relationship. And, renegotiating relational rules is most essential to restoring the relationship.

The communication tasks of forgiveness share much in common with the forgiveness process outlined by Gordon et al. (1999, 2000, 2003, 2005). Gordon and colleagues have created an interesting program of research focusing on couples that choose to work through marital affairs, or other major betrayals, using forgiveness. They suggest a three-stage process that parallels the general stages related to managing psychological trauma: impact, search for meaning, and recovery, or moving on.

Stage one, impact, is a time in which people recall details surrounding the betrayal in order to increase understanding. This stage is typically accompanied by emotions such as uncertainty, fear, hurt, or anger, that often alternate with a sense of numbness, disbelief, and increased risk. Punitive and erratic behaviors toward the offending partner are often typical. A therapist may help the wounded partner place boundaries, engage in self-care, and find appropriate ways to manage the emotion associated with remembering. Stage two, meaning, is characterized by discovering why the transgression happened and, subsequently, assigning meaning to the event. Meaning may involve learning (e.g., "I contributed to the cause of the transgression by..."), positive impact (e.g., spiritual growth), and rethinking one's own identity, one's partner's identity, and the relationship. Finally, stage three, recovery or moving on, is characterized by "moving on" psychologically, with reduced negative emotion. Hopefully, there is clearer thinking as a result of reduced arousal and the cognitive processing that occurred during stage two. At this stage individuals may decide that forgiveness, as opposed to revenge, provides better opportunities for psychological and future relational health. In addition, they choose to either move on in the current relationship, but with renegotiated rules and values, or to move on by ending or changing the nature of the relationship.

Integration of CTF with Gordon et al.'s three stages places a focus on the following elements (see Table 12.1): first, managing the impact of the transgression; second, making sense of one's self, one's partner, and one's relationship in the aftermath of the transgression; third, engaging the forgiveness process; fourth, negotiating reconciliation.

Table 12.1

Integration of Communication Tasks of Forgiveness* with Gordon et al.'s Three-Stage Forgiveness Process**

Stage	Key Motivation	Communication Task (CTF)	Communication Behaviors
Manging the impact	Restore well-being	Confront transgression-manage emotion	Confront transgressor, vent to a third party, questioning, identifying and expressing emotions
Making sense of one's self, partner, relationship	Restore moral order	Sense-making	Discussion, explanation, listening; perspective-taking; joint assessment of relational impact; contextualizing transgression in light of relational past
Engaging Forgiveness	Restore well-being and moral order	Seek/grant/accept forgiveness	Apology, nonverbal assurance, sensitvity, nondefensive listening, forgiveness request, empathy
Negotiating Reconciliation	Restore the relationship	Renegotiate rules/values Monitor transition	Negotiate: rules, values, relationship agreement, moral structure, conditions

*Waldron & Kelley (2008)
**Gordon et al. (1999, 2000, 2003, 2005)

Family Applications

Children typically learn forgiveness, as a positive communication strategy, from their parents (Denham, Neal, Wilson, Pickering, & Boyatzis, 2005). Forgiveness may be a result of interparental modeling or directly taught by parents. Regarding modeling, research by Denham et al. (2005) suggests that children who take part in their parents' conflicts are more likely to forgive. The authors suggest that children may learn resolution strategies from their parents' conflicts.

Related, research reveals children to understand forgiveness within the context of justice (Denham et al., 2005; Enright, Santos, & Al Mabuk, 1989). Denham et al.'s (2005) findings suggest that children consider forgiveness more likely when the transgression was accidental or accompanied by an apology or sincerity (e.g., the offender felt really bad). Interestingly, they found children to be most judgmental when an offender "made an excuse" (p. 134). The authors suggest that use of excuse fails to generate empathy, which we have seen to be closely related to forgiveness. They conclude that, "children's evaluations point to moral reasoning based on intentionality and motivation" (p. 134).

As suggested previously, moral reasoning regarding forgiveness may be taught directly. Based on The Adventure of Forgiveness (Enright, 2001; Knutson & Enright, 2002), Holter et al. (2008) suggest a forgiveness program for the education of young children. The program consists of five prescriptive processes (building blocks) taught in three parts: part one involves learning the five building blocks of forgiveness, "reframing and perspective taking for inherent worth, moral love, kindness, respect, and generosity" (Holter et al., 2008, pp. 78–79); part two provides concrete examples through story; part three focuses on practice of the five building blocks of forgiveness.

Based on our previous discussion of forgiveness motive, I suggest that children may learn forgiveness by focusing on the three functions (motives) of forgiveness: restoration of the relationship, well-being, and the moral order (see Table 12.2). These functions overlap with the basic building blocks suggested by Holter et al. (2008). For example, restoration of well-being overlaps with "reframing and perspective taking for inherent worth;" moral love is related to restoration of the moral order; and, kindness, respect, and generosity provide the skills necessary to restore the relationship.

First children may be taught to forgive by teaching them to restore the moral order. It appears that children naturally respond to the moral element of violations (Dehham et al., 2005). As such, teaching children to recognize that a "wrong" has happened is essential to training them to forgive. This initial step begins the process with a balance of mercy and justice. Although forgiveness is typically conceptualized as a merciful response to transgression, the acknowledgement and recognition of the transgression also begins the process of justice (Waldron & Kelley, 2008).

Second is the motive to restore well-being. To restore well-being, the parent teaches the child to process and release negative emotion, as well as to foster positive emotion. Essential to this stage of forgiveness training is the cultivation of positive emotion and behavior that can have a neutralizing effect on negative emotion (e.g., appropriate venting). Over time, negative emotions (e.g., bitterness and anger) should dissipate and be replaced with more positive feelings (e.g., peace and happiness).

Finally, children are encouraged to restore the relationship. Though reconciliation is not a necessary component of forgiveness, the typical goal within families is to restore relationship functioning between parent and child or between siblings. Typically, children are encouraged to return to "normal" or to renegotiate their relationship so as to improve relationship functioning. For example, parents may help children renegotiate relationship rules (e.g., only enter one another's room with permission). In addition, parents may teach the offender the nature of repentance. For example, in order to reestablish trust in the relationship, children can be taught the nature of full apology (Schlenker & Darby, 1981). Ideally, to move beyond the shallow "sorry" many of us heard from siblings growing up, children can learn to show sincerity, offer to fix or repay for damage done, and offer ideas for how or why the transgression will not reoccur (Kelley & Waldron, 2005).

Notice in this extended example in Table 12.2 that the parent leads them to all three types of restoration: moral, relational, and forgiver and offender well-being. Moral restoration is addressed twice as the parent helps the boys acknowledge that something "wrong" happened and makes sure the process seems "fair" to both boys. The parent also addresses well-being by helping them process their anger. In this way, the children are guided, but also given ownership of the process. Relational restoration occurs as the parent walks them through elements of a true apology: sincerity, verbalizing the transgression in a way that communicates an understanding of its effect, restitution (mow the lawn), and a plan to change things in the future.

Table 12.2

Sample Dialogue: Family Forgiveness

Parent: John, can you tell Brad why you are angry with him?
John: Because you're a creep and keep going into my room when I tell you not to.
Parent: John, can you rephrase what you just said and tell Brad why it bothers you when he goes into your room?
John: Well…I like to keep everything in my room just right. When you go into my room without my permission I feel like you mess things up and invade my space.
Brad: That's because you're too sensitive.
Parent: Brad, do you think John has the right to require his permission before going into his room?
Brad: I guess.
Parent: Then can you apologize for going into his room without permission?
Brad: Uh…sorry.
Parent: Okay, Brad can you say you're sorry like you mean it? And, can you tell John that you know what you did wrong?
Brad: John, sorry I went into your room without your permission.
Parent: Thank you, Brad. And John, what do you have to say?
John: You better not do it again.
Parent: Okay, we'll get to that. But John just apologized to you. That was pretty big on his part. What can you say in return?
John: No big deal.
Parent: Is that true? You thought it was a big deal at that time. How else can you say it?
John: Uhm, well, I know it might seem weird, but I really don't like people in my room, even Mom and Dad; so thanks for apologizing.
Parent: Great. Now Brad, what are you going to do about the mess you made?
Brad: I'll clean it up. I said I would before.
John: No! I don't want you to clean it up. I'll put everything back the way I like it.
Parent: Then, John, are we done here or is there something you'd like Brad to do?
John: Well, I don't want Brad in my room, but he could mow the yard for me since I have to clean up his mess.
Parent: Brad?
Brad: Okay, I'll do it.
Parent: Does that seem fair to you both?
John & Brad: I guess.
Parent: Now, just one more thing. Brad, what are you going to do next time you want to go into John's room?
Brad: …I'm going to ask.
Parent: Tell John, not me.
Brad: Okay. John, next time I'll ask first, okay?
John: That's cool.

Final Thoughts

This essay provides the theoretical grounding to understand forgiveness as a form of positive communication intended to restore. As positive communication, forgiveness is relational, recognizes a transgression, moves individuals' personal responses from negative to positive, and makes reconciliation possible. Seligman et al.'s (2005) three components of happiness (the pleasant life, the engaged life, the meaningful life) provide a basis for understanding positive-communication forgiveness motives as intended to restore personal and other well-being, the relationship, and the moral order. These three motivations (which may also be understood as forgiveness functions) can be used to guide couples and families in learning to develop forgiveness as a particular character strength. As such, forgiveness becomes more than just one among many conflict management strategies. It is a redemptive response to relational hurt that is able to heal and transform individuals and relationships, while providing an enlightened sense of relational justice.

References

Batson, C. D., & Oleson, K. C. (1991). Current status of the empathy-altruism hypothesis. In M. S. Clark (Ed.), *Prosocial behavior* (pp. 62–85). Newbury Park, CA: Sage Publications.

Denham, S. A., Neal, K., Wilson, B. J., Pickering, S., & Boyatzis, C. J. (2005). In E. Worthington (Ed.), *Handbook of forgiveness* (pp. 127–142). New York: Routledge.

de Waal, F. B. M., & Pokorny, J. J. (2005). Primate conflict and its relation to human forgiveness. In E. Worthington (Ed.), *Handbook of forgiveness* (pp. 17–32). New York: Routledge.

Duckworth, A. L., Steen, T. A., & Seligman, M. E. P. (2005). Positive psychology in clinical practice. *Annual Review of Clinical Psychology, 1*(1), 629–651.

Enright, R. D. (2001). *Forgiveness is a choice: A step-by-step process for resolving anger and restoring hope*. Washington, DC: American Psychological Association.

Enright, R. D., & Fitzgibbons, R. P. (2000). *Helping clients forgive: An empirical guide for resolving anger and restoring hope* (1st ed.). Washington, DC: American Psychological Association.

Enright, R. D., Santos, M. J., & Al Mabuk, R. (1989). The adolescent as forgiver. *Journal of Adolescence, 12,* 95–110.

Fredrickson, B. L. (2006). The broaden-and-build theory of positive emotions. In M. Csikszentmihalyi & I. S. Scikszentmihalyi (Eds.) *A life worth living: Contributions to positive psychology* (pp. 85–103). New York: Oxford University Press.

Freedman, S. R., & Enright, R. D. (1996). Forgiveness as an intervention goal with incest survivors. *Journal of Consulting and Clinical Psychology, 64,* 983–992.

Freedman, S. R., Enright, R. D., & Knutson, J. (2005). A progress report on the process model of forgiveness. In E. Worthington (Ed.), *Handbook of forgiveness* (pp. 393–406). New York: Routledge.

Gordon, K. C., & Baucom, D. H. (1999). A multitheoretical intervention for promoting recovery from extramarital affairs. *Clinical Psychology: Science and Practice, 6* 382–399.

Gordon, K. C., & Baucom, D. H. (2003). Forgiveness and marriage: Preliminary support for a measure based on a model of recovery from a marital betrayal. *American Journal of Family Therapy, 31,* 179–199.

Gordon, K. C., Baucom, D. H., & Snyder (2004). An integrative intervention for promoting recovery from extramarital affairs. *Journal of Marital and Family Therapy, 30,* 213–231.

Gordon, K. C., Baucom, D. H. & Snyder, D. K. (2005). Forgiveness in couples: Divorce, infidelity, and couples therapy. In E. Worthington (Ed.), *Handbook of forgiveness* (pp. 407–421). New York: Routledge.

Grewal, D. D., & Salovey, P. (2006). Benefits of emotional intelligence. In M. Csikszentmihalyi & I. S. Csikszentmihalyi (Eds.) *A life worth living: Contributions to positive psychology* (pp. 104–119). New York: Oxford University Press.

Hargrave, T. D. (1994). Families and forgiveness: A theoretical and therapeutic framework. *The Family Journal, 2*(4), 339–348.

Holter, A. C., Magnuson, C. M., & Enright, R. D. (2008). Forgiveness is a matter of choice: Forgiveness education for young children. In S. J. Lopez (Ed.), *Positive psychology: Exploring the best in people* (pp. 69–88). Westport, Connecticut: Praeger.

Kanz, J. E. (2000). How do people conceptualize and use forgiveness? The forgiveness attitudes questionnaire. *Counseling and Values, 44*(3), 174.

Kearns, J. N., & Fincham, F. D. (2004). Victim and perpetrator accounts of interpersonal transgressions: Self-serving or relationship-serving biases? *Personality and Social Psychology Bulletin, 31,* 321–333.

Kelley, D. L. (1998). The communication of forgiveness. *Communication Studies, 49*(3), 255–271.

Kelley, D. L. (2012). *Marital communication.* Cambridge, UK: Polity.

Kelley, D. L., & Waldron, V. (2005). An investigation of forgiveness-seeking communication and relational outcomes. *Communication Quarterly,* 53, 339–358.

Kelley, D. L., & Waldron, V. (2006). Forgiveness: Communicative implications in social relationships. *Communication Yearbook, 30,* 303–341.

Knutson, J., & Enright, R. D. (2002). *The adventure of forgiveness: A guided curriculum for early elementary classrooms.* Madison: University of Wisconsin-Madison.

Malcolm, W., Warwar, S., Greenberg, L. (2005). Facilitating forgiveness in individual therapy as an approach to resolving interpersonal injuries. In E. Worthington (Ed.), *Handbook of forgiveness* (pp. 379–391). New York: Routledge.

McCullough, M. E., Pargament, K. I., & Thorensen, C. E. (Eds.). (2000). *Forgiveness: Theory, research, and practice.* New York: Guilford.

McCullough, M. E., Worthington, E. L., Jr., & Rachal, K. C. (1997). Interpersonal forgiving in close relationships. *Journal of Personality and Social Psychology, 73,* 321–336.

Peterson, C., & Seligman, M. E. P. (2004). *Character strengths and virtues: A handbook and classification.* Washington, DC: American Psychological Association.

Rusbult, C. E., Hannon, P. A., Stocker, S. L., & Finkel, E. J. (2005). In E. Worthington (Ed.), *Handbook of forgiveness* (pp. 185–205). New York: Routledge.

Schlenker, B. R., & Darby, B. W. (1981). The use of apologies in social predicaments. *Social Psychology Quarterly, 44*, 271–278.

Seligman, M. E. P., & Csikszentmihalyi, M. (2000). Positive psychology: An introduction. *American Psychologist, 55*(1), 5–14.

Seligman, M. E. P., Rashid, T., & Parks, A. C. (2006). Positive psychotherapy. *American Psychologist, 61*(8), 774–788.

Seligman, M. E. P., Steen, T. A., Park, N., & Peterson, C. (2005). Positive psychology progress: Empirical validation of interventions. *American Psychologist, 60*(5), 410–421.

Smith, S. W., Smith, S. L., Pieper, K. M., Yoo, J. H., Ferris, A. L., Downs, E., & Bowden, B. (2006). Altruism on American television: Examining the amount of, and context surrounding, acts of helping and sharing. *Journal of Communication, 56*(4), 707–727.

Tsuang, T. M., Eaves, L., Nir, T., Jerskey, B. A., & Lyons, M. J. (2005). Genetic influences on forgiving. In E. Worthington (Ed.), *Handbook of forgiveness* (pp. 245–258). New York: Routledge.

Vangelisti, A. L., & Crumley, L. P. (1998). Reactions to messages that hurt: The influence of relational contexts. *Communication Monographs, 65*, 173–196.

Waldron, V. R., & Kelley, D. L. (2005). Forgiveness as a response to relational transgression. *Journal of Social and Personal Relationships, 22*, 723–742.

Waldron, V. R., & Kelley, D. L. (2008). *Communicating forgiveness*. Los Angeles: Sage.

Worthington, E. L. (1998). *Dimensions of forgiveness: Psychological research & theological perspectives*. Philadelphia: Templeton Foundation Press.

Worthington, E. L. (2001). Unforgiveness, forgiveness, and reconciliation and their implications for societal interventions. In R. G. Helmick & R. L. Petersen (Eds.), *Forgiveness and reconciliation* (pp. 171–192). Philadelphia: Templeton Foundation Press.

Worthington, E. L. (2005). Initial questions about the art and science of forgiving. In E. L. Worthington (Ed.), *Handbook of forgiveness* (pp. 245–258). New York: Routledge.

• CHAPTER THIRTEEN •

Supportive Communication: A Positive Response to Negative Life Events

Erina MacGeorge
Purdue University

Bo Feng
University of California, Davis

Kristi Wilkum
University of Wisconsin, Fond du Lac

Eileen Doherty
Purdue University

Recently, Erina (first author) was worried about whether to move her young son from one childcare center to another. Having recently moved to a different house in another part of town, she wanted to reduce her driving time (and gas expense!) by moving him to a center that was closer to their new home, but was also concerned about how he would handle even more change in his life. Erina shared the situation with her friend, Lisa, who expressed sympathy and understanding for Erina's concerns and shared some stories about when her son was in daycare. When Erina mentioned that she was leaning toward keeping her son at the old center for a while, Lisa said that she thought he was resilient enough to handle the change, but that Erina should "trust her instincts."

This interaction between Erina and Lisa provides an example of *supportive communication,* where this term refers to "verbal and nonverbal behavior produced with the intention of providing assistance to others perceived as needing that aid" (MacGeorge, Feng, & Burleson, in press). Thus, supportive communication is something that others can provide when life events, whether big or small, create emotional distress and challenge our ability to cope. If positive communication is defined as communication that promotes positive emotions and attitudes and benefits interpersonal relationships (see Socha & Pitts, chapter 1, this volume), then supportive communication certainly fits the definition. Erina's outcomes after interaction with Lisa exemplify some that are typical of high quality supportive communication, including reduced distress (Jones, 2004) and improved capacity to cope with the problem (MacGeorge et al., 2004). However, the beneficial influence of supportive interactions goes well beyond the short term: over time, the sustained receipt of high-quality supportive communication contributes substantially to psychological, physical, and relational well-being (MacGeorge et al., in press).

Researchers in communication and allied disciplines began giving focused attention to supportive communication in the early 1980s (e.g., Burleson, 1983). Since, there has been considerable growth in the quantity and sophistication of theory and research in this area. This chapter provides an overview of scholarship on supportive communication, organized into four sections. First, we situate the concept of supportive communication within the larger framework of research on social support. Second, we examine the influence of supportive communication on well-being. Third, we explicate the core of supportive communication research that has focused on identifying characteristics of messages and interactions which influence the effectiveness of support provision. Finally, we discuss factors influencing whether support providers give high-quality support, and discuss the development of supportive communication skills.

Social Support and Supportive Communication

Impetus for the study of supportive communication derives in part from research on *social support* that began in the 1970s. During this decade, scholars synthesized findings across disciplines showing that stressful conditions create greater risk for psychological disorder, disease, and death, but that social support (variously defined and measured) provided protection against these risks (Caplan, 1974; Cassel, 1976). Subsequently, there emerged three distinct approaches to conceptualizing and assessing social support: a sociological approach, a psychological approach, and somewhat later, a communication approach (for a fuller history, see Burleson & MacGeorge, 2002). Since the sociological and psychological approaches continue to support vigorous scholarly activity, and cross-pollinate with theory and research on supportive communication, we provide a brief overview of these traditions before focusing attention on the approach adopted by communication scholars.

The Sociological and Psychological Traditions

Within the sociological tradition, social support is conceptualized and measured as *social integration*—the extent to which individuals are embedded in relationships and groups, participate in social activities, or experience a sense of community and belonging (Brissette, Cohen, & Seeman, 2000). The positive association between social integration and longevity has been documented repeatedly in longitudinal, prospective research with large regional and national samples (Berkman et al., 2004), as have the positive effects of social integration on multiple facets of physical and psychological health (Ikeda & Kawachi, 2010). Social integration is theorized to protect health through various mechanisms, including social influence (network members encourage healthy behaviors and discourage unhealthy ones), social resources (network members provide goods, services, and information that are health-protective), and positive affect (interactions with network members result in positive emotions that promote psychological and physical health; for a review, see Cohen & Lemay, 2007). Social integration may also have a beneficial influence on physiological processes that include blood pressure, immune response, and inflammatory response (Kiecolt-Glaser, Gouin, & Hantsoo, 2010).

In the psychological tradition, there has been a historical progression in the conceptualization and measurement of social support. Some of the earliest research in this tradition examined what was termed *enacted support*, or helping behaviors directed from one person to another (Barrera, 1981). However, psychologists shifted rapidly to conceptualizations that were more perceptual in character. Some studies examine *received support*, or the perception of how much supportive behavior has been received in the recent past (e.g., Gleason, Iida, Shrout, & Bolger, 2008), but the more dominant construct is *perceived availability of support*, or the perception that caring behavior from others will be available if the need arises (e.g., Mak, Bond, Simpson, & Rholes, 2010). (For a fuller discussion of enacted, received, and perceived support within the psychological tradition, see MacGeorge et al., in press.)

Typically, the effects of perceived availability of support are explained with reference to appraisal theory (Lazarus & Folkman, 1984), which explains stress as arising from individuals' interpretation or "appraisal" of events, including evaluations of coping resources. Thus, to the extent that people perceive support as available to help them, they appraise negative events that arise as less stressful, and decreased stress contributes to better health outcomes (Uchino, 2009). Studies of perceived support availability and health outcomes have been conducted with a vast array of stressors, populations, and research designs. Although there is wide variation in the size and consistency of the observed effects, the research overwhelmingly supports the positive influence of perceived support availability on mental and physical health (Gruenewald & Seeman, 2010).

Supportive Communication

Research conducted within the sociological and psychological traditions was—and continues to be—valuable for establishing that social support makes an important contribution to well-being, and exploring theoretical mechanisms by which social integration and perceived availability of support produce positive outcomes. However, by the mid-1980s, scholars from multiple disciplines were beginning to recognize a shared interest in the way that people communicate to help one another deal with negative events, stress, and emotional upset. By the mid-1990s, this interest had coalesced into a distinct communication perspective (see Burleson, Albrecht, Goldsmith & Sarason, 1994).

Recently, MacGeorge et al. (in press) described the communication perspective on social support as having five distinguishing characteristics (see also Burleson & MacGeorge, 2002). The first of these is the centrality of communication. For scholars in the sociological tradition, communication is understood as a means by which social integration produces some of its positive effects. Similarly, scholars in the psychological tradition assume that perceptions of support availability arise from communication, either from recent supportive interactions, or in childhood, when we establish patterns of relating to others. However, communication is not the direct focus of theoretical or empirical attention in either of these traditions. In contrast, the communication perspective on social support gives primary attention to the messages that are used to provide (and seek) support, the interactions in which those messages occur, and the relationships that contextualize the interactions (Burleson et al., 1994).

The communication perspective on social support also involves a focus on *intentional* responses to others' perceived needs, and a normative orientation, which means being concerned with the quality rather than simply the quantity of support. The construct of perceived availability locates social support within an individual's cognitions, whereas the construct of social integration treats it as something that emerges from networks of positive social relationships. Thus, from both the sociological and psychological perspectives, social support can occur without anyone intending it to happen. In contrast, the communication perspective locates social support within the behaviors that one individual (a support provider) produces to address the needs of another (a support recipient). Correspondingly, the communication perspective on social support recognizes that not all behaviors intended to provide support are equivalent in quality. Some supportive communication is sensitive, effective, and otherwise well-designed for the individual, the need, and the context, but other communication, however well-intended, will be less effective on one or more dimensions, and can create greater distress and harm (Burleson, 2003; MacGeorge, Feng, & Thompson, 2008). Consistent with this recognition, a preponderance of theory and research from the supportive communication perspective is concerned with determining what constitutes more and less effective attempts to provide support, and with understanding factors that contribute to this variation in the quality of support providers' efforts.

The fourth and fifth characteristics of the communication perspective on social support are the assumption of a relatively direct connection between supportive communication and well-being, and a commitment to documenting these connections. Here, the term "well-being" is being used to refer to a wide range of emotional, cognitive, physiological, behavioral, and relational outcomes. Historically, research on supportive communication has focused most on immediate or "proximal" emotional, cognitive, and relational outcomes, but the past decade has seen increased attention to proximal physiological outcomes, and to longer-term or "distal" impacts on psychological and physical health. The next section of this chapter reviews some of the research evidence demonstrating the relationship between supportive communication and well-being.

Supportive Communication and Well-Being

A large part of the motivation for studying supportive communication is the evidence that it has important, even powerful, positive outcomes for recipients. A comprehensive review of the research documenting the benefits of supportive communication would exceed the space available (for a fuller review, see MacGeorge et al., in press), but this section highlights some of the key findings. At the end of the section, we also discuss the capacity for supportive communication to have negative outcomes.

Psychological Outcomes

Typically, supportive communication occurs in response to disclosure of a negative situation, or a display of distress. Thus, support providers are often specifically concerned with helping recipients deal with their emotional and psychological states, and researchers have been interested in the immediate or proximal impact of supportive communication on these states. There is ample evidence that high quality supportive communication can improve affect (Jones & Wirtz, 2006), increase coping capacity (MacGeorge et al., 2004), and aid decision-making (Feng & MacGeorge, 2010). Supportive communication is also a positive influence on a constellation of self-oriented feelings and perceptions, including confidence, self-efficacy, and self-esteem (Holmstrom & Burleson, in press).

In addition to these proximal outcomes, helpful supportive communication can substantially improve psychological outcomes as a cumulative result of interactions over time. In one longitudinal study, supportive communication from social network members predicted psychological adjustment and depression over a five week period (Saltzman & Holahan, 2002). Other long-term outcomes of receiving high quality support on a consistent basis include better psychological adjustment (Cramer, 2000), greater optimism (McNicholas, 2002), and higher life satisfaction (Wan, Jaccard, & Ramey, 1996).

Physical Outcomes

The positive influence of supportive communication is not limited to emotional or psychological outcomes. Research indicates that supportive communication influences physical health through a variety of mechanisms (Reblin & Uchino, 2008). Support providers can respond to recipients' needs for health information and advice, such as information about medical treatments, diet and nutrition, or exercise (Uchino, 2009). Supportive communication can also be "motivational," encouraging, persuading, or assisting recipients to adopt healthy behavior or discontinue unhealthy behavior (Padula & Sullivan, 2006).

However, these behavioral effects of informational and motivational support are only part of the picture. Over time, individuals receiving more high-quality emotional support tend to better resist disease onset, recover more quickly from various diseases and injuries, maintain their health for more extended periods, and live longer (for a review, see Uchino, 2009). Emotional support can also have relatively direct and immediate health effects. For example, studies of emotional support provided to women in labor by doulas (non-medical labor companions) show that, relative to women without doulas, women with doula support experience a range of desirable clinical outcomes, including shorter labors, less pain, reduced likelihood of forceps or caesarian delivery, and healthier newborns (Keenan, 2000; Klaus & Kennell, 1997). These physiological outcomes may stem from reduced anxiety during labor but may also reflect more direct physiological influences. Emotional support has been shown to reduce cardiovascular reactivity (a risk factor for heart attack and stroke; Uchino, Carlisle, Birmingham, & Vaughn, 2011) and the production of cortisol (which depresses the immune system; Priem & Solomon, 2009).

Relational Outcomes

In addition to its influence on psychological and physical health, supportive communication influences relationship quality across a broad array of social relationships, including those with friends (Samter, 2003), family members (Voorpostel & Blieszner, 2007), and co-workers (Stansfeld, Bosma, Hemingway, & Marmot, 1998). An impressive body of research shows that receiving high-quality supportive communication improves satisfaction and stability in marriages and other long-term romantic relationships (Cutrona, Russell, & Gardner, 2005), at least in part because it affects how relational partners solve problems together (Sullivan, et al., 2010). These effects are consistent with current theoretical models of intimate relationships, including attachment theory (Collins & Feeney, 2010), the relationship enhancement model (Cutrona et al., 2005), and the vulnerability-stress-adaptation model (Bradbury, Cohan, & Karney, 2000).

In sum, supportive communication can make a substantial contribution to its recipients' psychological, physical, and relational well-being. However, these benefits are contingent on the quality of the support received. Poor quality support can have a variety of negative consequences, including exacerbating stress, intensifying negative emotions, undermining relationships, and damaging health (e.g., Figueiredo, Fries, & Ingram, 2004). Further, there is ample evidence that giving sensitive and effective support is a challenging communication task (Holmstrom, Burleson, & Jones, 2005), and that a variety of problems can arise to undercut recipients' experience of support even when providers are well intended and motivated to help (Goldsmith, 2004). Correspondingly, the core of supportive communication research has focused on understanding effective support, identifying the features of supportive messages and interactions that lead to the most positive perceptions and outcomes for recipients, and exploring factors that explain variation in the quality of support provision. These issues are the subject of the last two sections of this chapter.

Effective Supportive Communication

Historically, scholars studying supportive communication have distinguished between between emotional support, or support intended to reduce emotional distress, and instrumental support, or support intended to address the problem or situation provoking the distress (for a fuller discussion of "types" of support, see MacGeorge et al., in press). Greater research attention has been given to emotional support or comforting messages than to instrumental forms of support such as advice, at least partly because of evidence that emotional support has a stronger impact on health outcomes than other forms of support (Barger, 2009). However, the past decade has seen greater attention to advice and esteem support, along with efforts to understand sequencing and other aspects of supportive interactions. Accordingly, each of these aspects of supportive communication is considered in turn.

Comforting

In research on supportive communication, the terms "comforting" and "emotional support" are often used synonymously to refer to communication behaviors intended to reduce the emotional distress of others. The dominant conceptualization of variation in the quality of comforting messages is that of "person centeredness." Comforting messages high in person-centeredness explicitly acknowledge and legitimate another's feelings by helping to articulate those feelings, elaborating on reasons why the other might feel that way, and trying to place the feelings within a broader perspective. Comforting messages moderate in person- centeredness implicitly recognize another's feelings by attempting to distract the other's attention from the distressing situation, offering expressions of sympathy, or presenting explanations of the situation that might function to reduce distress. Comforting messages that are low in person-centeredness deny another person's feelings and perspective by criticizing the feelings, challenging their legitimacy, or telling the other how he or she should act or feel. Overall, highly person-centered messages tend to be the most listener centered, emotion focused, and nonevaluative, with moderate- and low- person-centered messages exhibiting fewer of these qualities.

A substantial body of research indicates that highly person-centered comforting messages are rated highest in quality (i.e., more sensitive and effective); messages of moderate person centeredness are rated somewhat lower and messages low in person centeredness, considerably lower (for a review, see Burleson, 2003). Furthermore, recipients of comforting messages that are highly person-centered experience greater improvement in their emotional states than those receiving messages that are moderate or low in person centeredness (Jones, 2004; Jones & Guerrero, 2001). Burleson and Goldsmith (1998) argued that highly person-centered messages do a better job of reducing distress because they encourage support recipients to reflect on, talk about, and understand their feelings, leading to them to a more functional reappraisal of the negative situation. Experimental research has provided direct support for this theory of conversationally induced reappraisal (Jones & Wirtz, 2006). However, Burleson (2010) also criticized this reappraisal theory for failing to explain why messages lower in person centeredness (especially, those that are moderately person centered) can still have a positive influence on recipients, at least under certain conditions. Bodie and Burleson's dual-process theory of message production (Bodie & Burleson, 2008; Burleson, 2010) provides an explanation, suggesting that the evaluation and outcome of comforting messages is a function of how much recipients actually think about or "process" the content of the messages. Thus, messages that are lower in person centeredness may still be viewed positively and result in positive emotional change if recipients pay limited attention to the actual content of the message. This can occur either because of individual characteristics (e.g., masculinity, low cognitive complexity) or situational factors (e.g., distraction, low level of distress).

As the influence of person centeredness on comforting evaluations and outcomes has become increasingly well established, attention has turned to other factors that help to explain variation in the effectiveness of comforting messages. One factor receiving increased attention is nonverbal communication, with studies showing that various forms of nonverbal behavior are important influences on recipient outcomes in supportive interactions (Jones & Guerrero, 2001; Jones & Wirtz, 2007). Another factor of recent interest is religious content (see also Baesler et al., chapter 16, this volume). Wilkum and MacGeorge (2010) examined comforting messages for the bereaved and found that those containing "deferring" content (indicating that God was solely responsible for helping the bereaved person to cope) were evaluated more positively than those containing "collaborative" content (indicating that God would collaborate with the bereaved person to help them during the grieving process) or no religious content. These and other factors, such as humor (Bippus, 2000; Meyer, chapter 10, this volume), deserve greater research attention as scholarship on supportive communication proceeds.

Advice

As research on comforting began to mature in the early 1990s, supportive communication scholars began to pay more attention to instrumental support messages, and especially advice, defined as messages that make recommendations about what to do, think, or feel, in response to a problematic situation (MacGeorge et al., 2008). Research on advice was stimulated by the frequency of advice in supportive interactions and by wide variation in recipient reactions to advice (MacGeorge et al., 2004). Early theory and research focused on the style with which advice was given, especially the extent to which advice threatened or attended to the face needs of the recipient. Multiple studies have tested the influence of "politeness" or "facework" features and shown that advice presented in a more polite or face-saving manner is preferred to advice that is presented bluntly or with elements that increase face threat (Feng & Burleson, 2008; MacGeorge, Lichtman, & Pressey, 2002). Subsequently, researchers have begun to focus on the content of advice messages, especially the actions that are being recommended. A series of studies have shown that perceptions of an advised action's efficacy (whether it will work), feasibility (whether the advice recipient can do it), limitations (whether the action has risks or drawbacks), and confirmation (whether the advised action is something the recipient already intended to do) are important influences on outcomes that include coping, advice implementation, and perceived sufficiency of support (Feng & Burleson, 2008; Feng & MacGeorge, 2010; MacGeorge et al., 2004). Further, advice messages that contain explicit argument about the advised action's efficacy, feasibility, and (lack of) limitations are evaluated more positively than messages without these arguments (Feng & Burleson, 2008).

Recently, Feng and MacGeorge (2010) articulated an integrative theoretical framework they entitled advice response theory. This theory proposes that content and stylistic features of advice messages will vary in their degree of influence depending on characteristics of the source and the recipient. Consistent with the theory, Feng and MacGeorge found that message and source characteristics interacted to affect advice outcomes: message characteristics had a greater impact when source characteristics (liking, similarity, closeness, and expertise) had less impact, and message characteristics were more powerful influences when recipients had greater motivation to think carefully about the advice. They also found that the influence of source characteristics was substantially mediated by that of message characteristics. Further research is needed to test and develop the theory as a basis for understanding the range of advice outcomes.

Esteem Support

Esteem support is a form of supportive communication provided to enhance how recipients feel about themselves and their attributes, abilities, or accomplishments in the face of an esteem-threatening event (Holmstrom & Burleson, in press). Esteem support has typically been treated as a type of emotional support, but Holmstrom and Burleson argued that esteem-threatening events were distinct from other negative events, and that the concept of person-centered comforting does not adequately capture what makes esteem support effective. The cognitive-emotional theory of esteem support messages proposes that these messages are more effective when they are emotion-focused rather than problem-focused (i.e., concerned with the recipient's attributions and appraisals about the event rather than changing problematic behavior that contributed to the event). This is because the emotion-focused messages more directly address the negative emotions that arise with esteem threat (shame, guilt, embarrassment). Esteem support messages are also argued to be superior when they are inductive rather than assertive (designed to reason toward rather than force a change of perspective or behavior) because inductive reasoning leads to greater "ownership" of the outcome. Consistent with this theory, Holmstrom and Burleson's findings showed that emotion-focused and inductive messages were generally perceived as better than problem-focused and assertive messages on several outcomes, including self-esteem, self-efficacy, and feeling accepted.

Supportive Interactions

To date, a majority of supportive communication research has focused at the level of understanding supportive messages rather than the interactions in which these messages are exchanged. However, there has long been the recognition that comfort, advice, esteem support, and other forms of supportive communication (e.g., information, offers of assistance), are couched within larger interactional structures, and that these affect the outcomes of support provision even if the exact nature of that influence is not fully understood (Burleson et al., 1994). Gradually, research findings are accumulating to provide more detailed insight about how different elements of supportive interactions work together to affect recipients' outcomes. Some of this work has focused specifically on advice. For example, several studies suggest that when advice is actively solicited (or clearly desired) by recipients, it is evaluated more positively than when it is not (Goldsmith, 2000; MacGeorge et al., 2004). Advice is also evaluated more positively when support providers first provide emotional support and problem analysis (Feng, 2009). Yet another study provides intriguing evidence about *how* advice-giving helps recipients, showing that advice encourages recipients to express their own problem-solving ideas (Saitzyk, Floyd, & Kroll, 1997).

Other studies show that support recipients influence the quality of support they receive through their support-seeking behavior and response to the support they are given. In particular, direct support-seeking appears more likely to elicit emotional support, whereas indirect support seeking is more likely to elicit an avoidant reaction (Barbee & Cunningham, 1995). In addition, when support recipients reject or "spurn" assistance, providers become less interested in helping (especially, over time; Wong, Cheuk, & Rosen, 2007), but when recipients express gratitude for support received, support providers are more motivated to help in the future (Grant, 2010). All of this research supports the contention that supportive communication scholars need to increase attention to the interactions in which supportive messages occur, identifying behavioral sequences and contingencies that affect recipients' outcomes (MacGeorge et al., in press).

Factors Influencing Skill at Support Provision

In conjunction with research on characteristics of effective supportive messages and interactions, supportive communication scholars have exerted considerable effort to understand variation in the quality of support provision: why some support providers routinely provide higher quality comforting than others, or respond to some situations with a lower quality of support than others. A wide range of variables have been examined as influences on support providers (Barbee, Rowatt, & Cunningham, 1998; Burleson, 2003). A theoretically useful way of organizing this research is to recognize that the quality of any instance of supportive communication will be a joint product of the support provider's ability and motivation (Burleson, 1985), and that ability and motivation are themselves a function of multiple traits and situational factors. For example, interpersonal cognitive complexity is an extensively studied trait that influences the capacity to take the perspective of another, and consequently impacts the ability to produce highly person-centered comforting messages (Burleson, 2007). Ability can also be temporarily influenced by situational variables. If the environment is distracting, or the support provider is anxious, embarrassed, or otherwise distressed, these factors may interfere with the mental processes necessary to produce the quality of comfort or advice that the support provider would otherwise be able to generate (Burleson & Planalp, 2000). Similarly, motivation to provide support is affected by some traits (e.g., empathy; Tamborini, Salomonson, & Bahk, 1993) and a whole host of situational factors (e.g., the support recipient's responsibility for his or her problem; MacGeorge, 2001). Some variables, such as gender, appear to influence both ability and motivation to provide support (e.g., Burleson, Holmstrom, & Gilstrap, 2005; MacGeorge et al., 2003).

Recognizing ability and motivation as central influences on supportive communication highlights the fact that high-quality comforting, advice, esteem support, and so forth depend on support providers having the requisite skills *and* being sufficiently motivated to exercise them. Multiple skills are involved in producing a supportive message, including interpreting the situation, generating goals, planning behavior in pursuit of those goals, enacting the message, and monitoring its outcomes (Burleson, 2007; Burleson & Planalp, 2000). Thus, the ability to produce a highly person-centered comforting message will require (at a minimum) the awareness of another person's distress, goals such as providing sympathy and perspective, the articulation of those goals in a coherent message, and responding appropriately to whatever happens next—all of this in the course of on-going interaction. Motivation to provide support is also multi-faceted, involving goal motivation (the desire to pursue the primary goal, such as comforting or advising), normative motivation (the desire to behave in role-appropriate ways), and effectance motivation (self-efficacy, or the belief in the ability to achieve the goal). When support providers are lacking in one or more of these components of motivation, the quality of supportive communication declines (Burleson et al., 2005; MacGeorge, Clark, & Gillihan, 2002).

These analyses not only provide theory to explain variation in the quality of supportive communication, but are useful foundations for educational interventions. For example, women who have miscarried often report a low quality of supportive communication (e.g., Abboud, 2005). It appears that some support providers fail to recognize miscarriage as a significant or distressing event. This could not only undermine the capacity to formulate appropriate goals, but if the miscarriage is viewed as a trivial event, then the motivation to comfort is also reduced. Consequently, educational interventions for support providers to women who have miscarried need to address both the ability and motivation to produce messages appropriate to this context (MacGeorge & Wilkum, 2008). Overall, support providers' ability and motivation need to be taken into account in the design of any intervention, training program, or classroom effort to improve supportive communication skills.

Supportive Communication: Positive Communication

Negative events, stress, and emotional distress are a part of life, so we are fortunate when supportive communication is a part of our lives as well. As shown by research reviewed in this chapter, high-quality supportive interactions have a positive influence on psychological, physical, and relational outcomes both immediately and in the long term. Thus, providing support is a valuable form of positive communication, and one of the things we should strive to do as effectively as possible in our relationships with others. There is a significant body of scholarship identifying message and interactional features that contribute to the effectiveness of supportive communication, but ample room to extend knowledge in this domain. As communication scholars, we can contribute both theoretically and pragmatically by studying supportive communication, further specifying how best to provide support of different types, and identifying ways to improve the ability and motivation to provide sensitive, helpful support in multiple contexts.

References

Abboud, L. (2005). When pregnancy fails: Coping strategies, support networks, and experiences with health care of ethnic women and their partners. *Journal of Reproductive and Infant Psychology, 23*, 3–18.

Barbee, A. P., & Cunningham, M. R. (1995). An experimental approach to social support communications: Interactive coping in close relationships. In B. R. Burleson (Ed.), *Communication Yearbook 18* (pp. 381–413). Thousand Oaks, CA: Sage.

Barbee, A. P., Rowatt, T. L., & Cunningham, M. R. (1998). When a friend is in need: Feelings about seeking, giving, and receiving social support. In P. A. Andersen & L. K. Guerrero (Eds.), *Handbook of communication and emotion: Research, theory, applications, and contexts* (pp. 281–301). San Diego, CA: Academic Press.

Barger, S. D., Donoho, C. J., & Wayment, H. A. (2009). The relative contributions of race/ethnicity, socioeconomic status, health, and social relationships to life satisfaction in the United States. *Quality of Life Research, 18*, 179–189.

Barrera, M. (1981). Social support in the adjustment of pregnant adolescents. In B. H. Gottlieb (Ed.), *Social networks and social support* (pp. 69–96). Beverly Hills, CA: Sage.

Berkman, L. F., Melchior, M., Chastang, J. F., Niedhammer, I., Leclerc, A., & Goldberg, M. (2004). Social integration and mortality: A prospective study of French employees of Electricity of France—Gas of France. *American Journal of Epidemiology, 159*, 167–174.

Bippus, A. M. (2000). Humor usage in comforting messages: Factors predicting outcomes. *Western Journal of Communication, 64*, 359–384.

Bodie, G. D., & Burleson, B. R. (2008). Explaining variations in the effects of supportive messages: A dual-process framework. In C. Beck (Ed.), *Communication yearbook 32* (pp. 354–398). New York: Routledge.

Bradbury, T. N., Cohan, C. L., & Karney, B. R. (2000). Optimizing longitudinal research for understanding and preventing marital dysfunction. In T. N. Bradbury (Ed.), *The developmental course of marital dysfunction* (pp. 279–311). Cambridge, UK: Cambridge University Press.

Brissette, I., Cohen, S., & Seeman, T. E. (2000). Measuring social integration and social networks. In S. Cohen, L. G. Underwood, & B. H. Gottlieb (Eds.), *Social support measurement and intervention* (pp. 29–54). New York: Oxford University Press.

Burleson, B. R. (1983). Social cognition, empathic motivation, and adults' comforting strategies. *Human Communication Research, 10*, 295–304.

Burleson, B. R. (1985). The production of comforting messages: Social-cognitive foundations. *Journal of Language and Social Psychology, 4*, 253–273.

Burleson, B. R. (2003). Emotional support skills. In J. O. Greene & B. R. Burleson (Eds.), *Handbook of communication and social interaction skills* (pp. 551–594). Mahwah, NJ: Erlbaum.

Burleson, B. R. (2007). Constructivism: A general theory of communication skill. In B. B. Whaley & W. Samter (Eds.), *Explaining communication: Contemporary theories and exemplars* (pp. 105–128). Mahwah, NJ: Erlbaum.

Burleson, B. R. (2010). Explaining recipient responses to supportive messages: Development and tests of a dual-process theory. In S. W. Smith & S. R. Wilson (Eds.), *New directions in interpersonal communication* (pp. 159–179). Thousand Oaks, CA: Sage Publications.

Burleson, B. R., Albrecht, T. L., Goldsmith, D. J., & Sarason, I. G. (1994). The communication of social support. In B. R. Burleson, T. L. Albrecht, & I. G. Sarason (Eds.), *Communication of social support: Messages, interactions, relationships, and community* (pp. xi–xxx). Thousand Oaks, CA: Sage.

Burleson, B. R., & Goldsmith, D. J. (1998). How the comforting process works: Alleviating emotional distress through conversationally induced reappraisals. In P. A. Andersen & L. K. Guerrero (Eds.), *Handbook of communication and emotion: Research, theory, applications, and contexts* (pp. 245–280). San Diego, CA: Academic Press.

Burleson, B. R., Holmstrom, A. J., & Gilstrap, C. M. (2005). "Guys can't say *that* to guys": Four experiments assessing the normative motivation account for deficiencies in the emotional support provided by men. *Communication Monographs, 72*, 468–501.

Burleson, B. R., & MacGeorge, E. L. (2002). Supportive communication. In M. L. Knapp & J. A. Daly (Eds.), *Handbook of interpersonal communication* (3rd ed., pp. 374–424). Thousand Oaks, CA: Sage.

Burleson, B. R., & Planalp, S. (2000). Producing emotion(al) messages. *Communication Theory, 10*, 221–250.

Caplan, G. (1974). *Support systems and community mental health.* New York: Behavioral Publications.

Cassel, J. (1976). The contribution of the social environment to host resistance. *American Journal of Epidemiology, 104*, 107–123.

Cohen, S., & Lemay, E. P. (2007). Why would social networks be linked to affect and health practices? *Health Psychology, 25*, 410–417.

Collins, N. L., & Feeney, B. C. (2010). An attachment theoretical perspective on social support dynamics in couples: Normative processes and individual differences. In K. T. Sullivan & J. Davila (Eds.), *Support processes in intimate relationships* (pp. 89–120). New York: Oxford University Press.

Cramer, D. (2000). Social desirability, adequacy of social support and mental health. *Journal of Community and Applied Social Psychology, 10*, 465–474.

Cutrona, C. E., Russell, D. W., & Gardner, K. A. (2005). The relationship enhancement model of social support. In T. A. Revenson, K. Kayser, & G. Bodenmann (Eds.), *Couples coping with stress* (pp. 3–23). Washington, DC: American Psychological Association.

Feng, B. (2009). Testing an integrated model of advice-giving in supportive interactions. *Human Communication Research, 35*, 115–129.

Feng, B., & Burleson, B. R. (2008). The effects of argument explicitness on responses to advice in supportive interactions. *Communication Research, 35*, 849–874.

Feng, B., & MacGeorge, E. L. (2010). The influences of message and source factors on advice outcomes. *Communication Research, 37*, 576–598.

Figueiredo, M. I., Fries, E., & Ingram, K. M. (2004). The role of disclosure patterns and unsupportive social interactions in the well-being of breast cancer patients. *Psycho-Oncology, 13*, 96–105.

Gleason, M. E. J., Iida, M., Shrout, P. E., & Bolger, N. (2008). Receiving support as a mixed blessing: Evidence for dual effects of support on psychological outcomes. *Journal of Personality and Social Psychology, 94*, 824–838.

Goldsmith, D. J. (2000). Soliciting advice: The role of sequential placement in mitigating face threat. *Communication Monographs, 67*, 1–19.

Goldsmith, D. J. (2004). *Communicating social support.* New York: Cambridge University Press.

Grant, A. M. (2010). A little thanks goes a long way: Explaining why gratitude expressions motivate prosocial behavior. *Journal of Personalty and Social Psychology, 98*, 946–955.

Gruenewald, T. L., & Seeman, T. E. (2010). Social support and physical health: Links and mechanisms. In A. Steptoe (Ed.), *Handbook of behavioral medicine* (pp. 224–236). New York: Springer Science.

Holmstrom, A. J., & Burleson, B. R. (in press). An initial test of a cognitive-emotional theory of esteem-support messages. *Communication Research.*

Holmstrom, A. J., Burleson, B. R., & Jones, S. M. (2005). Some consequences for helpers who deliver "cold comfort": Why it's worse for women than men to be inept when providing emotional support. *Sex Roles, 53*, 153–172.

Ikeda, A., & Kawachi, I. (2010). Social networks and health. In A. Steptoe (Ed.), *Handbook of behavioral medicine: Methods and applications* (pp. 237–262). New York: Springer.

Jones, S. M. (2004). Putting the person into person-centered and immediate emotional support: Emotional change and perceived helper competence as outcomes of comforting in helping situations. *Communication Research, 31*, 338–360.

Jones, S. M., & Guerrero, L. K.. (2001). The effects of nonverbal immediacy and verbal person centeredness in the emotional support process. *Human Communication Research, 27*, 567–596.

Jones, S. M., & Wirtz, J. (2006). How *does* the comforting process work?: An empirical test of an appraisal-based model of comforting. *Human Communication Research, 32*, 217–243.

Jones, S. M., & Wirtz, J. (2007). "*Sad* monkey see, monkey do": Nonverbal matching in emotional support encounters. *Communication Studies, 58*, 71–86.

Keenan, P. (2000). Benefits of massage therapy and use of a doula during labor and childbirth. *Alternative Therapies, 6*, 66–74.

Kiecolt-Glaser, J. K., Gouin, J. P., & Hantsoo, L. (2010). Close relationships, inflammation, and health. *Neuroscience and biobehavioral reviews, 35*, 33–38.

Klaus, M. H., & Kennell, J. H. (1997). The doula: an essential ingredient of childbirth rediscovered. *Acta Paediatrica, 86*, 1034–1036.

Lazarus, R. S., & Folkman, S. (1984). *Stress, appraisal, and coping*. New York: Springer.

MacGeorge, E. L. (2001). Support providers' interaction goals: The influence of attributions and emotions. *Communication Monographs, 68*, 72–97.

MacGeorge, E. L., Clark, R. A., & Gillihan, S. J. (2002). Sex differences in the provision of skillful emotional support: The mediating role of self-efficacy. *Communication Reports, 15*, 17–28.

MacGeorge, E. L., Feng, B., & Burleson, B. R. (in press). Supportive communication. In M. L. Knapp & J. A. Daly (Eds.), *Handbook of Interpersonal Communication* (4th ed.). Thousand Oaks, CA: Sage.

MacGeorge, E. L., Feng, B., Butler, G. L., & Budarz, S. K. (2004). Understanding advice in supportive interactions: Beyond the facework and message evaluation paradigm. *Human Communication Research, 30*, 42–70.

MacGeorge, E. L., Feng, B., & Thompson, E. R. (2008). "Good" and "bad" advice: How to advise more effectively. In M. T. Motley (Ed.), *Studies in applied interpersonal communication* (pp. 145–164). Thousand Oaks, CA: Sage.

MacGeorge, E. L., Gillihan, S. J., Samter, W., & Clark, R. A. (2003). Skill deficit or differential motivation? Accounting for sex differences in the provision of emotional support. *Communication Research, 30*, 272–303.

MacGeorge, E. L., Lichtman, R. M., & Pressey, L. C. (2002). The evaluation of advice in supportive interactions: Facework and contextual factors. *Human Communication Research, 28*, 451–463.

MacGeorge, E. L., & Wilkum, K. C. (2008). *Supportive communication in the context of miscarriage: Rationale for a research agenda*. Paper presented at the annual convention of the International Communication Association.

Mak, M. C. K., Bond, M. H., Simpson, J. A., & Rholes, W. S. (2010). Adult attachment, perceived support, and depressive symptoms in Chinese and American cultures. *Journal of Social and Clinical Psychology, 29*, 144–165.

McNicholas, S. L. (2002). Social support and positive health practices. *Western Journal of Nursing Research, 24*, 772–787.

Padula, C. A., & Sullivan, M. (2006). Long-term married couples' health promotion behaviors: Identifying factors that impact decision-making. *Journal of Gerontological Nursing, 32*, 37–47.

Priem, J. S., & Solomon, D. H. (2009). Comforting apprehensive communicators: The effects of reappraisal and distraction on cortisol levels among students in a public speaking class. *Communication Quarterly, 57*, 259–281.

Reblin, M., & Uchino, B. N. (2008). Social and emotional support and its implication for health. *Current Opinion in Psychiatry, 21*, 201–205.

Saitzyk, A. R., Floyd, F. J., & Kroll, A. B. (1997). Sequential analysis of autonomy-interdependence and affiliation-disaffiliation in couples' social support interactions. *Personal Relationships, 4*, 341–360.

Saltzman, K. M., & Holahan, C. J. (2002). Social support, self-efficacy, and depressive symptoms: An integrative model. *Journal of Social and Clinical Psychology, 21*, 309–322.

Samter, W. (2003). Friendship interaction skills across the life span. In J. O. Greene & B. R. Burleson (Eds.), *Handbook of communication and social interaction skills* (pp. 637–684). Mahwah, NJ: Erlbaum.

Stansfeld, S. A., Bosma, H., Hemingway, H., & Marmot, M. G. (1998). Psychosocial work characteristics and social support as predictors of SF-36 health functioning: The Whitehall II study. *Psychosomatic Medicine, 60*, 247–255.

Sullivan, K. T., Pasch, L. A., Johnson, M. D., & Bradbury, T. N. (2010). Social support, problem-solving, and the longitudinal course of newlywed marriage. *Journal of Personality and Social Psychology, 98*, 631-644.

Tamborini, R., Salomonson, K., & Bahk, C. (1993). The relationship of empathy to comforting behavior following film exposure. *Communication Research, 20*(5), 723–738.

Uchino, B. N. (2009). Understanding the links between social support and physical health: A lifespan perspective with emphasis on the separability of perceived and received support. *Perspectives on Psychological Science, 4*, 236–255.

Uchino, B. N., Carlisle, M., Birmingham, W., & Vaughn, A. A. (2011). Social support and the reactivity hypothesis: Conceptual issues in examining the efficacy of received support during acute psychological stress. *Biological Psychology, 86*, 137–142.

Voorpostel, M., & Blieszner, R. (2007). Intergenerational solidarity and support between adult siblings. *Journal of Marriage and the Family, 70*, 157–167.

Wan, C. K., Jaccard, J., & Ramey, S. L. (1996). The relationship between social support and life satisfaction as a function of family structure. *Journal of Marriage and the Family, 58*, 502–513.

Wilkum, K., & MacGeorge, E. L. (2010). Does God matter?: Religious content and the evaluation of comforting messages in the context of bereavement. *Communication Research, 37*, 723–745.

Wong, K. S., Cheuk, W. H., & Rosen, S. (2007). Experience of being spurned: Coping style, stress preparation, and depersonalization in beginning kindergarten teachers. *Journal of Research in Childhood Education, 22*, 141–154.

Celebratory Support: Messages that Enhance the Effects of Positive Experience[1]

Jennifer Dane McCullough
Saginaw Valley State University

Brant R. Burleson
Purdue University

Imagine someone who just won the lottery, or just received a big promotion she/he has been working toward for a long time. Or, imagine someone just getting engaged to the person of his or her dreams, or perhaps she or he received some really good news from a doctor regarding test results that were a cause for concern. After experiencing any one of these wonderful events, what is likely the first thing someone might do? Look for someone to share the news with, of course! As human beings, it is natural for us to want to share our good news with others.

For various reasons, episodes of sharing good news may go well or poorly, depending on the event, the person we share with, and the kind of response we receive. We may find that sharing good news episodes is incredibly supportive, quite frustrating, or somewhere in between. Regardless, when good fortune knocks, our first response is often one of seeking significant others with whom to share the news. These interactions that occur when individuals share the news of an event they have interpreted positively, and another individual attempts to respond is precisely the subject of this chapter. This form of interaction, labeled celebratory support, is defined as the verbal and nonverbal signals a support provider uses to acknowledge, extol, and appreciate the significance of an event that has been interpreted as a good thing by the support recipient (McCullough, 2010).

Although this form of communication support has received comparatively little attention, versus emotional support (e.g., comforting messages) or instrumental support (e.g., advice), there are growing indications that these "positive" or "celebratory" communicative behaviors are important and may be fruitfully conceptualized as a genre of supportive communication (Vangelisti, 2009). This chapter provides a rationale for the study of celebratory support, a description of celebratory support message features that have the potential for success, and a review of past research that assesses the effectiveness of the message features of celebratory support

Why Celebratory Support Matters

The examination of celebratory support is worthwhile for numerous reasons including: the sheer volume of this form of interaction, the importance people place on their significant others being skilled at these interactions, the impact of these interactions on individuals and relationships, and the likelihood that celebratory messages used in these interactions vary in quality or skillfulness.

The Volume of Positive Interactions

According to Gable, Reis, and Elliot (2000) positive interactions tend to be more common than negative interactions in ordinary social behavior. Specifically, Gable et al. (2000) found that, on average, individuals tend to experience 11.4 positive events daily, but only 5.1 negative events per day. In another study, Gable et al. (2004) found that married couples report having more positive interactions than conflictual interactions. Specifically, couples reported experiencing positive activity on 40.1% of the previous 14 days whereas they reported a negative event or conflict occurring on only 21.3% of the previous fourteen days. On a related note, Gottman (1999) identified a "magic ratio" for martial satisfaction that suggests the importance of 5 positive interactions to 1 negative interaction. Celebratory support provides one opportunity in which individuals may engage in a positive interaction; of course, this is only the case if the support is provided skillfully. Thus, because positive events, and the sharing of these events, are quite prevalent and potentially consequential to relationships satisfaction, a better understanding of them should be valuable.

The Value People Place on the Celebratory Skills of Others

Another factor that motivates the study of celebratory support pertains to the value people place on these interactions. For example, numerous studies report that individuals rate the affectively oriented communication skills of their friends and partners as more important than their instrumental or interactional skills (Burleson, Kunkel, Samter, & Werking, 1996; MacGeorge, Feng, & Butler, 2003). That is, affectively oriented communication skills such as ego support and comforting are rated as more important than non-affectively oriented skills such as narrative and persuasive abilities (Burleson & Samter, 1990). These findings suggest that people value the communication skills that their associates use to help them feel good about happy events.

The Impact of Celebratory Interactions on Individuals and Relationships

Consistent with the research showing that people highly value the celebratory skills of their relationship partners, celebratory interactions and related forms of positive support have important effects for both individuals and relationships. This point is made quite nicely by Werner, Altman, Brown, and Ginat (1993):

> Celebrations are an important aspect of relationships; they occur across societies, are pervasive over time, and can include frequent or infrequent events and major or minor activities. All, nevertheless, are an integral part of relationship development and all serve as important symbols of the relationship. (p. 110)

For example, according to Langston (1994), when people share the news of a positive event with others or celebrate the event in some way, they experience positive affect beyond that associated with the event itself. Additionally, extensions of these findings, based on a diary study in which participants recorded the content and frequency of positive and negative event disclosure, suggest that positive affect and life satisfaction are higher on days people shared the occurrence of their most positive event of the day (Gable et al., 2004).

Partners' responses to positive event disclosures actually appear to be more predictive of relationship well-being and break-up than do their responses to negative event disclosures (Gable, Gonzaga, & Strachman, 2006). This claim is based on results of a study of 79 dating couples who participated in videotaped interactions in which they took turns discussing recent positive and negative events. Interactions were observed and coded and participants completed self-report measures in which they rated how understood, validated, and cared for they felt. Eight weeks later, both members of the couple independently answered follow-up questions. Results revealed a stronger correlation between partner's responses to the positive events, occurring eight weeks prior, and whether or not the couple was still together than partner's responses to negative events.

Aside from relational outcomes, celebratory interactions have potential consequences for individual well-being as well. For example, individuals who experience positive affect are more likely to: help other people (Isen, 1987); be flexible in their thinking (Ashby, Isen, & Turken, 1999); and generate effective problem-solving solutions (Isen, Daubman, & Nowicki, 1987). Additionally, Lewinsohn and Graf (1973) found that everyday pleasant events were associated with decreases in depressive symptoms as well as increases in self-esteem and perceived control (Nezlek & Gable, 2001). Research shows positive emotions are not just related to psychological well-being, but also physical well-being. For example, positive emotional states are thought to be related to enhanced defense against the common cold (Stone, Cox, Valdimarsdottir, Jandorf, & Neal, 1987) and better immune response against the cold virus once it infects (Stone et al., 1994).

Thus, responses to disclosures of positive events can lead to quite important intrapersonal and interpersonal outcomes. Clearly, even though celebratory support remains understudied, the research that does exist suggests that it is quite a consequential form of interpersonal communication.

Celebratory Interactions Vary in the Quality of the Supportive Messages Employed

Any personal and relationship benefits associated with the disclosure of good news to a relationship partner may vary substantially as a function of the quality of the support provider's response. For example, contentment with received celebratory support and perceptions that one's partner reacted appropriately to the disclosure are associated with greater relationship satisfaction, relationship closeness, and intimacy (Gable et al., 2006). This finding is based on a study in which fifty-nine heterosexual couples completed a survey that measured relationship variables including commitment, trust, and satisfaction as well as perceived responses to capitalization efforts. Results showed that perceived responses by a close relationship partner to the sharing of good news are reliably associated with relationship quality.

At this point, it is clear that the examination of celebratory support is a worthwhile endeavor. Celebratory support interactions are ubiquitous; they occur often and in various contexts. In addition to being a common form of communication, celebratory support messages are also consequential. Individuals do differentiate between better and worse forms of celebratory support messages and these variations impact both individual and interpersonal outcomes.

Message Features

It is probable that virtually all celebratory messages share a common core of features that are relevant to acknowledging, extolling, and appreciating another's good news, regardless of the particular character of that good news (i.e., whether it concerns an achievement, role transition, luck, etc.). These general features of effective celebratory messages are hypothesized to include: generic celebratory phrases, acknowledgement of the target's feelings, reciprocation of the target's feelings, encouragement or elaboration of the target's feelings, and offers to share the celebration.

Extending Congratulations. The act of extending congratulations is characterized by the expression of joy and pleasure. At its core, the extension of congratulations shows the target that the celebrant is happy for him/her. This message feature also lets the target know that the event he/she has just shared is in fact something that should be considered special. In essence, by extending congratulations to another, the celebrant is telling the target that he/she also recognizes the positive nature of the event and that it is, indeed, worthy of celebration. The extension of congratulations is important because it serves to validate, confirm, and/or recognize the significance of the news, or event, itself.

Generic celebratory phrases, including such statements as: "Wow, that's amazing," "Congratulations," and "What wonderful news" are specific behaviors one might use to perform this act. These are common phrases that individuals expect to hear in times of celebration; therefore, when the recipient hears such phrases, a positive reaction is triggered. Extensions of congratulations may also be performed nonverbally. For example, such behaviors as handshakes, hugs, and kisses may all be deemed appropriate methods for showing one's joy and pleasure to some good news.

Acknowledgement of Target's Feelings. The emotions experienced by someone sharing good news will typically include happiness as well as more specific positive feelings appropriate to the character of the particular event (e.g., pride for achievement, relief for stress reduction, excitement or satisfaction for role transitions, surprise or amazement for luck situations). The general act, of acknowledging these feelings, is characterized by recognition and understanding. In particular, the act involves the celebrant demonstrating that he/she heard what the target said and that he/she accepts it. In other words, this act is important because it demonstrates the celebrant: (a) understands and appreciates the significance of the event and (b) reaffirms the target's interpretation of the event.

A variety of behaviors can be performed in order to acknowledge the target's emotions. For example, phrases such as, "I can see you are very excited" and "you should be very proud of yourself" serve to acknowledge the target's feelings. Naturally, it is important that the celebrant acknowledge accurately the emotions experienced by the target. Whereas accurately reflecting the emotions that the target is feeling may show understanding and appreciation, inaccurately perceiving emotions may actually reflect misunderstanding and ineptitude.

Reciprocation of Emotions. It is important that celebrants also reflect the target's emotions. That is to say, celebratory messages should not just acknowledge the target's feelings, but also indicate a reciprocation of those feelings. The general act of reciprocating emotions is characterized by perceiving the symbolic behaviors of others, interpreting these behaviors to deduce the feelings they are meant to convey, and reflecting back these emotions through one's own behaviors.

The reflection of emotions is particularly important because it sends meta-communicative messages such as "I am pleased when you are pleased" and "I am excited because you are excited." These sentiments are likely experienced by the target as an expression of the closeness of the relationship between the celebrant and the target. Thus, one reason this message feature is effective is its ability to affirm the relationship between the celebrant and the target.

One specific behavior that demonstrates the reciprocation of emotion involves the use of "I" language. Using "I" language rather that "you" language ensures that the target realizes the celebrant not only understands the emotions he/she is currently feeling, but that the celebrant is also feeling these same emotions. For example, the celebrant might say, "I am so happy for you and proud of you" or "I am really excited about this." The reciprocation of emotions may also occur nonverbally. Nonverbal symbols that may reciprocate emotions might include jumping up and down, pumping one's fist, a large smile, or speaking quickly, loudly, and in a higher frequency (Scherer, 1986).

Encouragement of Elaboration. Encouragement of elaborations is characterized by attempts to create a conversational space through which extended, detailed versions of a story can be told and retold (Burleson, 2003). Explanation for the effectiveness of the encouragement of elaboration of emotions is provided by Burleson and Goldsmith's (1998) conversationally induced cognitive reappraisal model. This model suggests the comforting process occurs through the discursive construction of new assessments of and fuller appreciation for the emotional state of a distressed person, the reasons for the occurrence of this state, and an assessment of its appropriateness (Burleson & Goldsmith, 1998). Although the theory traditionally views conversation as a mechanism for helping the target to re-appraise a situation, it seems just as likely that conversation can be used to reinforce a target's current appraisal.

For example, in times of celebration, the encouragement of elaboration gives the target the opportunity to explicitly state everything he/she thinks is good about the positive event and this simple repetition might serve to enhance the target's positive feelings. Additionally, this message feature might allow the target to think about some of the great things about the event that he/she had yet to even think about and thus this expansion of details might serve to enhance the target's positive feelings. Finally, encouragement of elaboration could simply show the target that the celebrant is willing to take time to listen.

Behaviors that serve to encourage reflection and emphasize that the target should feel free to tell an extended story about the positive event include phrases such as: "Tell me more about this award," "I want to know all about your new house," or "What part of your new job are you most excited about?" Again, nonverbal signals can also be effective. Nonverbal cues that facilitate elaboration include: verbal tokens ("oh," "mm-hm," or "yeah") and nonverbal behaviors (e.g., head nods, eye contact, body lean).

Offers to "Go Celebrate. " Offers to go celebrate are categorized by efforts to mark an event as special by engaging in some pleasurable activity. These activities involve honoring or praising an individual with some form of public or formal display. These acts serve to tell the target, "you are important" and "you deserve extra recognition and/or additional attention." This validation of self is likely experienced by the target as rewarding and thus contributes, at least in part, to enhanced positive affect.

Offers to "go celebrate" may include: taking the target out for a celebration, buying the target a gift, or throwing the target a party. Although these behaviors do not explicitly state the acknowledgement and validation of the target's emotions, event's significance, or relationship's closeness, they implicitly recognize that something good has happened and that it should, indeed, be celebrated.

Each one of the suggested message features is a specific communicative act that can help create an interactional environment in which the target feels understood, valued, and cared for. More specifically, these message features express understanding by demonstrating awareness of the significance of the event. They express validation by reinforcing the target's self-views and make the target feel valued and special. Finally, they show caring by expressing feelings of affection for the target. The culmination of understanding, validating, and caring behaviors is best labeled as responsiveness (Reis & Patrick, 1996). Thus, the theoretical justification for the effectiveness of all five of these message features rests on the fact that the usage of them makes the target feel as though the celebrant is being responsive to him/her. Based on the previous suggestions, the following hypotheses were proposed:

H1: Celebratory support messages that explicitly *affirm the support recipient's emotions* will (a) be evaluated more positively, (b) lead to more positive evaluations of the celebrant, (c) lead to better feelings about the relationship with the celebrant, and (d) result in enhanced positive affect more than celebratory support messages that do not acknowledge the target's feelings.

H2: Celebratory support messages that explicitly *reciprocate the support recipient's emotions* will (a) be evaluated more positively, (b) lead to more positive evaluations of the celebrant, (c) lead to better feelings about the relationship with the celebrant, and (d) result in enhanced positive affect more than celebratory support messages that do not acknowledge the target's feelings.

H3: Celebratory support messages that explicitly *encourage elaboration* will (a) be evaluated more positively, (b) lead to more positive evaluations of the celebrant, (c) lead to better feelings about the relationship with the celebrant, and (d) result in enhanced positive affect more than celebratory support messages that do not acknowledge the target's feelings.

H4: Celebratory support messages that explicitly offer *to go celebrate* will (a) be evaluated more positively, (b) lead to more positive evaluations of the celebrant, (c) lead to better feelings about the relationship with the celebrant, and (d) result in enhanced positive affect more than celebratory support messages that do not acknowledge the target's feelings.

Method

Participants and Procedures

In order to test these hypotheses, a sample of college students (N = 503; men = 303, women = 191, missing = 9) were recruited from communication courses at a large Midwestern university. Participants ranged in age from 18 to 43 and averaged 20.33 years old. All participants received extra credit for their participation. A majority of the participants were European American (n = 363), but the sample also included Asian Americans (n = 50), African American (n = 21), and Hispanic Americans (n = 23).

Participants were asked to complete an on-line survey. Before starting the survey, they were asked to read an introductory message and click on a forward arrow button in order to continue. Upon agreeing to continue, participants were randomly assigned to complete one of the sixty-four versions of the questionnaire.

Specifically, participants were asked to read one of four hypothetical scenarios in which they were to imagine they have just experienced a positive event. The scenarios consisted of four celebratory contexts (achievement, luck, role transition, relief from stressor). Next, participants were asked to imagine they just shared the good news of this positive event with a special person in their lives (friend, family member, significant other) and that this person offered a celebratory message in response to the good news that they shared. They subsequently read one of the possible responses.

The messages all contained a generic congratulatory phrase "Wow! Congratulations, that is great news," but varied based on the specific message features including: acknowledging target's emotions, reciprocating target's emotions, encouraging elaboration, and offering to go celebrate. This design resulted in a total of 64 unique celebratory support messages; within each type of celebratory context, the set of 16 messages reflected a 2 (non-acknowledgement of target's feelings vs. acknowledgement of target's feelings) x 2 (non-reciprocation of target's feelings vs. reciprocation of target's feelings) x 2 (non-elaboration of target's emotions vs. elaboration of target's emotions) x 2 (non-articulation of offers to go celebrate vs. articulation of offers to go celebrate).

Each participant was randomly assigned one celebratory support message to evaluate. After reading the message, participants were asked to evaluate the message on a variety of scales which were used to assess the dependent measures. Participants also completed a set of manipulation checks and a demographic questionnaire.

Message Manipulations

Acknowledgement of feelings. Celebratory support messages that acknowledged the target's feelings referred to at least some of the potential emotions that the target might be feeling. For example, in response to the hypothetical situation of earning a scholarship, the message included the phrase "I can tell you are very excited, and you should be. Earning such a prestigious scholarship should make you proud."

Reciprocation of feelings. In celebratory support messages that reciprocate the target's emotions, the message indicated actually feeling the emotion. This is different than simply acknowledging the target's feelings because in this type of message the celebrant isn't just noticing that the target is experiencing certain emotions; the celebrant is actually experiencing the emotions as well. For example, in the achievement scenario, the message included the phrase "I am really happy for you and proud of you."

Encouragement of elaboration. In messages that encourage elaboration, the message asked the target to talk more about the good news he/she has just shared. In particular, these messages conveyed that the celebrant was interested in listening and encouraged the target to talk about and elaborate on the situation and his or her feelings. Again, using the achievement situation as an example, the message that encouraged elaboration stated, "I want to hear more about the scholarship. For example, do you know how many people applied for it?"

Offers to go celebrate. Finally, in messages that make an offer to go celebrate, the message told the target that the support provider wanted to take him/her out for something special. In all of the situations, the message included the phrase, "Let's go celebrate. I want to buy you dinner."

Each of these message manipulations was an illustration of a specific behavior that can be used to fulfill a message act. Certainly, these behaviors (specific phrases) did not represent every possible method for fulfilling each message act. For example, various phrases could be used to encourage a target to elaborate (e.g., "What else can you tell me about your award?" or "What is the best part about winning the award?"). Although this study cannot capture every possible behavior, it did provide a reasonable selection of behaviors that should allow the researcher to assess the impacts of different features.

Dependent Measures

Message evaluation. A message evaluation measure was adapted from a previously established measure of message effectiveness (Goldsmith &

MacGeorge, 2000). Specifically, the measure used adjective pairs: warm-cold, appropriate-inappropriate, sensitive-insensitive, kind-unkind, and responsive-unresponsive that were separated by 7-point scales. The overall measure of message evaluation was computed by averaging the scores for these adjective pairs ($\alpha = .85$).

Feelings toward celebrant. Participant perceptions of the celebrant was measured using a modified version of Feng and Burleson's (2008) measure. The scale asked participants to respond to the statement "I would think my friend was:" using 10 items (e.g., sincere, sensitive, understanding) based on a 7-point Likert scale (1 = strongly disagree; 7 = strongly agree). The scale revealed three distinct dimensions of feelings toward the celebrant: caring, unconcerned, and competent. Most relevant to this study were the items that pertained to caring dimension (i.e., caring, understanding, interested, sensitive). Thus, these four items were averaged to create an overall score for feelings toward the celebrant, $\alpha = .89$.

Feelings about relationship. Participants completed a measure assessing their feelings toward and liking for the celebrant. This scale was a modified version of measure developed by Holmstrom (2008) and asked participants to respond to items such as "My feelings toward this person became more positive as a result of what he/she said" on a 7-point Likert scale (1 = strongly disagree; 7 = strongly agree). Acceptable reliability was obtained for the three items ($\alpha = .79$).

Affect changes. Seven questions were used to assess changes in overall affect. Based on previous research suggesting positive affect and negative affect are relatively independent (Watson, Clark, & Tellegen, 1998; Gable et al, 2004) and the focus of this study, only the items pertaining to changes in positive affect were used. Changes in positive affect was assessed with three 7-point Likert items (1 = strongly disagree; 7 = strongly agree). Sample items included, "This message made me feel better" and "I felt happier after I read the message than I did before I read the message." Acceptable reliability was obtained for the three items ($\alpha = .89$).

Results

Before testing each individual hypothesis, preliminary analysis was conducted to examine differences between the most theoretically sophisticated messages (those containing all four features, including: the acknowledgment of target's feelings, reciprocation of target's emotions, encouragement of elaboration, and offers to go celebrate) and the least theoretically sophisticated message ("Wow! Congratulations, that is great news."). A 4 (type of celebratory context) x 2 (least sophisticated vs. most sophisticated message) multivariate analysis of variance (MANOVA) was conducted on the dependent variables of message evaluation, relationship evaluation, celebrant evaluation, and positive affect. A significant multivariate effect was observed, Wilks' $\Lambda = .84$, $F(4, 62) = 2.88$, $p = .03$.

Means and standard deviations for the dependent variables by message type are presented in Table 14.1. Univariate analyses for each dependent variable indicated that messages containing all of the manipulated features were rated as significantly better than messages containing none of the manipulated features: message evaluation, $F(1, 72) = 3.62$, $p = .06$, $\eta2 = .05$; relationship evaluation, $F(1, 72) = 8.17$, $p < .01$, $\eta2 = .10$; celebrant evaluation, $F(1, 72) = 11.55$, $p < .001$, $\eta2 = .14$; positive affect, $F(1, 72) = 5.99$, $p < .05$, $\eta2 = .08$. Results indicate messages containing the manipulated features have more desirable results than messages not containing these features.

Table 14.1

Means and Standard Deviations for Dependent Variables

	Most Sophisticated Message		Least Sophisticated Message	
	M	SD	M	SD
Message Evaluation	6.06	(0.91)	5.59	(1.14)
Relationship Evaluation	5.60	(1.12)	4.85	(1.06)
Celebrant Evaluation	6.00	(0.81)	5.21	(1.12)
Positive Affect	5.68	(1.04)	5.01	(1.25)

Assessment of Hypotheses and Research Questions

Hypotheses 1–4 made predictions regarding the impact of each individual message feature. Specifically, these hypotheses predicted that the presence of each individual feature would result in (a) more positive message evaluations, (b) more positive evaluations of the celebrant, (c) better feelings about the relationship with the celebrant, and (d) greater positive affect than celebratory support messages that did not contain each of these features. Given that these hypotheses predict each message feature will have a main effect on the dependent variables, analyses began with a one-way MANOVA on each message variable and was followed up with appropriate univariate one-way ANOVAs.

Acknowledgement feature. To assess the first hypothesis, a one-way MANOVA was conducted initially with the acknowledgement feature (present vs. absent) as the independent variable and message evaluation, relationship evaluation, celebrant evaluation, and positive affect as the dependent variables. The multivariate effect for the acknowledgement feature approached statistical significance, but did not reach the conventional .05 level, Wilks' $\Lambda = .02$, $F(4, 431) = 2.11$, $p = .08$.

However, univariate analyses indicated that the acknowledgement feature did have statistically significant effects for each dependent variable individually: message evaluation, $F(1, 434) = 3.94$, $p = .05$, $\eta 2 = .01$; relationship evaluation, $F(1, 434) = 6.06$, $p = .01$, $\eta 2 = .01$; celebrant evaluation, $F(1, 434) = 7.19$, $p < .01$, $\eta 2 = .02$; and positive affect, $F(1, 434) = 6.94$, $p < .01$, $\eta 2 = .02$. Specifically, messages that included this feature received more positive message evaluation ($M = 5.90$, $SD = 1.03$) than those that did not ($M = 5.77$, $SD - 1.03$); more positive relationship evaluation ($M = 5.43$, $SD = 1.20$) than those that did not ($M = 5.22$, $SD = 1.15$); more positive celebrant evaluation ($M = 5.72$, $SD = 1.05$) than those that did not ($M = 5.49$, $SD = 1.04$) and more positive affect ($M = 5.56$, $SD = 1.16$) than those that did not ($M = 5.32$, $SD = 1.17$). Thus, as predicted, the acknowledgement feature had a consistent, albeit small effect on all dependent variables. These results are consistent with Hypothesis 1.

In sum, it appeared acknowledging the feelings of someone who has just shared good news is, indeed, viewed as an important component of celebratory support. This feature had positive effects on all relevant dependent variables: message evaluation, relationship evaluation, celebrant evaluation, and positive affect.

Reciprocation feature. To assess the second hypothesis, a one-way MANOVA was conducted initially with the reciprocation feature (present vs. absent) as the independent variable and message evaluation, relationship evaluation, celebrant evaluation, and positive affect as the dependent variables. The multivariate effect for the reciprocation feature was not significant, Wilks' $\Lambda = .01$, $F(4, 431) = 1.24$, $p = .29$.

Although the means were in the expected directions for three of the four contexts, univariate analyses for each dependent variable indicated the reciprocation feature also had no main effect on any of the dependent variables. These results offer no support for Hypothesis 2.

Elaboration feature. To assess the third hypothesis, a one-way MANOVA was conducted initially with the elaboration feature (present vs. absent) as the independent variable and message evaluation, relationship evaluation, celebrant evaluation, and positive affect as the dependent variables. The multivariate effect for the elaboration feature was not significant, Wilks' $\Lambda = .01$, $F(4,431) = 1.16$, $p = .33$.

Univariate analyses for each dependent variable also revealed no significant main effects for this feature on any of the dependent variables. However, for each of the dependent variables, the effect of the elaboration feature approached statistical significance, and importantly, the direction of the means was opposite of that predicted, with messages lacking the elaboration feature tending to be rated more highly than messages exhibiting this feature. These findings offer no support for Hypothesis 3.

Offer to go celebrate feature. To assess the fourth and final hypothesis, a one-way MANOVA was conducted initially with the offer to go celebrate feature (present vs. absent) as the independent variable and message evaluation, relationship evaluation, celebrant evaluation, and positive affect as the dependent variables. The multivariate effect for the offer to go celebrate feature was near significant, Wilks' $\Lambda = .02$, $F(4,431) = 2.13$, $p = .08$.

Univariate analyses for each of the dependent variables indicated that messages containing the offer go celebrate feature had a significant, albeit small, effect on celebrant evaluation, $F(1, 434) = 7.25$, $p < .01$, $\eta2 = .02$ and positive affect, $F(1, 434) = 4.83$, $p = .03$, $\eta2 = .01$. More specifically, messages that included the offer to go celebrate feature led to more positive evaluations of the celebrant ($M = 5.75$, $SD = 1.02$) than message that did not include this feature ($M = 5.46$, $SD = 1.06$). Additionally messages including this feature also led the recipient to have more positive affect ($M = 5.59$, $SD = 1.11$) than messages that did not include this feature ($M = 5.30$, $SD = 1.21$) These findings appear to offer qualified support for Hypothesis 4 with regard to two of the four dependent variables.

Conclusion

This is one of the first studies conducted on celebratory support, the messages used in the effort to enhance the benefits of a positive event above and beyond the event itself. Thus, findings from this study provide a valuable foundation for this important form of positive interaction. Specifically, this study indicated that the most sophisticated celebratory support messages (those that contained all of the predicted messages features) receive more positive evaluations than the least sophisticated celebratory support messages (those that contained none of the predicted message features). These results confirm that generic celebratory support messages that simply say "congratulations" are not the most effective way to respond to another's good news. Rather, individuals expect and appreciate more refined responses.

Additionally, findings indicate that two particularly effective features of celebratory support messages include: the acknowledgement the target's feelings and an offer to go celebrate. Thus, despite what else is said or what type of celebration has been shared, celebratory support messages should first acknowledge the target's feelings. Results from this study indicated that this led to more positive evaluation of the message, relationship, and celebrant as well as more positive affect. In other words, messages that include phrases such as, "I can see that you are really happy and you should be, this is a big deal" or "I can see by the look on your face that this is truly a relief" are not only evaluated more positively by the recipient, but also lead the recipient to feel more positively about the individuals providing the support, better about his/her relationship with this person, and overall have more positive affect (in a similar vein, see Bodie, chapter 7, this volume).

Offers to go celebrate also appear to have particularly positive effects. Thus, messages that are used to respond to the good news that include phrases such as, "let me buy you a drink to celebrate" or "I'd like to help you commemorate the event, let me take you to dinner," generally lead to more positive outcomes than messages that do not.

Finally, this study indicates that the celebratory support message features of reciprocation and encouragement of elaboration are not as effective. Thus, when responding to another's news, a message may not need to contain these features. This recommendation is based on the fact that the reciprocation feature led to no significant main effects in this study. Although the elaboration effect did produce marginally significant main effects, these were in the opposite direction than expected. In other words, celebratory support messages that included this feature actually led to lower outcomes than messages that did not include this features.

In sum, the use of four specific message features (acknowledge, reciprocation, elaboration, and offer) is a more effective way to provide celebratory support than simply saying a generic phrase such as "congratulations." However, this study has also found that two message features, in particular, are especially effective at eliciting positive responses from celebratory support recipients: acknowledgment of target's feelings (across contexts) and offers to go celebrate (within at least two contexts).

In conclusion, this study has provided answers to the general research question, "what are the celebratory support message features that will elicit positive responses from celebratory support recipients?" However, important research questions remain. In particular, one might wonder, how is it that certain message features work, how does the nature of the celebratory event affect the evaluation of celebratory support, and how does the relationship between the support provider and recipient influence the evaluation of celebratory support. Research conducted in an attempt to answer these questions would continue to expand our understanding of the role of celebration within interpersonal communication and relationships.

Notes

1   This chapter is based on the PhD dissertation of the first author directed by the second author. McCullough, J.D. (2010). *"Celebrate good times, come on!": Defining effective features of celebratory support.* (Doctoral dissertation). West Lafayette: Purdue University.

References

Ashby, F. G., Isen, A. M., & Turken, U. (1999). A nueropsychological theory of positive affect and its influence on cognition. *Psychological Review, 106,* 529–550.

Burleson, B. R. (2003). Emotional support skills. In J. O. Greene & B. R. Burleson (Eds.), *Handbook of communication and social interaction skills* (pp. 551–594). Mahwah, NJ: Erlbaum.

Burleson, B. R., & Goldsmith, D. J. (1998). How the comforting process works: Alleviating emotional distress through conversationally induced reappraisals. In P. A. Andersen & L. K. Guerrero (Eds.), *Handbook of communication and emotion: Research, theory, applications, and contexts* (pp. 245–280). San Diego, CA: Academic Press.

Burleson, B. R., Kunkel, A. W., Samter, W., & Werking, K. J. (1996). Men's and women's evaluations of communication skills in personal relationships: When sex differences make a difference—and when they don't. *Journal of Social and Personal Relationships, 13,* 201–224.

Burleson, B. R., & Samter, W. (1990). Effects of cognitive complexity on the perceived importance of communication skills in friends. *Communication Research, 17,* 165–182.

Feng, B., & Burleson, B. R. (2008). The effects of argument explicitness on responses to advice in supportive interactions. *Communication Research, 3,* 553-575.

Gable, S. L., Gonzaga, G. C., & Strachman, A. (2006). Will you be there for me when things go right? Supportive responses to positive event disclosures. *Journal of Personality and Social Psychology, 91*(5), 904–917.

Gable, S. L., Reis, H. T., & Elliot, A. J. (2000). Behavioral activation and inhibition in everyday life. *Journal of Personality and Social Psychology, 78*(6), 1135–1149.

Gable, S. L., Reis, H. T., Impett, E. A., & Asher, E. R. (2004). What do you do when things go right? The intrapersonal and interpersonal benefits of sharing positive events. *Journal of Personality and Social Psychology, 87*(2), 228–245.

Goldsmith, D. J., & MacGeorge, E. L. (2000). The impact of politeness and relationship on perceived quality of advice about a problem. *Human Communication Research, 26,* 234–263.

Gottman, J. M. (1999). *The sound marital house: A theory of marriage.* In The marriage clinic (pp. 87–110). New York: Norton.

Holmstrom, A. J. (2008). The development and assessment of a cognitive-emotional theory of esteem support messages. (Doctoral dissertation). West Lafayette: Purdue University.

Isen, A. M. (1987). Positive affect, cognitive processes, and social behavior. In L. Berkowitz (Ed.), *Advances in experimental social psychology* (Vol. 20, pp. 203–253). New York: Academic Press.

Isen, A. M., Daubman, K. A., & Nowicki, G. P. (1987). Positive affect facilitates creative problem solving. *Journal of Personality and Social Psychology, 52,* 1122–1131.

Langston, C. A. (1994). Capitalizing on and coping with daily-life events: Expressive responses to positive events. *Journal of Personality and Social Psychology, 67,* 1112–1125.

Lewinsohn, P. M., & Graf, M. (1973). Pleasant activities and depression. *Journal of Consulting Clinical Psychology, 41,* 261–268.

MacGeorge, E. L., Feng, B., & Butler, G. L. (2003). Gender differences in the communication values of mature adults. *Communication Research Reports, 20,* 191–199.

McCullough, J.D. (2010). *"Celebrate good times, come on!": Defining effective features of celebratory support.* (Doctoral dissertation). West Lafayette: Purdue University.

Nezleck, J. B., & Gable, S. L. (2001). Depression as a moderator of relationships between positive daily events and day-to-day psychological adjustment. *Personality and Social Psychology Bulletin, 27*(12), 1692–1704.

Reis, H. T, & Patrick, B. C. (1996). Attachment and intimacy: Component processes. In E. T. Higgins & A. W. Kruglanski (Eds.), *Social psychology: Handbook of basic principles* (pp. 523–563). New York: Guilford Press.

Scherer, K. R. (1986). Vocal affect expression: A review and a model for future research. *Psychological Bulletin, 99,* 143–165.

Stone, A. A., Cox, D. S., Valdimarsdottir, H., Jandorf, L., & Neal, J. M. (1987). Evidence that secretory IgA antibody is associated with daily mood. *Journal of Personality and Social Psychology, 52,* 988–993.

Stone, A. A., Neale, J. M., Cox, D. S., Napoli, A., Valdimarsdottir, H., & Kennedy-Moore, E. (1994). Daily events are associated with secretory immune response to an oral antigen in men. *Health Psychology, 13,* 440–446.

Vangelisti, A. L. (2009). Challenges in conceptualizing social support. *Journal of Social and Personal Relationships, 26*(1), 39–51.

Watson, D., Clark, L.A., & Tellegen, A. (1988). Development and validation of brief measures of positive and negative affect: The PANAS scales. *Journal of Personality and Social Psychology, 54,* 1063–1070.

Werner, C.M., Altman, I., Brown, B.B., & Ginat, J. (1993). Celebrations in personal relationship: A transactional/ dialectical perspective. In S. Duck (Ed.), *Social context and relationships* (pp. 109–138). Newbury Park: Sage.

Section Three
Illustrative Applications

• CHAPTER FIFTEEN •

Engaging Health Communication

Gary L. Kreps
George Mason University

The Centrality of Communication in Health Promotion

Health communication is central to the delivery of health care and promotion of well-being. It is a complex social process that involves many different levels of communication (intrapersonal, interpersonal, group, organizational, and societal interactions), numerous channels for communication (including spoken interactions, written texts, telephone conversations, text messages, radio and television broadcasts, as well as many uses of computer-based information systems), and occurs within a variety of unique situations and contexts (such as hospital emergency rooms, surgical suites, medical offices, clinics, accident sites, workplaces, schools, and homes) (Kreps & Bonaguro, 2009; Kreps, Query, & Bonaguro, 2007). Health communication interactions are also often fast-paced, highly charged, intense, and emotional. Health care consumers and providers have urgent needs for relevant health information to help guide the difficult time-sensitive health decisions they need to make about treatment options, palliative care, and lifestyle choices (such as nutritional strategies, sexual practices, physical activity patterns, and drug/alcohol uses). Consumers and providers also depend on communication to encourage complex collaborative efforts between a broad range of health system participants (doctors, nurses, therapists, pharmacists, consumers and their family members) to provide coordinated care, relieve physical and emotional suffering, and extend well-being. Communication performs a central role in the achieving all of these goals and enabling the effective delivery of care and promotion of health. Moreover, the quality of health communication processes has been shown to be directly related to achieving desired health outcomes and can often mean the difference between life and death, and between wellness and suffering (Greenfield, Kaplan, & Ware, 1985; Kreps & Chapelsky Massimilla, 2002; Kreps & O'Hair, 1995).

On the positive front, doctors, nurses, and other health care providers depend on their abilities to communicate collaboratively with their patients (and with each other) to gather relevant information to diagnose and treat these patients' health problems. Providers must ask pertinent questions about patient symptoms, behaviors, and lifestyle factors, interpret patient responses, and probe for more detailed information. If the providers fail to fully engage their patients and encourage these patients to provide relevant information they will have a very difficult time diagnosing health care problems and the delivery of health will suffer. Health care providers also must engage with others to coordinate efforts with consumers in the delivery of care, encouraging their patients and co-workers to cooperate with the delivery of care and to follow treatment recommendations. If health care providers are not able to effectively explain treatment regimens to their patients and encourage these patients to follow therapeutic procedures and take prescribed medications, even the best medical strategies are not likely to work very well (Kreps et al., 2011). Furthermore, it is often a challenge to elicit cooperation between health team members (providers, consumers, and support personnel) to deliver coordinated care, and there are many instances in the delivery of care when communication is not ideal, providers and consumers do not have the best information for guiding their health decisions, and there are breakdowns in the health care/promotion process (Kreps & Thornton, 1992; Kreps, 1988a; 1988b).

Consumers also depend on their abilities to communicate effectively with heath care providers to seek help, identify health problems, interpret health recommendations and treatment strategies, and negotiate their ways through the many complex and bureaucratic modern health care systems. However, it is often difficult for consumers to communicate their needs and concerns to health care providers. Patients are often intimidated by the health care system, have difficulties expressing their health concerns, and feel challenged to participate fully in directing their own health care (Kreps, 1999; 1996; Kreps & Thornton, 1992). It is critically important to equalize the communication dynamics between consumers and providers, encouraging more active exchange of information and influence over the delivery of care and promotion of health.

In health promotion efforts (campaigns designed to influence public health knowledge, attitudes, and behaviors to help reduce health risks and encourage the adoption of healthy behaviors and lifestyles), communication is the primary campaign process by which influential messages about relevant health risks and appropriate health preserving behaviors are directed to targeted public health audiences. Yet, many health promotion efforts are not designed to communicate effectively with targeted audiences, engage these audiences, and motivate them to make good health decisions. Care must be taken in health promotion efforts to craft messages that are appropriate and compelling to target audiences, deliver these messages through the most effective communication channels, and reinforce adoption of healthy behaviors over time.

A large and developing body of research illustrates the centrality of communication processes in achieving important health care and health promotion goals. Kreps and O'Hair (1995) review studies showing the influences of communication strategies and programs on health knowledge, behaviors, and outcomes. For example, Greenfield and colleagues (1985) clearly demonstrated the positive influences of increased patient/provider communicative involvement in directing health care treatment in achieving desired health outcomes. Dearing and colleagues (1996) illustrated the positive influences of social marketing and diffusion-based communication campaign strategies in encouraging at-risk populations to adopt important health risk prevention behaviors. Large-scale multi-year communication intervention programs, such as the Stanford Five City Heart Health Program (Flora, Maccoby, & Farquhar, 1989) and the Minnesota Heart Health communication program (Pavlik et al., 1993) also demonstrate the positive influences of these campaigns on promoting adoption of lifestyle changes to prevent cardiovascular disease and reducing gaps in public health knowledge. Within health care/promotion delivery systems, communication is the central social process that can help connect and coordinate all the diverse, yet interdependent, health care professionals and providers, helping to guide their activities to promote health. There is great potential for the use of sensitive and compelling health communication to provide health care consumers and providers with needed health information and to help address important public health needs. However, it is critically important for these health communication efforts to effectively engage audiences, capture their attention, and positively influence their health beliefs, attitudes, and behaviors.

A Need to Strengthen Current Health Communication Practices

More attention needs to be paid to the quality of communication in the delivery of care and promotion of health. Typically the focus in health care and health promotion is on health care procedures and technologies and not on the ways health care information is communicated. This often results in poor quality health communication that inhibits, rather than facilitates, the achievement of desired health outcomes. As a form of positive interpersonal communication, several qualitative factors in the delivery of health care and promotion of health need to be taken into consideration. How engaging are health communication efforts? Do health communication efforts capture audiences' attention (exposure)? Do they communicate clearly (taking into account individual audience differences and levels of health literacy)? Do they communicate humanely (sensitivity)? Do they communicate persuasively? Do they adapt well to unique individuals? Do they promote immediacy (relational closeness and dynamism)? Unfortunately, answers to these questions about the quality of health communication processes are often very disappointing. If we are to advance a positive, strengths-based approach to interpersonal communication in healthcare settings, we must focus on ways to augment positive experiences that emphasize patient strengths, coping, and resilience (e.g., see Seligman, 2002; Seligman & Csikszentmihalyi, 2000, for discussions about positive psychology). Such efforts should, in general, feature communication facilitative of positive states found to be significant in health and wellness, in particular, hope (Snyder, 1994; 2004).

Too often, health communication efforts are boring and unimaginative. Health care providers can often appear robotic and emotionally unattached to their patients. There is a focus on filling out forms, standardized interview formats, and having the same basic questions asked over and over again in health-care settings. Health-care personnel are often required to treat many different patients and have limited time, which can lead them to be rushed and to appear to be superficial when communicating with individual patients. Health promotion efforts often focus more on presenting scientific facts and directives than on connecting the information in personally engaging way to individual consumers.

There is common overuse of technical medical language (jargon) that is difficult for laypeople to understand (sometimes referred to as medicalese or medspeak). This jargon is used by health care personnel when delivering information about diagnoses, treatment options, and therapeutic recommendations. The use of jargon is also widespread in many of the written materials provided to consumers on websites, in pamphlets, in treatment direction handouts, and in medication package inserts. Due to the overuse of technical terminology and jargon it is often difficult for consumers to understand the information presented to them by health care providers, which leads to confusion and disengagement, and impedes the provision of informed consent for care. The entire health care system can appear to be overly complex and formal (bureaucratic), with lots of rules and regulations that constrain health care consumers and providers (Kreps, 1996).

Sometimes, the messages sent to consumers can be disempowering, suggesting that the consumers' behaviors are the primary causes of their health problems. This negative communication strategy tends to blame the victim of health care problems (patients), alienating them and making them feel bad about themselves. Worse, the ways that questions are asked of consumers about their health behaviors and health histories can be intimidating and insulting. (Are you still smoking? How much exercise do you get? How often do you bathe? How much alcohol do you drink? Do you eat a balanced diet? Are you following your doctor's recommendations?). The medical recommendations presented to patients often sound like negative directives for consumers to clean up their acts. These health messages sent to consumers are often very prescriptive, suggesting that health care professionals know what's best for consumers, and individual consumers do not have much say in the matter. The messages are often very static, without providing consumers with many (or any) options. (Often the directives are presented as "It is our way or the highway.") For all of these reasons, health communication is far from "fun" for consumers. The quality of health communication is often disempowering and alienating. This kind of health communication discourages patient participation and cooperation, leads to problems with understanding and following health care recommendations, and limits informed and cooperative health care decision making.

Increasing Immediacy to Promote Engaging Health Communication

The effectiveness of health communication processes depends upon multiple communication factors, including the accuracy, timeliness, fidelity, persuasiveness, and sensitivity of messages exchanged. One of the most important, and largely unrecognized, dimensions of effective health communication relates to how engaging the communication is, a process often referred to in the communication literature as "immediacy." Immediacy is a critical factor in determining whether communication processes capture attention, connects health care participants, and encourages these participants to work together to achieve important health goals (Andersen, 1979). Immediacy is a relational dimension of human communication that influences physical and emotional closeness, comfort, engagement, caring, personal involvement, intensity, enthusiasm, authenticity, and enjoyment in human interactions (Andersen, 1979).

There is a large body of research literature on the influences of communication immediacy on instructional outcomes that suggests that instructors that communicate with high levels of immediacy can promote relational closeness and cooperation with students, enhance the expression of affect to students, increase cognitive and affective learning by students, improve students' perceptions of instructor credibility, enhance motivation and participation with students, encouraging active communication and feedback between students and instructors, as well as reduce student resistance and verbal aggression (see, Andersen, 1979; Arbaugh, 2001; Chesebro & McCroskey, 2001; Gorham, 1988; Kelley & Gorham, 1988; Pogue & AhYun, 2006). These communication outcomes in the instructional domain all sound like they would also be most valuable for use in the health care/promotion arena. Yet, there has been very limited attention to communication immediacy in health care and health promotion research. In fact, there has been limited attention given to the whole spectrum of relational dimensions of health communication in health care and health promotion, despite the importance of relational communication in achieving desired health outcomes (Kreps, 1988a, 2001; Query & Kreps, 1996; Weathers, Query, & Kreps, 2010). Based upon the instructional communication research findings about the influences of immediacy on instructional outcomes, there appears to be great potential for examining the health influences of immediacy on increasing consumer and provider access to relevant health information, improving the quality of health communication and care, increasing consumer-provider participation and involvement, promoting coordination of health care services, relieving demands on health care staff, reducing health care costs and increasing efficiency, and influencing health behaviors and outcomes.

Communication Strategies for Enhancing Immediacy and Engagement

Research has shown that there are a variety of relatively simple verbal and nonverbal communication strategies that can be used to enhance the immediacy of interactions in instructional contexts that can be applied very well to health care and health promotion settings (Andersen, 1979; Arbaugh, 2001; Chesebro & McCroskey, 2001; Gorham, 1988; Kelley & Gorham, 1988; Pogue & AhYun, 2006). There are several straightforward verbal strategies that can be used for promoting immediacy in health care contexts. For example, it is a good idea to use the consumer's (or providers') names when interacting with them to personalize communication. Providers can use collective terms (such as "we" and "us") to enhance a sense of inclusion and cooperation with consumers. Providers can use familiar terms and explain complex concepts (eschewing the use of medical jargon, and increasing the use of culturally and educationally appropriate terms and examples). Health personnel can provide opportunities for casual interaction with consumers to break the ice, reduce tension, and help to build rapport. Health personnel should strive to provide specific and appropriate feedback to consumers to make sure they understand the information being provided and their different treatment options. Providers should ask for patient input on health care decisions, seek feedback about reactions to recommendations, and encourage patients to express their personal preferences and concerns. These positive verbal communication strategies can help humanize health care interactions, encourage participation, and help to build meaningful consumer-provider relationships (also see Mirivel, chapter 4, this volume).

There are also a number of straightforward nonverbal message strategies that have been found to enhance immediacy in instructional communication settings that can be easily adapted to health care and health promotion contexts. For example, it is important for health care providers to communicate in ways that show concern and empathy (caring) for consumers. This can be done by smiling appropriately while talking to show friendliness, gesturing in an animated way while talking to enhance the active and dramatic nature of health communication, maintaining good eye contact with patients to demonstrate personal involvement, using vocal variety when speaking to consumers (avoiding the use of monotone speech), using a relaxed body posture to increase perceptions of comfort and accessibility, and using touch appropriately to express feelings and connect with consumers personally. Interestingly, past research has shown that most uses of touch by health care providers with their patients are used for instrumental (moving the patient, giving the patient a shot, adjusting an IV line, etc.), rather than to express emotions (Kreps & Thornton, 1992). Research has also shown that that ways that instructors dress influences immediacy, with casual appearance increasing immediacy in the classroom (Andersen, 1979). A recent hospital-based intervention project where colorful hats were created for patients, health care personnel, and family members to wear demonstrated that wearing the colorful hats helped to enhance health communication and increase engagement between consumers and providers (Khorsand, Desens, & Kreps, 2011). Furthermore, health care delivery systems can use engaging design features that enhance consumer privacy, increase warm room colors, add comfortable furniture and carpeting to enhance immediacy and comfort in health communication.

Paying attention to the quality of communication in the delivery of care and the promotion of health can increase engagement between health care providers and consumers, increase active participation, and enhance health outcomes. The immediacy of communication appears to be a particularly important aspect of effective health communication. The strategic use of relationally and culturally sensitive verbal and nonverbal communication can help increase immediacy. This can enhance the energy, excitement, and salience of health communication activities across multiple channels and health settings so participants are likely to be fully engaged, involved, and motivated to promote health and well being.

References

Andersen, J. F. (1979). Teacher immediacy as a predictor of teaching effectiveness. In D. Nimmo (Ed.), *Communication Yearbook*, 3 (pp. 543–559). New Brunswick, NJ: Transaction.

Arbaugh, J. B. (2001). How instructor immediacy behaviors affect student satisfaction and learning in web-based courses. *Business Communication Quarterly*, 64, 42–54.

Chesebro, J. L., & McCroskey, J. C. (2001). The relationship of teacher clarity and immediacy with student state receiver apprehension, affect, and cognitive learning. *Communication Education*, 50, 59–68.

Dearing, J. W., Rogers, E. M., Meyer, G., Casey, M. K., Rao, N., Campo, S., & Henderson, G. M. (1996). Social marketing and diffusion-based strategies for communicating with unique populations: HIV prevention in San Francisco. *Journal of Health Communication*, 1(4), 342–364.

Flora, J. A., Maccoby, N., & Farquhar, J. W. (1989). Communication campaigns to prevent cardiovascular disease: The Stanford community studies. In R. E. Rice & C. K. Atkin (Eds.), *Public communication campaigns* (2nd ed.) (pp. 233–252). Newbury Park, CA: Sage.

Gorham, J. (1988). The relationship between verbal teaching immediacy behaviors and student learning. *Communication Education*, 17, 40–53.

Greenfield, S., Kaplan, S., & Ware, J. Jr. (1985). Expanding patient involvement in care: Effects on patient outcomes. *Annals of Internal Medicine, 102*, 520–528.

Kelley, D. H., & Gorham, J. (1988). Effects of immediacy on recall of information. *Communication Education, 37*, 198–207.

Khorsand, S., Desens, L., & Kreps, G.L. (2011, April). The Glories HATS Project®—"Stay healthy to help others:" Increasing adolescent self-efficacy through altruistic action and positive youth development. Presented to the DC-area Health Communication (DHHC) conference, Fairfax, VA.

Kreps, G. L. (1988a). Relational communication in health care. *Southern Speech Communication Journal, 53*, 344–359.

Kreps, G. L. (1988b, May). *The homeostatic function of communication training for health care providers: Facilitating interprofessional respect, sensitivity and cooperation.* Paper presented to the International Communication Association conference. New Orleans, LA.

Kreps, G. L. (1996). Promoting a consumer orientation to health care and health promotion. *Journal of Health Psychology, 1 (1), 41–48.*

Kreps, G. L. (1999). Social responsibility and the modern health care system: Promoting a consumer orientation to health care. Salem, P. (Ed.). *Organizational communication and change* (pp. 293–304). Cresskill, NJ: Hampton Press.

Kreps, G. L. (2001). Consumer/provider communication research: A personal plea to address issues of ecological validity, relational development, message diversity, and situational constraints. *Journal of Health Psychology, 6(5), 597–601.*

Kreps, G. L. (2011). Translating health communication research into practice: The influence of health communication scholarship on health policy, practice, and outcomes. In T. Thompson, R. Parrott, & J. Nussbaum, (Eds.), *The handbook of health communication,* (2nd ed.) (pp. 595–608). New York: Routledge.

Kreps, G. L., & Bonaguro, E. (2009). Health communication as applied communication inquiry. In L. Frey & K. Cissna (Eds.), *The handbook of applied communication Research* (pp. 970–993). Hillsdale, NJ: Lawrence Erlbaum.

Kreps, G. L., & Chapelsky Massimilla, D. (2002). Cancer communications research and health outcomes: Review and challenge. *Communication Studies, 53(4), 318–336.*

Kreps, G. L., & O'Hair, D. (Eds.). (1995). *Communication and health outcomes.* Cresskill, NJ: Hampton Press

Kreps, G. L., Query, J. L., & Bonaguro, E. W. (2007). The interdisciplinary study of health communication and its relationship to communication science. In L. Lederman (Ed), *Beyond These Walls: Readings in Health Communication,* (pp. 2–13). London: Oxford University Press.

.Kreps, G. L., & Thornton, B.C. (1992). *Health communication: Theory and practice* (2nd. ed.). Prospect Heights, IL: Waveland Press.

Kreps, G. L., Villagran, M. M., Zhao, X., McHorney, C., Ledford, C., Weathers, M., & Keefe. B. P. (2011). Development and validation of motivational messages to improve prescription medication adherence for patients with chronic health problems. *Patient Education and Counseling, 83*, 365–371.

Pavlik, J.V., Finnegan, J.R., Strickland, D., Salman, C. T., Viswanath, K., & Wackman, D.B. (1993). Increasing public understanding of heart disease: An analysis of the Minnesota heart health program. *Health Communication, 5(1), 1–20.*

Pogue, L., & AhYun, K. (2006). The effect of teacher nonverbal immediacy and credibility on student motivation and affective learning. *Communication Education, 55*, 331–344.

Query, J. L. & Kreps, G.L. (1996). Testing a relational model of health communication competence among caregivers for individuals with Alzheimer's disease. *Journal of Health Psychology, 1(3),* 335–352.

Seligman, M. E. P. (2002). *Authentic happiness.* New York: Free Press.

Seligman, M. E. P, & Csikszentmihalyi, M. (2000). Positive psychology: An introduction. *American Psychologist, 55*, 5–14.

Snyder, C. R. (1994). *The psychology of hope.* New York: Free Press.

Snyder, C. R. (2000). *Handbook of hope: Theory, measures, and applications.* San Diego, CA: Academic Press.

Weathers, M., Query, J. L., & Kreps, G. L. (2010). A multivariate test of communication competence, social support, and coping among Hispanic lay caregivers for loved ones with Alzheimer's disease: An extension of the Relational Health Communication Competence Model. *Journal of Participative Medicine, 2e14,* http://www.jopm.org/evidence/research/2010/12/05/a-multivariate-test-of-communication-competence-social-support-and-coping-among-hispanic-lay-caregivers-for-loved-ones-with-alzheimers-disease-an-extension-of-the-relational-health-communication/.

• CHAPTER SIXTEEN •

Positive Religious/Spiritual Coping Among African American Men Living with HIV in Jails and/or Prisons

E. James Baesler
Old Dominion University

Valerian J. Derlega
Old Dominion University

James Lolley
Virginia Consortium Program in Clinical Psychology,
Virginia Beach, VA

About one million people in the United States live with the human immunodeficiency virus (HIV) that causes acquired immunodeficiency syndrome (AIDS), according to recent estimates from the Center for Disease Control (2009). Since the mid-1990s, medical treatment for HIV offers life extending possibilities, shifting the focus away from anticipating an early death to creating a positive quality of life. Yet, HIV still remains a life-threatening chronic illness with multiple, severe, and unrelenting stressors (Bosworth, 2006) that impact on individual's physical, psychological, social, and spiritual life. Coping with HIV stressors leads many individuals to explore religion/spirituality[1] as a way to positively improve their quality of life (Siegel & Schrimshaw, 2002; Somlai & Heckman, 2000).

To conceptualize the ways persons living with HIV use religious/spiritual coping to enhance their quality of life, we turn to the emerging area of *positive communication* (Socha, 2008). One way to conceptualize the new area of "positive communication" is to expand the psychological orientation that has focused on positive experiences, traits, and emotions (Peterson & Seligman, 2004) and consider the types of "positive messages" that influence these psychological outcomes.

In this chapter, we focus on a particular type of positive communication: religious/spiritual messages that assist in coping with stress. We define religious/spiritual communication broadly, from particular communications to/with God [2], as in interpersonal prayer, to any number of communication contexts that incorporate religious/spiritual content. Religious/spiritual communications span a continuum, from those having a positive quality (e.g., intercessory prayer for the ill) to communications having a more dark quality (e.g., curses against enemies that invoke the name of a deity). We are exploring the possibility of positive religious/spiritual coping communication resulting from the combined force of two unique stressors: living with HIV in a prison or jail environment.

Religious/Spiritual Coping among Inmates

A substantial number of individuals living with HIV are in prison. Of the 1.5 million individuals in the United States incarcerated in federal and state prisons in 2006, approximately 22,000 persons (19,842 being male) were identified as HIV positive (Bureau of Justice Statistics, 2006). Many individuals in prison use religion/spirituality to cope with the stressors of life (O'Connor & Perreyclear, 2002). Combining a serious personal illness like HIV with the challenges of living in prison provides a potent interaction of stressors for exploring the possibility of positive religious/spiritual coping messages. In the following sections, we introduce the literature on religion/spirituality in the prison, and suggest how this literature is related to positive communication as religious/spiritual coping behind prison walls while living with HIV.

Prison is a harsh, stressful environment that includes the loss of many freedoms, but in 1987 the Supreme Court of the United States ruled that prison inmates retain constitutional rights, including that of religion. This ruling was reinforced in 1993 by the Religious Freedom and Restoration Act (Turner, 2008). Currently, several general religious/spiritual programs are represented by institutional religions in prisons (e.g., Buddhist Peace Fellowship, Prison-Ashram Project, Prison Fellowship), and a wide variety of specific religious/spiritual programs available at most large prisons (e.g., Bible study, Catholic Mass, Islamic Ta-Leem, Native American Sweat Lodge Ceremony) (Dammer, 2002). At least one study indicates a sizeable proportion of inmates are regularly involved in some type of religious/spiritual activity, and that these activities are associated with positive social behavior (O'Connor & Perreyclear, 2002).

Inmates report a number of reasons for being involved in organized and personal religion/spirituality: (a) providing meaning and direction in life, (b) cultivating feelings of faith, hope, and peace through religious/spiritual experiences like personal meditation and prayer, and (c) providing opportunities for social support through community worship and interaction (Dammer, 2002; Turner, 2008). Several of these reasons could be the result of positive communications to or with God and/or with others.

Religious/Spiritual Coping with HIV

We note that many of the benefits of religion/spirituality for inmates parallel benefits of religion/spirituality for persons living with HIV outside of the prison context. For instance, those with HIV, in and outside prison, can both benefit from cultivating faith and finding direction and meaning in life through religion/spirituality. We hypothesize that the prison environment, when combined with a serious illness like HIV, accentuates the number of overall life stressors, thereby activating and increasing the relevance of religious/spiritual coping pathways. We were not able to find any published research on the religious/spiritual coping strategies of prisoners living with HIV, but we highlight some of the growing literature on religious/spiritual coping with HIV.

One consistent and reliable finding across a number of studies is the positive role of religion/spirituality in living with HIV. For example, those living with HIV report: (a) increases in prayer and meditation (Greene, Berger, & Reeves, 1999), (b) the importance of religious/spiritual beliefs like "a higher power cares for me" (Somlai & Heckman, 2000, p. 65), and (c) emotional comfort derived from religion/spirituality (Siegel & Schrimshaw, 2002). Many types of religious/spiritual coping for individuals living with HIV have been identified in a review of the literature on religion/spirituality and HIV (Pargament et al., 2004): belief in a higher power, prayer, collaboration with God/higher power, and to a lesser extent attendance of religious services. One or more of these religious/spiritual coping strategies have been associated with positive outcomes: decreased emotional distress, lower depression, greater optimism, sense of peace, finding meaning in life, increased spiritual growth, and stronger spiritual beliefs.

Theoretical Framework

Having reviewed the general methods of religious/spiritual coping with HIV, we turn to the special case of prayer as an interpersonal religious/spiritual communication strategy to cope with HIV. The importance of prayer as a method of religious/spiritual coping with a variety of health issues is well documented (e.g., Levin, 2004; McCullough & Larson, 1999). In the research on persons living with HIV, several studies incorporate prayer as one of several components of religious/spiritual coping (Carson, Soeken, Shanty, & Terry, 1990; Cotton et al., 2006; Greene et al., 1999; Somlai & Heckman, 2000; Szaflarski et al., 2006), but none of these investigations explore the potential importance of prayer in religious/spiritual coping by specifying the type, content, or function of prayer. Based on the foundational work of Bade and Cook (2008), we propose that prayer may serve a variety of functions in the religious/spiritual coping process including, petition for assistance, forgiveness of self and others, and adoration/worship.

Our previous work in the area of prayer and religious/spiritual coping combines two theories to understand how mothers living with HIV use interpersonal prayer to cope (Baesler, Derlega, Winstead, & Barbee, 2003). In the present investigation, we add to our previous work in the interpersonal private prayer context by considering religious/spiritual coping methods, as a type of positive communication, in other prayer contexts like small and large groups. In the prison environment, often characterized by isolation, loneliness, and depression, we anticipate that those with HIV will use prayer as a primary method of religious/spiritual coping in the private interpersonal context with God. We also anticipate that prayer will play some type of supportive role in small and larger religious/spiritual groups, but we do not know the specific nature of this support.

In summary, the general literature on HIV and health outcomes consistently shows that persons living with HIV are confronted with a variety of stressors, and that these stressors, when combined with medical advances that increase the life span of those living with HIV, motivate individuals to focus on quality of life issues. Religion/Spirituality provides a context for responding to the stressors of HIV and addressing quality of life issues. Those living in prison also use religion/spirituality to cope with a variety of stressors that impacts their quality of life. The combined stresses of living in prison with HIV should provide a rich source of data for exploring religious/spiritual coping methods. In particular, we anticipate that positive religious/spiritual communications in personal, interpersonal, and social contexts will be part of the religious/spiritual coping methods exercised by those living with HIV behind prison walls. Given the review of the literature on religious/spiritual coping in prison, religious/spiritual coping with HIV, and the theoretical frameworks of the Social Interaction Model of Coping with HIV infection, and the Relational Prayer Theory, we propose the following hypotheses and research questions:

> H1: Those living with HIV will use one or more religious/spiritual methods to cope with their life in prison.
>
> H2: The most frequently used religious/spiritual coping method, among the personal, interpersonal, and social contexts, for those living with HIV in a prison context, will be some type of prayer.
>
> R1: What do the different types of prayer tell us about the needs and concerns of those living with HIV in prison?
>
> R2: How do the religious/spiritual coping methods compare in terms of emotional affect/valence?

Methods

Participants

Qualitative semi-structured interviews, lasting from one to two hours in length, were conducted over a one year period (2002–2003) with 17 African American men between the ages of 32–54 who were former inmates at a state or federal adult prison or jail in the southeastern region of the United States. Within the general protocol of questions that focused on interpersonal coping, privacy, and stigmatization issues, a series of questions asked participants about their religious/spiritual beliefs and practices as they related to coping with the challenges of living with HIV while in prison.

Coding Scheme and Procedures

The content of five well validated measures of religious/spiritual was the conceptual basis for us to code participants' religious/spiritual beliefs and practices. These measures were: the Duke Religion Index (Koenig, Parkerson, & Meador, 1997), the Functional Assessment of Chronic Illness Therapy—Spiritual Well-Being—Expanded Scale (Peterman, Fitchett, Brady, Pharm, & Cella, 2002), the Religious Coping Scale (Pargament, Koenig, & Perez, 2000) [3], Ironson-Woods Spirituality/Religiousness Scale (Ironson et al., 2002), and the Religious Involvement Scale (Taylor, Chatters, & Levin, 2004). All five measures include several overlapping categories: an organizational or institutional aspect of religion/spirituality, a personal or private dimension of religion/spirituality, and a belief/attitude dimension that underlies both the public and private expression of religion/spirituality. Thus, our coding scheme includes all three of these general dimensions represented in the literature.

In addition, the coding scheme we used categorizes types of prayer as specific forms of religious/spiritual coping based on a typology of active and receptive prayers derived from Relational Prayer theory (Baesler, 2003). The final coding scheme consisted of three dimensions: personal/private religious/spiritual coping, social religious/spiritual coping, and religious/spiritual cognitions associated with coping. Each of these dimensions, and their respective categories, are defined in the following sections with examples in Table 16.2.

Personal/Private Religious/Spiritual Dimension. Those religious/spiritual coping activities performed by the individual, and not in the company of others, are coded personal/private religious/spiritual activities. The second category for the personal/private religious/spiritual dimension is receptive prayer. Receptive prayers are characterized by a slowing down of bodily and mental processes, a quiet awareness, a willingness to listen, and an attitude of openness (Baesler, 2003). The third category included personal/private religious/spiritual coping activities other than active and receptive types of prayer.

Social Religious/Spiritual Dimension. The social dimension included religious/spiritual coping activities performed in the company of others. The religious/spiritual social dimension is not simply "social" in the sense of "socializing" but includes religious/spiritual content.

Cognitions: Religious/Spiritual Beliefs and Experiences Dimension. Beliefs are statements about religious/spiritual realities characterized by a cognitive component and imply the truth or falsity of a religious/spiritual statement.

Religious/Spiritual Affective Dimension. In addition to the three dimensions for coding religious/spiritual coping, we developed a coding scheme for assessing the affect or valence associated with the religious/spiritual dimensions. To determine affect/valence, we searched for one or more "qualifying" terms associated with religious/spiritual statements in the interview transcripts. If a qualifying term was found, then we judged the affect/valence of the qualifier as positive or negative; or, in the absence of a clear qualifier, we coded the affect/valence neutral. We also coded the number of participants who reported affect/valence one or more times in association with a particular religious/spiritual dimension/category. We report the percentage of use of a particular dimension/category based on the total number of thought units generated from the interviews, and the number of participants using a particular dimension/category one or more times.

Inter-Rater Reliabilities for Coding

Transcripts were highlighted for portions of the interviews where participants responded to religious/spiritual questions. Each thought unit, a complete thought represented as a phrase, sentence, or multiple sentences (an extension of the "key word in context idea," Krippendorff, 1980), for each participant, was given a unique number. A seven page coding manual with definitions of categories and illustrative examples was provided to coders to study before they began their coding.[4] Inter-rater reliability (Phi coefficient, Scott, 1955) for coding the thought units into the religious/spiritual categorization scheme was highly reliable at .91. The second and third author independently coded the 361 thought units into positive, negative, or neutral valence to assess affect/valence. The resulting inter-rater reliability was .97.

Results

Hypothesis one, predicting that African-American men would engage in one or more religious/spiritual methods to cope with their HIV while incarcerated, received moderate support. Collectively, participants used all religious/spiritual coping dimensions, but not all dimensions were employed with equal frequency. Table 16.1 reports two types of percentages: percentage of use based on total number of thought units, and percentage of use based on affect/valence. Both of these percentages are accompanied by the number of participants using a particular category, and the number of participants associated with each of the three affect/valence categories for each category.

Table 16.1

Religious/Spiritual Dimensions and Categories: Percentage of Use and Affect/Valence

Use of Religious/Spiritual Dimensions/Categories			Affect/Valence		
			Negative	*Neutral*	*Positive*
Personal/Private	Total	37.8			
Active Prayers	subtotal	31.7			
Adoration		2.8 (5)	0 (0)	1.0 (4)	1.8 (3)
Confession		5.5 (7)	0 (0)	5.4 (5)	<1.0 (2)
Thanksgiving		2.8 (4)	0 (0)	1.2 (1)	1.6 (3)
Petition—Self					
Physical/Material		13.6 (13)	0 (0)	10.1 (12)	2.5 (4)
Psychological		1.4 (5)	0 (0)	1.3 (3)	<1.0 (2)
Spiritual		2.8 (5)	0 (0)	2.7 (5)	<1.0 (1)
Petition—Other					
Physical/Material		2.2 (10)	0 (0)	1.1 (10)	1.1 (1)
Psychological		0.3 (1)	0 (0)	0.2 (1)	<1.0 (1)
Spiritual		0.3 (2)	0 (0)	0.2 (1)	<1.0 (1)
Receptive Prayers	subtotal	1.7 (2)	0 (0)	1.7 (2)	0 (0)
Other Activities	subtotal	4.4			
Studying R/S Texts		2.8 (4)	0 (0)	2.7 (4)	<1.0 (1)
Reading R/S Literature		0.5 (2)	0 (0)	0.5 (2)	0 (0)
Listening R/S Music		0.8 (1)	0 (0)	0.8 (1)	0 (0)
Watching R/S Programs		0.3 (1)	0 (0)	0.3 (1)	0 (0)
Social	Total	15.0			
Interpersonal		4.9 (6)	0 (0)	4.8 (4)	<1.0 (3)
Small Group		5.2 (7)	0 (0)	5.1 (7)	<1.0 (1)
Large Group		4.9 (7)	0 (0)	4.9 (7)	0 (0)
Cognitions	Total	32.0			
Beliefs		26.8 (17)	1.6 (5)	16.4 (17)	8.8 (14)
Experiences		5.2 (13)	<1.0 (1)	3.7 (7)	1.4 (4)
Other	Total	3.0			

Note. Percentages in the first column were compiled by dividing the number of thought units associated with a particular religious/spiritual dimension/category by the total number of thought units (361). Next to these percentages (in parentheses), is the number of participants,

Table 16.1 Continued

out of 17 total, that reported using a particular religious/spiritual dimension/category one or more times. The three affect/valence columns also summarize the percentage of thought units divided by the total number of thought units coded as negative, neutral, or positive for a particular dimension/category as well as the number of participants who expressed affect/valence one or more times (in parentheses). The "other" category represents thought units that could not be categorized into one of the religious/spiritual dimensions/categories. R/S is an abbreviation for Religious/Spiritual. The column of percentages for the religious/spiritual dimensions does not sum to 100 because 12.2 % (44 of the 361 thought units) were too general to classify into the active prayer categories for the personal/private dimension (e.g., "I prayed before bedtime" was too general to classify into a particular type of active prayer like adoration, thanksgiving, or petition).

Table 16.2 provides illustrative quotes from transcripts representing the religious/spiritual dimensions and categories. Eighty-two percent of participants used all three religious/spiritual dimensions (personal, social, and cognitive) at least once. Almost all of the remaining participants used two of the three general religious/spiritual dimensions. No participants reported using none of the religious/spiritual dimensions.

Table 16.2

Quoted Excerpts from Transcripts that Illustrate Religious/Spiritual Dimensions

Religious/Spiritual Dimensions	Quoted Excerpts from Participants' Disclosures
Personal/Private	
Active Prayers	
Adoration	*Love you Lord; I glorify and praise your name*
Confession/Reconciliation	*I would pray for forgiveness for catching it [HIV]*
	Forgive me for all my sins
Thanksgiving	*Thank you for helping me through another day*
	Thank you Lord [for blessings]
Petition—Self	
Physical/Material	*Praying for the medication to work*
	Don't let me have no relapses
Psychological	*Keep my sanity; Keep my head up*
	Cope with this illness

Table 16.2 Continued

	Spiritual	*God watch over me; God guide me*
		Change so that I can have faith...in you [God]
	Petition—Other	
	Physical/Material	*Pray that my family don't get sick*
	Psychological	*That my family understand when I tell them I was positive [with HIV]*
	Spiritual	*[God] look over my family*
		Keep my family in good spirit
	Receptive Prayers	*I had a meditation thing...block out everything;*
		[alone while praying] I'd hum to myself...moan
Social		
	Interpersonal	*[a "guy"] giving me hope...telling me not to worry*
		[chaplain] give me hope, encouragement
	Small Group	*[bible study] these guys who helped me pick myself up and on*
		up and begin to move on; they were my buddies
	Large Group	*[church services] took me away from...my troubles*
		I would get a little bit more spirituality in me
Cognitions		
	Beliefs	*[hope from religious speaker] Gave me hope;*
		[faith] I still...have enough faith
		[trust] the more I did it [prayer] the more you learn to trust it; Trust in God
		[strength] God...a big factor in my life to just hold on
	Experiences	*I would talk to God and I'd do a lot of crying*
		Usually that [my prayer time] ended in sobbing

As predicted by hypothesis two, prayer, in comparison to the other religious/spiritual dimensions, was the most frequently utilized religious/spiritual coping strategy when considering the total number of thought units. Participants reported using active prayers associated with the personal/private religious/spiritual dimension (43.9%) more frequently than other religious/spiritual dimensions based on total number of thought units. The next most frequently occurring religious/spiritual coping strategy was religious/spiritual cognitions (32 %) including religious/spiritual beliefs and experiences.

Examining the content of active prayers reveals some of the needs and concerns of participants (RQ1). Physical/material concerns expressed through petitionary prayers were more frequently used (both as percentage of total thought units and the number of participants) than petitionary prayers for psychological or spiritual health. This pattern was prominent in both petitionary prayers for *self* and petitionary prayers for *others*.

Finally, there are social needs that can be inferred through the fifteen percent of total thought units associated with religious/spiritual social contexts, and the six to seven (35–41%) participants that reported using these social religious/spiritual dimensions. See Table 16.2 for illustrative content. The interpersonal context shows mostly supportive communications. The majority of responses in the small group context involved some type of "Bible study" in which several participants reported developing bonds and finding support. The large group context comprised almost exclusively attendance at "church services."

Research question two compared affect/valence for the religious/spiritual dimensions and categories. Among the set of 361 religious/spiritual idea units, affect/valence was coded 2% negative, 22% positive, and 64% neutral (12% of the unclassifiable thought units were not included in the affect/valence coding). The majority of responses associated with religious/spiritual content were expressed as neutral affect/valence while the ratio of positive to negatively valenced responses was about 11:1. This ratio indicates that, when participants expressed affect/valence in relation to religious/spiritual content, there was a preference for positive over negative affect/valence.

While small in total number, there were a variety of positive affect/valence themes for cognitive beliefs including hope, faith, trust, and strength (See Table 16.2 for participant disclosures). Negatively valenced idea units were not sufficient in number to suggest themes.

Discussion

The African American men in this sample used a variety of religious/spiritual coping methods to deal with the combined stressors of living with HIV while incarcerated. This finding is consistent with two separate literatures previously reviewed (refer to sections in the introduction entitled: Religious/Spiritual Coping in Prison, and Religious/Spiritual Coping with HIV) showing that individuals often use religious/spiritual coping methods to cope with incarceration (e.g., O'Connor & Perreyclear, 2002; Turner, 2008) and to cope with living with HIV (e.g., Somlai & Heckman, 2000; Pargament et al., 2004). One interpretation of the combined stress of living with HIV while incarcerated is that the stressors may intensify a search for meaning and understanding. Following is a discussion of religious/spiritual coping in the personal, social, and cognitive dimensions.

The use of particular religious/spiritual coping dimensions based on number of participants in this sample varied considerably. The number of participants using different religious/spiritual dimensions could be related to the ease of accessing religious/spiritual resources. For instance, many of the personal religious/spiritual activities, like religious beliefs and prayer, do not require any special equipment or personnel, only a convenient time to recall a religious belief, or engage in a prayer. The ease of access to private religious/spiritual beliefs and prayer explanation, when combined with the personal search for meaning, supports the second hypothesis that prayer is the most frequently used religious/spiritual coping strategy when considered as a percentage of total thought units. However, when considering the number of total participants that use particular religious/spiritual categories, religious/spiritual beliefs and prayers of petition appear to be the preferred coping strategies.

Overall, active prayers of petition for physical/material concerns were the most frequently reported type of active prayer when measured as percentage of total thought units. In contrast, receptive types of meditative and contemplative prayer were rarely used (less than two percent). One explanation for this finding could be that the length of time taken to "pray" an active prayer of petition, perhaps less than a minute, is less effortful than the time needed for meditative types of receptive prayer that might last for a half hour or more. Perhaps one reason for the small percentage of receptive prayers is the lack of knowledge about methods of engaging in receptive prayer. Future research might assess participants' knowledge of receptive prayer methods; and, if appropriate, provide opportunities for educational spiritual enrichment.[5] It is worth noting that all but one type of prayer was associated with positive affect/valence for at least one or more participants, and that prayers were never associated with the expression of negative affect/valence. Thus, prayers may serve as a source of positive affective communication in religious/spiritual coping.

In addition to active prayers of petition, about one-quarter to over one-third of the seventeen participants reported engaging in other types of active prayer, specifically prayers of thanksgiving (four or 23% of participants), adoration (five or 29% of participants), and reconciliation (seven or 41% of participants). These particular types of active prayers can be indicative of individuals with a well-integrated religion/spirituality, and perhaps a high need for religion/spirituality (Baesler, 2003); but, without further data, this interpretation remains speculative. Future research might include variables about religious/spiritual identity and religious/spiritual growth to test the merit of this interpretation, especially if those with a high need for religion/spirituality show greater *religious/spiritual integration* (Pargament, 2007), and positive character traits like *gratitude* from prayers of thanksgiving (Emmons & McCullough, 2003), and *peace* from prayers of forgiveness and reconciliation (Worthington, 2006).

While individual prayer is the most frequently used type of religious/spiritual practice, results suggest a low to modest level of interest in social dimensions of religion/spirituality. Future research might explore the some of the themes found in this study: the types of interpersonal support "ministers" provide, the camaraderie and prayers of support during small group "bible studies," and the religious/spiritual experiences inmates may have during "church services." Further, the coding for affect/valence was consistent with a neutral interpretation of the social dimension of religious/spiritual coping. There was only limited evidence for the use of positive affect/valence associated with the social religious/spiritual coping categories. We expected a greater use of positive affect/valence in referring to the social aspects of religion/spirituality. Perhaps the nature of the interviews could partially explain the absence of positive affect/valence in association with social religious/spiritual coping. Respondents were not prompted to provide affect/valence information for the content that they provided in the interview. Thus, many of the thought units for the social dimension are simple reports of participant behavior.

Beyond individual prayers and social religious/spiritual contexts, participants reported more positive than negative affect/valence associated with the use of religious/spiritual cognitive beliefs and experiences. All participants made use of religious/spiritual beliefs. Of the 26.8% of total number of thought units related to religious/spiritual beliefs, 8.8% of these are positively valenced. The small but meaningful percentage of positively valenced religious/spiritual beliefs is comparable to the overall percentage of positively valenced active prayers (about 10%). Perhaps there is some connection between the types of religious/spiritual beliefs and types of active prayers. Future research might devise questions that address the potential relationship between religious/spiritual beliefs and types of prayer.

The positive and negatively valenced responses for the cognition dimension are consistent with previous research which found that religious/spiritual coping is characterized by both positive and negative cognitive appraisals (Pargament et al., 2004). While positive outweighed negative affect/valence by a ratio of 2:1 or more, it is worth noting that religious/spiritual *cognitions* is the only religious/spiritual dimension that included negatively valenced responses dealing with guilt, fear, and sin. Without additional data, and given the small overall percentage of negative responses, these specific negatively charged responses are difficult to interpret. We suggest that future research take into account how individuals cope with negative affect/valence related to guilt, fear, and sin. In contrast, there were a number of positively valenced beliefs that seem particularly relevant to the literature on positive psychology and positive communication. Several positively valenced beliefs describe a relationship with God imbued with faith, hope, and trust. This finding is consistent with other research conceptualizing God as an ultimate attachment figure (Sim & Loh, 2003) with infinite resources to draw upon. Other positively valenced beliefs further support an attachment to God as a source of strength to, for example, "hold on to" through troubled times. Further research might explore the nature of positive and negative relationships with God through the theoretical lens of the attachment literature.

About two-thirds of participants' religious/spiritual responses were coded as neutral affect/valence. The large number of neutrally valenced responses creates a degree of uncertainty about our conclusions. However, we can at least say that participants did not use negative affect/valence in reference to the personal/private and social dimensions of religion/spirituality. There was also a clear preference by participants to use either neutral or positive affect/valence in association with *all* of the religious/spiritual dimensions. Conservatively, in the absence of specific data for the neutrally valenced responses, we can only suggest that there is a trend for positive over negatively valenced religious/spiritual coping strategies based on the affective data provided by participants. Future research might include questions that provide opportunities for participants to disclose affect/valence associated with religious/spiritual activities.

The participants in the present investigation of inmates living with HIV were all African American men. The widespread use of multiple religious/spiritual dimensions by African American men to cope with their situation affirms previous literature that indicates the import of religion/spirituality for African Americans with HIV. In an African American sample with HIV, religion/spirituality was found to be particularly important for their psychological health (Boyle, Ferrell, Hodnicki, & Muller, 1997). Results from Cotton et al.'s (2006) study of 347 adults with HIV/AIDS found that African Americans were more likely to have an increase in religious/spiritual activity after their diagnosis, and that their belief that religion/spirituality helped them live longer was stronger than for their Caucasian counterparts.

In summary, we note the pervasiveness of multiple religious/spiritual coping strategies for African American men living with HIV in prison, in particular the prevalence of active forms of prayer that suggest a positive relationship with God characterized by faith, hope, trust, and strength. The religious/spiritual social dimension also appears to contribute to religious/spiritual coping for a small percentage of those incarcerated with HIV. For the responses that included information on affect/valence, positive affect/valence associated with cognitions and personal religious/spiritual surpass negative affect/valence by at least a two to one margin. Some of the more important areas for future research in religious/spiritual coping as positive communication include: (a) exploring how religious/spiritual identity, particularly relationship with God, functions in prayers that promote positive coping with stress, including the active prayers associated with gratitude, forgiveness, and adoration, (b) developing an phenomenological interview protocol that explicitly explores the affect/valence dimension associated with religious/spiritual beliefs and experiences related to positive coping strategies, and (c) comparing the religious/spiritual positive coping strategies among a more culturally diverse sample of participants with other serious health issues.

Notes

1   "Religion" is often defined as the organizational/institutional search for the sacred, consisting of beliefs and behaviors that are legitimized by a community of believers while "spirituality" is frequently contrasted with religion by emphasizing a more personal and subjective search for the sacred without necessarily referencing a larger community (Hill & Pargament, 2003). However, the two terms, religion and spirituality, are not unrelated. In the national Baylor religion survey of 2007, 57 % of Americans reported that they view themselves as both "spiritual and religious" (Stark, 2008, p. 89). In the present study, we are more concerned with capturing the breadth of religious and spiritual communications used to cope with HIV than we are with labeling particular beliefs or practices as "religious" or "spiritual." Therefore, we have opted for using the notation "religion/spirituality" (religious/spiritual) as an inclusive term that recognizes personal, interpersonal, and communal searches for the sacred.

2   The term "God" is understood in the broadest sense possible, encompassing conceptualizations such as: Ultimate Reality, Ground of Being, Higher Self, True Self, Goddess, Trinitarian Godhead, Divine Other, and so forth. While we did not specifically ask par-

ticipants to identify their religious/spiritual affiliation, the content of address for many of the prayers (e.g., Heavenly Father, Jesus, Lord, and God) combined with the data on "Bible" studies and attending "church" services, suggests that the majority of participants are oriented toward a western Christian religious/spiritual worldview.

3   Pargament, Koenig, and Perez's scale on Religious Coping (2000) is based on Carver, Scheier, and Weintraub's (1989) COPE scale. A shorter version of this well validated scale is Carver's (1997) "COPE" scale. The measure describes 14 different types of coping that have been applied to various health contexts. One type of coping is labeled "religious coping" and includes two items: "I've been trying to find comfort in my religion or spiritual beliefs," and "I've been praying or meditating." The original COPE scale contained two additional religious coping items: "I put my trust in God," and "I seek God's help" (Carver et al., 1989). Four HIV studies are cited by Carver that use one or more of the COPE subscales. Unfortunately, none of these studies report using the religion subscale as a method to cope with HIV. The coding manual is available from the first author.

4   Initial coding of two independent raters for affect/valence resulted in inter-rate reliability of .78. Close inspection of the ratings showed a recurring inconsistency in coding petitionary prayer. After author collaboration, we decided to code petitionary prayers that ask for something "good" (for oneself or another) as positive valence. These petitionary prayers indicate some degree of "faith in God," and they may also engender positive thoughts of hope, optimism, and positive expectations (Levin, 2001).

5   There are many possible methods of receptive prayer that could be introduced for persons living with HIV. Three viable options having widespread use, and having stood the test of time, are: (a) centering prayer (Keating, 1986), a type of Christian prayer that can be adapted to other faith traditions, (b) a Buddhist based form of mindfulness meditation that can be adapted to other religious traditions (Kabat-Zin, 1990), and (c) the relaxation response when combined with the "faith factor," also applicable to a number of religious traditions (Benson, 1987).

References

Bade, M., & Cook, S. (2008). Functions of Christian prayer in the coping process. *Journal for the Scientific Study of Religion, 47,* 123–133.

Baesler, E. J. (2003). *Theoretical explorations and empirical investigations of communication and prayer.* Lewiston, NY: Edwin Mellen Press.

Baesler, E. J., Derlega, V. J., Winstead, B., & Barbee, A. (2003). Prayer as interpersonal coping in the lives of mother with HIV. *Women and Therapy, 26,* 283–295.

Benson, H. (1987). *Your maximum mind.* New York: Random House.

Bosworth, H. B. (2006). Editorial: The importance of spirituality/religion and health-related quality of life among individuals with HIV/AIDS. *Journal of General Internal Medicine, 21,* S3–S4.

Boyle, J., Ferrell, J. Hodnicki, D., & Muller, R. (1997). Going home: African-American care giving for adult children with human immunodeficiency virus disease. *Holistic Nursing Practice, 11,* 27–35.

Bureau of Justice Statistics (2006). *Prison Statistics.* Retrieved from: http://bjs.ojp.usdoj.gov/content/pub/pdf/hivp06.pdf

Carson, V., Soeken, K., Shanty, J., & Terry, L. (1990). Hope and spiritual well-being: Essentials for living with AIDS. *Perspectives in Psychiatric Care, 26,* 28–34.

Carver, C. S. (1997). You want to measure coping but your protocol's too long: Consider the Brief COPE. *International Journal of Behavioral Medicine, 4,* 92–100.

Carver, C. S., Scheier, M., & Weintraub, J. (1989). Assessing coping strategies. *Journal of Personality and Social Psychology, 56,* 267–283.

Center for Disease Control, Department of Health and Human Services (2009). Retrieved from: http://www.cdc.gov/hiv/topics/basic/index.htm

Cotton, S., Puchalski, C., Sherman, S., Mrus, J., Peterman, A., Feinberg, & J., Tsevat, J.(2006). Spirituality and religion in patients with HIV/AIDS. *Journal of General Internal Medicine, 21,* S5–S13.

Dammer, H. R. (2002). The reasons for religious involvement in the correctional environment. *Religion, the Community, and the Rehabilitation of Criminal Offenders, 35,* 35–58.

Emmons, R., & McCullough, M. (2003). Counting blessings versus burdens. *Journal of Personality and Social Psychology, 84,* 377–389.

Greene, K., Berger, J., & Reeves, C. (1999). Most frequently used alternative and complementary therapies and activities by participants in the AMCOA study. *Journal of the Association of Nurses in AIDS Care, 10,* 60–73

Hill, P. C., & Pargament, K. I. (2003). Advances in the conceptualization and measurement of religion and spirituality: Implications for physical and mental health research. *American Psychologist, 58,* 64–74.

Ironson, G., Solomon, G., Balbin, E., O'Cleirigh, C., George, A., Kumar, M., &Woods, T. (2002). The Ironson-Woods spirituality/religiousness index is associated with long survival, health behaviors, less distress, and low cortisol in people with HIV/AIDS. *Annuals of Behavioral Medicine, 24,* 34–48.

Kabat-Zin, J. (1990). *Full catastrophe living.* NY: Delta.

Keating, T. (1986). *Open mind, open heart.* NY: Amity House.

Koenig, H., Parkerson, G., & Meador, K. (1997). Religion index for psychiatric research. *American Journal of Psychiatry, 154,* 885–886.

Krippendorff, K. (1980). *Content analysis.* Thousand Oaks, CA: Sage.

Levin, J. (2001). *God, faith, and health: Exploring the spirituality-healing connection.* NY: John Wiley and Sons.

Levin, J. (2004). Prayer, love, and transcendence. In K. Schaie, N. Krause, & A. Booth (Eds.), *Religious influences on health and well-being in the elderly* (pp. 69–95). NY: Springer.

McCullough, M. E., & Larson, D. B. (1999). Prayer. In W. R. Miller (Ed.), *Integrating spirituality into treatment* (pp. 85–110).Washington, DC: American Psychological Association.

O'Connor, T., & Perreyclear, M. (2002). Prison religion in action and its influence on offender rehabilitation. *Religion, the Community, and the Rehabilitation of Criminal Offenders, 35,* 11–33.

Pargament, K. (2007). *Spiritually integrated psychotherapy: Understanding and addressing the sacred.* NY: Guilford Press.

Pargament, K., Koenig, H., & Perez, L. (2000). The many methods of religious coping: Development and initial validation of the RCOPE. *Journal of Clinical Psychology, 56,* 519–543.

Pargament, K., McCarthy, S., Shah, P., Ano, G., Tarakeshwar, N., Wachholtz, A., & Duggan, J. (2004). Religion and HIV: A review of the literature and Clinical implications. *Southern Medical Journal, 97*, 1201–1209.

Peterman, A., Fitchett, G., Brady, M., Pharm, L., & Cella, D. (2002). Measuring spiritual well-being in people with cancer: The Functional Assessment of Chronic Illness Therapy—Spiritual Well-Being Scale (FACIT-Sp), *Annals of Behavioral Medicine, 24,* 49–58.

Peterson, C., & Seligman, M. (2004). *Character strengths and virtues: A handbook and classification.* NY: Oxford University Press; Washington, DC: American Psychological Association.

Scott, W. A. (1955). Reliability of content analysis. *Public Opinion Quarterly, 19,* 321–325.

Siegel, K., & Schrimshaw, E. (2002). The perceived benefits of religious and spiritual coping among older adults living with HIV/AIDS. *Journal for the Scientific Study of Religion, 41,* 91–102.

Sim, T., & Loh, B. (2003). Attachment to God: Measurement and dynamics. *Journal of Social and Personal Relationships, 20,* 373–389.

Socha, T. (2008, November). *Building positive communication pedagogy: Positive experiential communication learning in human relating.* Paper presented at the annual meeting of the National Communication association, San Diego, CA.

Somlai, A., & Heckman, T. (2000). Correlates of spirituality and well-being in a community sample of people living with HIV disease. *Mental Health, Religion and Culture, 3,* 57–70.

Stark, R. (2008). *What Americans really believe.* Waco, TX: Baylor University Press.

Szaflarski, M., Ritchey, P., Leonard, A., Mrus, J., Peterman, A., Ellison, C., . . . Tsevat, J. (2006). Modeling the effects of spirituality/religion on patients' perceptions of living with HIV/AIDS. *Journal of General Internal Medicine, 21,* S28–S38.

Taylor, R., Chatters, L., & Levin, J. (2004). *Religion in the lives of African Americans: Social, psychological, and health perspectives.* Thousand Oaks, CA: Sage.

Turner, R. G. (2008). *Religion in prison: An analysis of the impact of religiousness/spirituality on behavior, health and well-being among male and female prison inmates in Tennessee.* (Doctoral dissertation). Available from ProQuest Dissertations and Theses database. (UMI No. 3307301).

Worthington, E., Jr. (2006). *Forgiveness and reconciliation: Theory and application.* New York: Routledge.

• CHAPTER SEVENTEEN •

Nurturing Children as Assets: A Positive Approach to Preventing Child Maltreatment and Promoting Healthy Youth Development

Steven R. Wilson
Purdue University

Patricia E. Gettings
Purdue University

Child abuse and neglect are serious, persistent social problems. The National Child Abuse and Neglect Data System, which analyzes reports from Child Protective Services (CPS) agencies in all 50 states, estimates that these agencies received 3.3 million allegations of child maltreatment in 2009 (USDHHS, 2010). Such statistics can seem overwhelming, especially when we know that many incidents of child maltreatment never come to the attention of CPS agencies (Straus, Hamby, Finkelhor, Moore, & Runyan, 1998). How can we, as interpersonal communication scholars, contribute to helping prevent child abuse and neglect? And for that matter, why would a volume devoted to the "positive side of interpersonal communication" include a chapter on child maltreatment?

In this chapter, we advocate taking a positive approach by reframing the issue from "stopping child abuse" to "nurturing children as assets." In part, this chapter describes shifts in our own thinking. The first author of this chapter, Steve, is a professor who studies patterns of parent-child interaction associated with child maltreatment. In 2005, a brutal child abuse fatality shocked Steve's local community. He analyzed his community's response to that incident (Wilson, 2006) and became actively involved with "Our Kids Are Our Community," a network of individuals and organizations in the Greater Lafayette, Indiana area working together to support youth. Our Kids sponsors an annual summit that initially focused on preventing child abuse but has moved to a broader focus on healthy youth development. The second author, Patricia, is a master's student who recently participated in this summit; her master's thesis is exploring adult mentors' commitment to youth mentoring relationships.

In making the case for reframing approaches to child abuse prevention, we divide this chapter into four sections. The first elaborates on Wilson's (2006) analysis of first- and second-order change in how communities respond to child abuse, whereas the second shows how this distinction is premised on a deeper difference between "risk-reduction" and "asset-building" models of youth development. The third suggests directions for interpersonal communication research couched in asset-building models (using youth mentoring relationships as an exemplar), while the final section lays out broader implications of asset-based thinking.

The Framing of Aiyana's Story: First- and Second-Order Change

In March 2005 police responded to a 911 call and found 4-year old Aiyana Gauvin lying dead in the Lafayette area home of her stepmother and biological father. Police discovered bruises all over her body, and an autopsy showed that she had died from a head injury. Interviews revealed that Aiyana's stepmother and biological father had severely abused her, physically and psychologically, for months prior to her death (Wilson, 2006). Aiyana's case generated tremendous local media coverage, due in part to the severity of the abuse but also because her case shares features with others that receive widespread media attention-miscues by CPS and law enforcement (Kirkpatrick, 2004).

To analyze his community's reaction to the case, Steve read numerous stories and editorials that focused on mistakes made by CPS and the local sheriff's department, the trials of Aiyana's stepmother and father, three forums organized by the Community Foundation of Greater Lafayette to educate the public about child abuse, and the first Our Kids summit. Based on the press coverage, Steve sensed that public discourse shifted over time. Early stories and editorials expressed shock and anger at what had happened, characterized Aiyana's stepmother and father as monsters, and blamed institutions that should have protected her. Although these themes continued, some later stories expressed a more complex view by discussing a host of risk and protective factors associated with child maltreatment (e.g., access to affordable prenatal healthcare). Steve struggled to find a framework to analyze these shifting stories until a colleague suggested that what he was describing sounded similar to Watzlawick, Weakland, and Fisch's (1974) distinction between first- and second-order changes.

First- and second-order responses imply different conceptions of child maltreatment. From a first-order perspective, if the "problem" is that government institutions sometimes fail to protect children from deviant parents or caretakers, then the "solution" is to provide these institutions with sufficient resources, improve coordination between them, and hold them accountable. On the face of it, these first-order changes make sense. Tippecanoe county CPS case managers were handling nearly three times the maximum recommended number of families at the time of Aiyana's death, and CPS and law enforcement failed to share information in her case (Wilson, 2006); hence, responses such as allocating additional state funds to hire more CPS staff, creating a confidential database where local institutions could share information about child abuse allegations, and recruiting more Court Appointed Special Advocates (CASA) volunteers to represent abused and neglected children seem like "common sense."

Although these first-order changes are vital for protecting children in immediate danger and coordinating services for maltreated children, they are insufficient to prevent child abuse within a community. First-order responses occur only after a child already has been maltreated (intervention); they do little to address the range of factors that place children at risk for abuse or neglect (prevention). They are premised on the idea that child abuse and neglect can be attributed to single causes (e.g., drug-addicted or mentally-ill parents) whereas the scholarly consensus is that child maltreatment arises from a complex interplay of factors associated with children, parents, families, neighborhoods, and societies (Belsky, 1993; Cicchetti, 2004; National Research Council, 1993). Because much of child maltreatment never comes to the attention of legal and mental health professionals (Straus et al., 1998), these institutions cannot be solely responsible for addressing the issue.

Second-order responses occur when communities rethink their assumptions about child abuse and neglect. They reflect a more complex understanding of the nature and etiology of child maltreatment, and emphasize prevention as well as intervention. As one example of second-order change, more than 250 community leaders and citizens attended the first Our Kids summit, the focus of which was adopting the Search Institute's 40 developmental assets as a framework for preventing child maltreatment. The Search Institute is a non-profit organization that conducts large-scale survey research and provides materials and training for organizations and communities. Developmental assets are experiences and qualities that children and youth need to avoid risks and thrive (Scales, 1999). Like most asset-based models, the Search Institute draws a distinction between external and internal assets. External assets refer to "the relationships and opportunities that adults provide young people" (e.g., families, schools, youth-serving organizations) whereas internal assets refer to "the values, skills, and competencies young people develop to guide themselves [and] become self regulating" (Scales, 1999, p. 113). The community sent individuals for training at the Search Institute; these individuals in turn conducted workshops with local CPS, police, and CASA volunteers, but also with teachers, healthcare professionals, and social service and faith-based organizations.

As is evident from this example, second-order responses focus attention on a broader range of risk and protective factors and presume a broader range of institutions and individuals are responsible for preventing child maltreatment than do first-order responses. First- and second-order responses are not mutually exclusive, but too often communities focus only on first-order changes when heinous cases of child abuse occur. Second-order responses lead to the paradoxical conclusion that in order to prevent child maltreatment, public attention may need to focus on issues that seem tangential (e.g., children's access to high-quality healthcare and early childhood education programs). Communities need to focus consistently on what they can do to support all children's healthy development rather than paying attention to child abuse only when cases like Aiyana's occur (Kirkpatrick, 2004).

This analysis of first- and second-order changes mirrors a larger debate about "risk reduction" versus "asset-building" models for addressing a host of social problems and promoting healthy youth development. The following section compares these two models.

Reducing Risks and Building Developmental Assets

Similar to the emerging field of positive psychology (Seligman & Csikszentmihalyi, 2000), as well as communicative approaches to resiliency and positive agency (Buzzanell, 2010; Socha, 2009), scholars from several disciplines advocate a shift from risk-reduction to asset-building models of youth development (e.g., Edwards, Mumford, Shillingford, & Serra-Roldan, 2007; Hamilton, Hamilton, & Pittman, 2004; Scales, 1999). This section describes the Search Institute's 40 developmental assets and compares it to risk-reduction models.

Developmental Assets: Typologies and Measures

Numerous typologies of assets have been proposed, most of which display overlap (Constantine, Benard, & Diaz, 1999; Hamilton et al., 2004; National Research Council and Institute of Medicine, 2002). Table 17.1 displays a summary of the Search Institute's 40 developmental assets for adolescence grouped into eight categories.

Grounded in theories of child development that focus on prevention, resiliency, and protective factors, the list includes both external and internal assets. Interpersonal skills and relationships feature prominently on the list; for example, many of the external assets focus on relationships between adolescents and parents as well as other caring adults (e.g., whether parents display responsiveness and demandingness; Wilson & Morgan, 2004), and the internal asset category of social competence includes a variety of skills and processes studied by interpersonal communication scholars (e.g., empathy, social support, resistance and conflict management).

Table 17.1

The Search Institute's Developmental Assets for Adolescent Youth (Grades 6–12)

External Assets

1.	Support	Family provides acceptance/support; youth seek advice from parents; youth receive support from non-parent adults; parents help youth succeed at school
2.	Empowerment	Young person perceives adults in community value youth; youth given useful roles, serve others, and feel safe at home, school, and community
3.	Boundaries and Expectations	Family has clear/consistent rules and monitors youth; school has clear rules/consequences; adults model responsible behavior; close friends model responsible behavior; adults have high expectations for youth
4.	Constructive Use of Time	Youth involved in music/art/drama/creative writing, participate in structured after-school or community programs, and attend religious programs or services; youth do not spend most weeknights "hanging out" with peers

Table 17.1 Continued

Internal Assets

5.	Commitment to Learning	Youth motivated to do well at school, hand in homework on time, care about teachers, read for pleasure, enjoy learning activities outside school
6.	Positive Values	Parents communicate importance of helping others, working for equality, standing up for one's beliefs, telling the truth, accepting personal responsibility, and understanding healthy sexuality
7.	Social Competencies	Youth display skills relevant to decision making, friends, interacting with diverse others, resisting unwanted requests, and nonviolent conflict management
8.	Positive Identity	Youth feel have some influence over life events, proud of self, think about life's purpose, optimistic about future

Note: Condensed from Leffert et al. (1998, p. 212).

Researchers from the Search Institute have developed the Profiles of Student Life—Attitudes and Behavior (PSL-AB) measure, a self-report survey that assesses youth perceptions of developmental assets (Leffert et al., 1998). Thirteen of the 40 developmental assets are tapped by one Likert-type item per asset; the remaining 27 each are tapped by 2–4 items. Leffert et al. (1998) reported PSL-AB results from 99,642 youth in grades 6–12. Regarding reliability, 19 of the 27 assets tapped by multiple items have internal consistency coefficients (alphas) from .60 to .80 whereas reliabilities for the other 8 assets are lower (Leffert et al., 1998). Search Institute researchers acknowledge that "reliability of the asset items...in some cases could be better" but argue that "there is a tradeoff between getting some information about a lot of dimensions in the ecologies or children and youth, or getting a lot of information on just a few aspects" (Scales, 1999, p. 116). Critics have questioned the PSL-AB's reliability, factor structure, and relevance for diverse populations of adolescents (Howard, Dryden, & Johnson, 1999; Price, Dake, & Kucharewski, 2002) and several alternative measures for assessing assets have been developed (Constantine et al., 1999; Klein et al., 2006; Oman et al., 2002).

Despite potential measurement limits, research using the PSL-AB has shown that developmental assets are inversely associated with high-risk adolescent behavior (e.g., alcohol, tobacco, and drug use; shoplifting or vandalism; peer aggression; suicide attempts) and positively associated with measures of thriving (e.g., school success, leadership, helping others, physical health, delay of gratification; Leffert et al., 1998). In a study of 6000 adolescents (1000 from each of six racial/ethnic groups), Scales, Benson, Leffert, and Blyth (2000) showed that developmental assets accounted for between 10% and 43% of the variance in seven different indices of thriving even after controlling for demographic factors. The predictive power of assets was similar for all six racial/ethnic groups. Scales, Benson, Roehlkepartain, Sesma, and Dulmen (2006) reported data from a longitudinal study of 370 adolescent students who were followed for 3 years. Developmental assets, assessed via the PSL-AB when students were in 7th–9th grade, significantly predicted students' school GPA three years later in 10th–12th grade, over and above those students' school GPA in 7th–9th grade.

Comparing Risk Reduction and Asset Building

Table 17.2 frames a number of distinctions between risk-reduction and asset-building models. It is important to emphasize that these models are not mutually exclusive. Somewhat like first- and second-order change, advocates of asset-building models recognize the importance of reducing risk factors associated with a host of social problems, but argue that focusing only on risks is insufficient and tends to lead to fragmented community responses.

At their core, the two models differ in how they conceptualize child wellbeing in terms of problems versus strengths as well the degree to which they embrace a holistic perspective (see Table 17.2). Asset-based approaches encourage holistic thinking by moving away from a fragmented focus on "one social problem at a time" and instead exploring connections between social problems as well as thriving indicators. In his chapter calling for a positive ontology of applied family communication research, Socha (2009) argues that "studies that focus on a single problem, close up, are necessary, of course, but studies that examine connections between and among problems also are needed" (pp. 313–314). Asset-based models thus focus on creating and maintaining relationships and opportunities that all children and adolescents—not just those designated "at risk"—need to avoid a host of social problems and thrive (see Table 17.2).

Table 17.2

Risk-Reduction and Asset-Building Models for Promoting Child/Adolescent Health/Well-Being

Basis for Comparison	Risk Reduction Model	Asset Building Model
Primary Theme	Alleviating problems	Building on strengths
Conception of Healthy Child	Free from risk, absence of problems or pathologies	Well-being, thriving, positive outcomes
Issues Emphasized	Social problems (child abuse teen pregnancy, drug/alcohol abuse, gangs, suicide...)	Indicators of thriving (school success, leadership, helping others, physical health...)
Approach to Addressing Issues	Name problems and try to reduce them, address problems one at a time	Create relationships and opportunities children need to avoid risks and thrive
Children/Youth who are Targeted	Children and youth "at-risk" or already in the "system"	All children/youth (universal)
Basic Response	Develop additional programs for at-risk children/youth and families	Strengthen relationships between adults/youth and their youth-serving organizations
Implied Functions of Interpersonal Communication	Discipline, conflict	Discipline, conflict, social support, listening, advice relationship maintenance...

Note: This table is based on distinctions drawn by Edwards et al. (2007), Hamilton et al. (2004), Scales (1999), and Socha (2009).

From the perspective of asset building "relationships are key" (Search Institute, 2011). The list of external assets in Table 17.1 highlights the importance of family relationships as well as relationships children develop with other caring non-parent adults. Asset-rich communities occasionally may create new programs to connect families, schools, neighborhoods, businesses, and other contexts where inter-generational communication occurs. But as the next section on youth mentoring will demonstrate, the quality of adult-youth relationships matters far more than the mere presence of formal youth programs.

Finally, asset-based models highlight the wide range of functions that interpersonal communication can serve. According to Socha (2009), risk-reduction models begin with:

> the negative assumption that communication in families is, in some way, deficient and that it is up to family communication scholars to generate research that can inform the development of interventions (e.g., courses, textbooks, and campaigns) designed to help families overcome their communication deficiencies. (p. 317)

As an example, risk-reduction models might focus on teaching parents alternatives to physical discipline when responding to perceived child misbehavior. By focusing on strengths, however, asset-based models highlight a broader range of communicative functions. In addition to responding to difficult child behavior, interactions in which parents and other adults listen to a child, follow a child's lead, encourage a child's creativity, and support and challenge a child's developing abilities are highlighted by asset-based models (Socha, 2009).

From the perspective of asset-based models, comprehensive attempts to prevent child abuse and neglect need to supplement targeted interventions for children at the highest risk with efforts to create "asset-rich communities" where relationships and opportunities exist for all children to thrive. In this chapter's next section, we describe one example of research where interpersonal communication scholars could address fundamental questions about relationships, emphasize asset-based assumptions, and collaborate with youth-serving organizations.

Youth Mentoring Programs and Relationships

In 2008, the Our Kids network in Greater Lafayette, influenced by asset-based models, expanded the annual summit to include a broader focus on promoting healthy child development. Formal youth mentoring was identified as a promising approach for preventing juvenile delinquency and promoting a number of thriving outcomes, and hence Our Kids decided to focus on what various institutions in the community (e. g., schools, social service organizations, businesses) could do to help support the work of existing mentoring programs in the local community. The Our Kids group asked Steve to investigate evaluation research on the impact of youth mentoring programs and present back to the group (and eventually, to the 2010 annual summit) on a series of best practices for mentoring. Steve suggested that Patricia join him in this exploration and complete an independent study under his supervision in which they would review scholarly literature on youth mentoring.

Formal youth mentoring programs are a popular approach used to promote healthy child development. In fact, according to MENTOR/National Partnership (2009), three million young people in the United States currently are involved in formal mentoring relationships. In light of this, researchers are focusing attention on understanding which elements of the mentoring process yield the most positive results for youth (e. g., increased self-esteem, improved grades, or enhanced social skills). One such component—the formation of an *enduring* relationship between a mentor and mentee—has been associated with a range of benefits for youth (Grossman & Rhodes, 2002). In contrast, some youth involved in relationships that end prematurely experience negative outcomes as a result of the mentoring process (DuBois, Holloway, Valentine, & Cooper, 2002; Grossman & Rhodes, 2002). Thus, it quickly became clear to us that identifying best practices for youth mentoring organizations could only be done by focusing on adult mentor-youth mentee *relationships*. In what follows, we provide formal definitions of youth mentoring, review the literature on best practices, and suggest directions for interpersonal communication research.

Defining Youth Mentoring

MENTOR/National Mentoring Partnership (2009) defines youth mentoring as "a structured and trusting relationship that brings young people together with caring individuals who offer guidance, support, and encouragement aimed at developing the competence and character of the mentee." Most definitions of youth mentoring, like this one, include three central elements (DuBois & Karcher, 2005). First, most definitions suggest that the mentor has more experience or wisdom than the mentee counterpart. Second, definitions imply that mentors provide guidance to mentees in an effort to facilitate positive development. Finally, and integral to this chapter, is that there is a strong "emotional bond" that develops between mentor and mentee, "a hallmark of which is a sense of trust" (DuBois & Karcher, 2005, p. 3).

Scholars also distinguish between natural and formal mentoring relationships. Natural mentoring relationships are those that sometimes evolve—albeit, not necessarily—out of a variety of roles that adults play in the lives of youth (e.g., extended family members, coaches) (Zimmerman, Bingenheimer, & Behrendt, 2005). It is often these natural mentors that individuals recall when asked if anyone has served as a mentor in their lives. In contrast, formal mentoring relationships result when a program pairs youths and adults together *specifically* for the purpose of developing a bond. Formal mentoring programs—our focus here—aim to foster relationships that benefit youth in the same ways as natural mentoring relationships.

Best Practices: Characteristics of Effective Youth Mentoring Organizations

DuBois et al. (2002) conducted a meta-analysis as a way to bring together the results of individual program evaluation studies and develop conclusions regarding the impact of formal youth mentoring programs on a larger scale. Through these analyses, they compared the impact of mentoring programs on different outcomes (social versus academic), and clarified which aspects of mentoring programs influence their ability to impact youth.

The authors identified fifty-nine independent samples ranging in size from 373 to 47,775 youths for inclusion in the meta-analysis (inclusion criteria: mentoring must occur in a one-on-one relationship, mentors must be older or more experienced than mentees, mentees must be youth, and programs must assess outcomes). The meta-analysis resulted in two primary conclusions: (a) youth mentoring programs on average should anticipate *modest* impacts on mentees (the meta-analysis revealed an overall mean weighted effect size of $d = .18$ across outcomes), and (b) programs that incorporate best practices have greater positive impacts on youth (DuBois et al., 2002). Specifically, programs that followed 50% or more of a list of "best practices" identified by the authors had positive impacts on youth outcomes (mean weighted $d = .25$) whereas those that followed fewer than 50% had virtually no impact (average $d = .09$).

Best practices can be grouped into four categories: (a) recruiting, matching and training mentors, (b) developing mentoring relationships, (c) evaluating program implementation and impact, and (d) planning at the program level. Several of these practices relate—either directly or indirectly—to the development of the mentoring relationship itself. For example, the meta-analysis suggested that programs that included pre-match and ongoing training of mentors revealed a larger impact. Training can help encourage relationship development, for example, by providing mentors with guidance on the types of issues they may face in getting to know their mentee and how to best address these. Findings also identified setting expectations for how frequently mentors should meet with youth as a best practice. Regular interactions are necessary, though arguably not sufficient, to foster an enduring relationship.

Directions for Future Research: Equity and Relational Maintenance

Clarifying communicative processes associated with the development and maintenance of close, trusting, and enduring adult mentor-youth mentee relationships is central to understanding when youth mentoring programs help build children's developmental assets. This section briefly describes relevant potential directions for future research, couched in equity theory.

Equity theory focuses on a partner's perception of the fairness of exchanges in a relationship (Walster, Walster, & Berscheid, 1978). Individuals feel under-benefitted when they contribute more than they receive from a partner and over-benefitted when they receive more than they contribute to a partner. When an imbalance is experienced, individuals typically work to restore equity by adjusting their own contributions and/or encouraging their partner to adjust his/her contributions. However, if the dyad is unable to reestablish equity, one of the partners may choose to terminate the relationship. Research generally supports the prediction that distress experienced as a result of perceived inequity is associated with lower levels of relational satisfaction and commitment (e.g., Sprecher, 1988; Utne, Hatfield, Traupmann, & Greenberger, 1984). The presence of an underbenefitted individual, though, is typically more destructive to positive relational outcomes than that of an over-benefitted individual (Sprecher, 1986).

Some research suggests that perceived inequity may be a factor in the early termination of adult mentor-youth mentee relationships. Spencer (2007) interviewed 31 male and female participants (20 adults and 11 adolescents) from two Big Brother Big Sisters of America programs to explore relationship failures (defined as a relationship that did not last through the one year commitment required by the program). Semi-structured interviews were conducted.

Most adults described their desire to form a close and lasting relationship with a young person as a reason for becoming involved in a mentoring program (Spencer, 2007). Specific reasons include the hope to "give something back," "make a difference," or to give a young person "new experiences" (Spencer, p. 340). Mentors, then, enter into mentoring relationships with established ideas about what they hope to put into and get out of the mentoring experience. The mentor anticipates what resources she is prepared to put into the relationship and expects to get something in return. Such ideas might be based on the mentor's past experiences of mentoring relationships or even based on portrayals of mentoring relationships from popular culture. However, it seems that not all mentors are prepared for the realities of developing a relationship with a younger, and often very different, mentee.

Perceived inequality of relational exchanges may upset the fragile balance of a budding mentoring relationship. For example, many mentors entered mentoring relationships expecting to feel rewarded as a result of the relationship but expressed disappointment when this did not occur. Spencer (2007) described the experiences of a mentor who revealed: "Obviously, when you volunteer, you're not expecting . . . the world back . . . But you want something . . . you at least want to leave with a feeling . . . a good feeling" (p. 343). This mentor felt underbenefitted in the relationship because she perceived that she was putting more into the relationship than she was getting. Another mentor expressed a similar sentiment of feeling underbenefitted: "My expectation was, 'Gosh . . . I know a lot of young people who'd really appreciated me just calling them up [chuckling]!. . .If I'm gonna do that for. . .a young person I'm not related to, then it needs to be appreciated" (Spencer, 2007, p. 345). Again, these mentors referred to a perceived imbalance of inputs and outputs when accounting for relationship termination. This termination might also suggest that the pair may not have engaged in relational maintenance strategies that could have prevented the relationship's termination.

Individuals involved in relationships they perceive as equitable are likely to engage in communicative relational maintenance strategies to prolong the relationship (Canary & Stafford, 1992). Such strategies include assurances (messages stressing commitment to the partner and relationship), openness (self-disclosure and direct discussion of the relationship), positivity (behaving in an optimistic, cheerful manner), sharing tasks (equal responsibility for accomplishing tasks that face the couple), and social networks (relying upon common friends and affiliations), as well as offering advice and managing conflict (Stafford & Canary, 1991; Stafford, Dainton, & Haas, 2000). Several studies have demonstrated that increased use of these strategies is associated relational variables such as liking, love, satisfaction and commitment (Dainton, Stafford, & Canary, 1994; Stafford & Canary, 1991). Perceived inequity, in turn, tends to erode the use of relational maintenance strategies (Canary & Stafford, 1992).

Much of the research on equity and maintenance strategies has been conducted in romantic relationships, but Vogl-Bauer, Kalbfleisch, and Beatty (1999) examined both in the context of parent-child relationships. Findings indicated that parents were most satisfied in equitable relationships with their adolescent children, and used several maintenance strategies more often in equitable than inequitable relationships. Interestingly, teens reported higher levels of satisfaction and greater use of maintenance strategies when they felt over benefitted. Vogl-Bauer et al. posit that this finding, which runs contrary to the predictions of equity theory, may be the result of the adolescent stage of development. This suggestion is particularly interesting to the present context because many mentees are approaching—or have reached—adolescence.

In sum, equity theory offers one framework for understanding perceptions and communicative behaviors that may be associated with problems in developing closeness in youth mentoring relationships. Adults may volunteer to mentor for largely altruistic reasons, but still hope to get certain things out of the experience and hence may not employ communicative strategies that otherwise might sustain the relationship when perceived inequity occurs in the early stages of relationship development. Patricia is exploring these questions in her master's thesis by surveying adult volunteers from several local youth mentoring programs about their perceptions of equity, use of maintenance strategies, and levels of relational satisfaction and commitment to sustaining their mentoring relationships. Future research might explore the timing, phrasing, and sequencing of specific relational maintenance strategies. For example, although giving assurances may be associated with satisfaction and commitment at any stage of the mentoring relationship, adults who attempt to offer advice too early may be perceived by youth as being judgmental rather than as expressing caring; such perceptions also would likely depend on the way in which the advice was offered (MacGeorge, Feng, & Thompson, 2008).

This discussion has practical as well as theoretical implications. For example, mentoring programs need to assist mentors in developing a realistic view of what can (and cannot) be expected from their relationship with a mentee. Adult mentors may need to be reminded that they are more socially experienced than their mentee counterpart and that these differences will impact the way the relationship progresses. Mentors should anticipate giving more than they receive, especially in the earliest stages of the relationship, and be prepared to make repeated—and sometimes unreturned—contact with their mentees. Finally, mentors should be aware that they need to be patient about receiving explicit signs of appreciation from their mentees.

Conclusion

This chapter calls for a "positive" approach to preventing child maltreatment by focusing on how communities can "nurture children as assets." We end with four broader implications of asset-based perspectives for how interpersonal communication scholars approach their work.

Implication #1: Focus on Developmental Assets, Not Just Social Problems

In the past two decades, interpersonal communication has seen an explosion of "applied" scholarship as well as research exploring the "dark side" of personal relationships (Smith & Wilson, 2010). Scholars have shown how interpersonal communication theory and research can speak to social problems such as child maltreatment, drug and alcohol abuse, teen pregnancy and STDs, and stalking (Socha, 2009). This work has challenged simplistic assumptions about relationships (e.g., families are not always safe havens), addressed socially meaningful issues, encouraged interdisciplinary collaboration, and led to extramural funding. Despite this, our argument is that focusing only on risk reduction tends to: (a) reinforce perceptions that problems such as child maltreatment are intractable, (b) turn attention away from connections between social problems as well as indicators of thriving, and (c) divert attention from what our hopes and aspirations are for all children and adolescents (see the list of internal assets in Table 17.1). As interpersonal communication scholars, we need to highlight developmental assets in our theories and include asset measures in our research.

Implication #2: Explore a Broad Range of Communicative Processes and Functions Associated with Developmental Assets

Our metaphor of "nurturing children as assets" is more than a call for being "warm and fuzzy." The external assets in Table 17.1 focus attention on how parents and other adults monitor, advise, and challenge youth as much as how they offer affection, caring, warmth, and support. This broad conception of "nurturing" is consistent with ideas such as that: (a) relational communication is multidimensional (Burgoon & Hale, 1984); (b) authoritative parenting involves demandingness as well as responsiveness (Wilson & Morgan, 2004); (c) confirmation involves challenge as well as acceptance (Dailey, 2010), and (d) relationships are maintained via advice and conflict management as well as assurances and positivity (Stafford et al., 2000). Interpersonal communication scholars should explore a variety of communication processes associated with children's developmental assets, including how these processes are connected (e.g., how interpretations of advice vary depending on levels of closeness or trust; MacGeorge et al., 2008).

Implication #3: Investigate Communication and Relationship Processes as Mediators of Program Success

As was highlighted in the previous section, the key question about youth mentoring programs is "how, and under what conditions, do they produce positive impacts for youth?" Understanding how mentor-mentee relationships develop is central to answering this question. The same thing is true for many other programs designed to support children and families. For example, program evaluation studies have shown that parenting programs "work" (i.e., lead to positive impacts for children such as decreased peer aggression and increased social competence) when they help parents alter their own contributions to behavioral patterns that define the parent-child relationship, through such best practices as having parents focus on how they respond to positive as opposed to only aversive child behavior and coaching parents as they practice skills with their child (see Wilson, in press). Interpersonal communication scholars can play an important role in clarifying relationship processes that mediate program impact.

Implication #4: Pursue Opportunities for Participating in Engaged Research

Second-order change and asset-based models tell us that a broad range of institutions and individuals—including but not limited to child protection, law enforcement, and healthcare professionals, social-service and faith-based organizations, and schools and universities—share a collective responsibility for nurturing children as assets. Although definitions of "engaged scholarship" vary, they typically emphasize research that involves meaningful collaboration between academics and other community stakeholders in terms of what questions to ask, what methods to employ, how to make sense of data, and how to present findings to various audiences (Barge & Shockley-Zalabak, 2008; Dempsey, 2010). As our involvement with the Our Kids network hopefully illustrates, engaged research requires a commitment of time and a willingness to step outside of one's comfort zone, but it also offers opportunities for interpersonal communication scholars to ask theoretically—and practically—important questions while building relationships with others in their local communities.

References

Barge, J. K., & Shockley-Zalabak, P. (2008). Engaged scholarship and the creation of useful organizational knowledge. *Journal of Applied Communication Research, 36,* 251–265.

Belsky, J. (1993). Etiology of child maltreatment: A developmental-ecological analysis. *Psychological Bulletin, 114,* 413–434.

Burgoon, J. K., & Hale, J. L. (1984). The fundamental topoi of relational communication. *Communication Monographs, 51,* 193–214.

Buzzanell, P. M. (2010). Resilience: Talking, resisting, and imagining new normalcies into being. *Journal of Communication, 60,* 1–14.

Canary, D.J., & Stafford, L. (1992). Relational maintenance strategies and equity in marriage. *Communication Monographs, 59,* 243–267.

Cicchetti, D. (2004). An odyssey of discovery: Lessons learned through three decades of research on child maltreatment. *American Psychologist, 59,* 731–741.

Constantine, N. A., Benard, B., & Diaz, M. (1999, June). Measuring protective factors and resilience traits in youth: The Healthy Kids Resilience Assessment. Paper presented at the seventh annual meeting of the Society for Prevention Research, New Orleans.

Dailey, R. M. (2010). Testing components of confirmation: How acceptance and challenge from mothers, fathers, and siblings are related to adolescent self-concept. *Communication Monographs, 77,* 592–617.

Dainton, M., Stafford, L., & Canary, D. J. (1994). Maintenance strategies and physical affection as predictors of love, liking, and satisfaction in marriage. *Communication Reports, 7,* 88–98.

Dempsey, S. E. (2010). Critiquing community engagement. *Management Communication Quarterly, 24,* 359–390.

DuBois, D. L., Holloway, B. E., Valentine, J. C., & Cooper, H. (2002). Effectiveness of mentoring programs for youth: A meta-analytic review. *American Journal of Community Psychology, 30(2),* 157–197.

DuBois, D. L. & Karcher, M. J. (2005). Youth mentoring: Theory, research, and practice. In D. L. DuBois & M. J. Karcher (Eds.), *Handbook of youth mentoring* (2–11). Thousand Oaks, CA: Sage Publications, Inc.

Edwards, O. W., Mumford, V. E., Shillingford, M. A., & Serra-Roldan, R. (2007). Developmental assets: A prevention framework for students considered at risk. *Children & Schools, 29,* 145–153.

Grossman, J. B., & Rhodes, J. E. (2002). The test of time: Predictors and effects of duration in youth mentoring programs. *American Journal of Community Psychology, 30,* 199–219.

Hamilton, S. F., Hamilton, M. A., & Pittman, K. (2004). Principles for youth development. In S. F. Hamilton & M A. Hamilton (Eds.), *The youth development handbook: Coming of age in American communities* (pp. 3–22). Thousand Oaks, CA: Sage.

Howard, S., Dryden, J., & Johnson, B. (1999). Childhood resilience: Review and critique of the literature. Oxford Review of Education, 25, 307–323.

Kirkpatrick, K. T. (2004). *Reframing child abuse and neglect for increased understanding and engagement: Defining the need for strategic reframing.* Chicago: Prevent Child Abuse America. Retrieved on May 22, 2011 from http://www.preventchildabuse.org/about_us/reframing/downloads/reframing%20revised.pdf.

Klein, J. D., Sabaratnam, P., Matos Auerbach, M., Smith, S. M., Kodjo, C., Lewis, K., et al. (2006). Development and factor structure of a brief instrument to assess the impact of community programs on positive youth development: The Rochester Evaluation of Asset Development for Youth (READY) Tool. *Journal of Adolescent Health, 39*, 252–260.

Leffert, N., Benson, P. L., Scales, P. C., Sharma, A. R., Drake, D. R., & Blyth, D. A. (1998). Developmental assets: Measurement and prediction of risk behaviors among adolescents. *Applied Developmental Science, 2,* 209–230.

MacGeorge, E. L., Feng, B., & Thompson, E. R. (2008). "Good" and "bad" advice: How to advise more effectively. Motley, M. (Ed.), *Applied interpersonal communication: Behaviors that affect outcomes (pp. 145–164)*. Thousand Oaks, CA: Sage.

MENTOR. (2009). *MENTOR's Mission.* Retrieved May 24, 2011 from http://www.mentoring.org/about_mentor/mission.

MENTOR. (2009). *What is Mentoring?* Retrieved November 11, 2009 from http://www.mentoring.org/mentors/about_mentoring/.

National Research Council. (1993). *Understanding child abuse and neglect.* Washington, D.C.: National Academy Press.

National Research Council and Institute of Medicine. (2002). *Community programs to promote youth development.* Washington, DC: National Academy Press.

Oman, R. F., Vesely, S., McLeroy, K. R., Harris-Wyatt, V., Aspy, C., Rodine, M. et al. (2002). Reliability and validity of the Youth Asset Survey (YAS). *Journal of Adolescent Health, 31,* 247–255.

Price, J. H., Dake, J. A., & Kucharewski, R. (2002). Assessing assets in racially diverse, inner-city youths: Psychometric properties of the Search Institute Asset Questionnaire. *Family and Community Health, 25,* 1–9.

Scales, P. C. (1999). Reducing risks and building developmental assets: Essential actions for promoting adolescent health. *Journal of School Health, 69,* 113–119.

Scales, P. C., Benson, P. L., Leffert, N., & Blyth, D. A. (2000). Contribution of developmental assets to the prediction of thriving among adolescents. *Applied Developmental Science, 4,* 27–46.

Scales, P. C., Benson, P. L., Roehlkepartain, E. C., Sesma, A., & van Dulmen, M. (2006). The role of developmental assets in predicting academic achievement: A longitudinal study. *Journal of Adolescence, 29,* 691–708.

Search Institute. (2011). *Principles for asset-building communities.* Retrieved on May 23, 2011 from http://www.search-institute.org/key-themes-asset-building-communities.

Seligman, M. E. P., & Csikszentmihalyi, M. (2000). Positive psychology. *American Psychologist, 55,* 5–14.

Smith, S. W., & Wilson, S. R. (2010). Evolving trends in interpersonal communication research. In S. W. Smith & S. R. Wilson (Eds.), *New directions in interpersonal communication research* (pp. 3–23). Thousand Oaks, CA: Sage.

Socha, T. J. (2009). Family as agency of potential: Toward a positive ontology of applied family communication theory and research. In L. R. Frey & K. N. Cissna (Eds.), *Routledge Handbook of applied communication research* (pp. 309–330). New York, NY: Routledge.

Spencer, R. (2007). "It's not what I expected": A qualitative study of youth mentoring relationship failures. *Journal of Adolescent Research, 22(4),* 331–354.

Sprecher, S., (1986). The relationship between inequity and emotions in close relationships. *Social Psychology Quarterly, 49,* 309–321.

Sprecher, S. (1988). Investment model, equity, and social support determinants of relationship commitment. *Social Psychology Quarterly, 51*, 318–328.

Stafford, L., & Canary, D. J. (1991). Maintenance strategies and romantic relationship type, gender, and relational characteristics. *Journal of Social and Personal Relationships, 8*, 217–242.

Stafford, L., Dainton, M., & Haas, S. (2000). Measuring routine and strategic relationship maintenance: Scale revision, sex versus gender roles, and the prediction of relational characteristics. *Communication Monographs, 67 (3)*, 306–323.

Straus, M. A., Hamby, S. L., Finkelhor, D., Moore, D. W., & Runyan, D. (1998). Identification of child maltreatment with the Parent-Child Conflict Tactics Scales: Development and psychometric data for a national sample of American parents. *Child Abuse & Neglect, 22*, 249–270.

USDHHS. (2010). Child maltreatment 2009. Retrieved on May 18, 2011 from http://www.childwelfare.gov/systemwide/statistics/can.cfm.

Utne, M. K., Hatfield, E., Traupmann, J., & Greenberger, D. (1984). Equity, marital satisfaction, and stability. *Journal of Social and Personal Relationships, 1*, 323–332.

Vogl-Bauer, S., Kalbfleisch, P. J., & Beatty, M. J. (1999). Perceived equity, satisfaction, and relational maintenance strategies in parent-adolescent dyads. *Journal of Youth and Adolescence, 28*, 27–49.

Walster, E., Walster, G.W., & Berscheid, E. (1978). *Equity: Theory & Research*. Boston, MA: Allyn and Bacon, Inc.

Watzlawick, P., Weakland, J., & Fisch, R. (1974). *Change: Principles of problem formation and problem resolution*. New York: W. W. Norton.

Wilson, S. R. (2006). First and second-order changes in a community's response to a child abuse fatality. *Communication Monographs, 73*, 481–487.

Wilson, S. R. (in press). Social-interactional perspectives on child maltreatment: How can they contribute to relationship science? In O. Gillath, G. Adams, & A. Kunkel (Eds.), *New directions in close relationships: Integrating across disciplines and theoretical perspectives*. Washington, DC: American Psychological Association.

Wilson, S. R., & Morgan, W. M. (2004). Persuasion and families. In A. L. Vangelisti (Ed.), *Handbook of family communication* (pp. 447–472). Mahwah, NJ: Lawrence Erlbaum.

Zimmerman, M. A., Bingenheimer, J. B., & Behrendt, D. E. (2005). Natural mentoring relationships. In D. L. DuBois & M.J. Karcher (Eds.), *Handbook of youth mentoring* (143–157). Thousand Oaks, CA: Sage Publications, Inc.

• CHAPTER EIGHTEEN •

Promoting Personal, Interpersonal, and Group Growth through Positive Experiential Encounter Communication Pedagogy

Lawrence R. Frey
University of Colorado, Boulder

Angie B. White
University of Colorado, Boulder

Given the pleasures and joys, along with the stresses and strains, of personal relationships in the postmodern world, coupled with the reliance on and benefits of, as well as problems associated with, working in groups/teams, the need for people to have positive, high-quality interpersonal and group communication skills never has been more apparent and important. To move beyond basic competencies and toward communication excellence (see Miczo, chapter 5, this volume), people need experience creating and sustaining positive, high-quality interpersonal and group relationships. Attaining those optimal experiences, however, can be difficult, as people may shy away from working to become better communicators (e.g., learning how to express emotional closeness or managing conflict constructively; see Kellett, chapter 11, this volume) because of fear of failure, and they often feel locked into ongoing, unwanted, problematic patterns of interactions that they cannot break (e.g., parents who cannot express love to their children or romantic partners who push each other's buttons; see Mirivel, chapter 4, this volume). Moreover, universities (and other educational levels) often promote a didactic, cognitively oriented, indirect approach to learning about communication that stresses theory and research over application and practice. As a result, academic instruction rarely provides opportunities for students to experientially acquire positive communication competencies (for an exception, see Socha, 2008).

Responses to this dearth of practical communication education have stressed the need for experiential learning (for an overview in the communication discipline, see Katula & Threnhauser, 1999). However, most classroom-based experiential learning tends to be highly structured, via, for instance, examining case studies of other people's interpersonal communication successes and failures (see, e.g., Braithwaite & Wood, 2000), or engaging in experiential "activities" (see, e.g., Gordon, 2004; in positive psychology, see, e.g., Peterson, 2006), such as icebreakers, to practice group/team communication skills. Other forms of experiential learning (e.g., internships, service-learning, and study abroad) immerse students in "real-world" experiences, but typically offer little guided instruction about developing communication skills from those experiences, and they frequently do not provide a safe classroom environment for students to practice those new skills.

Although these forms of experiential learning are valuable for "learning-by-doing," they also can be indirect (e.g., case studies) and artificial (e.g., experiential activities), resulting in limited development of the positive communication competencies that people need to create and sustain high-quality relationships. Moreover, because there is no formula for creating high-quality relationships, those relationships must emerge from people's communicative practices, in line with a constitutive (as opposed to transmission) view of communication (see, e.g., Carey, 1989, Mokros & Deetz, 2006). Hence, to learn how to form such relationships, people must have opportunities to experience and practice such constitutive communication.

This chapter describes a course, called *Communication and Human Relations*, that provides opportunities for students to practice positive constitutive communication by participating in creating and understanding how they collaboratively develop a group in which they experience high-quality relationships that facilitate personal, interpersonal, and group growth. We first explain the purposes, processes, and practices of the course. We then point out similarities and differences between the course and tenents of positive psychology. We conclude by offering suggestions for how the course and its pedagogy might inform other communication courses.

The Communication and Human Relations Course

Do you *really w*ant to know how others see you?
Communicate better in relationships?
Work directly on your communication weaknesses?
*Do you **really** want a very practical course that could transform your life?*
—Flyer for Course

Communication and Human Relations (*CHR*) is an advanced course (typically taught as a senior seminar) that develops participants' abilities to understand, evaluate, and improve their interpersonal and group communication abilities. Specifically, *CHR* provides opportunities for students to understand more fully, critically reflect on, and enact alternatives to taken-for-granted communication principles and practices in dyadic and group settings by participating in creating and understanding how they constitutively constructed high-quality relationships with other course members.

Although the goals of this course are somewhat similar to and extend those addressed in introductory interpersonal and group communication courses,[1] the processes by which those goals are accomplished make this course unique. First, the course meets for 2.5 hours one evening each week to provide the continuous extended time needed to accomplish the work. Second, except for some sessions toward the middle of the semester in which small groups present an overview of salient topics (e.g., self-disclosure and communication of emotions) and lead the class in relevant experiential activities, the class interacts as a single group seated in a circle,[2] a configuration that makes clear participants are there to engage with each other rather than to get a message from an authority figure.

Third, except for an opening-day lecture that explains the course, the teacher/facilitator[3] gives no lectures; instead, after briefly introducing each class period, the group engages in an open discussion for the entire time. That discussion is purposefully not structured to reflect that in everyday life, no facilitator tells people what to do or sets up experiences for them; rather, people must initiate and respond "on the spot" to communication situations that arise spontaneously. Class members, thus, create what occurs by their actions and then examine effects of those choices to learn what communicative behaviors contributed to developing what interpersonal and group qualities.

Fourth, although the group discussions are not prestructured, they are guided by a commitment to "here-and-now" communication (see, e.g., Egan, 1973) of talking only about what is occurring in the classroom within and between members (e.g., perceptions and feelings toward other members), in contrast to "there-and-then" communication about, for instance, current events in society or in participants' personal lives (unless those are directly relevant to their behavior in the group).[4] The facilitator keeps the group focused on here-and-now communication by, for instance, asking questions and making statements about members' communicative practices (e.g., asking what members intended to accomplish by particular speech acts directed toward other members); offering alternative interpretations to traditional, taken-for-granted communicative practices (e.g., pointing out how questions asked of other members, such as "Do you think you reacted the best way when ____ [member's name] confronted you?," function as statements about those members, such as "I do not think you reacted the best way when ____ confronted you"); directing members' communicative behavior (e.g., having them talk to each other rather than to the entire group and through the facilitator); or proposing structured activities to meet members' specific needs (e.g., asking a member who wants to learn to distinguish cognitions from emotions to go around the group and, for each person, complete the phrase, "I see you as ____, which makes me feel ____"); as well as by role modeling the communication desired (e.g., sharing his or her perceptions of group members).[5]

Fifth, members are encouraged to experiment with new communicative behaviors (e.g., initiating communication with others by those who are shy or expressing strong emotions by those who appear emotionless) and to receive feedback from fellow group members, to better enact those communicative behaviors both inside and outside the group. Doing so challenges people in ways beyond what they face in their everyday lives, involving more than what occurs ordinarily at parties, bars, or school. In fact, such a group experience has little value unless participants go beyond their typical everyday interactional patterns and try previously unattempted ways of relating that, at first, are unfamiliar and uncomfortable, but which they sense are harmonious with their deeper values regarding who they want to be and how people best can be together. Thus, when the group is working most effectively, members sense that they are taking risks, being more honest and open than usual, by trying to put into words (and nonverbal actions) what is hard to express and difficult to say nicely or in a controlled, tactful fashion (specifically, what is going on inside them and among them in the group). As individuals practice this process and become better able to communicate what often eludes expression, they reduce the likelihood of alienation, confusion, misunderstandings, and other causes of breakdowns in relationships.

These processes are employed to accomplish the overriding goal of promoting members' increased communication excellence, with a more general procedural goal of members working together to establish a supportive community where they feel free to investigate their communication style and experiment with behaviors that normally are not part of that style. An even more specific goal is for members to establish a relationship of some closeness/intimacy with every other group member. Together, the three goals of personal, interpersonal, and group growth comprise the primary intended outcomes of the course.

Importantly, course members are not graded on their ability to successfully achieve these goals, or on the practices that are involved in their creation (e.g., the group discussions). Instead, grades are based on the small group oral presentation (mentioned previously, constituting 25% of the course grade) and the following written assignments: (a) response papers written after every session (30%); (b) two analysis papers [15% each, with one comparing the beginning stages of the group's development with relevant readings (e.g., Bennis & Shepard, 1956), and the other comparing the behavior of the facilitator and, when applicable, facilitator-in-training, with relevant readings (e.g., Lakin & Costanzo, 1975)]; and (c) an application paper (15%) that involves students engaging in and critically analyzing an encounter-based interaction with a person who is not in the course. Additionally, students can miss only one class session, after which, each additional unexcused absence results in the lowering of their final course grade by an entire grade. Lastly, at the end of the semester, members self-evaluate their participation in the group discussions and are evaluated by all other members and by the teacher. If those evaluations indicate that a member consistently contributed significant leadership to the group discussions, that person's course grade is raised an entire grade. Thus, active participation in the group discussions can help, but not hinder, students' course grade.[6]

This course, thus, is a form of positive experiential education in which students learn and grow by moving themselves from a condition of being strangers to collaboratively developing a group that is as growthful and as gratifying as they can create and maintain. Participants learn by interacting with and encountering others, seeing how their efforts turned out, and perceiving how their ways of communicating affected the outcomes. Thus, through participation, members become aware of and assess their interpersonal communicative behaviors, and experiment with new ways of relating with others. In the process, they develop, together, appropriate beliefs, values, procedures, and behaviors for creating high-quality relationships.

The Positive Psychology of Experiential Encounter Communication Pedagogy

Using the method described above to nurture personal, interpersonal, and group growth can be traced back to the T-groups ("training" groups; sometimes called "sensitivity" or "laboratory training" groups) that developed when Kurt Lewin, Ronald Lippitt, Leland Bradford, and Kenneth Benne (from the Research Center for Group Dynamics at the University of Michigan) conducted a 2-week group dynamics training program for the Connecticut State Interracial Commission in 1946. During that program, the group facilitators and researchers regularly met to process the dynamics taking place during group work. Lewin, setting a precedent, allowed some group participants to attend a processing session and to comment on the observations being made, which, in some cases, were different from interpretations offered by the facilitators and researchers. Word quickly spread about the interesting processing session, and by the end of the training program, more than half of the group participants were attending them. Recognizing the value of having participants comment on their group's processes (that is, engaging in "metacommunication," communication about communication), the following year, the researchers (although Lewin died later that year) officially established the National Training Laboratory for Group Development (later changed to the NTL Institute for Applied Behavioral Science) in Bethel, Maine to conduct T-groups. Hence, what originally was conceived as a research method became a new pedagogy (see Bradford, Gibb, & Benne, 1964).

T-groups essentially had two purposes: (a) teaching participants how to encourage planned changes in systems, especially to promote social justice (see Bradford, 1976; NTL Institute, 2008), and (b) facilitating personal, interpersonal, and group growth. The first focus, often called "human relations," was incorporated into organizational management training (see, e.g., Highhouse, 2002), but did not last very long (probably because it called for drastic changes that were incompatible with for-profit organizations). The second focus, called "encounter groups," derived from existential philosophy and meaning "a real meeting between people, where each treats the other as a full human being" (Rowan, 2011, Encounter section, para. 1), stressed the expression of emotions (see, e.g., Lieberman, Yalom, & Miles, 1973; Rogers, 1970), and became popular during the 1960s and 1970s, as part of the general interest in humanistic psychology and, more specifically, the personal growth movement. In fact, during that time period, human relations and encounter groups were well integrated into the study of interpersonal and group communication,[7] but those fields shifted, respectively, to the quantitative study of strategic communicative behaviors in heterosexual romantic dyads (primarily, marriages) and the relationship between group communication and decision making. Although T-groups (and related groups) are not practiced much today, many of their principles, processes, and practices live on in self-help/support groups that aid people in coping with problems (e.g., living with cancer), as well as in conflict management, dialogue, and peace-building groups.

CHR focuses on facilitating personal, interpersonal, and group growth, and, hence, is closer to encounter groups than to T-groups. Most important for the purposes of this chapter is that, in many ways, the course's pedagogical principles, processes, and practices (and those of the historical groups that informed the course) are in line with the tenets of positive psychology, although there are some important differences as well.

First, a primary "aim of positive psychology is to begin to crystallize a change in the focus of psychology from preoccupation only with repairing the worst things in life to also building positive qualities" (Seligman & Csikszentmihalyi, 2000, p. 5). To do so, positive psychology puts "as much focus on strengths as on weaknesses, as much interest in building the best things in life as in repairing the worst, and as much attention to fulfilling the lives of healthy people as to healing the wounds of the distressed" (Peterson, 2006, p. 5).

CHR, in line with the design of T-groups as "group therapy for normals" (Yalom, 2005, p. 530), which represented a shift away from a "sickness" model that characterized earlier psychotherapy groups, starts from the premise that participants have many communication strengths and are functioning in a healthy manner. Moreover, during the initial group sessions, the facilitator explicitly asks participants to articulate their communication strengths, thereby identifying themselves as resources for members who have difficulty enacting those communicative behaviors.

Second, positive psychology has three central concerns/foci: (a) positive subjective experiences/emotions (e.g., well-being, joy, happiness, and pleasure), (b) positive individual traits (e.g., authenticity, bravery, capacity for love, and interpersonal skill), and (c) positive institutions (e.g., strong families, schools, and communities). *CHR* certainly promotes positive subjective experiences/emotions; indeed, a seminal book that informed encounter groups was *Joy* (Schutz, 1967) and stressed the importance of experiencing that feeling, primarily via "peak experiences" (see Maslow, 1962) and basking in those moments, rather than the more typical tendency to race out of them. For example, a participant in the course wrote in a response paper:

> What a session. Tonight was powerful and, strangely, I came out of it feeling really happy. I've had some issues with that lately, so I'm encouraged and relieved to have found such an intense happiness tonight. I think it came from connecting with the other participants. We had some good laughs during the break, but the entire session made our group feel like more of a close-knit group for me.

Simultaneously, however, the course joins positive psychology to challenge the traditional assumption that "negative" emotions are detrimental (see Fredrickson, 2009, 2011). Instead, experiencing any emotion in the here-and-now within a supportive group context is viewed as a "positive" experience insofar as it is through the use of signature strengths to manage inevitable obstacles that people increase thriving and resiliency. For instance, in a response paper, a course participant described in a very different way what, in many contexts, would be considered a negative emotion:

> I felt comfortable crying in the class. I was not embarrassed or ashamed. If I cried in a class in a different situation, or if I cried in front of people I do not know well in another situation, I could have been judged and thought of very differently. In this case, I felt respect, care, and interest from everyone in the group. I also got the feeling that everyone found my reason for crying as legitimate, even though they did not really know what I was talking about. This was a profound realization for me because that support usually comes from people who know exactly what I am experiencing.

Members, thus, acquire emotional communication literacy by creating a supportive climate in which they become aware of their emotions, experience those emotions, and express those emotions in the group setting (see Egan, 1973). Such a process is grounded in an inherent trust in people's ability to learn how to handle any emotion rather than being overwhelmed by uncomfortable emotions that they avoid or bury (e.g., anger or sadness), leading, in some cases, to devastating consequences (e.g., violence and suicide).

CHR also promotes positive character traits (see Mirivel, chapter 4, this volume). At the heart of the course's pedagogy is the notion of members being "authentic," by being "true" to themselves (genuine) and in their communication with other members (despite being in a classroom setting). That authenticity cannot be preestablished or mandated; it must be cultivated via members' communicative practices, as a participant recognized in a response paper written after the very first session:

> We as communicators are striving to be authentic. The basis of that authenticity is contingent on six things: inclusion, knowing one another, cared/supported, mutual openness, influence/control, and being heard. This group is under a lot of pressure, because what we share needs to communicate a deeper expression of who we are.

In this context, authenticity means that people acknowledge/own and express their positive traits and skills to other group members, but it also means engaging in the courageous act of facing themselves and others, in spite of their fears. Within the supportive group climate that participants create, one main reason that members do not express certain positive traits and skills is because they hold themselves back, for instance, from showing the warmth that they feel for other members or from developing skills to handle feedback constructively (e.g., not judging feedback as "positive" or "negative," leading to the dismissal of the latter). People have many reasons for not engaging in behaviors that would lead them to become more positive persons (e.g., they have not behaved that way much in the past, they fear not being good at expressing a behavior, and/or they fear that others will not like them if they behave that way), revealing that they are their worst enemies. More important, those fears reside in the there-and-then realm of reflecting on action (either before or afterwards), and a key learning of the course is that there is no fear in the moment but only action, and that members have the communication resources to handle whatever consequences may occur.

Furthermore, when such fears arise, rather than shutting them down, exploring reasons why people have them (as if there were particular reasons or that knowing those reasons would change behavior), or offering advice (which people usually know), experiential encounter communication pedagogy explores what people are doing, how they feel about doing it (thereby exacerbating their uncomfortableness), and what they *need* (not halfheartedly want) to be doing. The first steps, then, are for members to own what they need to do and to recognize the ensuring need to risk engaging in new communicative behavior. As a student explained in a response paper:

> I usually do not take risks in my personal interactions with strangers. As I mentioned in class, I am really nervous to share an intimate experience with people I do not know. Usually, when I first meet people, I ask questions about them to get a feel for how they interact and gauge the way that I will proceed in the interaction. After the syllabus was explained in more depth, I began to realize that this class would finally allow me to take the risks that are necessary for me to grow as a person.

Once members own and are ready to risk doing what they need to do, letting down their well-developed defenses and acting in spite of their uncomfortableness, they need opportunities within a safe, supportive group context to practice that behavior, receive feedback about it, and then practice it more. That opportunity may be as simple as letting someone initiate a previously untried communicative behavior. As a group member, using the metaphor of learning to swim, explained:

> What I noticed is that under the pressure of risk, I safeguard or do the opposite of what I feel the most. In the "waters of this course," the biggest failure I can do is to not speak or to buckle to my fear of not being accepted. So what did I do? I spoke

first. I set the precedent for speaking. This is alarming (even to me), when I took a risk that I am not comfortable doing. In essence, I was learning how to swim in my environment.

In other cases, to practice and receive feedback on untried or underused communicative behaviors, the facilitator (or, sometimes, other members) offers structured activities to meet members' needs. For instance, when a member expressed that she had difficulty nonverbally expressing her warm feelings for other group members, Larry asked her to go around the room and hug each person. She did so in a superficial manner, giving each person a quick, perfunctory hug. When she claimed afterwards that the activity had not helped her, another member pointed out her lack of engaging the activity and challenged her to do it again and put herself fully into it. Accepting the challenge, she hugged each person in a deep way, and in the subsequent metacommunication processing of that activity, she realized that she could choose to show affection that way.

In still other cases, the facilitator offers activities to meet the needs of the entire group. For instance, because the issue of how members were being treated based on their gender emerged repeatedly in a group, Larry suggested temporarily dividing into all-male and all-female subgroups, to explore relationships among the same-gender members and to surface perceptions and feelings about the opposite-gender members to share when everyone got back together. A member of the women's group noted in her response paper about this activity:

> The absence of men really allowed us to open up and talk in a way that may not have been deemed appropriate for our [entire coed] circle. There was much more laughter and rapid-fire conversation without what we've come to consider "proper" responses.

Moreover, the women had written on a chalkboard comments about each male, which, if even done in another context, likely would be erased and not shared (constituting gossip by talking about people not in the room), but which, in this context, as that same member explained, became a means of providing feedback and demonstrating the high-quality relationships that members had formed:

> One moment that impressed me was the girls' debate over whether to erase the board. We were a bit hesitant because complete exposure hadn't been considered [when doing it] but in the spirit of group honesty, we decided to leave it up. This choice reflected stronger bonds between both women and women (placing trust in our combined decisions with no concerns of exposing specific members) and wom-

en and men (leaving the highly personal material on the board for evaluation and discussion).

In each of these (and many more) cases, members identified what they needed to work on, initiated or were offered opportunities to work, and worked in spite of their fears and uncomfortableness. They learned from that process that they have the internal resources (positive traits and skills) needed to achieve their goals; as one member wrote in a response paper after taking such initiative, "Mission accomplished!"

Although *CHR* creates opportunities to develop even more positive traits and skills than members currently possess, the experiential encounter communication pedagogy views the locus for such growth as residing in members' relational communicative behaviors rather than in individuals per se (as positive psychology appears to do, at least for two of its three central concerns). For instance, as Schmid (2001) maintained:

> Being authentic is a precondition to enter dialogue—the way of communicating between persons where the other is truly acknowledged as an Other (in the sense of encounter philosophy), who is opening up, revealing him- or herself. Thus, in an epistemological perspective, it is the foundation of personal and facilitative communication. (p. 217)

Being authentic can lead to dialogue but it is not a precondition for it per se, for, from a constitutive experiential encounter communication perspective, the reverse also is true: Dialogue with others (encounter communication) produces authenticity, with people discovering their genuine self by engaging in the communication described in this course. Hence, communication is not just a tool that people use to display authenticity (or any other positive trait); more important, it also is a medium through which positive traits and skills can be produced and acquired.

Moreover, a constitutive communication perspective views subjective positive experiences/emotions, traits, and skills as being fundamentally relational. As Schmid (2001) claimed, "Authenticity is the response-ability which answers the call to respond to another person's needs, whether in therapy, or in any personal relationship" (p. 217). In line with research showing that communicative acts have both content and relational dimensions (see, e.g., Watzlawick, Beavin, & Jackson, 1967; in the context of T-group communication, see Fisher & Beach, 1979), although what members talk about during class discussions is important (i.e., the content dimension), what is more significant in experiential encounter communication is the relational dimension. Hence, the fact that people care enough about each other to initiate genuine human contact—that is, encounter one another—regardless of whether that contact is based, for instance, on happiness or unhappiness with the other person, makes their communication "positive" in this context. As a participant described in a response paper, "This course helped me realize that responding to the content is not as effective as responding to the individual." Consequently, rather than viewing interpersonal (communication) skills as one of many positive traits, the experiential encounter communication pedagogy views positive relationships (meaning positive relational communication) as another fundamental (and currently overlooked in the extant literature) domain of positive psychology.

Finally, to a much lesser extent, *CHR* focuses on promoting positive institutions. The course models forms of group interaction and educational experience that are significantly different from students' prior academic experiences, and although the focus on personal, interpersonal, and group growth should translate into systemic social change (see, e.g., Foss & Foss, 2011), whether such change occurs as a result of this course remains an empirical question.

Although the effects of the course and its pedagogy on macrolevel systems remains unknown, as the comments above demonstrate, students learn and grow substantially from the course, and they enthusiastically describe the beneficial impacts in their writing during and after the course.[9] Course evaluations always are very high, with students' open-ended comments documenting positive effects on their lives. For instance, a student claimed, "This class helped me to look inside myself. No other class on this campus has done that." Another student wrote, "I have learned so much about myself. It's ridiculous how much this class has helped me grow as a person with my self-confidence and my abilities to handle interpersonal relationships." Many students have noted, as captured in the words of one student, that "this has been, and I assume will be, the most significant undergraduate course that I have taken," and, as another said succinctly, "Simply put, this class was life-changing." Angie credits her facilitator-in-training experience in the course to positively affecting, in momentously significant ways, her interpersonal relationships and her desire as a teacher to interact genuinely and without defenses with her students, and to "risk" interacting with them as equals (e.g., by sharing personal stories in the classroom) rather than maintaining a distanced, hierarchical teacher–student power dynamic. In many cases, course participants and those who have served as facilitators-in-training continue to express such positive comments, even many years after taking the course; indeed, Larry receives e-mails from students who took the course long ago (some as many as 35 years ago) that say, undoubtedly overstating the claim but showing the impact on their lives, they think virtually every day about the course and try to put into practice what they learned in it.

Applying Experiential Encounter Communication Pedagogy

We recognize that not all educators have the desire, skill, or opportunity to teach this type of course. However, there are at least two ways that this pedagogy can be applied to other communication education efforts to offer students experiential opportunities to practice positive constitutive communication to promote personal, interpersonal, and group growth: (a) by adopting some of the processes and practices that characterize this pedagogy, and (b) by integrating the pedagogy more fully into a lecture-based, learning-centered course.

First, communication courses (perhaps some more than others) could adopt some of the experiential encounter communication pedagogical processes and practices, in general, or as employed in *CHR*, specifically (e.g., extended class length, sitting in a circle, open discussion, here-and-now communication, experimentation with new communicative behaviors coupled with member feedback, and writing response papers), to develop a positive classroom climate that encourages personal, interpersonal, and group growth. For example, teachers of public speaking courses, after a round of speeches, could employ these strategies to discuss speakers' communication strengths and how the audience supported and encouraged speakers.

As another example, in teaching an interpersonal communication course, in conjunction with lectures and course activities on the topics of self-concept and competence, Angie employs an activity (occurring later in the semester, after a strong classroom community has been established) that aligns well with the experiential encounter communication processes of receiving feedback and engaging in authentic communication. Students receive pieces of paper labeled with every other class member's name, and they anonymously write a few words/phrases that honestly describe how they perceive each classmate (e.g., outgoing and happy-go-lucky, or shy and introspective). After receiving such feedback, students engage in a group discussion about whether it confirmed their self-concept and how it felt to give honest, anonymous feedback to others. Students often note that this was the first time they ever received such direct, honest feedback from peers, and that the experience was both rewarding but tough (particularly when the feedback disconfirms students' self-concept, such as students who view themselves as outspoken leaders receiving feedback that describes them as frequently interrupting others). Furthermore, many students express that simply knowing how they are honestly perceived by others brings a sense of relief (by reducing anxiety and uncertainty that comes with managing face) and that the feedback will guide their future self-presentation.

Second, the experiential encounter communication pedagogy could be integrated more fully into a traditional course design, with lecture and group work used together during class periods (e.g., 45 minutes of lecture and 45 minutes of experiential encounter group discussion, or a day of the week devoted to each). In this integration, experiential group discussion is employed, but rather than being relatively free-form (as in *CHR*), it focuses on here-and-now communication related to course topics (e.g., expression of emotion in an interpersonal communication course) and then analyzes the effects of doing so on individuals, class members' relationships, and the class as a group.[10] Thus, these (and other) practices can be employed in communication courses to achieve some of the benefits associated with this experiential, communication-based pedagogical approach to personal, interpersonal, and group growth.

Conclusion

The encounter communication pedagogy described in this chapter represents an important type of experiential education for teaching students positive communicative practices. Whether taught as a separate communication course, woven into the fabric of current communication courses, or appropriated with regard to particular course practices, experiential encounter communication is a powerful pedagogy that offers students opportunities to develop their positive potential as human beings to constitutively and collectively create and sustain high-quality relationships.

Notes

[1] At the University of Colorado Boulder, there are required introductory interpersonal and group communication prequiste courses for the CHR course.

[2] In earlier course versions, participants sat on the floor, but because of health concerns, they now sit in chairs (preferably, ones with no writing arm), with no tables in front of them, to prevent putting their energy there. Participants cannot take notes during the group discussions (but are encouraged to write notes during the 15-minute break and to complete response papers immediately after sessions).

[3] In some cases, a graduate student (as Angie White did in fall 2008) or an undergraduate student who has taken the course and demonstrated excellent communication skills serves as a "facilitator-in-training."

⁴ Towards the end of the course, as students transition out of the classroom, some discussion of their lives outside of the group occurs; by that time, they have created the positive, caring group climate to effectively talk about their lives.

⁵ There are two basic approaches to the facilitation of such groups: the one described of being an active facilitator and member, and one in which the facilitator does not intervene to direct group processes and does not share as a member, to frustrate participants' traditional dependence on a leader and, thereby, develop leadership skills. Although we recognize the importance of the second approach and incorporate it into our facilitation style, we adopt the first approach under the assumption that people should not be asked to do what we are not prepared to do.

⁶ To minimize the potential for grading to adversely affect students' learning, students are encouraged to take the course, if possible, on a pass–fail basis.

⁷ Indeed, Larry's doctoral degree from the University of Kansas is in Speech Communication and Human Relations.

⁸ There is much research documenting benefits and potential problems of T-groups (and related groups; see, e.g., Bennan & Zimpfer, 1980; Cooper & Mangham, 1971).

⁹ For an example of how the course (and, more specifically, a structured activity employed) changed a student's life, see Silipigni (1979; esp. chapter 5).

References

Bennan, J. J., & Zimpfer, D. G. (1980). Growth groups: Do the outcomes really last? *Review of Educational Research, 50,* 505–524. doi:10.3102/00346543050004505

Bennis, W. G., & Shepard, H. A. (1956). A theory of group development. *Human Relations, 9,* 415–437. doi:10.1177/001872675600900403

Bradford, L. P. (1976). The laboratory method: A historical perspective. *Group & Organization Management, 1,* 415–429. doi:10.1177/105960117600100404

Bradford, L. P., Gibb, J. R., & Benne, K. D. (Eds.). (1964). *T-group theory and laboratory method: Innovation in re-education.* New York: John Wiley.

Braithwaite, D. O., & Wood, J. T. (Eds.). (2000). *Case studies in interpersonal communication: Processes and problems.* Belmont, CA: Wadsworth.

Carey, J. W. (1989). *Communication as culture: Essays on media and society.* Boston, MA: Unwin Hyman.

Cooper, C. L., & Mangham, I. L. (Eds.). (1971). *T-groups: A survey of research.* New York: Wiley-Interscience.

Egan, G. (1973). *Face to face: The small-group experience and interpersonal growth.* Monterey, CA: Brooks/Cole.

Fisher, B. A., & Beach, W. A. (1979). Content and relationship dimensions of communicative behavior: An exploratory study. *Western Journal of Communication, 43,* 201–211. doi:10.1080/10570317909373969

Foss, S. K., & Foss, K. A. (2011). Constricted and constructed potentiality: An inquiry into paradigms of change. *Western Journal of Communication, 75,* 205–238. doi:10.1080/10570314.2011.553878

Fredrickson, B. L. (2001). The role of positive emotions in positive psychology: The broaden-and-build theory of positive emotions. *American Psychologist, 56,* 218–226. doi:10.1037/0003-066X.56.3.218

Fredrickson, B. L. (2009). *Positivity: Groundbreaking research reveals how to embrace the hidden strength of positive emotions, overcome negativity, and thrive*. New York, NY: Crown.

Gordon, J. (Ed.). (2004). *Pfeiffer's classic activities for improving interpersonal communication: The most enduring, effective, and valuable training activities for improving interpersonal communication*. San Francisco, CA: Pfeiffer.

Highhouse, S. (2002). A history of the T-groups and its early applications in management development. *Group Dynamics: Theory, Research, and Practice, 4,* 277–290. doi:10.1037//1089-2699.6.4.277

Katula, R. A., & Threnhauser, E. (1999). Experiential education in the undergraduate curriculum. *Communication Education, 48,* 238–255. doi:10.1080/03634529909379172

Lakin, M., & Costanzo, P. R. (1975). The leader and the experiential group. In C. L. Cooper (Ed.), *Theories of group processes* (pp. 205–234). London: John Wiley.

Lieberman, M. A., Yalom, I. D., & Miles, M. B. (1973). *Encounter group: First facts*. New York, NY: Basic Books.

Maslow, A. H. (1962). *Toward a psychology of being*. Princeton, NJ: Van Nostrand.

Mokros, H. B., & Deetz, S. (1996). What counts as real? A constitutive view of communication and the disenfranchised in the context of health. In E. B. Ray (Ed.), *Communication and disenfranchisement: Social health issues and implications* (pp. 29–44). Mahwah, NJ: Lawrence Erlbaum.

NTL Institute. (2008). *About NTL: NTL mission statement and values*. Retrieved from http://www.ntl.org/inner.asp?id=177&category=2

Peterson, C. (2006). *A primer in positive psychology*. New York: Oxford University Press.

Rogers, C. (1970). *Carl Rogers on encounter groups*. New York, NY: Harper & Row.

Rowan, J. (2011). *A guide to humanistic psychology*. Petaluma, CA: Association for Humanistic Psychology. Retrieved from http://www.ahpweb.org/rowan_bibliography/index.html

Schmid, P. F. (2001). Authenticity: The person as his or her own author. Dialogic and ethical perspectives on therapy as an encounter relationships. And beyond. In G. Wyatt (Ed.), *Rogers' therapeutic conditions: Evolution, theory and practice: Vol. 1. Congruence* (pp. 217–232). Ross-on-Wye UK: PCCS Books.

Schutz, W. C. (1967). *Joy: Expanding human awareness*. New York, NY: Grove Press.

Seligman, M. E. P., & Csikszentmihalyi, M. (2000). Positive psychology: An introduction. *American Psychology, 55,* 5–14. doi:10.1037///0003-066X.55.1.5

Silipigni, R. (1979). *6:16*. New York: Vantage Books.

Socha, T. J. (2008, November). *Building positive communication pedagogy: Positive experiential communication learning in human relating*. Paper presented at the meeting of the National Communication Association, San Diego, CA.

Watzlawick, P., Beavin, J. H., & Jackson, D. D. (1967). *Pragmatics of human communication: A study of interactional patterns, pathologies, and paradoxes*. New York, NY: Norton.

Yalom, I. D. (with Leszcz, M.). (2005). *The theory and practice of group psychotherapy*. New York: Basic Books.

EPILOGUE

The Power of the Dark Side

Brian Spitzberg
San Diego State University

William Cupach
Illinois State University

In his poem, *September 1, 1939*, W. H. Auden envisioned an impending world in which "Waves of anger and fear circulate over the bright and darkened lands of the earth, obsessing our private lives." Despite such apparent pessimism, he continued:

> Defenseless under the night
> Our world in stupor lies;
> Yet, dotted everywhere,
> Ironic points of light
> Flash out wherever the Just
> Exchange their messages:
> May I, composed like them
> Of Eros and dust,
> Beleaguered by the same
> Negation and despair,
> Show an affirming flame.

We always have, and continue, to be drawn toward what we believe is a positive and affirming light in the study of the dark side of interpersonal communication and relationships. We continue to champion its value, not in contradiction to the positive side, but in an attempt to dissolve the arbitrary imputation of a wall between the metaphorical "sides" that delimits our collective ability to see the entire landscape of interest, and promotes unproductive polarizations among those who inhabit the territories divided by such barriers. There are others who will attack the underlying ideological and rhetorical architecture of positive psychology (McDonald &

O'Callaghan, 2008). There are others still who will demonstrate that the negative and the bad are far stronger and more compelling in affecting our lives compared to the positive and the good (Baumeister, Bratslavsky, Finkenauer, & Vohs, 2001). Instead, we elect to seek, as we always have, a rapprochement among those who still see the "dark" and the "light" as oppositions. Our view goes beyond the mere juxtapositioning of positive and negative communication (Kinney & Pörhölä, 2009). We advocate an integrative view that appreciates simultaneously the positive and negative aspects of human relating, and seeks to reveal, or at least direct others to look for, their dynamic interplay.

Toward this end, we are unabashedly ambivalent about our mission in this epilogue. On the one hand, the idea of this book, and the authors' contributions, are both long overdue and of consistently extraordinary quality and thoughtfulness. On the other hand, many of the insights pursued and achieved we believe are already encompassed by the dark side perspective. This irony seems only appropriate, however, given that we will be arguing that ambivalence is a fundamental dark side facet of human and relational experience.

Of Dualities and Dialectics

The late Stephen Jay Gould (1995) often speculated that humans are, by their nature, "beset by dualities, perhaps because nature favors pairings," but perhaps more "because our mind works as a dichotomizing machine" (p. 133). We are certainly examples of his observations. When we began our journey on the dark side, it was under what was partly a (probably mistaken) supposition that most scholarly research was biased toward the "good" and the "positive" (e.g., love, satisfaction, desire, well-being, mental health, etc.). Our interest was also partly motivated by a (probably accurate) sense that undergraduate textbooks in communication, sociology, and psychology tended toward banal optimism in claims about the value of honesty, clarity, understanding, empathy, cooperation, compatibility, love, harmony, openness, and the like. As we matured in our own understanding of research and theory in dark side books by ourselves and others, we came to recommend viewing the dark side as a topography defined by two dimensions: normative and functional (Spitzberg & Cupach, 2007). The *normative* dimension is defined by subjective individual or collective judgments of what is good, desirable, moral, and ethical on the one side, and bad, undesirable, immoral, and unethical on the other side. This dimension capitalizes on people's judgments of the appropriateness and inappropriateness of experiences and actions. The *functional* dimension is defined by experiences that increase the vitality, thriving, and survival of an organism or system on one side, and experiences that increase disease, disruption, decay and death of an individual or system on the other side. This dimension capitalizes on the effectiveness or ineffectiveness with which actors and institutions pursue their objectives and lives.

From this dualistic typology, four domains of scholarly interest are configured: (1) those processes that we normatively tend to think of as positive, which nevertheless can produce dysfunctional outcomes (what once was bright is now dark; e.g., fatal attractions); (2) those processes that we normatively think of as immoral or bad, yet sometimes produce positive outcomes (what once was dark is now bright; e.g., post-traumatic growth); (3) those processes that we think are dark and are indeed dysfunctional (evil incarnate; e.g., genocide); and (4) those processes that we think are bright and are indeed functionally enhancing. We have speculated that the last cell of the typology may well be a mythical or a null set (and thus, no exemplar is yet provided).

We cannot claim this typology is theoretical, scientific, or exhaustive. Despite some who have suggested the scientific and theoretical status of "the dark side" (Perlman & Carcedo, 2011), we prefer to consider this a heuristic, and at best, meta-theoretical framework. And, despite efforts by some to propose a third dimension (see Baxter, chapter 2, this volume), we would instead suggest that there are many potential dualities or dialectics that could be added (e.g., rationality vs. narrative; Fisher, 1985).

(De)Constructing the Wall Between Good and Bad

The vagaries and complexities implied by this typology require great subtlety in extracting the functions of positive and negative experiences. For example, some time ago Jahoda (1953) warned against mistaking "psychological health" with such simple formulations as "absence of mental disease" or "psychological well-being," warning further that "the unit of analysis when investigating psychological health can never be the individual in artificial isolation. It must be simultaneously the individual and the social matrix" within which the individual interacts (p. 351).

The self and its identities are embedded in social networks and systems. Social networks and systems are functionally ambivalent—some close ties are experienced as primarily dysfunctional, and some as primarily functional, but most are experienced as mixed bags (Fingerman, Hay, & Birditt, 2004). That is, many of our important social relations are close, important, but both positive and negative in their influence on our state of well-being. Given that much of our identity and sense of worth is in turn a significant function of our relations with others we value, it follows that the experience of ambivalence in our relations is likely to create a sense of ambivalence about self (Knee, Canevello, Bush, & Cook, 2008).

There is evidence that our connections with others mediate our mortal health and vitality (Okun & Lockwood, 2003)—that is, it is the social and not the self that determines what is positive and what is negative. It might be assumed that ambivalent social networks and experiences would be a bad thing, but there is reason to expect otherwise. Despite a predominant tendency for research and theory to presume that adverse experiences are cumulatively and univocally adverse in their effects (e.g., Anda et al., 2006), when data are decomposed and examined with sensitivity and longitudinal detail, there is evidence that the experience of adversity is curvilinear to well-being—that is, a moderate level of adversity tends to produce resilience—at the extremes (i.e., little or no adversity, very high adversity), it appears that life satisfaction suffers (Seery, Leo, Holman & Silver, 2010).

The Interplay of Positive and Negative

The suppositions of ambivalence and curvilinearity are not necessarily the same things (Spitzberg, 1994). So, for example, *ambivalence* implies that the experience of a given emotion, cognition, or behavior has at least some of *both* positive and negative effects. A related concept, *dialectic* (see Baxter, chapter 2, this volume) refers to a simultaneous experienced opposition that creates some tension or pull in different but incompatible directions. Whereas ambivalent experiences may be averaged, summed, or weighted to produce a summary evaluation, dialectics reflect ongoing dynamic experiential dilemmas. In contrast, *curvilinear* relationships imply univocal relations between experiences and their valence, but these unitary relations change at different types, levels, or times of experience.

As an exemplar of curvilinear concerns, there is extensive evidence that negative or adverse experiences tend to disproportionately influence judgments of well-being, satisfaction, and health (Baumeister et al., 2001). Yet, the curvilinearity of adverse experiences in relation to life satisfaction (Seery et al., 2010) could reflect that various thresholds alter the cumulative impact of such experiences on the self's ability to cope, and that some level of stress-reactive coping helps mature a person's ability to both manage adverse events and appreciate life in light of such experiences.

Other experiences may better reflect ambivalence or dialectical dynamics than curvilinearity. For example, despite decades of research presumptively claiming and empirically demonstrating the advantages of physical attractiveness and attraction, those who might be considered extremely attractive may experience ambivalent effects of their beauty, or experience personal and interpersonal conflicts about their attributed adorations (e.g., Meyer, Enström, Harstveit, Bowles, & Beevers, 2007). More extreme examples of ambivalence might be reflected in findings that psychopaths are often surprisingly successful in life pursuits, and often even well-liked and accomplished in social contexts (Hall & Benning, 2006). In all these instances, humans seem drawn to the prospects of making deals with the devil—seeking that which seems to sparkle, only to discover the costs of such desire.

Working Toward a Science of Functionalist Integration

The potential for taking into account multiple levels or types of emotional experience, in relational context, is illustrated by the results of a study by Sanford and Rowatt (2004), in which hard (e.g., anger), soft (e.g., feeling sad or hurt), and fear-based (e.g., anxiety, feeling threatened) emotions were distinguished. Although positively correlated, hard and soft emotions related in opposite ways to relationship functioning, such that higher levels of soft emotions were associated with higher satisfaction, lower conflict, and lower avoidance, whereas higher levels of hard emotions were associated with no change in, or lower, satisfaction, higher conflict, and higher avoidance. In contrast, higher levels of fear-based emotions were uniquely associated with greater relationship anxiety.

The complexity of these relationships is only revealed when considering factors such as time and perspective (Spitzberg, 1994). As an example of the chronological dimension, going through the trauma of a bad relationship and the chaos of a relationship breakup may be traumatizing, but we often emerge having learned important lessons in which we see the silver linings of our difficult relational journeys (e.g., Tashiro & Frazier, 2003). As an example of the perspective dimension, studies of support providers tend to find that whereas giving companionship support (e.g., affection, appreciation) was associated with less depression for the provider, giving helping support (e.g., listening to worries, giving advice, intervening into conflicts on the receiver's behalf, etc.) was associated with greater depression for the provider (Strazdins & Broom, 2007).

A more potentially dialectic appreciation of phenomena might be illustrated by research on socio-evaluative or communal concerns. There is evidence that along with many of the personal and relational benefits of interpersonal competence that arise from empathy and socioemotional abilities also arise greater risks of depression (Rudolph & Conley, 2005), and that some forms of accommodating others come with many maladaptive costs (Hennig & Walker, 2008). We often seek greater intimacy and closeness, but with such closeness, the experience of interdependencies, sacrifices, and costs accumulate, which require continuous trade-offs of one value against another (Parks, 1982). Conversely, excessive concern for self presents other potential dialectics (Crocker, 2002). Those with acutely high self-esteem are at elevated risks of narcissistic defensiveness, revealing a brittle need to react with hypersensitivity and aggressiveness to perceived slights or criticisms (Baumeister, Boden, & Smart, 1996).

Normative Deviance

As fascinating as these perambulations down the paths of ambivalence, dialectics, and curvilinearity may be, they cannot fully describe the topography of the dark side. These dimensions reflect primarily *functional* questions—how experience functions to affect some personal, relational, or group outcome. A second dimension is a more subjective and moral crucible of concern. The domain of the dark side can also be understood along a continuum of subjective judgments of "good" and "bad" (or evil). Although functionalist (Baumeister & Campbell, 1999) and structural (Bringsjord, Khemlani, Arkoudas, McEvoy, Destefano, & Daigle, 2005) perspectives toward evil have been posited, we are here more interested in evil as one pole of a *normative* dimension, along which people's judgments of good and bad are aligned. It is along such a dimension that the appropriateness of scholarly inquiries into the "positive" outcomes of childhood sexual experiences with adults (e.g., Okami, 1991) or the maladaptiveness of closeness in family systems (e.g., Green & Werner, 1996) can be gauged.

If researching the competence of interpersonal violence (Spitzberg, 2011), or sexual abuse of children (McMillan, Zuravin, & Rideout, 1995) seems distasteful, or beyond the pale, it illustrates the potential value of the normative dimension. It seeks to draw attention to the ways in which even our research interests sometimes shy away from pushing the boundaries of science. In researching the bright or positive side of relationships, it is equally important to ask what the implications are of people pursuing the logical extensions of such research. For example, efforts to diffuse the importance of self-esteem to our children in our culture may have contributed to an "epidemic" of narcissism (Twenge, Konrath, Foster, Campbell, & Bushman, 2008), and the promotion of western notions of agency and achievement may have correspondingly diminished orientations toward communion and community (Twenge, 2009). In our rush to pursue scientific and purely functionalist questions, we often overlook the more ideological, cultural and practical implications of such work.

(Dis)Satisfactions With the Dark and Bright Sides

As he has before (Duck, 1994) in an appreciation of the "dark side," Duck (Foreword, this volume) emphasizes that any serious journey on or toward the bright or positive sides of relationships is fraught with constraints, historical, ideological, and theoretical. A legitimate science will account for the fact that humans and their relationships are inherently both good and bad, positive and negative. This observation, in and of itself, is now well-evidenced. The larger question is how our theories and science can plant the seeds of such ambivalence, duality, and dialectic into its foundational assumptions, and cultivate theories and methods that can appreciate such complexity. It will be a richer science for the harvesting of such fruits.

> The artist, the scientist, the founder of a religion, are able to perform truly great achievements only if they abandon themselves completely to their work, if they neglect their own being for it. But, as soon as it finally stands before its creator, the finished product is never simply a thing of satisfaction; it is, at the same time, a disappointment. (Cassirer, 1961, p. 193)

If future research on the positive and dark sides of human action is to avoid disappointment, we recommend the following heuristic meta-theoretical questions be addressed in any research program:

- Might the results of research provide resource to parties who might commit normative (i.e., moral) or functional harm, and if so, what might these uses and harms be? For example, might the discovery of post-traumatic growth provide defense attorneys the ability to deny justice or compensation to victims of abuse?
- If there is any implicit or explicit "valence" to the concepts being theorized or the constructs being operationalized, what is the possibility that the opposite valence is also involved? For example, if it is theorized that abuse is traumatizing, is the possibility of post-traumatic growth conceived, and does the measurement scheme provide for this possibility?
- Can the conditions be identified under which one valence or another will occur and thereby incorporated into the propositional structure of the theory? For

example, if post-traumatic growth can occur, can the specific conditions be identified under which such growth is likely to occur?

Such guideposts are suggestive of the potential value of the dark side. Pursuit of the dark side can indeed be illuminating, positively.

References

Anda, R. F., Felitti, V. J., Bremner, J., Walker, J. D., Whitfield, C., Perry, B. D., & ... Giles, W. H. (2006). The enduring effects of abuse and related adverse experiences in childhood: A convergence of evidence from neurobiology and epidemiology. *European Archives of Psychiatry and Clinical Neuroscience, 256*, 174–186.

Baumeister, R. F., Boden, J. M., & Smart, L. (1996). Relation of threatened egotism to violence and aggression: The dark side of high self-esteem. *Psychological Review, 103*, 5–33.

Baumeister, R. F., Bratslavsky, E., Finkenauer, C., & Vohs, K. D. (2001). Bad is stronger than good. *Review of General Psychology, 5*, 323–370.

Baumeister, R. F., & Campbell, W. K. (1999). The intrinsic appeal of evil: Sadism, Sensational threills, and threatened egotism. *Personality and Social Psychology Review, 3*, 210–211.

Bringsjord, S., Khemlani, S., Arkoudas, K., McEvoy, C., Destefano, M., & Daigle, M. (2005). *Proceedings of the Sixth International Conference on Intelligent Games and Simulation* (pp. 31–39). Ghent-Zwijnaarde, Belgium: European Simulation Society.

Cassirer, E. (1961). *The logic of the humanities.* Newhaven, CT: Yale University Press.

Crocker, J. (2002). The costs of seeking self-esteem. *Journal of Social Issues, 58*, 597–615.

Duck, S. (1994). Stratagems, spoils, and a serpent's tooth: On the delights and dilemmas of personal relationships. In W.R. Cupach & B.H. Spitzberg (Eds.), *The dark side of interpersonal communication* (pp. 3–24). Hillsdale, NJ: LEA.

Fingerman, K. L., Hay, E. L., & Birditt, K. S. (2004). The best of ties, the worst of ties: Close, problematic, and ambivalent social relationships. *Journal of Marriage and the Family, 66*, 792–808.

Fisher, W. R. (1985). The narrative paradigm: An elaboration. *Communication Monographs, 52*, 347–367.

Gould, S. J. (1995). *Dinosaur in a haystack: Reflections in natural history.* New York: Harmony Books.

Green, R. J., & Werner, P. D. (1996). Intrusiveness and closeness-caregiving: Rethinking the concept of family "enmeshment." *Family Process, 35*, 115–136.

Hall, J. R., & Benning, S. D. (2006). The "successful" psychopath: Adaptive and subclinical manifestations of psychopathy in the general population. In C. J. Patrick (Ed.), *The handbook of psychopathy* (pp. 459–478). New York: Guilford.

Hennig, K. H., & Walker, L. J. (2008). The darker side of accommodating others: Examining the interpersonal structure of maladaptive constructs. *Journal of Research in Personality, 42*, 2–21.

Jahoda, M. (1953). The meaning of psychological health. *Social Casework, 34*, 349–354.

Kinney, T. A., & Pörhölä, M. (Eds.) (2009). *Anti and prosocial communication: Theories, methods, and applications.* New York: Peter Lang.

Knee, C. R., Canevello, A., Bush, A. L., & Cook, A. (2008). Relationship-contingent self-esteem and the ups and downs of romantic relationships. *Journal of Personality and Social Psychology, 95*, 608–627.

McDonald, M., & O'Callaghan, J. (2008). Positive psychology: A Foucauldian critique. *The Humanistic Psychologist, 36*, 127–142.

McMillen, C., Zuravin, S., & Rideout, G. (1995). Perceived benefit from child sexual abuse. *Journal of Consulting and Clinical Psychology, 63*, 1037–1043.

Meyer, B., Enström, M. K., Harstveit, M., Bowles, D. P., & Beevers, C. G. (2007). Happiness and despair on the catwalk: Need satisfaction, well-being, and personality adjustment among fashion models. *The Journal of Positive Psychology, 2*, 2–17.

Okami, P. (1991). Self-reports of "positive" childhood and adolescent sexual contacts with older persons: An exploratory study. *Archives of Sexual Behavior, 20*, 437–457.

Okun, M. A., & Lockwood, C. M. (2003). Does level of assessment moderate the relation between social support and social negativity? A meta-analysis. *Basic and Applied Social Psychology, 25*, 15–35.

Parks, M. R. (1982). Ideology in interpersonal communication: Off the couch and into the world. In M. Burgoon (Ed.), *Communication yearbook 5* (pp. 79–107). New Brunswick, NJ: Transaction/International Communication Association.

Perlman, D., & Carcedo, R. J. (2011). Overview of the dark side of relationships research. In W. R. Cupach & B. H. Spitzberg (Eds.), *The dark side of close relationships II* (pp. 1–37). New York, NY: Routledge.

Rudolph, K. D., & Conley, C. S. (2005). The socioemotional costs and benefits of social-evaluative concerns: Do girls care too much? *Journal of Personality, 73*, 115–137.

Sanford, K., & Rowatt, W. C. (2004). When is negative emotion positive for relationships? An investigation of married couples and roommates. *Personal Relationships, 11*, 329–354.

Seery, M. D., Leo, R. J., Holman, E., & Silver, R. (2010). Lifetime exposure to adversity predicts functional impairment and healthcare utilization among individuals with chronic back pain. *Pain, 150*(3), 507–515.

Spitzberg, B. H. (1994). The dark side of (in)competence. In W. R. Cupach & B. H. Spitzberg (Eds.), *The dark side of interpersonal communication* (pp. 25–49). Hillsdale, NJ: LEA.

Spitzberg, B. H. (2011). Intimate partner violence and aggression: Seeing the light in a dark place. In W. R. Cupach & B. H. Spitzberg (Eds.), *The dark side of close relationships II* (pp. 327–380). New York, NY: Routledge.

Spitzberg, B. H., & Cupach, W. R. (2007). Disentangling the dark side of interpersonal communication. In B. H. Spitzberg & W. R. Cupach (Eds.), *The dark side of interpersonal communication* (2nd ed., pp. 3–28). Mahwah, NJ: LEA.

Strazdins, L., & Broom, D. H. (2007). The mental health costs and benefits of giving social support. *International Journal of Stress Management, 14*, 370–385.

Tashiro, T., & Frazier, P. (2003). "I'll never be in a relationship like that again": Personal growth following romantic relationship breakups. *Personal Relationships, 10*, 113–128.

Twenge, J. M. (2009). Status and gender: The paradox of progress in an age of narcissism. *Sex Roles, 61*, 338–340.

Twenge, J. M., Konrath, S., Foster, J. D., Campbell, W. K., & Bushman, B. J. (2008). Egos inflating over tie: A cross-temporal meta-analysis of the narcissistic personality inventory. *Journal of Personality, 76*, 875–902.

• CODA •

Positive Interpersonal Communication as Child's Play

Thomas J. Socha
Old Dominion University

Margaret J. Pitts
University of Arizona

Early inspiration for work on the positive side of interpersonal communication came over six years ago to the first author during a summer in Iowa on the campus of Luther College (Decorah, Iowa), not far from the *Field of Dreams* movie site (in Dyersville, Iowa). In a keynote speech given at the NCA Summer Faculty Development Institute (held at Luther College), Socha (2005) reported that, relative to adults, the field of communication had been neglecting young children (a situation that has changed little, see Socha & Yingling, 2011). He noted that parents and teachers put forth extensive effort to create positive communication environments that are supportive of children's communication development and learning. They endeavor to display patience and understanding when children make communication mistakes. They go to great lengths to prevent exposing children to harmful messages, work hard to make sure that children understand, and, desiring the best possible communication, they set high communication standards when communicating with children. And, like good parents, adult interactions today could display more patience, forgiveness, communication playfulness, and nurturing and support. Rather than valorizing incivility, disparagement, and degradation (as we often see in political and entertainment media), we should venerate communication that supports human potential, recognizes weaknesses while enhancing strengths, and displays positive regard even in the face of communication challenges.

What then might be imagined in prototypical "positive interpersonal communication?" We of course argue that the key qualities discussed in this volume such as relational aesthetics, synchrony, excellence, positive virtues, and intimacy; as well as the many positive communication processes covered in this volume, including engaged listening, affection, play, humor, positive conflict, forgiveness, support, and celebration in some way all play a role, along with recognizing potential applications of positive interpersonal communication in the contexts of health, spirituality, peace, and ongoing positive communication learning.

And, if adults do in fact aspire to be at their communication best when interacting with the littlest communicators, perhaps it is conceptually useful to imagine "communicating with children" as a kind of prototype of positive interpersonal communication. That is, positive interpersonal communication would include communicative processes and forms which we would be proud to model and teach to children; processes that would likely serve our children (and all of us) well across the human lifespan, of which many are discussed in this volume. For Socha and Yingling (2010), positive interpersonal communication is first learned at home and features message forms and processes that facilitate the development of human potentialities and avoid processes that inhibit or diminish human capacities to develop, learn, and grow; positive communication processes that are indeed kind and gentle.

Thus, it is our hope that this volume reminds us all of our higher and positive interpersonal communication selves, inspires new interpersonal communication scholarship on the positive side, and, perhaps, may begin to convince those on the dark side (e.g., Spitzberg & Cupach, epilogue, this volume) that bright and functionally enhancing interpersonal communication is not an empty, nor a mythical cell, but rather is more like child's play.

References

Socha, T. J. (2005, July). *Towards a positive ontology of communication theorizing: Lessons from Pollyanna.* A keynote address presented at the National Communication Association's Summer Faculty Development Institute Conference (Hope at Luther), Luther College, Decorah Iowa [written version available from the author.]

Socha, T. J., & Yingling, J. A. (2010). *Families communicating with children: Building positive developmental foundations.* Cambridge, UK: Polity.

Socha, T. J., & Yingling, J. A. (2011, November). *What can family communication learn from children's laughter? Un-muting the voices of children in families and integrating positive lifespan development into family communication theory and research.* Paper to be presented at the National Communication Association, New Orleans, LA.

Contributors

Editors-Authors

Thomas J. Socha, Ph.D., Professor of Communication, Graduate Program Director, Old Dominion University, Norfolk, Virginia

Margaret J. Pitts, Ph.D., Assistant Professor of Communication, University of Arizona

Authors

Krystyna Aune, Ph.D., Interim Associate Dean, College of Arts & Humanities and Professor of Communication, University of Hawaii at Manoa

E. James Baesler Ph.D. Associate Professor of Communication, Old Dominion University', Norfolk, Virginia

Leslie Baxter, Ph.D., F. Wendell Miller Distinguished Scholar of Communication Studies, University of Iowa

Graham Bodie, Ph.D., Assistant Professor of Communication Studies, Louisiana State University

Brant Burleson (1952–2010), Ph.D., University of Illinois, Urbana-Champaign, 1982) was a Professor of Communication and an Affiliate Professor of Psychological Sciences at Purdue University

William Cupach, Ph.D., Professor of Communication, Illinois State University

Douglas Deiss, M.A., Ph.D. student, Hugh Downs School of Human Communication, Arizona State University

Valerian Derlega, Ph.D., Professor of Psychology, Old Dominion University, Norfolk, Virginia

•CONTRIBUTORS•

Eileen Doherty, Ph.D. student at Purdue University

Steve Duck, Ph.D., Daniel and Amy Starch Distinguished Research Chair, University of Iowa

Bo Feng, Ph.D., Assistant Professor, University of California, Davis

Carla Fisher, Ph.D., Assistant Professor of Communication Studies, George Mason University

Kory Floyd, Ph.D., Professor and Associate Director of the Hugh Downs School of Human Communication, Arizona State University

Lawrence Frey, Ph.D., Professor, Department of Communication, University of Colorado at Boulder

Patricia Gettings, M.A., graduate student in Communication, Purdue University

Peter Kellett, Ph.D., Associate professor and Head of the Department of Communication studies, University of North Carolina at Greensboro

Douglas Kelley, Ph.D., Associate professor of communication, Arizona State West

Young Yun Kim, Ph.D., Professor of Communication, University of Oklahoma

Gary Kreps, Ph.D., Eileen and Steve Mandell Professor of Health Communication, Chair of the Department of Communication, Director of the Center for Health and Risk Communication, George Mason University

Erina MacGeorge, Ph.D., Associate Professor of Psychology, Purdue University

Jennifer Dane McCullough, Ph.D., Assistant Professor in the Communication Program, Saginaw Valley State University, Michigan

•CONTRIBUTORS•

John Meyer, Ph.D., Professor of Speech Communication, University of Southern Mississippi

Nathan Miczo, Ph.D., Associate Professor of Communication, Western Illinois University

Michelle Miller-Day, Ph.D., Associate Professor of Communication Arts & Sciences, faculty affiliate with the Center for Human Development and Family Research, Pennsylvania State University

Julien Mirivel, Ph.D., Associate Professor in the Department of Speech Communication, University of Arkansas at Little Rock

Sarah Nebel, MA., doctoral student in Communication Studies at the University of Iowa.

Kristen Norwood, Ph.D., Assistant Professor of Communication, Trinity University

John Nussbaum, Ph.D., Professor of Communication Arts & Sciences and Human Development & Family Studies, Pennsylvania State University

Brian Spitzberg, Ph.D., Professor of Communication, San Diego State University

Angie White, MA., Doctoral student, Department of Communication, University of Colorado at Boulder

Kristi Wilkum, MA., PhD. candidate at Purdue, teaching at University of Wisconsin, Fond du Lac

Steve Wilson, Ph.D., Professor of Communication, Purdue University

Norman Wong, Ph.D., Assistant Professor of Communication, University of Oklahoma

Author Index

•A•

Abboud, L., 223–224
Abraham, R., 31, 35, 54
Abramis, D. J., 143, 158
Adair, N., 179, 191
Adams, G., 295
AhYun, K. 254–255, 258
Akkoor, C., 26, 36
Al Mabuk, R., 204, 207
Albers, J. J., 141
Alberts, J. K., 166–167, 175
Albom, M., 68, 70
Albrecht, T., 122, 214, 225
Allen, G., 28, 35
Altman, I., 231, 245
Amico, J. A., 137, 141
Anda, 316, 320
Andersen, J. 254–256
Andersen, P. A., 224–225, 244
Anderson, R., 25, 36, 88–89, 190
Anderson, S. E., 121
Andrejevic, M., xii, xix
Andrews, G., 133, 141
Ano, G., 276
Applegate, J., 47, 52, 118, 123
Aquino, K., 33, 38
Arbaugh, J. B., 254–256
Arendt, H., 73, 75, 78, 80–83, 87–88
Argyle, M., 109, 121, 144–145, 158
Aristotle, xiv, xvi, 57, 69–71, 73, 103
Arkoudas, K., 318, 320
Arnett, R., 10, 14, 36
Ashby, F. G., 232, 244
Asher, G. R., 245
Aspy, C., 294
Atkin, C. K., 256
Aubin, M., 105
Aune, K., 2, 11, 13, 130, 143, 145, 150, 158–159, 174, 325

Aune, R., 144, 158
Austin, W., 55–56
Averbeck, J. M., 174, 176

•B•

Babrow, A. S., 169, 176
Bade, M., 262, 274
Baesler, E. J., 3, 7, 10, 12, 14, 219, 259, 262, 264, 271, 274, 325
Bage, G., 182, 190
Bahk, C. 223, 228
Bakhtin, M. M., 19–30, 34, 36–37
Balbin, E., 275
Barbee, A. P., 222, 224, 262, 274
Barber, B. K., 132, 139
Barge, J. K., 292–293
Barger, S. D., 218, 224
Barker, D. R., 114, 121
Barker, L. L., 111–112, 114, 121, 125
Barker, M., 46, 53
Barrera, M., 213, 224
Basso, K. H., 31, 36, 44, 52
Bateson, G., 37, 55
Batson, C. D., 195, 207
Baucom, D. H., 197, 200, 208
Bauman, R., 31, 34, 36
Baumeister, R. F., 77, 79, 82, 88, 131, 139, 314, 316, 318, 320
Bavelas, J., 41, 52
Baxter, L. A., v, xvi, xviii, 2, 9, 11–12, 19–20, 23, 25–29, 32–33, 36–37, 70, 80, 88–89, 122–123, 144–145, 148, 150, 152–153, 156–158, 190, 315–316, 325
Beach, W. A., 72, 259, 307, 311
Beatty, M. J., 123, 289, 295

Beavin, J. H., 307, 312
Beck, C., 225
Beckman, M., 98, 103, 139
Beevers, C. J., 317, 321
Behrendt, D. E., 286, 295
Bell, L., 10, 14
Bell, N. J., 165, 175
Bell, R., 47, 52
Bellah, R. N., 26, 37
Belsky, J., 279, 293
Benard, B., 281, 293
Bengtson, V. L., 132, 141
Benigni, R., 103
Bennan, J. J., 311
Benning, S. D., 317, 320
Bennis, W. G., 301, 311
Benson, H., 274
Benson, P. L., 283, 294
Berge, J., 49, 55
Berger, C. R., 45, 52, 116, 122, 163, 175, 261, 275
Berkman, L. F., 133, 139, 213, 224
Berkson, D. M., 139
Bernieri, F. J., 40–41, 52, 125
Berscheid, E., xiv, xix, 288, 295
Betcher, R. W., 143–144, 152, 158
Bhaduri, S., 103
Bies, R. J., 33, 38
Biesta, G. J. J., 179, 182, 191
Billig, M., 47, 52
Bingenheimer, J. B., 286, 295
Bippus, A. M., 165–167, 175, 177, 219, 224
Birditt, K. S., 315, 320
Birdwhistell, R., 44, 52
Birmingham, W. A., 137, 140, 217, 228
Black, A., 41, 52–53, 66
Blieszner, R., 217, 228
Bloch, L. R., 66, 70
Blommaert, J., 55
Blumen, D. L.. 181, 191
Blyth, D. A., 283, 294
Bochner, A. P., 79, 88
Boden, J. M., 318, 320
Bodenmann, G., xix, 226
Bodie, G. D., 2, 7, 67, 109–118, 120, 122–123, 219, 225, 243, 325
Bodley-Tickell, A. T., 100, 103
Bolger, N., 213, 226
Bombar, M. L., 144, 158

Bommelje, R. K., 120, 125
Bonaguro, E. W., 249, 257
Bond, M. H., 213, 227
Booker, C., 181, 190
Booth, A., 164, 167, 177, 275
Booth-Butterfield, M., 164, 167, 177
Booth-Butterfield, S., 164, 167, 177
Boren, J. P., 140
Bortz, W., 103
Bosma, H., 217, 228
Bostrom, R. N., 110, 112, 122, 125
Bosworth, H. B., 259, 274
Bowden, B., 209
Bowlby, J., xiv, xix
Bowles, D. P., 317, 321
Boyatzis, C. J., 204, 207
Boyle, J., 273–274
Bradbury, T. N., xix, 217, 225, 228
Bradford, L. P., 301–302, 311
Brady, M., 263, 276
Braithwaite, D. O., 29, 36, 37, 122–123, 298, 311
Brann, M., 57, 70
Braschi, G., 91, 103
Brashers, D. E., 163, 175
Bratslavsky, E., 314, 320
Bremner, J., 320
Brewer, M., 46, 53
Brickman, P., 5, 14
Bringsjord, S., 318, 320
Brissette, I., 213, 225
Broadhead, P., 143, 158
Brooks, P., 181, 190
Brooks, G. P., 175
Broom, D. H., 317, 321
Brown, B. B., 231, 245
Brown, J. I., 110–111, 122
Brown, M. H., 125
Brown, P., 59, 70
Brown, R., 164, 176
Broyles, F. C., 141
Bruess, C. J. S., 144, 159
Bruneau, T. J., 80, 85, 88
Brunner, C., 53
Buber, M., 25–26, 37, 52, 53, 68, 70
Buck, R., 47, 53
Buckley, T. C., 136, 139
Buhrmester, D., 117, 125, 141
Buka, S., 141
Bureau of Justice Statistics, 260, 274

Burgoon, J. K., 45, 53, 115–116, 123, 144, 150, 291, 293
Burgoon, M., 89, 321
Burleson, B., ix, xv, 2–3, 12, 25, 37, 68, 93, 113, 115, 116–118, 122–123, 125, 211–212, 214–217, 219, 220–229, 231, 235, 239, 244
Burton, L., 94, 104
Bush, A. L., 316, 321
Butler, R. N., 98, 104, 227, 231, 245
Buzzanell, P. M., 280, 293
Byrne, S., 191

•C•

Caffrey, J. G., 112, 123
Cahn, D., 175
Cain, R., 63, 70
Calabrese, R. J., 163, 175
Callan, V., 46, 53
Campbell, W. K., 318–321
Canary, D. J., 73, 88, 145, 159, 289, 293, 295
Canevello, A., 316, 321
Cann, A., 167, 175
Caplan, G., 212, 225
Caplan, S. E., 118, 123
Cappella, J., 40–41, 45, 53
Carbaugh, D., 52–53
Carcedo, R. J., 315, 321
Carey, J. W., 298, 311
Carlisle, M., 217, 228
Carlsen, G. R., 111, 122
Carlson, R. E., 181, 191
Carnegie, D., xiv, xix
Carpenter, B. M., 143, 159
Carrere, S., 93, 104
Carson, V., 262, 275
Carstensen, L. L., 95, 104, 124
Carver, C. S., 274–275
Carwile, A. M., 166, 176
Casey, M. K., 256
Cassel, J., 212, 225
Cassirer, E., 319–320
Castleberry, S., B., 109, 123
Caughlin, J. P., 63, 71

Cegala, D., J., 47, 53, 115, 123
Cella, D., 263, 276
Center for Disease Control, 259, 275
Chadwick, M., 49, 54
Chapelsky Massimilla, D., 250, 257
Chapple, E., 41–43, 45, 53
Charles, S. T., 95, 104
Chartrand, T., 41, 53
Chastang, J. F., 224
Chatters, L., 263, 276
Chen, L., 45, 53
Chesebro, J. L., 254–256
Cheuk, W. H., 222, 228
Chiang, H., 54
Cicchetti, D., 279, 293
Cicirelli, V. G., 94, 104
Cissna, K., N., 15, 25, 36–37, 88–89, 190, 257, 294
Clandinin, D., 182, 190
Clark, L. A., 239, 245
Clark, M. C., 182, 190
Clark, M. S., 207
Clark, R. A., 223, 227
Coakley, C. G., 25
Coates, D., 5, 14
Coatsworth, J. D., 109, 123
Cody, M. J., 73, 88
Cohan, C. L., 217, 225
Cohen, S., 133, 136, 139–140, 213, 225
Coker, D. A., 115–116, 123
Collins, N. L., 217, 226
Comstock, J., 145, 158
Comte-Sponville, A., 58–59, 61–62, 64, 66–70, 74–77, 88
Condon, W., 41, 43, 53
Conley, C. S., 318, 321
Connelly, F., 182, 190
Conrad, A., 53
Constantine, N. A., 281–282, 293
Contractor, N., 153, 159
Cook, A., 316, 321
Cook, G., 30, 37
Cook, M., 109, 121
Cook. S., 262, 274
Cooper, C. L., 311–312
Cooper, H., 286, 293

Cooper, L. 113, 122–123
Corbin, J., 169, 177
Cordini, G., 159
Corman, S. R., 166, 175
Costanzo, P. R., 301, 312
Cotton, S., 262, 273, 275
Coupland, J., 96, 104
Cox, D. S., 232, 245
Cramer, D., 216, 226
Crick, N., 19, 31, 37
Crisp, R., 47, 53
Crocker, J., 318, 320
Cronen, V. E., 19, 35, 37
Crumley, L. P., 194, 209
Csikszentmihalyi, I. S., 207–208
Csikszentmihalyi M., 1, 4, 7, 14–15, 20–24, 37, 40, 53, 74, 88, 194, 207–209, 252, 258, 280, 294, 303, 312
Cunningham, M. R., 222, 224
Cupach, W. R., vii, 1, 4, 8–9, 14–15, 19, 33, 35, 37, 57, 72, 78–88, 313–314, 320–321, 324–325
Cupples, L. A., 140
Cutrona, C. E., 217, 226
Czarniawaska, B., 182, 190

•D•

Daigle, M., 318, 320
Dailey, R. M., 291, 293
Dainton, M., 289, 293, 295
Dake, J. A., 282, 294
Dalton, D., G., 179–180, 182, 191
Daly, J. A., 52, 115, 123, 225, 227
Daniel, J., 44, 53, 326
Darling, R., 110, 125
Darwin, C., 130, 139
Daubman, K. A., 232, 245
Daughton, S. M., 115, 123
Dauria, A. F., 181, 191
Davies, P., 49, 54
Davis, H. B., 167, 175
Davis, K., 65, 70
Davis, M., 53, 54
Dawson, E. J., 158
de Ruyter, K., 109, 123

de Waal, F. B. M., 198, 207
Dean, K. W., 162, 176, 325
Dearing, J. W., 251, 256
Deetz, S., 83, 88, 298, 312
DeGood, D., 137, 139
DeGooyer, D., 19, 23, 26, 32, 36
Delaney, P., 141
Delia, J. G., 118, 123
Dempsey, S. E., 292–293
Denham, S. A., 204, 207
Derlega, V. J., vi, 3, 259, 262, 274, 325
Destefano, M., 318, 320
DeSteno, D., 40, 55
Dewey, J., 20–24, 30–31, 34, 37–38
Diamond, L. M., 137, 139
Diaz,M., 281, 293
diBattista, P., 45, 52
Dillard, J. P., 25, 37, 80, 88, 117, 123
Dindia, K., 63, 70, 71, 88
Dion, K. K., xiv, xix
Dixon, L., 48, 54
Donoho, C. J., 224
Doster, J. A., 143, 159
Downs, V. C., 133, 139, 209, 325–326
Drake, D. R., 294
Dryden, J., 282–293
DuBois, D. L., 286–287, 293, 295
Duck, S. W., v, xi–xiii, xvii, xix, 1, 4, 8–9, 14, 22, 37, 88, 158, 245, 319–320
Duckworth, A. L., 196–197, 207
Duffey, N. S., 165, 175
Duggal, H. V., 103
Duggan, J., 276
Dun, T., 158
Duncan, H. D., 162, 175
Duncan, L. G., 109, 123
Duong, D., 55
Dutton, J. E, xv, xix, 71
Dyer, A. R., 136, 139

•E•

Eadie, W. F., 123, 181, 191
Eaves, L., 209
Ebesu Hubbard, A. S., 115, 123
Eckholm, E., 66, 71
Eden, J., 140
Educational Testing Service, 123

Edwards, O. W., 280, 284, 293
Egan, G., 299, 304, 311
Eisenberg, E. M., 24, 37
Eisenberger, R., 120, 123
Elliot, A. J., 230, 244
Ellis, C., 79, 88
Emerson, C., 24, 36, 37
Emmers-Sommer, R. M., 150, 159
Emmons, R., 271, 275
Enright, R. D., 194–195, 197–199, 204, 207–208
Enström, M. K., 317, 321
Epstein, R., 128, 139
Essex, M., 133, 141
Ethier, N., 55
Exline, J. J., 77, 88

•F•

Farinelli, L., 140
Farquhar, J. W., 251, 256
Feeney, B. C., 217, 226
Fehr, B., 104
Feinberg, J., 275
Feldman, R. S., 52, 136, 140
Feldstein, S., 40, 53
Felitti, V. J., 320
Feng, B., 211, 215–216, 220, 222, 226–227, 231, 239, 244–245, 290, 294, 326
Ferrell, J., 273–274
Ferri, E., 91, 103
Ferris, A. L., 209
Figueiredo, M. L., 217, 226
Figueroa-Muñoz, A., 89
Fingerman, K. L., 315, 320
Finkel, E. J., 198, 209
Finkelhor, D., 277, 295
Finkenauer, C., 314, 320
Finnegan, J. R., 257
Fisch, R., 279, 295
Fisher, B. A., 307, 311
Fisher, C. L., 104
Fisher, W. R., 315, 320
Fishman, E., 137, 139
Fitch-Hauser, M., 112, 114, 120–122
Fitzgibbons, R. P., 195, 198, 207
Fitzpatrick, M. A., 118, 123–124
Flora, J. A., 251, 256

Floyd, F. J., 222, 228
Floyd, K., 1–2, 6, 11, 13, 73, **88**, 116–117, 120, 123, 129–130, 132, 134–138, 140
Foley, M., 26, 36
Folkman, S., 213, 227
Foss, K. A., 308, 311
Foss, S. K., 308, 311
Foster, J. D., 319, 321
Foucault, M., 62, 71
Frank, A. W., 67, 71
Frazier, P., 317, 321
Fredrickson, B. L., 13–14, 196, 207, 304, 311–312
Freedman, S. R., 197, 199, 207–208
Frey, L., 3, 7, 15, 257, 294, 297, 326
Fries, E., 217, 226
Frost, P. J., 71

•G•

Gable, S. L., 230–232, 239, 244–245
Gallo, L. C., 141
Gallois, C., 46–47, 53–54
Gardner, K. A., 217, 226
Garsoffky, B., 182, 190
Gattegno, C., 159
Gavrilova, N., 99, 104
Gayle, B. M., 164, 176
Gearhart, C. G., 113, 123
George, A., 91, 249, 275, 326
Gergen, K., 191
Gibb, J. R., 302, 311
Giles, H., 9–10, 14, 46–47, 54, 320
Gillath, O., 295
Gillihan, S. J., 223, 227
Gillum, R. F., 136, 140
Gilmour, R., xix
Gilstrap, C. M., 223, 225
Ginat, J., 231, 245
Gingell, C., 104
Glaser, M., 135, 141, 182, 190
Glaser, R., 135, 141
Glasser, D. B., 104
Gleason, M. E. J., 213, 226
Goff, P., 49, 54
Goffman, E., 47, 54, 59, 71
Goldberg, M., 224

Goldsmith, D. J., 122, 214, 217, 219, 222, 225–226, 235, 238, 244–245
Golish, T. D., 63, 71
Gonzaga, G. C., 231, 244
Goodall, H. L., 180–181, 190
Goodson, I. F., 179–180, 182, 191
Goody, E. N., 70
Goold, P., 103
Gordon, J., 298, 312
Gordon, K. C., 197, 200, 201–203, 208
Gordon, U. L, 133, 139,
Gorham, J., 254–257
Goss, B., 114, 123
Gottlieb, B. H., 224–225
Gottman, J. M., 8, 13–14, 93, 104, 124, 230, 245
Gouin, J. P., 213, 227
Gould, S. J., 314, 320
Goven, A. J., 159
Graen, G. B., 116, 119, 123
Graf, M., 232, 245
Graham, E. E. 109, 164–165, 173, 175
Grant, A. M., 222, 226
Green, V. A., 132, 140, 318, 320
Greenberg, M. T., 109, 123, 195, 208
Greenberger, D., 288, 295
Greene, J. O., 45, 53, 81, 88, 125, 225, 228, 244
Greene, K., 261–262, 275
Greenfield, S., 250–251, 257
Grewal, D. D., 196, 208
Grewen, K. M., 137, 141
Grossman, J. B., 286, 293
Gruenewald, T. L., 142, 214, 226
Gruner, C. R., 161–162, 175
Gudykunst, W. B., 52, 54
Guerrero, L. K., 219, 224–226, 244
Gunn, G., 55
Gurung, R. A. R., 142
Gustafson, D., 98, 103, 139

•H•

Haas, S., 289, 295
Haberman, M. R., 128, 142
Habermas, J., 117, 124
Hagestad, G., 94, 104
Haidt, J., 88

Hale, J., 45, 53, 144, 159, 291, 293
Hall, E. T., 43–45, 54
Hall, J. R., 317, 320
Hall, J. A., 125
Halone, K. K., 113, 124, 140
Hamby, S. L., 277, 295
Hamilton, G. V., xiv, xix
Hamilton, M. A., 280–281, 284, 293
Hamilton, S. F., 280–281, 284, 293
Hammack, P. L., 182, 191
Hammerschmidt, H., 96, 104
Hampes, W. P., 165, 176
Hanasono, L. K., 122
Hancks, M., 47, 55
Handler, L. 143, 159
Hangerup, L. M., 136, 141
Hannawa, A. F., 140
Hannon, P. A., 198, 209
Hantsoo, L., 213, 227
Harden-Fritz, J. M., 10, 14
Hargrave, T. D., 198, 208
Harrington, K. V., 165, 176
Harrison, J., 49, 54
Harrison, R., 53
Harris-Wyatt, V., 294
Harstveit, M., 317, 321
Hart, R. P., 181, 191
Hatfield, E., 288, 295
Hause, K. S., 159
Hay, E. L., 315, 320
Hazan, C., xiv, xix
Hecht, M. L., 74, 89
Heckman, T., 259, 261–262, 270, 276
Helmick, R. G., 209
Hemingway, H., 61, 217, 228
Henderson, A. S., 133, 141
Hendeson, G. M., 256
Henderson, M., 144–145, 158
Hendrick, 26, 37, 154, 159
Henley, N., 72
Henneberger, M., 100, 104
Hennig, K. H., 318, 320
Herberman, R., 136, 142
Herbert, T. B., 136, 140
Herrick, L. R., 109, 117, 124
Hess, J., 140
Hesse, C., 130, 134, 140
Hetherington, E. M., 104
Hewstone, M., 47, 53
Higgins, E. T., 245

Highhouse, S., 302, 312
Hill, P. C., 54, 88, 128, 141, 273, 275
Hjelmquist, E., 80, 88
Hobbs, S. A., 74, 88
Hodgson, F. M., 159
Hodnicki, D., 273–274
Holahan, C. J., 216, 228
Holloway, B. E., 286, 293
Holman, E., 316, 321
Holmstrom, A. J., 122, 216–217, 221, 223, 225–226, 239, 245
Holquist, M., 36
Holter, A. C., 194, 196, 197, 204, 208
Holt-Lunstad, J., 137, 140
Honeycutt, J, M., 122, 164, 176
Horowitz, M., 48, 54
Houldin, A., 142
Howard, S., 289–293
Hughes, C. F., 135, 141
Huntington, R., 120, 123
Husband, R. L., 113, 123
Hutchison, S., 120, 123

•I•

Iida, M., 213, 226
Ikeda, A., 213, 226
Imhof, M., 115, 122, 124
Impett, E. A., 245
Ingram, K. M., 217, 226
Innes, J. M., xiii–xix
International Listening Association, 121, 123–125
Ipe, M., 63, 71
Ironson, G., 263, 275
Isen, A. M., 232, 244–245

•J•

Jaccard, J., 216, 228
Jackson, D. D., 307, 312
Jacobi, L., 10, 14
Jahoda, M., 315, 320
Jandorf, L., 232, 245
Jannoff–Bulman, R., 14
Janov, A., 132, 140
Janusik, L., 110, 114, 124

Javidi, M., 133, 139
Jayson, S., 66, 71
Jensen, M., 57, 71
Jeong, H. K., 182, 191
Jerskey, B. A., 209
Johnson, M. D., 228, 282, 293
Jones, E., 46, 53
Jones, S. M., 25, 37, 109–110, 113, 122, 124, 212, 216–217, 219, 226–227
Jones, W. H., 74, 88
Judd, J., 140

•K•

Kabat-Zin, J., 274–275
Kalbfleisch, P. J., 164, 176, 289, 295
Kaloupek, D. G., 136, 139
Kannel, C., 136, 140
Kanov, J., 68, 71
Kanz, J. E., 198, 208
Kaplan, A., 110, 114, 124
Kaplan, S., 250, 257
Karcher, M. J., 286, 293, 295
Karney, B. R., xiii, xix, 217, 225
Kaslow, F. W., 96, 104
Kassing, J. W., 62, 71
Katula, R. A., 298, 312
Katz, P. 53
Kaufmann, W., 37, 89
Kawachi, I., 213, 226
Kayser, K., xix, 226
Kearns, J. N., 198, 208
Keating, T., 274–275
Keefe, B. P., 257
Keenan, P., 217, 227
Kellar-Gunther, Y., 166, 175
Kellett, P. M., 2, 12, 179–182, 190–191, 297, 326
Kelley, D. L., 2, 12, 57, 193–200, 203, 205, 208–209, 254–255, 257
Kelly, B., 165, 177
Kelly, C. M., 111–112, 121, 124
Keltner, D., 166, 176
Kendon, A., 40, 54
Kennedy-Moore, E., 245
Kennell, J. H., 217, 227
Kent, M. L., 116, 124
Kessler, R. C., 133, 139, 141

Key, M., 55
Keyes, C. L. M., 88
Khemlani, S., 318, 320
Khorsand, S., 256, 257
Kiecolt-Glaser, J. K., 135, 141, 213, 227
Kikihara, C., 77, 89
Kilborne, B., 89
Kim, H-K., 25, 37, 57, 71
Kim, Y. Y., 2, 11, 46–49, 52, 54, 79
Kinney, T. A., 1, 8, 9, 14, 314, 320
Kirkpatrick, K. T., 278, 280, 293
Klaus, M. H., 217, 227
Klein, J. D., 282, 294
Klein, L. C., 142
Knapp, M., 225, 227
Knee, C. R., 316, 321
Knopp, R. H., 141
Knutson, J., 199, 204, 208
Kodjo, C., 294
Koenig, H., 263, 274–275
Koerner, A. F., 118, 124
Komisaruk, B. R., 132, 141
Konrath, S., 319, 321
Kramarae, C., 72
Krause, N., 275
Kreps, G. L., 2, 3, 7, 249–251, 253–254, 256–258
Krippendorff, K., 265, 275
Kroll, A. B., 222, 228
Kruglanski, A. W., 245
Kubota, S., 113, 124
Kubzansky, L., 141
Kucharewski, R., 282, 294
Kumar, M., 275
Kunkel, A. W., 231, 244, 295

•L•

La Valley, A. G., 140
LaFrance, M., 41, 54
Lakens, D., 39, 54
Lakin, M., 301, 312
Langer, E., 47, 54
Langess, L. L., 89
Langston, C. A., 231, 245
Larson, D. B., 262, 275
Laumann, E. O., 97, 104
Lazarus, R. S., 49, 54, 213, 227

Leary, M. R., 131, 139
Lebel, U., 57, 72
Leclerc, A., 224
Ledbetter, A. M., 119, 124
Lederman, L., 257
Ledford, C., 257
Leets, L.. 66, 72
Leffert, N., 282–283, 294
Lemery, E. P., 41, 52
Leo, R. J., 316, 321
Leonard, A., 276
Leszcz, M., 312
Levasseur, D. G., 162, 176
Levenson, R. W., 124
Levin, J., 262–263, 274–276
Levinger, G., xv, xix
Levinson, R. W., 59, 70, 104
Lewinsohn, P. M., 232, 245
Lewis, B. P., 142
Lewis, C. S., 127, 141
Lewis, K., 294
Lewis, M. I., 98, 104
Liapunov, V., 36
Lichtman, R. M., 220, 227
Lieberman, M. A., 302, 312
Light, K. C., 137, 140–141
Lilius, J., 71
Lin, Y. C., 143, 159
Lindau, S. T., 97–99, 104
Lindberg, H. A., 139
Lindholm, K., 49, 55
Lindquist, R., 109, 125
Lindsey, 80, 88
Lipari, A. E., 113, 124
Lipsitt, L. 141
Littig, L. W., 144, 158
Lockwood, C. M., 316, 321
Loh, B., 272, 276
Long, H. 45, 54
Lopez, S. J., 208
Luborsky, L., 142
Luecken, L. J., 141
Lujan, P., 48, 54
Lundsteen, S. W., 112, 124
Lutgen-Sandvik, P., 66, 71
Lyon, A., 64, 71
Lyons, M. J., 209
Lyubomirsky, S., 6, 15

•M•

Maccoby, M., 251, 256
MacGeorge, E. L. 2, 4, 13, 93, 211–216, 218–220, 222–223, 225–228, 231, 239, 245, 290–291, 294, 326
MacIntyre, A., 57, 71
Mackinnon, A., 133, 141
Macrae, C. N., 40, 54
Madsen, R., 37
Magee, M. S., 141
Magnuson, C. M., 194, 208
Maitlis, S., 71
Mak, M. C. K., 213, 227
Makuc, D. M., 136, 140
Malcolm, W., 195, 208
Mangham, I. L., 311
Manusov, V. L., 73, 88
Mariani, T., 174, 176
Markowitcz, L. E., 105
Marmot, M. G., 217, 228
Martin, D. M., 164, 176
Martin, M., 123
Maselko, J., 128, 141
Maslow, A. H., 49, 54, 303, 312
Matejka, L., 38
Matlin, M., 13, 15
Matos, M., 294
Matyok, T., 191
McCann, B. S., 136, 141
McCarthy, S., 276
McCarthy, T. A., 124
McCroskey, J. C., 52, 123, 254–256
McCullough, J. D., 2, 4, 12, 68, 93, 122, 229, 244–245
McCullough, M. E., 195–196, 198, 208, 262, 271, 275
McDonald, M., 313, 321
McEvoy, C., 318, 320
McEwan, B., 140
McGhee, P. E., 165, 175
McHorney, C., 257
McKay, J. R., 142
McLaughlin, M. L., 88
McLeroy, K. R., 294
McMillen, C., 321
McNicholas, S. L. 216, 227
Meador, K., 263, 275
Mechanic, D., 109, 124
Melchior, M., 224

MENTOR, 286, 294
Metts, S., 78, 88, 154, 159
Meyer, B., 317, 321
Meyer, G., 256
Meyer, J. C., 1, 2, 12–13, 161, 163, 165, 176, 219
Meyer, S. 109, 124
Miczo, N., 2, 9, 12, 73, 87–88, 140, 164–165, 174, 176, 297, 327
Mielke, R. K., 159
Mikkelson, A. C., 140
Miles, L., 40, 54, 302, 312
Miller, K. I., 25, 37, 57, 68, 71
Miller, L., 46, 55
Miller, N., 53
Miller, W. R., 275
Miller-Day, M., ix, 91, 93, 104
Mills, C. B., 166, 169, 176
Mirivel, J. C., 2, 6, 9, 11, 57, 60, 64, 71, 76, 255, 297, 304, 327
Mishima, N., 113, 124
Mokros, H. B., 298, 312
Monge, P., 153, 159
Montgomery, B. M., 70
Moore, D. W., 277, 295
Moorefield, R., 159
Moreria, E., 104
Morgan, W. M., 281, 291, 295
Morman, M. T., 130, 140
Morreall, J., 161–162, 165, 174, 176
Motley, M., 227, 294
Mrus, J., 275, 276
Muircheartaigh, C. A., 104
Muller, R., 273–274
Mullett, J., 41, 52
Mumford, V . E., 280, 293
Murdoch, K., 109, 124
Musselman, D. L.,133, 142
Myers, K. A. 66, 71
Myers, S. A., 57, 70, 109, 124

•N•

Nagata, S., 113, 124
Nakamura, J., 74, **88**
Napoli, A., 245
National Research Council, 279, 281, 294
Neal, K., 204, 207, 232, 245

Nebel, S., 19, 33, 36, 327
Neck, C. P., 165, 176
Nepo, M., 61, 72
Nesdale, D., 49, 55
Nezleck, J. B., 245
Nichols, R., 111, 124
Nicholson, N. A., 133, 141
Nicolosi, A., 104
Niedhammer, I., 224
Nietzsche, F., 76–77, 89
Nilsen, T. R., 64, 72
Nind, L., 40, 54
Nir, T., 209
Norton, R., 55, 147, 159, 245, 295, 312
Norwood, K. M., xiv, xix, 19, 33, 36, 38, 125, 159, 327
Notarius, C. I., 109, 117, 124
Nowicki, G. P., 232, 245
NTL Institute, 302, 312
Nussbaum, J., ix, 2, 7, 91–97, 101–102, 104, 125, 257, 327

•O•

O'Callaghan, J., 314, 321
O'Cleirigh, C., 275
O'Connor, T., 260–261, 270, 275
O'Heeron, R. C., 135, 141
Ogay, T., 47, 54
Ogston, W., 41, 53
Okami, P., 318, 321
Okun, M. A., 316, 321
Oleson, K. C., 195, 207
Oliver, J. M., 133, 141
Olowokure, B., 103
Oman, R. F., 282, 294
Oudenhoven, J. P., 49, 55

•P•

Padilla, A., 49, 55
Padula, C. A., 216, 227
Paffenbarger, R. S.,140
Paik, A., 104
Palagi, E., 143, 159
Palmer, M. T., 117, 123, 190
Papa, M. J., 175

Pargament, K. I., 195, 208, 261, 263, 270–276
Park, N., xix, 37, 52–53, 207, 209, 245, 256
Parker, R. G., 81, 88
Parkerson, G., 263, 275
Parks, A. C., 197, 209
Parks, M. R., 78, 89, 318, 321
Parrott, R., 257
Pasch, L. A., 228
Pasupathi, M., 109, 113, 124
Patrick, B. C., 236, 245, 320
Paul, O., xiii, 101, 139
Pauley, P. M., 130, 134, 140
Pausch, R., 58, 72
Pavlik, J. V., 251, 257
Pearson, J. C., 144, 156, 159, 191
Pecchioni, L. L., 93, 104, 113, 124
Pelzer, D., 66, 72
Pena, E. F., 158
Pence, M., 122
Pendell, S. D., 117, 125
Pennebaker, J. W., 135, 141
Perez, L., 263, 274–275
Perlman, D., 158, 315, 321
Perreyclear, M., 260–261, 270, 275
Perrin, F. A. C., xiv, xix
Perry, B. D., 171–172, 320
Persky, V., 139
Peterman, A., 263, 275–276
Peters, F. H., 70
Petersen, R. L., 209
Peterson, C., 1, 4–7, 11–12, 15, 52, 55, 70, 72, 194, 208–209, 260, 276, 298, 303, 312
Petronio, S., 62, 72, 78, 89
Pharm, L., 263, 276
Piaget, J., 143, 159
Pickering, S., 204, 207
Pieper, K. M., 209
Pirsig, R., 57–58, 72
Pittman, K., 280, 293
Pitts, L., 1, 15
Pitts, M. L. ix, xvi, 1, 3, 15, 212
Planalp, S., 223, 225
Pogue, L., 254, 255, 258
Pokorny, J. J., 198, 207
Polek, E., 49, 55
Pörhölä, M., 1, 8, 9, 14, 314, 320
Potter, J., 66, 72

Powers, W. G., 115–116, 125
Prager, K. J., 93, 104, 117, 125, 132, 141
Pressey, L. C., 220, 227
Price, J. H., 282, 294
Priem, J. S., 217, 227
Proyer, R. T., 85, 89
Ptacek, K. M., 110, 125
Puchalski, C., 275
Punyanunt, N. M. 164, 176

•Q•

Query, J. L., 249, 254, 257–258
Quinn, W. H., 132, 141
Quyang, J., 40, 55

•R•

Rachal, K. C., 195, 208
Rack, J. J., 25, 37, 117, 122–123
Raftery, M., 141
Ragins, B., xv, xix
Ramey, S. L., 216, 228
Rao, N., 256
Rashid, T., 197, 209
Ray, E. B., 312
Reblin, M., 216, 227
Reeb, A., 141
Reeves, C., 261, 275
Reis, H. T., 113, 125, 230, 236, 244–245
Revenson, T. A., xix, 226
Reznick, J., 40, 52

Rhodes, J. E., 286, 293
Rhodes, S. C., 112–113, 125
Rholes, W. S., 213, 227
Rice, R. E., 256
Rich, C. O., 164, 176
Rideout, G., 318, 321
Ridge, A., 112, 121, 125
Riforgiate, S., 134, 140
Riley, C. A., 159
Rime, B., 52
Ritchey, P., 276
Rittenour, C. E., 57, 70
Roberts, C. V., 112, 115, 125

Roberts, J. D., 112, 125
Roberts, R. E. L., 132, 141
Roberts, K. G., 36
Robinson, J. D., 37, 93, 104
Robinson, R. E., 20–21
Roblin, R., 24, 37
Rodine, M., 294
Roehlkepartain, E. C., 283, 294
Rogers, C., 61, 67, 72, 302, 312
Rogers, E. M., 256
Rold, M., 122
Ronel, N., 57, 72
Rosen, S., 222, 228
Rosenfeld, H., 47, 55
Rosenthal, R., 40–41, 52, 55, 142
Rosier, J. G., 122
Ross, J. D. C., 103
Rossiter, M., 182, 191
Rowan, J., 302, 312
Rowatt, T. L., 222, 224
Rowatt, W. C., 317, 321
Rubin, M., 47, 53
Ruch, W., 85, 89
Rudolph, K. D., 318, 321
Ruesch, J.. 40, 47, 55
Runyan, D., 277, 295
Rusbult, C. E., 198, 209
Russell, D. W., 217, 226

•S•

Sabaratnam, P., 294
Sabee, C. M., 115, 125
Sadler, P., 40–41, 55
Sahlstein, E., 158
Saitzyk, A. R., 222, 228
Salem, P., 257
Salman, C. T., 257
Salomonson, K., 223, 228
Salovey, P., 196, 208
Saltzman, K. M., 216, 228
Samter, W., 175, 217, 225, 227–228, 231, 244
Sandage, S. J., 128, 141
Sanders, R., 47, 55
Sanford, K., 317, 321
Santiago-Rivera, A. L., 92, 104
Santos, M. J., 204, 207

Sarason, I. G., 122, 214, 225
Sassi, M., 81, 88
Savage, G., 53
Scales, M., 49, 54
Scales, P. C., 280, 282–284, 294
Schaie, K., 275
Scheier, M., 274, 275
Scherer, K. R., 234, 245
Schillinger, J. A., 105
Schkade, D., 6, 15
Schlenker, B. R., 205, 209
Schmais, A., 41, 55
Schmais, C., 41, 55
Schmid, P. F., 307, 312
Schmidt, K., 142
Schon, D., 190
Schrader, S. M., 191
Schrimshaw, E., 259, 261, 276
Schrodt, P., 110, 116, 119, 124–125
Schroll, M., 136, 141
Schumm, L. P., 104
Schutz, W. C., 303, 312
Schwan, B., 182, 190
Schwartz, J., 66, 72
Sclafani, R., 24, 37
Scott, W. A., 265, 276
Search Institute, 279–282, 284, 294
Seeger, M. W., 62, 72
Seeman, T. E., 213–214, 225–226
Seery, M. D., 316, 321
Seibert, J. H., 110, 125
Seligman, M. E. P., 1, 4, 5, 11–12, 15, 40, 52, 55, 70, 72, 94, 103–104, 194, 196–197, 207–209, 252, 258, 260, 276, 280, 294, 303, 312
Sellnow, T. L., 64, 72
Selye, H., 133, 141
Serra-Roldan, R., 280, 293
Sesma, A., 283, 294
Shah, P., 276
Shanty, J., 262, 275
Shapiro, R. M., 132, 142
Sharlin, S. A., 95–97, 104
Sharma, A. R., 294
Sharples, T., 101, 104
Shaver, P., xiv, xix
Shekelle, R. B., 139
Sheldon, K. M., 6, 15
Shepard, 301, 311
Shepherd, H. A., 109, 123

Sherman, S., 275
Shillingford, M. A., 280, 293
Shively, C. A., 133, 142
Shockley-Zalabak, p. 292–293
Shrout, P. E., 213, 226
Shuntich, R. J., 132, 142
Shurcliff, A., 161, 176
Sieburg, E., 25, 37
Siegel, K., 259, 261, 276
Siegman, A., 53
Silipigni, R., 311–312
Silver, R., 316, 321
Sim, T., 272, 276
Simpson, J. A., 83, 88, 213, 227
Skoog, I., 98, 103, 139
Sleight, C., 25, 37
Slote, M., 75, 79, 89
Smart, L., 318, 320
Smith, G., 103
Smith, P., 46, 54
Smith, S. L., 195, 209
Smith, S. W., 195, 209, 225, 291, 294
Smith, W. J., 165, 176
Smitherman, G., 44, 53
Snyder, C. R., 13, 15, 125, 197, 200, 208, 252, 258
Socha, T. J., ix, xvi, 1, 3, 5, 7, 10, 15, 165, 177, 212, 259, 276, 280, 283–285, 291, 294, 297, 312, 323–325
Soeken, K., 262, 275
Solomon, D. H., 117, 123, 217, 227
Solomon, G., 275
Somera, L., 25, 37
Somlai, A., 259, 261–262, 270, 276
Sowa, D., 120, 123
Speer, R., 9, 10, 14
Spencer, R., 288, 289, 294
Spiro, M. E., 79, 89
Spitzberg, vii, 1, 4, 8–9, 14–15, 19, 33, 35, 37, 57, 72, 74, 89, 313–314, 316–318, 320–321, 324, 327
Sprecher, S., 104, 288, 294–295
St. Clair, R., 54
St. Cyr, K., 116, 122
St. Louis, M. E., 105
Stafford, L., 159, 289, 291, 293, 295
Stallworth, L. M., 109, 124
Stamler, J., 139
Stang, D., 13, 15
Stansfeld, S. A., 217, 228

Stark, R., 273, 276
Steele, C., 49, 54
Steele, S., 52, 55
Steen, T. A., 196, 207, 209
Steil, L. K., 120, 125
Steptoe, A., 256
Sternberg, R. J., 145, 159
Stiff, J. B., 25, 37
Stocker, S. L., 198, 209
Stone, A. A., 232, 245
Story, L, B., xix, 278
Strachman, A., 231, 244
Straus, M. A., 277, 279, 295
Strauss, A., 169, 177
Strazdins, L., 317, 321
Strickland, D., 257
Strom, B., 85, 89
Stroud, S. R., 19, 21, 23, 31, 38
Sullivan, K. T., 226, 228, 217
Sullivan, M., 216, 227
Sullivan, W. M., 37,
Sunwolf, 66, 72
Swidler, A., 37
Sypher, B. D., 110, 125
Sypher, H. 47, 52
Szaflarski, M., 262, 276

•T•

Tafoya, M. A., 140
Tajfel, H., 48, 55
Tamborini, R., 223, 228
Tannen, D., 31–32, 38, 70, 72
Tarakeshwar, N., 276
Tardy, C., 159
Tarli, S., 143, 159
Tashiro, T., 317, 321
Tax, A., 142
Taylor, D., 53
Taylor, J. R., 81, 89
Taylor, M., 116, 124
Taylor, R., 263, 276
Taylor S. E., 131, 142
Tedder, M., 179, 182, 191
Tellegen, A., 239, 245
Temerson, C., 70
Terry, L., 262, 275
Thatcher, M., 26, 36

Thijs, J., 48, 50, 55
Thomas, D. L., 132, 139
Thompson, E. R., 215, 227, 290, 294
Thompson, T. L., 93, 104, 257
Thorensen, C. E., 195, 208
Thorne, B., 72
Thornton, B. C., 250, 256–257
Threnhauser, E., 298, 312
Tieu, T., 63, 71
Tillich, P., 61–62, 72
Tillmann–Healy, L. M., 88
Tipton, S. M., 37
Titunik, I. R., 38
Toledo, J. R., 159
Tracy, K., 59, 72
Tracy, M. F., 109, 125
Tracy, S. J., 50, 72
Traupmann, J., 288, 295
Trent, J. S., 37
Tripp, T. M., 33, 38
Trout, D., 40–41, 55
Tsevat, J., 275–276
Tsuang, T. M., 195, 209
Turken, U., 232, 244
Turkheimer, E., 137, 139
Turkle, S., 11, 15
Turner, J., 48, 55
Turner, L., 15
Turner, R. G., 260–261, 270, 276
Tusing, K., 140
Twenge, J. M., 319, 321

•U•

Uchino, B. N., 214, 216, 227–228
Uhl-Bien, M., 116, 119, 123
Ulmer, R. R., 64, 72
Underwood, L. G., 92, 104, 225
University of Pennsylvania Positive Psychology Center, 7, 15
Updegraff, J. A., 142
USDHHS, 277, 295
Utne, M. K., 288, 295

•V•

Valdesolo, P., 40, 55

Valdimarsdottir, H., 232, 245
Valentine, J. C., 286, 293
van Baaren, R., 41, 53
van Dulmen, M., 294
van Lear, C., 53
Vangelisti, A. L., 115, 123, 194, 209, 230, 245, 295
Vaughan, M., 141
Vaughn, A. A., 217, 228
Veatch, T. C., 163, 177
Veksler, A. E., 140
Verschueren, J., 55
Vesely, S., 294
Villa, D., 84, 86, 89
Villagran, M. M., 257
Villaume, W. A., 110, 125
Vinson, L., 115, 125
Viswanath, K., 257
Vogl-Bauer, S., 289, 295
Vohs, K. D., 314, 320
Voloshinov, V. N., 20, 27, 38
Voorpostel, M. 217, 228

•W•

Wachholtz, A., 276
Wackman, D. B., 257
Waern, M., 98, 103, 139
Wagatsuma, Y., 49, 55
Waite, J., 104
Waldhart, E. S., 112, 122
Waldron, V., 194–200, 203, 205, 208–209
Walker, J. D., 320
Walker, L. J., 318, 320
Wallace, L. A., 159
Walster, G. W., 288, 295
Walton, R. E., 179, 191
Walton, S., 49, 55
Wan, C. K., 216, 228
Wang, T., 104
Wanzer, M. B., 164, 167, 177
Ward, D., 103
Ward, S. A., 181, 191
Ware, J., 250, 257
Warwar, S., 195, 208
Watanuki, S., 109, 125
Watson, D., 239, 245
Watson, K. W., 111–112, 122, 125

Watt, J., 53
Watzlawick, P., 279, 295, 307, 312
Wayment, H. A., 224
Weakland, J., 37, 279, 295
Weathers, M., 254, 257–258
Weaver, C., 110, 112, 115, 125
Weiner, B., 77, 89
Weintraub, J., 274–275
Weisberg, J., 128, 142
Welkowitz, J., 40, 53
Welter, R. E., 164, 176
Werking, K. J., 231, 244
Werner, P. D., 231, 245, 318, 320
West, C., 70, 72
West, L., 26, 37
West, R., 15
Wetherell, M., 66, 72
Wetzels, M. G. M., 109, 123
Whaley, B. B., 175, 225
Wheeless, L. R., 110, 125, 147, 159
Whipple, B., 132, 141
Whiteside, T., 136, 142
Whitfield, C., 320
Wiemann, J. M., 53, 125
Wilder, C., 37
Wildermuth, N. L., 132, 140
Wilkum, K. C., vi, 211, 219, 223, 227–228, 327
Willard, S. L., 133, 142
Williams, A., 20, 93, 94–95, 104
Williams, L. J., 120–121
Williams, R., 38
Williamson, P., 66, 71
Wills, T. A., 133, 139
Wilson, B. J., 204, 207
Wilson, J., 140
Wilson, S. R., vi, 3, 4, 7, 10–11, 77, 89, 115, 125, 225, 277–279, 281, 291–292, 294–295, 327
Winstead, B., 262, 274
Wirtz, J., 216, 219, 226–227
Witt, A. D., 115–116, 125
Wolvin, A. D., 122, 124–125
Wong, K. S., 222, 228
Wong, N. C. H., vi, 2, 11, 13, 130, 143–144, 150, 158, 174, 327
Wood, J. T., xii, xix, 84, 89, 298, 311
Woods, T., 263, 275
Woody, E., 55
Worchel, S., 49, 55–56

Worline, M. C., 71
Worthington, D. L., 112–113, 122
Worthington, E. L., 195–196, 198, 207–209, 271, 276
Wyatt, G., 294, 312

Xu, F., 101, 105

Yalom, I. D., 302–303, 312
Yingling, J. A., 10, 15, 323–324
Yoo, J. H., 209

Young, S. L., 166, 177

•Z•

Zapata, C. L., 167, 175
Zebrowitz, L. A., 114, 125
Zezima, K., 66, 71
Zhao, X., 257
Zimbardo, P. G., 63, 72
Zimmerman, D. H., 70, 72
Zimmerman, M. A., 286, 295
Zimpfer, D. G., 311
Ziv, A., 165, 177
Zorrilla, E. P., 136, 142
Zuravin, S., 318, 321

Subject Index

•A•

acknowledgement
    behavioral instructors, 60–61
    forgiveness, 201, 205
    support, 218, 230, 233
    See celebratory support
activity theories, 95
advice, 216, 218, 220–223
    advice response theory, 220–221
    in mentor relationships, 289–291
aesthetic moments, 21, 29–30
aesthetic performance, 31
aesthetic relating,
    creative action, 20–21
    definition, 19–20
    experience, 20–22, 30
    noninstrumentality, 22–23, 34
    process, 22
    structural approach, 30
    unity, 20, 23–26, 34
    See also goal driven communication
affection exchange theory, 116, 136, 138
    and listening, 117
    as explanation for affection
        behaviors, 130–131
affection
    and humor, 165
    and lifespan, 128
    and nurturing children, 291
    definition, 128–129
    vs. affectionate communication, 129
affectionate behaviors
    and relationships, 139
    as adaptive, 130–132
    as stress management, 133–135
    mental health benefits, 132–133
    physical competence, 135–137
affectionate communication, 128–129
    tripartite model, 129–130
altruism
    and mentorship, 290
    as forgiveness, 195–196, 198
ambivalence, 26, 314–319
anger, 13, 58, 60, 197, 201–202, 205, 304, 314, 317
    See forgiveness
    See negative emotions
apology, 198, 200, 203–205
appraisal theory, 213–214
appreciation of beauty/excellence, 12
    See aesthetic relating
archetypal conflict story, 179–181, 184
Aristotle, xvi, 57–58, 69, 73, 103
asset–building model vs. risk reduction model, 278, 280–285, 291
assurances
    See relational maintenance
asynchronous intercultural
    communication, 44–45
attachment, 131, 174
    and God, 272
    attachment theory, xiv, 217
attraction, xv, 315, 317
attractiveness, xiv, xvi, 317
authentic communication, 309
authenticity, 11, 2545, 303–308, 309

•B•

balance (positive and negative), xvi–xvii
bravery, 11, 194, 303, 304
Brown–Carlsen Listening Test, 111
bullying, 4, 66, 292, 283

•C•

Caesar, Julius, xi–xii
celebratory support, 93
    acknowledge target feelings, 233–234, 238, 241, 243–244
    and positive relational outcomes, 231–232
    and well–being, 232
    defined, 229
    encourage elaboration, 234–235, 238, 242, 243
    extending congratulations, 233, 238, 243
    frequency, 230
    offer to celebrate, 235–236, 238, 242, 243–244
    reciprocate emotions, 234, 238, 241–243
child abuse, 277
    dark side, 291, 318
    Gauvin, Aiyana, 278–280
    sexual, 318
    statistics, 277
child abuse prevention, 279–281, 285, 290–292
child maltreatment
    See child abuse
children
    adult children, 118–119
    and affection, 291
    and communication, 3, 42, 44, 74, 214, 323
    and forgiveness, 204–206
    and humor, 165, 173
    and listening, 118–119
    as assets, 277, 208–285 289–292
    behavioral instruction, 60–61
    play, 143–144
Cicero, xvi
citizen/ship, 76, 84, 87
closeness
    See immediacy
    See intimacy
cognition, 80, 82,
    and humor, 163
    and religion/spirituality, 264, 266, 268–269, 272–273
cognitive complexity
    and interpersonal communication, 118, 222–223
    and listening, 115, 118
cognitive reappraisal model, 235
cognitive–emotional theory of esteem support messages, 221
comforting messages, xv, 3–4, 117–118, 218–224, 230–231, 235
    and humor, 165, 167
    See compassion
    See immediacy
    See social support
commitment, 145, 150–151
communication and human relationships course, 298–301, 303–310
    positive psychology, 303–307
communication as a verbal art, 19, 31, 34
communication as performance, 31, 74, 144, 157
communication competence, 46–49, 86, 114–115, 181, 281
    and listening, 113
    competence model, 84, 86–87
    risks, 318
    See social competence
communication effectiveness, 84–87
    and conflict, 185
    and goals, 73, 78, 84, 86–87
    and health care, 249–251, 253–254, 256
    and humor, 9, 165–167
    and listening, 113, 118, 120
    and play, 149–151
    and support, 13, 215, 218, 220
    celebratory messages, 233–236, 243–244
communication engagement, 22–23, 48, 50–51, 74–75, 80, 85
    and immediacy, 255–256
communication ethics, 10, 57–58, 63–65, 78–79
communication excellence, 57–58, 73–74, 297, 300
    See virtues
communication skills, 73, 93, 308
communication strengths, 303–304, 309, 323
communication tasks of forgiveness, 200–203
community, xi, 27, 42–44, 52, 81

and abuse, 277–280, 283, 285, 290–292
compassion, 9, 25
    communication, 68
    empathy, 195
    virtue, 57-58, 67-68, 69, 75-76, 78
conflict
    and humor, 165–166, 167
    as bright side, 179, 190
    as co–constructed, 183–184, 190
    as dark side, 190
    as positive experience, 179–181, 184–185
    management of, 207, 281–282, 303
    narratives and antecedents, 182–183
    narratives and change, 187–190
    narratives and possibilities, 185–187
conformity orientation, 118–119
congratulations, 233, 243
    See celebratory support
constructivism, 116–119
continuity theories, 95
conversational flow, 32
conversational involvement, 74, 115
    See engagement
conversational orientation, 118
cooperation, 39–40, 46–47, 49
    and health, 250–255
coping
    and HIV, 259–262
    and prayer, 261–262
    elder adults, 93–94
    health, 252
    support, 213–214, 216, 220
    See religious/spiritual coping
courage, 11, 57–58, 61–63, 67, 69, 78, 194, 304–305
creativity, 11, 20–21, 25, 28–29, 31, 194
    and children, 143, 285
    and conflict, 179–180
    and culture, 47, 49
    and forgiveness, 196
    and play, 144
culture
    and affection, 130–131
    and communication, 31, 79. 81, 85
    and intimacy, 91–92
    and marriage, 95–96
    and sexuality, 97
    and virtue, 11, 196

dominant culture, 28
    See intercultural synchrony
curiosity, 11

•D•

dark side of interpersonal communication, 1–2, 8–10, 313–320
    abuse, 4, 190, 291
    conflict, 183, 190
    functional, 315, 318–319
    history, 4, 314
    normative, 314–315, 318–319
    poetic justice, 33–34
    vs. affection, 138
    vs. bright side, 19–20, 34
    See child abuse
dehumanizing communication, 62, 64, 66, 69, 67
depression, 6, 66, 132–133, 216, 262, 317–318
developmental assets for adolescence, 281–283
    See asset–building model vs. risk reduction model
dialectics, 316
    positive–negative communication 314–315
dialogic communication approach, 86–87, 180–181, 188
    and forgiveness, 199
    and listening, 67–68, 75
dialogue, 76, 78, 84–87, 307
    idealized, 28–29
    silent dialog, 80–83, 84, 89
dichotomous communication, xvi–xvii, 9, 314
difference as positive communication, 24–26
disclosure
    as courage, 62–63, 69
    celebratory support, 231–232
    supportive communication, 206
    interpersonal, 62–63, 69, 76–78
    medical/health, 64, 67, 250
discourse of rationality, 28
disease
    buffering disease, 133–136, 216

HIV, 259–262, 269–273
    sexually transmitted, 100–101
disengaged healthcare, 252–253
    medical language, 252–253, 255
disengagement theories, 95
dysfunctional communication, 315–316

•E•

Eichmann, Adolf, 82–83
emotion
    acknowledgment, 233–235, 239–240
    and affection, 117, 128–130, 131, 137–138
    and ambivalence, 316
    and bonding, 286
    and elaboration, 234–235, 238–240
    and expression, 300, 302, 304, 310
    and forgiveness, 195–197, 201–203, 205
    and health, 249–250
    and play, 143–144
    and reciprocation, 234, 238, 239–240
    and religion/spirituality, 261
    and rhythm, 30
    and support, 94, 96, 133, 212–219, 222, 230
    emotional communication literacy, 304
    emotional distress, 212
    emotional intelligence, 196
    emotion–focused messages, 221–222
    hard/soft emotions, 317–318
    negative emotions, 13, 196–197, 201–203, 205, 224, 304
    positive emotions, 13, 20, 195–197, 205, 212–213, 232, 259–260, 303–304, 307
    See affection
    See attachment
    See comforting messages
    See immediacy
empathy, 281
    and engagement, 75
    and intercultural communication competence, 49
    and listening, 47, 113, 115
    and love, 24–26
    in forgiveness, 195–196, 198, 203, 204
    in healthcare, 255
    See compassion
empowerment, 253, 281
encounter groups, 302–303, 310
engaged healthcare, 251, 253–256
engaged life, 196–197, 207
engaged research, 292
equity theory, 288–290
esteem support, 218, 221, 223
ethics, 78–79
    compassion, 68
    ethical life, 58
    interpersonal communication ethics, 8, 10
    medical ethics, 64–65
    Nicomachean ethics, 57–58
    responsibility, 64
eudemonia, 5–11, 14
expectations, 162–163
    and humor, 162–163, 164
    and intercultural communication, 45, 51
    and mentoring, 287, 289
    normative, 51, 75
experiential learning, 6–7, 297–299, 301, 305, 307–308
    pedagogy, 307, 309–310
external assets, children as, 281, 284, 291

•F•

Face, 58–59, 74–75, 77, 309–310
    and advice, 220
    attentiveness, 58–59, 69
fairness, 11–12, 288
    See justice
family communication patterns, 116, 118–119
family communication research, 5, 283
fidelity, 39, 76–78, 81, 85, 116, 253
first– and second–order change, 278–280
flourish, 7, 13, 128, 197
flow, 7–8, 20–21, 22–23, 40
    conversational flow, 32, 87
forgiveness, xii, 12, 57, 78
    and creativity, 194, 196

as positive communication, 194–197
defined, 194–194
family, 193–194, 200, 204–206
parent–child relationships, 193–194, 204–206
siblings, 193–194, 205–206
three stage forgiveness process, 200–203
to restore moral order, 194, 199, 201, 204–205
to restore relationships, 194, 198–199, 201, 204
to restore well–being, 194, 197, 201, 204
friendship, 94–95, 144–146
and play, 150–152, 156–158
dark side, xii
future mindedness, 194

•G•

Gauvin, Aiyana, 278–280
generosity, 51–58, 59–61, 69, 76, 85, 204
gentleness, 58–59
goal driven communication, 22–23, 25, 28, 31, 34–35, 73, 78, 80–87
and forgiveness, 199, 205
in supportive communication, 222–224
See aesthetic relating, noninstrumentality
goals, 7, 13
grandparent–grandchild relationship, 94
gratitude, 6–7, 12, 58, 222, 271, 273
group communication, 11
See communication and human relations course

•H•

happiness, xvi, 1, 5–9, 12–14, 196–197, 200, 207
and affection, 132, 139
and celebration, 233–234
and conflict, 180
and narrative, 182
authentic happiness, 40

eudemonic happiness, 8–10, 12
hedonic happiness, 12–14
harmony, 23, 41, 44
health
and intimacy, 93–96, 103
and sexuality, 98–101, 103
as positive communication outcome, 1
health decisions, 64–65, 249
See affectionate behaviors
See supportive communication
See well–being
health care
communication as central role, 249, 251
health communication, 249, 252
as positive interpersonal communication, 252
strengths–based approach, 252
health information, 216, 249, 250–251, 254
health promotion, 249, 250–251, 256
target audience, 251, 256
help
and reflective conversation, 75–76, 78, 82–84, 86
dark side, 317
helping others, 8–9
See empathy
See supportive communication
self help, 302–303
here–and–now communication, 299, 304, 309–310
high and low context communication, 44
high–risk adolescent behavior, 282–283
hope, 12, 194
in healthcare, 252
Snyder's hope theory, 13
and forgiveness, 194, 196, 199–200
religion/spirituality, 261, 268–269, 272–273
and positive psychology, 6–7, 194
humanistic psychology, 302
humanity, 11
humor, 12
and affection, 165
and ambivalence, 165–167
and children, 165
and expectation violation, 162–165, 173

and health, 165
and intimacy, 165
and mentor relationships, 289–290
and play, 165–166, 174
and sharedness, 163–164, 175
and unity, 161
appreciation, 165, 167, 174
as cognitive incongruity, 162, 173
as physiological relief, 161–162, 165
as psychological superiority, 162, 173
as relationship enhancer, 167, 175
as social cohesion, 164–165
at work, 163
dark side, 9
humor categories, 169–174
humor orientation, 164, 162
sources of, 161–163
teasing, 157, 162, 166
See play
hurtful communication, xvi, 8–9
and humor, 167, 169
relational hurt, 193–196, 198, 202, 207

•I•

identity
and humor, 164, 166, 174
dark side, 315
inclusivity and security, 40, 47–52
relational, 35, 151, 202
religious/spiritual identity, 271, 273
sexual identity, 63, 69
social identity, 48, 77, 157
See face
See intercultural synchrony
immediacy
and involvement, 75, 85
and listening, 115
in healthcare, 254–256
nonverbal, 255–256
verbal immediacy, 255
implicit communication, 39, 50–51
forgiveness, 199
listening, 115, 119, 121
support, 218, 236
individualism

as discourse, 27
in goals–plans–actions model, 86
informed decisions, 64–66, 69
instrumental support, 94, 218
as advice, 220–222, 230
intercultural synchrony
as biological, 42–43
as cultural, 43–45
as sociocultural, 42–43
asymmetric synchrony, 40–41
concurrent asymmetric synchrony, 41
defined, 39–40
in positive interpersonal communication, 40
individuation and convergence, 40, 46–47, 51
reciprocal asymmetric synchrony, 41
symmetric synchrony, 39, 40–41
See identity
See rhythm
intergenerational transmission of
communication, 118
forgiveness, 204
internal assets, children as, 280, 281–282
interpersonal cohesion, 40, 46–47, 50, 164–165
interpersonal revenge, 4, 33–35, 199, 202
interpersonal violence, 58–60
see child abuse
interpretive intelligence, 181, 185, 187, 190
intimacy, 92–93, 145
and humor, 165
and marriage, 96
and play, 144–145, 150–151, 156
elder adults, 93–95
health benefits, 93, 135–136
See affection

•J•

joy, 13, 20, 30, 233, 303
justice, 11–12, 204–204, 207

•K•

kindness, 11, 60, 120, 196, 204

•L•

laughter, 9, 163, 165, 173
    dark side, 66–67, 162
leadership, 11, 196
    leader–member–exchange theory, 119–120
life satisfaction, 5, 7, 94, 216, 316
lifespan
    and affection, 128
    and communication, 3, 10, 324
    and forgiveness, 201
    and intimacy, 92–96
    and marriage, 96
listening
    active listening, 68, 113
    and children, 285
    and forgiveness, 203
    and prayer, 264
    and support, 218, 235
    as compassion, 67–68, 69
    as complex of skills, 112
    as dialogic response, 75
    as lecture comprehension, 111
    as multidimensional construct, 115
    as positive interpersonal communication, 109–110
    as relating, 113
    as responding, 112–113
    as theory, 114–120
    cognitive phenomenon, 115, 117, 120–121
    history of, 111–113
    theories of, 116–120
longitudinal research
    and affection, 128
    and development, 283
    and play, 157
    and support, 213, 216
love, 127, 303
    aesthetic love, 20, 24–27, 32, 34–35
    as positive virtue, 11
    attachment, xiv
    compassionate love, 92
    forgiveness, 200
    moral love, 204
    romantic, 26–27
    See affection
    See intimacy
love–of–learning, 11

•M•

management communication, xv, 302
marital/romantic forgiveness, 193, 200–204,
marriage, 29
    older adult, 95–96
    satisfaction, 103, 131, 164, 217
meaningful life, 196–197, 200, 207
medical decision–making, 66, 69, 249–251, 253, 255
    See health
meditation, 261
mental health
    and affection, 132–133
    and intimacy, 94
    relationships, xv, 103
    See health
    See well-being
mentor, 58, 110
    See youth mentor
mercy, 12, 57, 194–196, 205
modesty/humility, 12, 196
morals
    appropriateness/functionality, 19, 35, 318
    moral order, 35, 163
    moral order and forgiveness, 194, 197, 199, 201, 204–205
    moral transgression, 193–194, 195, 199
    morality, 78–80
    See ethics

•N•

narrative, 91–92, 79
    narrative learning, 181–190
national training laboratory for group development, 302

need to belong theory, 131
negative emotions, 196–197, 202, 205, 304
   See anger
nonverbal communication
   and affection, 130, 134, 138
   and expectancy, 45
   and forgiveness, 201
   and immediacy, 255–256
   and listening, 112
   and play, 148, 156
   and support, 211, 219, 229, 233–234, 235
   and synchrony, 39, 41, 46, 48, 50

•O•

open–mindedness, 11
openness, 75–78
   and maintenance, 145, 289
optimal experiences, 7, 20–24, 93, 180, 297, 303
Our Kids, 277–280, 285

•P•

parent–child communication, 323–324
parent–child relationships, 193–194, 204–206, 118–119
   and abuse, 277–279, 285, 289–292
   and adult children, 94–97, 100
peace, 180, 182, 185, 261, 271
perseverance, 62, 194
persistence, 11
person–centered communication, 25, 47, 118, 218–219, 221–223
perspective, 11
physician–patient communication, 64, 249–250, 253
play
   adult typology, 144, 148–149, 154–156
   and humor, 165–166, 173, 174–175
   appropriateness, effectiveness, and uniqueness, 149, 151, 157
   child, 143
   creativity, 143–144
   frequency, 149–150, 154, 156
   functions, 150–152
   solidarity and satisfaction, 149, 152
   within adult friendships, 144–146
   within adult romantic relationships, 144–146
playfulness, 155–156
pleasant life, 196–197, 207
pleasure
   aesthetic pleasure, 20–21, 34–35
   See happiness
poetic justice, 33–34, 35
politeness, 74–78
politeness theory, 59
   See face
Pollyanna principle, 12–13
positive affect, 6, 213, 231–232, 235, 242–244
   religious/spiritual, 270–271, 273
positive attitudes, 12–13
positive character strengths, 8, 11–12, 52, 196, 200, 207
positive character traits, 271, 304–305, 307–308
positive individual traits, 303, 308
   See positive character strengths
positive institutions, 197, 285–286, 303, 308
   neighborhoods, 279, 284
   schools, 280–284, 285, 292, 303
positive interpersonal communication, 1–5, 7, 9–12, 13–14, 323–324
   and health, 252
   and listening, 109, 114–115
positive psychology, 1, 4–8, 11–14, 128, 194–197, 280, 301–309
positive/negative communication, 314, 316, 317–320
positivity bias, 4, 314
positivity ratio
   relationships, 13, 230
   religious/spiritual, 269, 272
prayer, 259–261, 262, 270–271
prison
   and religion/spirituality, 261
   as stressor, 260, 269–270
   statistics, 260–261
pro–social/anti–social communication, xvi, 1, 5, 8–10, 12
Protean self, 86–87

prudence, 12, 57–58, 96
psychological health, 73, 213, 143, 232, 272–273, 315
See mental health

•Q•

quality of life, 93, 95, 139, 259, 262

•R•

racist language, 62, 66–67
reconciliation, 188–189, 198–199, 202–203, 205, 207
redemption, 200
relational maintenance
    and humor, 163
    and play, 157–158
    in mentor relationships, 289–290
    strategies, 11, 288–290
relational prayer theory, 263–264
religious/spiritual communication
    and forgiveness, 194, 202
    and positive communication, 3, 5, 8, 10–12, 259–260
    See religious/spiritual coping
religious/spiritual coping
    cognitions, 264, 266–270, 272
    in prison, 261
    personal/private, 264, 266–270
    social, 264, 266–269, 270–271
    with HIV, 260–261
    See prayer
religiousness/spirituality as virtue, 12, 194
resilience, 252, 316, 280–281, 304
respect, 39, 59, 64, 189, 204
responsibility, 85, 194
    ethical responsibility, 64–65
responsiveness, 25–26, 236, 281, 291
rhythm, 23, 30–32, 42–45, 50
    See intercultural synchrony
ridicule, 157, 162, 166
risk–reduction, 278, 280–285, 291

•S•

sadness, 6, 304, 317
    See negative emotions
satisfaction
    and humor, 164
    and play, 150–151, 156–158
    and support, 217, 230
    dark side, 316–317
    friendship, 94, 144–145
    life, 5, 7, 93, 216, 231
    marriage, 103, 131, 164, 217
    physical, 101
    relational maintenance, 289–290
    romantic, 27, 95, 113, 138, 144
    workplace, xv, 119–120
self–esteem, 6, 49–50, 66, 132, 216, 221
    dark side, 318–319
self–regulation, 12, 194
semantic beauty, 27–30, 34–35
sexual abuse, 318
    See child
Sexuality, 6, 95–102
    and humor, 169–170, 172–174
    and intimacy, 96
    and older adults, 96–103
    as adaptive, 131
    dark side, 129, 138
    sexual identity, 63, 69
sexually transmitted diseases, 100–101
    as stressor, 260, 269–270
    HIV, 259
sibling relationship, 94, 193–194, 205–206
silence, 42, 44, 68, 80–81, 85
social competence, 281, 292
    See communication competence
social integration, 213–214
social intelligence, 11
social interaction, 92, 117–118
    model of coping with HIV, 263
    theory, 42–43, 45
social networks, 134, 151, 216, 289
    dark side, 315–316
    elder adult, 93–95
social problems, 277, 280, 283, 291
social support, 212–213, 281
    communication approach, 214–215
    listening, 110, 113, 115, 120

sociological/psychological approach, 213–214
See comforting messages
See supportive communication
socioemotional selectivity theory, 95
Socrates, xvi, 75–76, 79, 82–84, 86–87
space of appearance, 75
speech/communication accommodation, 9, 43–46, 48, 318
strengths–based approach, 285
See asset–building model vs. risk reduction model
stress
 and social support, 221–214, 217, 224
 buffer, 93, 133–134, 139–140
 coping, 316
 HIV and prison, 259, 260–262, 269–270
 management, 135–137
 recovery, 134–135
 reduction, 131
 response, 174
 stressors, 133–134
 threat, 133
 work stress, 169
supportive communication
 and physical well–being, 216–217
 and psychological well–being, 215–216
 and relational well–being, 217
 challenges, 217–218
 defined, 211–212
 history, 212–215
 interactions, 221–222
 skills, 222–224
 See comforting messages
 See social support
survival, 131–132, 315
symmetry in interpersonal communication, 30–34, 40–41
 See rhythm
 See intercultural synchrony

•T•

t–groups, 301–303, 307
teamwork, 11

telesmatic communication, 180–181, 182–183
 defined, 181
 intelligence, 181–182, 184–185, 188–189
 telesmatic moments, 180, 188
temperance, 12, 196–197
tend and befriend theory, 131
thinking, 80–83, 85
 dichotomous thinking, xvi, 9, 84
 thoughtfulness, 80–83
 positive thinking, 12–13
 See cognition
thriving, 279–280, 283, 285, 291, 304, 315
touch, 68, 102, 137, 255–256
 See nonverbal communication
transcendence, 12
 See transformation
transformation, 28, 29–30, 180, 195, 200
 transformational learning, 180
 transformational meaning, 28–30
transgression, 193–194, 196–198, 201–203, 205, 207
 and children, 204
 moral, 195, 199
 See forgiveness
trust, 269, 272–273, 286 304
 and humor, 163, 165
 restoration, 198–199, 201, 205
 self–trust, 49
truth, 76–79, 82, 83–84, 86
 as courage, 62–63
 parrhesia, 62

•U•

understanding, 46, 86, 98, 118–119, 202
 and support, 233–234, 236
 healthcare, 253
 religious/spiritual, 270
 See comforting communication
 See empathy
unethical, 10, 63, 314–315
 See ethics

•V•

victim, 82–83, 138, 183–185, 190
    and forgiveness, 196–198
    and revenge, 33
virtue, 11–12, 196–197
    and communication, 57–58, 69, 73–80, 83–87
    and happiness, xvi, 5

•W•

Well-being, 20, 256, 315–316
    and affection, 128, 132–133, 137–138
    and compassion, 68
    and friendship, 94–95
    and intimacy, 92–93, 100
    and listening, 117
    and marriage, 94–96
    and play, 143
    and support, 212, 214–2158, 231–232
    other well–being, 198
    relational well–being, 110, 193, 198, 212, 217, 231
    relationships, 73
    restoring well–being, 194, 197–198, 200–201, 204–205, 207
    See health
wisdom, 11, 194, 196
workplace, 62, 119–120

•Y•

youth development, 278, 280–285
youth mentoring, 285–290, 292
    and equity, 288–289
    best practices, 278
    define, 286–287

•Z•

zest, 11

Howard Giles,
GENERAL EDITOR

This series explores new and exciting advances in the ways in which language both reflects and fashions social reality—and thereby constitutes critical means of social action. As well as these being central foci in face-to-face interactions across different cultures, they also assume significance in the ways that language functions in the mass media, new technologies, organizations, and social institutions. Language as Social Action does not uphold apartheid against any particular methodological and/or ideological position, but, rather, promotes (wherever possible) cross-fertilization of ideas and empirical data across the many, all-too-contrastive, social scientific approaches to language and communication. Contributors to the series will also accord due attention to the historical, political, and economic forces that contextually bound the ways in which language patterns are analyzed, produced, and received. The series will also provide an important platform for theory-driven works that have profound, and often times provocative, implications for social policy.

For further information about the series and submitting manuscripts, please contact:

> Howard Giles
> Department of Communication
> University of California at Santa Barbara
> Santa Barbara, CA 93106-4020
> HowieGiles@cox.net

To order other books in this series, please contact our Customer Service Department at:

> (800) 770-LANG (within the U.S.)
> (212) 647-7706 (outside the U.S.)
> (212) 647-7707 FAX

Or browse online by series at:

> www.peterlang.com